THE VICTORIA HISTORY OF THE COUNTIES OF ENGLAND

A HISTORY OF DORSET

VOLUME III

THE VICTORIA HISTORY OF THE COUNTIES OF ENGLAND

EDITED BY R. B. PUGH

THE UNIVERSITY OF LONDON
INSTITUTE OF
HISTORICAL RESEARCH

Oxford University Press, Ely House, 37 Dover Street, London, W.1

GLASGOW NEW YORK TORONTO MELBOURNE WELLINGTON
BOMBAY CALCUTTA MADRAS KARACHI LAHORE DACCA
CAPE TOWN SALISBURY NAIROBI IBADAN ACCRA
KUALA LUMPUR HONG KONG TOKYO

19 722718 x

PRINTED IN GREAT BRITAIN

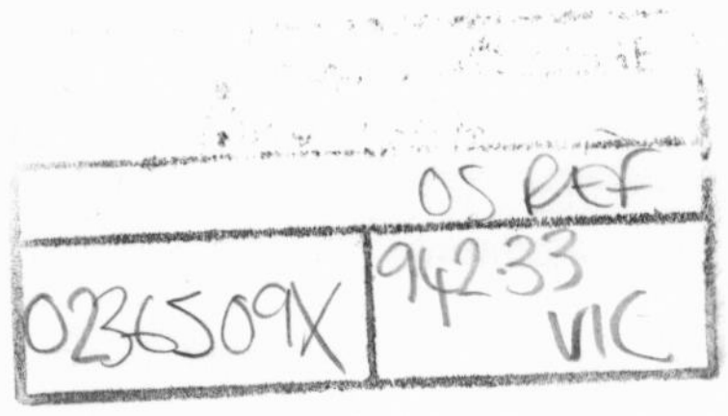

INSCRIBED TO THE

MEMORY OF HER LATE MAJESTY

QUEEN VICTORIA

WHO GRACIOUSLY GAVE THE TITLE TO

AND ACCEPTED THE DEDICATION

OF THIS HISTORY

Knowlton in the Parish of Woodlands
The ruined 12th-century church stands within one of the prehistoric circles of Knowlton Rings; the site is thought to be that of a deserted village and the meeting-place of Knowlton hundred.

A HISTORY OF THE COUNTY OF DORSET

EDITED BY R. B. PUGH

VOLUME III

WITH INDEX TO VOLUME II

PUBLISHED FOR
THE INSTITUTE OF HISTORICAL RESEARCH
BY THE
OXFORD UNIVERSITY PRESS
1968

Distributed by the Oxford University Press until 1 January 1972
thereafter by Dawsons of Pall Mall

CONTENTS OF VOLUME THREE

LIST OF ILLUSTRATIONS

The frontispiece is from an air photograph by J. K. St. Joseph, Cambridge University Collection, copyright reserved. The Domesday map was drawn by H. A. Shelley from a draft by Ann Williams and Celia B. Clarke, and is based on the Ordnance Survey with the sanction of the Controller of H.M. Stationery Office, Crown Copyright reserved.

EDITORIAL NOTE

The *Victoria History of Dorset*, Volume II, containing most of the 'general' articles for that county, appeared in 1908. Articles on natural history, pre-history, and schools, and the translation, with commentary, of the county section of Domesday Book then remained to be published in order to complete the 'general' volumes. Though a volume to contain those articles was in preparation at the time, it was not proceeded with, and the First World War put a stop to all further activity on Dorset. An opportunity arose in 1965 to publish separately the Domesday section, which had been prepared for another purpose, and it was decided to do so and not to await the completion of any other 'general' articles. The Royal Commission on Historical Monuments are in any case actively engaged in surveying the county's prehistoric monuments and the case for compiling a partially overlapping survey did not seem compelling. There is, moreover, no strong probability that natural history articles, apart from a survey of physique, will now be needed. They have been omitted from the *Victoria History* scheme in recent years. It is possible that accounts of ancient endowed grammar schools will in Dorset's case eventually be incorporated in the 'topographical' articles.

The structure and aims of the *History* as a whole are outlined in an article published in the *Bulletin of the Institute of Historical Research*, Vol. XL (No. 101, May 1967). In preparing the present volume for the press much valuable work has been done by Miss Celia B. Clarke, formerly an Assistant to the Editor.

DOMESDAY SURVEY[1]

I. The procedure of the Domesday survey—the Exchequer text and the Exon. Domesday—the Domesday commissioners and the hearing of claims—assessment of the shire for geld—teamlands and ploughs—land-values, 1066 and 1086—the peasants—manorial adjuncts, meadow, pasture, woodland, and others—the Dorset boroughs, pp. 00–00. II. The land of the king, 1086 and 1066—the pre-Conquest landowners of Dorset—the survival of the English—the lands of the religious houses, in 1086 and before the Conquest, pp. 00–00. III. The lay tenants in 1086—the king's thegns and the king's serjeants—the later history of the fiefs, pp. 00–00.

I

DORSET, Wiltshire, Somerset, Devon, and Cornwall, the five counties covered by the Exon. Domesday, probably comprised one of the circuits into which England was divided for the making of the Domesday survey.[2] Each circuit was assigned its own bodies of commissioners[3] and, from a passage in the account of Somerset, it has been assumed that William, Bishop of Durham, headed the group of commissioners for the south-west, but the passage could be otherwise construed.[4] The commissioners seem to have held special sessions of the shire court, at which the juries of the shire and the hundreds gave sworn evidence, but there is little in the accounts of the south-western shires to illustrate this process. There are several references to the testimony of the English and the thegns of the shire,[5] none of which occurs in the Dorset section, and in Devon there is a single reference to the men of the hundred.[6] In Dorset there are four references to oral testimony, but the hundred juries are not mentioned.[7] It is noticeable that in Domesday there are no hundred rubrics for any of the five south-western shires, although the rest of the English counties were so rubricated. Two hundreds in Dorset are mentioned incidentally, Buckland hundred, where there were 3½ virgates attached to the manor of Bingham's Melcombe (no. 30), and Purbeck hundred, where William of Briouze held 7 hides less ½ virgate (no. 296). It is possible partially to reconstruct the Dorset hundreds by collating the Dorset section of the Domesday survey with the Dorset Geld Rolls.[8] It then emerges that the manors of each tenant-in-chief in Domesday are arranged in a fairly consistent order of hundreds, or rather groups of hundreds.[9] Whether this order indicates that the records of the court proceedings were originally arranged hundred by hundred, as in the *Inquisitio Comitatus Cantabrigiensis*, is conjectural. It is possible that when the original returns were sent to Winchester, they were already in feudal order. The arguments for this view largely turn on the relationship between the Exchequer Domesday and the Exon. Domesday, preserved in Exeter cathedral library.

Exon. Domesday in its original form must have covered all five south-western counties, but the Wiltshire section, with the exception of one manor, and four-fifths

[1] The author wishes to thank Professor R. R. Darlington for his invaluable assistance in preparing this article, the ensuing translation, and the text of the Geld Rolls.

[2] Eyton distinguished 9 circuits in all, which A. Ballard (*Domesday Inquest* (1906), 12–13) reduced to seven; see *Domesday Re-Bound* (H.M.S.O., 1954), App. II.

[3] Robert, Bp. of Hereford, in his contemporary account of the survey, says that there were 2 sets of commissioners, one sent to check on the other: W. H. Stevenson, 'A Contemporary Description of the Domesday Survey', *E.H.R.* xxii. 74, translated in *Eng. Hist. Doc.* ii. 851.

[4] *Dom. Bk.* (Rec. Com.), i, f. 87b; see R. W. Eyton, *Domesday Studies: Somerset*, i. 12–13; V. H. Galbraith, *Making of Dom. Bk.* 87, 94, 207; *V.C.H. Wilts.* ii. 42, n. 2.

[5] F. W. Maitland, *Dom. Bk. and Beyond*, 11, n. 1; Galbraith, op. cit. 70 sqq. For the Wilts. evidence on this matter, see *V.C.H. Wilts.* ii. 43.

[6] *Dom. Bk.* (Rec. Com.), i, f. 107; iv. 277.

[7] See nos. 263, 308, 369, 378 and cx.

[8] See p. 115 sqq.

[9] R. Welldon Finn, 'The Making of the Dorset Domesday', *Proc. Dorset Nat. Hist. and Arch. Soc.* lxxxi. 150–1.

of the Dorset section have not survived. Apart from the incomplete descriptions of the five counties of Wiltshire, Dorset, Somerset, Devon, and Cornwall, the Exon. Domesday contains the Geld Rolls for all five counties, including three distinct versions of the Wiltshire Rolls, lists of *terre occupate* for Somerset, Devon, and Cornwall, and summaries of the fiefs of some barons, notably the Abbot of Glastonbury. The descriptions of the manors in Exon. Domesday are fuller than those in the Exchequer text, especially in recording the livestock statistics which the author of the Anglo-Saxon Chronicle found so shocking.[10] Many surnames and occupations are recorded in Exon. Domesday and omitted in the Exchequer text. Exon. Domesday regularly distinguishes between the demesne, which the Exchequer text records sporadically, and the land of the *villani*,[11] which the Exchequer text does not mention at all. The phraseology of Exon. Domesday is very diffuse, in strong contrast to the brevity of the Exchequer text, and the numerous differences in terminology and the spelling of place and personal names have given rise to the belief that the two versions are 'independent copies of the same original'.[12] It was also suggested by Reichel that the sections for Cornwall, Devon, and Somerset were compiled at Exeter from the original returns, while the sections for Dorset and Wiltshire were made at Winchester, from an Exchequer digest of the original returns.[13] This view, which seems on the face of it unlikely, is not borne out by any significant differences between the Dorset section and the rest of Exon. Domesday. More recently, however, the theory has been adopted that the Exchequer text for the south-western counties was derived from Exon. Domesday.[14]

Apart from the question of place and personal names there are discrepancies between the two texts which are difficult to explain if one is based upon the other although on balance the general resemblance of the two texts makes it difficult to believe that they are quite independent of each other. The Exon. Domesday for Dorset covers the land of the king, with the exception of the two manors formerly held by Countess Goda, the land of the Countess of Boulogne, the lands of Cerne Abbey, Abbotsbury Abbey, Athelney Abbey, Tavistock Abbey, and Milton Abbey, the lands of William of Moyon, Roger Arundel, Serle of Burcy, the wife of Hugh fitz Grip, and Walter de Claville. In all, 160 of the 515 manors recorded in the Exchequer text are also in Exon. Domesday, covering about one-third of the total hidage of the county. As has been said above, Exon. Domesday contains information not in the Exchequer text; it is also true that the Exchequer text contains items of information which do not appear in Exon. Domesday. At Spetisbury (nos. 274 and lxxxiv) there were two pieces of pasture, one piece measuring 5½ furlongs by 2 furlongs and *in alio loco* another piece measuring 2½ furlongs by 1½ furlong. According to the Exchequer text this second piece of land lay *super aquam* but these words do not appear in the Exon. entry. There is a more serious omission in the Exon. account of the borough of Shaftesbury. The Exchequer text says that the Abbess of Shaftesbury had there 151 burgesses, 20 *mansiones vacuas*, and a garden, the whole rendering 65*s*., but none of these details is in the Exon. account of the borough.

The most serious discrepancy in the arrangement of manors concerns the land of the king. In the Exchequer text the six manors which had belonged to King Edward, beginning with Portland, come first, followed, with a separate heading, by the

[10] '. . . nor indeed (it is a shame to relate but it seemed no shame to him to do) one ox nor one cow nor one pig which was there left out, and not put down in his record': *Anglo-Saxon Chron.*, a revised translation ed. D. Whitelock and others, 161–2.

[11] For a discussion of *villani* and other classes of peasants, see pp. 14–20.

[12] O. von Feilitzen, *Pre-Conquest Personal Names of Dom. Bk.* 9, n. 1.

[13] *V.C.H. Devon*, i. 375–80.

[14] R. Welldon Finn, 'The Immediate Sources of the Exch. Domesday', *Bull. John Rylands Libr.* xl. 47–78; Galbraith, *Making of Dom. Bk.* cap. VIII.

manors of Earl Harold and Little Puddle, belonging originally to Earl Harold's mother. In the Exon. Domesday Earl Harold's manors come first, with no heading to distinguish them from the land of King Edward, which follows. Countess Gytha's manor of Little Puddle is included among her son's manors, next to Puddletown, and Portland is placed between the manors of Ibberton and Fleet, both belonging to Earl Harold. In addition the lands of Bollo the priest, Bristuard the priest, and the abbey of St. Wandrille are interspersed with the king's manors, whereas in the Exchequer text they are entered separately. A virgate of reeveland, held by Aiulf the sheriff, is also entered among the king's manors, but it does not appear at all in the Exchequer text. The manors of Queen Maud are entered in almost the same order in both texts except that one of the manors of *Tarente* (nos. 26 and xxxv), which in the Exchequer text lies fifth among the manors held by Hugh fitz Grip of the queen, lies eighth in Exon. Domesday. Abbotsbury, the chief manor of the abbey of that name, comes third in the Exon. arrangement of the abbey's fief, and first in the Exchequer arrangement, and Milton Abbas, the *caput abbatie* of Milton Abbey, lies eighth among the abbey's manors in Exon. Domesday and second in the Exchequer text.[15]

Of the discrepancies in actual content the most serious relates to the wood of *Hauocumbe*, attached to the manor of Burton Bradstock (nos. 2 and x). According to the Exchequer text one-third of the wood was held by Earl Edwin, which Exon. Domesday says belonged to Earl Godwin. The Exon. version is probably correct, since this portion of the wood was appurtenant to Frampton (no. 121) which was held T.R.E. by Countess Gytha, Earl Godwin's widow. The value of Nettlecombe (nos. 88 and li) is also a matter of disagreement between the two texts. According to Exon. Domesday the manor *reddit abbati viii libras et prefato militi l solidos et v et quando abbas recepit valebat xx solidos plus*. The former value of the manor must therefore have been £11 15*s*. 0*d*. The Exchequer text, however, gives the former value of the manor as £12 0*s*. 0*d*. There are numerous other small discrepancies, which could have been due to mistakes in copying. At Child Okeford (nos. 7 and i) the king had 9 (viiii) bordars according to Exon. Domesday but 8 (viii) bordars according to the Exchequer text. At Creech (nos. 412 and cxlv) the pasture measured 7 furlongs by 4 (iiii) furlongs according to Exon. Domesday and 7 furlongs by 3 (iii) furlongs according to the Exchequer text. In all these cases it is easy to see how a misreading may have occurred. Similarly at Hampreston (nos. 19 and xxv) there were 2 *villani* according to Exon. and 5 *villani* in the Exchequer text, which could be explained by a misreading of *ii* as *v*. At another manor in the same vill of Hampreston (nos. 389 and cxxi) the wife of Hugh had 1 *villanus* and 1 bordar according to Exon. Domesday, but 1 *villanus* and 2 bordars according to the Exchequer text. At *Cerne* (nos. 108 and lxxxii) 7 bordars in Exon. have become 5 bordars in the Exchequer text. At Winterborne Stickland (nos. 403 and cxxxvi) the former and present values of the manor have become transposed. A mistake like this could arise through the difference in arrangement between the two texts, since Exon. always places the 1086 value first, whereas the Exchequer text gives the former value first.

There are frequent instances of omissions in the Exchequer text. Exon. Domesday records that William of Moyon's manor of Hammoon (nos. 277 and lxxxvii) was held of him by Torstin, but the Exchequer text omits this and treats the manor as if William

[15] The rearrangement of the lands of Abbotsbury Abbey and Milton Abbey in the Exch. text has disarranged the hundredal order. Abbotsbury lay in Uggescombe hundred, along with Portesham and Shilvinghampton, which it immediately precedes in Exon. Domesday, and Milton lay in *Haltone* hundred, with Lyscombe and Woolland, its neighbours in Exon. Domesday. Similarly Little Puddle, in Puddletown hundred, follows the manor of Puddletown in Exon. Domesday, but is isolated from it in the Exchequer text. This is not the case with the queen's manor of *Tarente*, where the position is reversed; it is in the Exon. arrangement that the hundredal order is upset, and it is rectified in the Exchequer text.

held it in demesne. At Turners Puddle (nos. 391 and cxxiv) there was ½ hide, 4 acres, and a garden which did not pay geld, which are recorded in Exon. Domesday but not in the Exchequer text, and the same is true of a piece of woodland 1 league and 8 furlongs long and 1 league wide in Puddletown (nos. 8 and ii), 15 acres of wood at North Poorton (nos. 329 and ci), 8 cottars at Frome St. Quintin (nos. 15 and xxi), 2 cottars at Chilfrome (nos. 278 and lxxxviii), and a *villanus* with ½ virgate at Winterborne Houghton (nos. 275 and lxxxv). Exon. Domesday reveals that only half of the 2 mills at Child Okeford (nos. 7 and i) was held by the king, and that the wood at Nettlecombe (nos. 88 and li) *nullum fructum fert*. At Cruxton (nos. 279 and lxxxix), Durweston (nos. 401 and cxxxiv), and Ringstead (nos. 409 and cxlii) the Exchequer text does not record the men's ploughs, although they are entered in Exon. Domesday. Other minor omissions include leaving out the words *et dimidia* in some cases, for instance at Cranborne (nos. 16 and xxii) where there were 2½ leagues of pasture in length according to Exon. Interlineations in Exon. Domesday are not always reproduced in the Exchequer text. At *Cerne* (nos. 108 and lxxxii) the mill was worth xx(v)*d*. in Exon. Domesday and xx*d*. in the Exchequer text. In the case of North Poorton (nos. 329 and ci) the geld assessment is left out by the Exchequer text, although it is given by Exon. Domesday, but this appears to be due to a scribal error. The Exchequer entry reads *Wido tenet de Rogerio POVERTONE. Alwinus et Ulf tenuerunt* [*T.R.E.*] *pro ii hidis*. As it stands this makes little sense and it seems plain that the scribe intended to write something like *Alwinus et Ulf tenuerunt pro ii maneriis T.R.E. et geldabat pro ii hidis*.[16] At Affpuddle (nos. 80 and xliii), where the Exchequer text breaks off short, the Exon. entry is complete but makes little grammatical sense.[17] It seems as if the Exchequer entry, if taken from Exon., was left incomplete until this could be clarified. At Nettlecombe (nos. 88 and li), where Exon. Domesday records a knight with two hides of land, the knight was at first left out in the Exchequer text, but was added in the margin. Several of these marginal additions occur in the Exchequer text, possibly left out in the first place because of haste in the compilation of the Exchequer Domesday, but none of the other entries involving such marginalia survives in the existing Exon. Domesday.[18]

Some omissions, such as that of the hundred rubrics mentioned above, occur in both the Exchequer text and Exon. Domesday. Apart from this it is noticeable that in many cases where a gap has been left in the Exchequer text for some item of information to be inserted, the relevant information is missing from Exon. Domesday also. It is not stated how many teamlands there were at Portland (nos. 1 and vi), Nettlecombe (nos 88 and li), or Winterborne Stickland (nos. 403 and cxxxvi), although spaces have been left in each case for the relevant information which is not recorded in the Exon. entries either. Spaces have also been left for ploughs at *Torne* (nos. 419 and clii), for the men's ploughs at *Tarente* (nos. 26 and xxxv) and Renscombe (nos. 91 and liv), and for the number of *villani* at Morden (nos. 385 and cxvii). At Stafford (nos. 383 and cxv) there is some confusion over the manorial adjuncts. The Exchequer text says that there were 24 acres of meadow, and 16 furlongs of pasture, and 8 acres, leaving a space after acres, which would logically be filled by woodland, since meadow and pasture have already been enumerated. This obscurity also exists in the Exon. text which states that the manor was divided between two men, each of whom held *xii agros prati et viii quadragenarias pascue et iiii agros*, without indicating to what the *iiii agros* refer. There are

[16] Cf. the entry for Milborne St. Andrew (no. 477), where the hidage is not given, and the entry for Petersham (Farm) (no. 375), where there is no value. In both these cases over-compression seems to be the cause. Neither is covered by Exon. Domesday.

[17] The 2 manors referred to in this entry are Affpuddle and Bloxworth (nos. 79 and xlii). The Bloxworth entry is complete in both texts.

[18] See below.

many such entries in the Dorset survey which cannot be checked against Exon. Domesday, because the relevant portion has not survived. At Cheselbourne (no. 138) a space has been left for the teamlands, at Pulham (no. 146) for the number of ploughs in demesne, at Lulworth (no. 198) for the ploughs belonging to the men, at Wimborne St. Giles (no. 499) for the account of the mill, at Stalbridge (no. 42) for the former value of the manor, and at Knighton (no. 298) there is a space between the bordars and the men's ploughs where one would normally expect to find cotsets or cottars. The entry concerning Kingcombe (no. 485) is unfinished with room left to complete it, and Herston (no. 512), the last manor entered in the Dorset survey, is not completed. The account of Blackmanston (no. 476) is unfinished, since the value is omitted, but, instead of inserting the value in the space provided, the scribe has repeated the whole entry, with the value, later in the text (no. 489). Cases like this seem to indicate haste in the compilation of the Exchequer Domesday. This is borne out by the marginal additions, one of which, the knight with 2 hides of land at Nettlecombe, has already been mentioned. The other instances are a virgate of land which did not pay geld at Catsley (no. 229), the name of the T.R.E. owner (Burde) at Rushton (no. 292), a burgess at Wareham, rendering 2*s*., attached to Povington (no. 242), and a virgate at Kington Magna (no. 245). The account of the woodland at Iwerne Minster (no. 131) was omitted and entered at the end of the following entry, and the T.R.E. tenure of Bricsrid at Frome Billet (no. 491) was added by interlineation. Apart from these the interlineations are few and confined mostly to titles, like *Heraldus* (*comes*), surnames, and the words *et dimidia*.

Not only small items of information but whole manors, and in some cases groups of manors, have been omitted from their correct position in the Exchequer text, and added in other places. A group of eight manors belonging to William of Moyon was left out and is recorded on the lower part of the dorse of a folio inserted (f. 81b). In Exon. Domesday *Poleham* (nos. 276 and lxxxvi), the first of the manors misplaced in the Exchequer text, is entered on the page which begins with part of the account of Winterborne Houghton (nos. 275 and lxxxv). Winterborne is entered in the correct place in the Exchequer text, and it cannot be argued that the Exchequer scribe mislaid a sheet or series of sheets of the Exon. Domesday and found them later. The land of the Countess of Boulogne is entered almost as an afterthought in the Exchequer text, after the land of the king's serjeants. In Exon. Domesday the three manors of the countess are entered on one sheet only (f. 33), the other side of which is blank, and they follow the king's land and immediately precede the land of Cerne Abbey. It is possible that the misplacing of this leaf caused the omission of the countess's manors from the places where it would be more appropriate to find them, that is, with the lands of the Count of Mortain and Earl Hugh, or with the lands of the wife of Hugh fitz Grip. Other displaced manors are Iwerne Courtney (no. 316), the single Dorset manor of Baldwin of Exeter which appears on folio 81 inserted in the Exchequer volume and having William of Moyon's manors on the dorse; the king's manor of Hinton Martell (no. 31), inserted on a special sheet (f. 76); Compton Valence (no. 357), the manor of Hugh de Port, entered at the foot of folio 83; Kingston (no. 134) and Farnham (no. 135), belonging to Shaftesbury Abbey, added at the foot of folio 78b; North Poorton (no. 249), belonging to Ernulf of Hesdin, added at the foot of folio 80b, and three manors (nos. 510–12), belonging to the king's serjeants, which were omitted and added after the land of the Countess of Boulogne.

It is noticeable in the Dorset survey, as in other parts of the Exchequer Domesday, that the index given on the first folio of the survey, after the account of the boroughs, does not tally with the headings in the text either in arrangement or in terminology.

Aiulf is called *vicecomes* in the index and *camerarius* in the heading. Baldwin is Baldwin *de Execestre* in the index but Baldwin alone in the heading, and similarly Waleran is Waleran *Venator* in the index but Waleran alone in the heading. *Maci de Moretanie* in the index becomes *Mathiu de Moretania* in the text. The heading in the index *Reinbaldus presbyter et alii clerici* becomes *terra elemosinariorum regis* in the text. In the same way *Gudmund et alii taini* and *Willelmus Belet et alii servientes regis* in the index become *terra tainorum regis* and *terra servientium regis* in the text. Alvred of Epaignes has a heading and a number in the text but not in the index, with the result that the numbers do not tally, and the discrepancy was solved only by omitting heading and number from the entry of Iseldis's land in the text, although they appear in the index. The lands of the abbey of St. Wandrille and of Hugh de Boscherbert have no headings in the text, the relevant numbers being inserted in the margin. The heading *Hugo de Luri et alii franci* is omitted in the text, the number being inserted in the margin by the land of Hugh de Lure. The index lists first the land of the king (I), then the land of the Bishop of Salisbury (II), and then the land of the monks of Sherborne (III) but in the text the lands of the monks are entered as part of the bishop's fief, with the words *hec novem descripta maneria sunt de victu monachorum Scireburnensium* at the end of the section relating to the monks' land, and the number 'III' inserted in the margin at the point where the lands of the monks begin, half way through the account of Sherborne itself (no. 37). The manors of the bishop both precede and follow the lands of the monks. According to the index the land of the abbey of Montevilliers precedes that of the canons of Coutances, but in the text the positions are reversed.

Despite the difference in nomenclature and phraseology and the inclusion in the Exchequer text of some items not in Exon. Domesday, the relationship of the two texts seems to be closer than some authorities would allow. With exceptions most of the discrepancies could be put down to the speed at which the Exchequer text was compiled, and the fact that the Exchequer text often leaves spaces just where the information is lacking in Exon. Domesday seems to indicate that the Exchequer text was compiled either from Exon. Domesday or a fair copy.

The Domesday commissioners were required to ascertain the name of each manor (*mansio*), who held it T.R.E., who held it in 1086, how many hides there were, how many ploughs in demesne and among the men, how many *villani*, cottars, *servi*, free men, and sokemen, how much wood, meadow, and pasture, how many mills and fishponds, how much had been added or taken away, how much it used to be worth, and how much it was worth, and how much each freeman and sokeman had. All this information was to be recorded for three different times, *scilicet tempore regis Aedwardi et quando rex Willelmus dedit et quomodo sit modo et si potest plus haberi quam habeatur.*[19] Where the question of tenure was concerned, the commissioners in their capacity as justices heard conflicting claims. In Dorset the son of Odo the chamberlain claimed the manor of Chelborough (nos. 280 and xc) held by William of Moyon. According to Exon. *rex vero iussit ut inde rectum habeat*, but William continued to hold the manor. The Abbess of Shaftesbury had been more fortunate in respect of her manors of Cheselbourne and Stour (nos. 127, 138), which Earl Harold had taken T.R.E., for King William *eas fecit resaisiri quia in ipsa ecclesia inventus est brevis cum sigillo regis Edwardi precipiens ut ecclesie restituerentur*. The writ, however, also ordered the return of Bingham's Melcombe (no. 30), but *rex adhuc tenet*. At Povington (no. 242), belonging to Robert fitz Gerold, the mill was claimed *ad opus regis*, and at Friar Waddon (no. 143),

[19] The commissioners' terms of reference are preserved in the preamble to the Ely Inquest: see *Dom. Bk.* (Rec. Com.), iv. 496; *Inquisitio Comitatus Cantabrigiensis*, ed. N. E. S. A. Hamilton, 97.

which Hugh fitz Grip had given to the abbey of Montevilliers, the Abbot of Abbotsbury had been entitled to *vi acras messis et iii circscez de consuetudine sed Hugo nunquam dedit*. Two hides in Tatton (nos. 398 and cxxxi), which were *de dominio abbatie de Cernel T.R.E.*, were held by the wife of Hugh fitz Grip in 1086. Hugh is said to have taken them from the church (*has Hugo super abbatem accepit*).[20] Farnham (no. 135), belonging to the Abbess of Shaftesbury, was held in 1086 by the wife of Hugh fitz Grip and Aiulf the chamberlain, and is recorded again among their manors.[21] Little Cheselbourne (nos. 378 and cx), held by the wife of Hugh in 1086, had apparently belonged formerly to the Abbot of Abbotsbury. It was claimed that Hugh had held this land of the abbot *ut homines eius dicunt sed abbas negat*. The inference is that Hugh fitz Grip had taken possession of the property and then alleged that he had been enfeoffed by the abbot. At Abbotsbury itself (nos. 109 and lviii) Hugh held one hide which *T.R.E. ad victum monachorum erat* and at Portesham (nos. 112 and lxix) one virgate which *erat in victu monachorum T.R.E.* Both pieces of land were held by his wife in 1086. At Winterborne Houghton, a divided vill held partly by the wife of Hugh and partly by William of Moyon, the wife of Hugh held one virgate *iniuste que pertinet ad Willelmum de Moione* (nos. 392 and cxxv). William Rufus (*filius regis*) had taken 3 virgates at Stalbridge (no. 42) *sine consensu episcopi et monachorum* and had given them to Manasses.

At Swyre (no. 263) there was a piece of land which did not pay geld *sed erat in dominio et in firma regis*. The land had been let to Toxus T.R.E. by a king's reeve who later took it back into the king's hand. *Toxus vero per regem Edwardum iterum fuit saisitus sicut dicit et ita tenuit eam in vita et in morte regis Edwardi et tempore Heraldi*.[22] A similar entry concerns a piece of land in Gillingham, which Hugh fitz Grip received from the king's farm and gave to Cranborne Abbey.[23] This land also was not assessed in hides. Half a hide at *Cerneli* (no. 212) belonging to the Count of Mortain was *de dominica firma Cerne T.R.E.*[24] Land held in pledge (*vadimonium*) is occasionally recorded. At *Tarente* (nos. 24 and xxx), a manor of Queen Maud, there was a virgate which Alvric, who held the land T.R.E., had in pledge for $\frac{1}{2}$ mark of gold and *necdum est redempta*. At Blandford St. Mary (no. 261) William of Eu had $\frac{1}{2}$ hide which Toli his predecessor had in pledge *et fuit adquietata*, but Ralph de Limesi had taken it *cum ista alia terra*. Stock Gaylard (no. 269), another of William of Eu's manors, had been held in pledge by Toli *de terra Scireburne*. At Silton (no. 271), belonging to William of Falaise, there was a hide and $\frac{1}{2}$ virgate which Wulfweard White, the previous holder, had in pledge from one of his reeves, and attached to the same manor was a hide which Wulfweard had bought from the Bishop of Exeter *sed non pertinebat ad ipsum manerium*. Eadnoth the staller, the predecessor of Hugh, Earl of Chester, had bought two manors, Catsley (no. 229) and South Perrott (no. 228), from Aelfwold, Bishop of Sherborne, on condition that at his death they should revert to the church, but Earl Hugh held them in 1086. Exchanges of land had also taken place. Five of the Bishop of Salisbury's manors in Dorset and one in Wiltshire were held in exchange for *Scipeleia*, which cannot be identified. The king had given the church of Gillingham to the Abbess of Shaftesbury in exchange for one hide of Kingston (no. 134) in which to build Corfe Castle. Hugh fitz Grip had given Little Waddon (no. 460) to Brictuin, a thegn, in exchange for a manor worth twice as much (*ipsum scambium valet duplum*). Although this manor is

[20] Another part of Tatton (no. 345) was held by Aiulf the chamberlain. T.R.E. 1 thegn had held it of Cerne Abbey *et non poterat ab ea separari*.

[21] See nos. 352 and 396.

[22] The phrase *sicut dicit* appears to imply that Toxus gave evidence. This seems unlikely, but it is difficult to see who other than Toxus can be the subject of *dicit*. If it was he who gave evidence, he presumably held of William of Eu in 1086.

[23] See no. 70: *Hanc terram accepit Hugo de firma regis et dedit ecclesie*.

[24] In the Geld Roll for Whitchurch hundred the Count of Mortain had $\frac{1}{2}$ hide which was *de firma regis*, which seems to be this $\frac{1}{2}$ hide in *Cerneli*: see pp. 125, 126.

supposed to have been held by the Count of Mortain in 1086, it cannot be identified among his manors. From the Somerset survey it appears that the Count of Mortain gave to Athelney Abbey the manor of Purse Caundle (nos. 118 and lxiv) in Dorset in exchange for Bishopston (Montacute) in Somerset.[25] This exchange is not recorded in the Dorset survey. Some of the tenants-in-chief in 1086 had been given their land by the queen. Anschitil fitz Ameline held Tyneham (no. 369) of the queen *ut dicit sed post mortem eius regem non requisivit*. Dodo held ½ hide, in an unspecified locality, of the queen in alms (no. 444). Torchil held part of Hampreston (no. 443) which Schelin had held of the queen, but which in 1086 the king had in demesne (*modo habet rex in dominio*).[26] William fitz Osbern had apparently once held land in Dorset, since Waleran the huntsman had held Church Knowle (no. 308) of Earl William but *modo ut dicit tenet de rege*.

Land disputed between two tenants is sometimes entered under each tenant's name, but this only happens twice in the Dorset survey. Farnham is entered under Shaftesbury Abbey (no. 135) and under Aiulf (no. 352) and the wife of Hugh fitz Grip (nos. 396 and cxxix), and the disputed virgate at Winterborne Houghton is entered under William of Moyon (nos. 275 and lxxxv) and the wife of Hugh fitz Grip (nos. 392 and cxxv). One manor, Blackmanston, belonging to Alvric, seems to be entered twice. One entry (no. 476) gives the name of the manor, the holder T.R.E., the hidage, and the teamland, but is unfinished. The other entry (no. 489) omits the hidage but adds the value. The fact that there are so few double entries makes it easier to calculate the assessment of the shire for geld. The total hidage recorded in Domesday amounts to 2,304 hides.[27] This can be compared with the hidage recorded in the Dorset Geld Rolls. There were 39 hundreds and, according to the figures given for the number of hides in each hundred, there should have been 2,298 hides. The details of each hundred account, however, do not always amount to the figure given for the number of hides in the hundred. The figures derived from the actual details of each hundred account yield a total of 2,307 hides, which is much closer to the Domesday figure.[28] There was in addition a substantial amount of land which was not assessed in hides and not liable to geld. The six manors which had belonged to King Edward, and which were plainly very large, had never paid geld. There were 25½ carucates (*carucate*) at Sherborne (no. 37) which had never paid geld, 16 belonging to the Bishop of Salisbury and 9½ to the monks of Sherborne. The bishop had 2 carucates at Beaminster and 2 at Netherbury (nos. 46, 47), and 2 teamlands (*quantum possunt arare ii caruce*) at Charminster (no. 32), 2 more at Alton Pancras (no. 33), 6 at Yetminster (no. 35), and 1 at Lyme Regis (no. 36). None of this land had ever paid geld. The monks of Sherborne had 2 carucates at Stoke Abbott (no. 45) which did not pay geld. The Abbot of Glastonbury had 14 teamlands at Sturminster Newton (no. 63) and 8 at Buckland Newton (no. 65), which were exempt from geld. Aiulf the chamberlain had 4 carucates in demesne at Wootton Fitzpaine (no. 347). Some manors were beneficially hidated. Puddletown (nos. 8 and ii) was assessed at ½ hide but had land for 15 ploughs. Okeford Fitzpaine (no. 64) was assessed at 8 hides, but had land for 16 ploughs and Stanton St. Gabriel (no. 210) was assessed at ½ hide with land for 6 ploughs. Another part of Wootton Fitzpaine (no. 211) was assessed at 2 hides, but had land for 7 ploughs. The king's manor of Wimborne

[25] *Dom. Bk.* (Rec. Com.), i, f. 93.

[26] The queen had enfeoffed Hugh fitz Grip in several manors, all in the king's hand in 1086, and had probably given the 2 manors of Edmondsham (nos. 353 and 354) to Humphrey the chamberlain.

[27] Maitland (*Dom. Bk. and Beyond*, 505) gives this figure as 2,321 hides, a figure apparently based on Eyton (*Key to Domesday: Dorset*, 144). Eyton's total includes 8 hides, 3 virgates, in Badbury hundred, belonging to Earl Aubrey, which must refer to the manor of Gussage St. Michael, which is in Dorset, but which is treated as part of Wilts. in Domesday; and 8 hides in *Glochresdone* hundred, which cannot be identified with any manor recorded in Domesday. When these 16 hides, 3 virgates, are deducted from Eyton's total, 2,304 hides, 1 virgate, remain.

[28] Eyton (op. cit. 144) gives these totals as 2,295 hides and 2,301 hides respectively.

Minster (nos. 21 and xxvii), assessed at $\frac{1}{2}$ hide, never paid geld although it did not belong to the night's farm of Wimborne, and other exemptions are occasionally recorded.[29] The four Dorset boroughs were assessed at a total of 45 hides, but they contributed to the upkeep of the royal housecarls and were not included in the total assessment of the shire.

There were 39 hundreds in Dorset at this period, which may suggest an original assessment of about 3,900 hides, but this seems unlikely. The hidages recorded in the various earlier charters which can be compared with Domesday assessments do not suggest any reduction in the hidage. The abbey of Shaftesbury, for example, received from King Alfred 100 hides, consisting of Donhead St. Andrew (Wilts.) and the manors which in 1086 formed the hundreds of Handley and Sixpenny. The hundred of Handley consisted solely of the manor of that name, assessed at 20 hides, the hundred of Sixpenny contained 53 hides, and Donhead St. Andrew was assessed at 40 hides, which is rather more than the total hidage given by Alfred, not less.[30] Only three Dorset hundreds contained more than 100 hides, Uggescombe with 104 hides, Beaminster with 105 hides, and Cullifordtree with 109 hides, while the tiny hundred of Redhone contained only 7 hides.

Several hundreds contained approximately 50 hides,[31] and it is noticeable that some of these hundreds were later amalgamated. The Domesday hundred of *Celberge* (51 hides) became part of Winfrith hundred (49 hides), thus forming one unit of 100 hides; *Stane* (63 hides) was amalgamated with Modbury (63 hides); and *Canendone* (48 hides) became part of Badbury (32 hides). This suggests that there had been a division of the original hundreds (if indeed the Dorset hundreds ever did approximate to 100 hides) rather than a reduction in the assessment, which in any case is not indicated by any earlier evidence. Dorset was not included in the County Hidage, compiled earlier in the 11th century, but the earliest text of the Burghal Hidage, dating from the early 10th century,[32] includes Wareham, to which it assigns 1,600 hides, and *Brydian* (which may be identified with either Bridport or Bredy), to which it assigns 760 hides. These figures yield a total of 2,360 hides, some 56 more than the Domesday figure. The four Dorset boroughs in 1086 were assessed at a total of 45 hides, which would largely account for this discrepancy. Later texts of the Burghal Hidage omit Wareham and *Brydian*, but include Shaftesbury, to which they assign 700 hides. The Domesday hidage can also be compared with the actual amount of geld collected in 1084. At the end of the Dorset Geld Rolls it is stated that the king received £415 8*s.* 9$\frac{1}{2}$*d.*, the geld on approximately 1,394 hides. The money recorded in the individual hundred accounts amounts to £422 6*s.* 5$\frac{1}{2}$*d.*, the geld on approximately 1,407 hides. About 900 hides were therefore exempt in 1084, which can be accounted for by the baronial demesnes, amounting to approximately 750 hides, and by the various exemptions and defaults, amounting to approximately 130 hides.

The system of assessment in Dorset shows traces of artificiality in the number of manors assessed at multiples or fractions of 5 hides. About one-fifth of all the manors in Dorset were assessed on this principle, and this figure can be broken down as follows:

2$\frac{1}{2}$ *h.*	5 *h.*	10 *h.*	15 *h.*	20 *h.*	25 *h.*	30 *h.*
21	44	25	5	5	1	2

In all, 103 out of 515 manors were assessed on a 5-hide basis, and in addition some divided vills add up to 5-hide units as is shown in Table 1.

[29] See pp. 119–20.

[30] See p. 42.

[31] Yetminster (47 hides); *Albretesberge* (47); *Canendone* (48); Badbury (32); *Stane* (63); Tollerford (59); Bere (49); *Celeberge* (41); Newton (47); Knowlton (36); Sixpenny (50); Brownshall (32); Winfrith (49); *Celberge* (51).

[32] A. S. Robertson, *Anglo-Saxon Charters*, 246–8 and nn.

Table 1
Divided Vills Assessed on a 5-Hide Basis

Edmondsham: 5 hides		*Shilvinghampton: 5 hides*	
The king	2 h.	Abbotsbury Abbey	1 h. 1 v.
Humphrey the chamberlain	1 h. 2 v.	Edwin	2 h. 2 v.
Eddeva of Humphrey	1 h. 2 v.	Count of Mortain	1 h. 1 v.
Farnham: 5 hides		*Creech: 5 hides*	
Aiulf the chamberlain	2 v.	Bretel of the Count of Mortain	2 h.
Wife of Hugh fitz Grip	2 v.	Roger de Beaumont	2 h.
Odo fitz Eurebold	2 h.	Walter of William of Briouze	2 v.
Aiulf the chamberlain	2 h.	Robert of the wife of Hugh	2 v.
Nyland: 5 hides		*Warmwell: 5 hides*	
Drew of the Count of Mortain	2 h.	Robert of the Count of Mortain	1 h.
Ralph of Turstin fitz Rolf	2 h.	William of Earl Hugh	2 h. 2 v.
Bernard of Turstin fitz Rolf	1 h.	Turold of the wife of Hugh	1 h. 2 v.
Tatton: 5 hides		*Little Windsor: 5 hides*	
Aiulf	3 h.	William of Moyon	4 h.
Wife of Hugh fitz Grip	2 h.	Hunger fitz Odin	1 h.
Mayne: 5 hides		*Glanvilles Wootton: 5 hides*	
William of Earl Hugh	3 h.	Ralph of William of Briouze	3 h.
The same	2 h.	The same	2 h.
Church Knowle: 7½ hides		*Milton on Stour* (in Gillingham)*: 7½ hides*	
Beulf of Waleran	1 h.	Roger of William of Falaise	3 h.
Walter de Claville	2 h.	Godmund	4 h. 2 v.
Walter of William of Briouze	1 h.		
Roger de Beaumont	3 h. 2 v.		
Mappowder: 7 hides, 1½ virgate, 7 acres		*Morden: 10 hides, 1 virgate*	
Count of Mortain	3½ v. 7 a.	Robert of the Count of Mortain	1 h.
Hugh of William of Eu	3 v.	Walter de Claville	3 h. 2½ v.
Bollo the priest	5 h. 3 v.	Aiulf the chamberlain	3 v.
		William of the wife of Hugh	1 h. 1 v.
		Ulvric	2 h. 2 v.
		Wife of Ulvric's brother	1 h. 0½ v.
Hampreston: 10 hides, ⅓ virgate		*Worth Matravers: 17 hides, 3½ virgates*	
The king	2 h. 1 v.	Roger Arundel	16 h. 2½ v.
Aiulf the chamberlain	6 h.	The same	2 v.
William of the wife of Hugh	1 h.	Robert of the wife of Hugh	3 v.
Torchil	3½ v.		

The divided vill was quite a common feature in Dorset, where manors were mostly small and hamlets more common than vills. Sometimes only one part of a divided vill is recorded. William of Eu had 1 hide in *Hiwes* (no. 258), but no one else is said to have any land there, and the place is not otherwise mentioned. Similarly, the Count of Mortain had 2 hides in Mannington (no. 186) and a mill and ½ hide of land in Stoborough (no. 201), but neither place occurs again. William Malbank had 3 hides in Trill (no. 225), attached to Clifton Maybank, but Trill is not mentioned elsewhere. About a quarter of the manors in Dorset in 1086 were parts of divided vills. A large proportion of the manors amounted to no more than 2 or 3 hides, and even the large manors were not as extensive as those in other south-western counties. Sherborne (no. 37), the largest manor in Dorset, was assessed at 43 hides, Piddletrenthide (no. 69) and Sturminster Marshall (no. 232) were each assessed at 30 hides, and Sydling St. Nicholas (no. 93) was assessed at 29 hides. Apart from these only 11 manors were assessed at 20 hides or over.[33] Most of them belonged to ecclesiastical tenants, but Loders (nos. 13 and ix), assessed at 20 hides, had belonged to Earl Harold and was held by the king in 1086, Canford Magna (no. 243), assessed at 25 hides, belonged to Edward of Salisbury, and Broadwindsor (no. 505), assessed at 20 hides, belonged to Hunger fitz Odin.

After the assessment in hides is recorded the number of ploughs which could be employed on the manor. Occasionally it happens that the number of hides and the number of ploughs which could be employed are identical. At Frampton (no. 121) there were 25½ hides and there was land for the same number of ploughs (*terra est totidem carucarum*). In a few cases the number of teamlands exceeds the number of hides, usually as a result of beneficial hidation. At Puddletown (nos. 8 and ii) there was land for 15 ploughs, but the manor was assessed at ½ hide. Beneficial hidation is more usual in the case of ecclesiastical than lay land but two manors of the Count of Mortain, Stanton St. Gabriel (no. 210), and Wootton Fitzpaine (no. 211), were beneficially hidated. In the majority of cases, however, the number of hides exceeds the number of teamlands. This sometimes appears to affect the value of the manor. Stalbridge (no. 42) was assessed at 20 hides, but had land for only 16 ploughs. It was worth £13. Similarly Tolpuddle (nos. 110 and lxvi), assessed at 18 hides, had land for 12 ploughs and was worth £12 and Stour (no. 127), assessed at 17 hides, had land for 10 ploughs and was worth £10. On the other hand Piddletrenthide (no. 69), assessed at 30 hides, but with land for only 17 ploughs, was worth £30.

There is no discernible relation between the hidage of a manor, representing the geld assessment, and the number of teamlands, representing an estimate of agricultural capacity. The relation between the teamlands and the number of ploughs actually at work on the manor is likewise not constant. Sometimes their numbers coincide. At Dorchester (nos. 4 and xii) there was land for 56 ploughs and 56 ploughs were actually being used there. In some instances there were more ploughs than teamlands. At Chardstock (no. 49) there was land for 20 ploughs, but 21 ploughs were actually there, and the same figures apply in the case of Cerne Abbas (nos. 76 and xxxix). At Stockland (nos. 106 and lxxx) there was land for 16 ploughs, but 22 ploughs were actually there, and at Abbotsbury (nos. 109 and lviii) there was land for 16 ploughs, but 21 ploughs were actually there. It is worth noting that Abbotsbury was assessed at 21 hides. In most cases, however, the number of ploughs falls short of the number of teamlands. Some 180 manors had fewer ploughs than teamlands, as compared with 150 manors where there were equal numbers, and 24 with an excess of ploughs. A considerable number of entries (110), referring to the smaller manors, record teamlands but no ploughs. The values of these manors do not seem to be affected. Woolgarston (no. 297) was assessed at 2 hides and had land for 2 ploughs, and was worth £2, although no ploughs are actually recorded. The teamlands are given for the manor as a whole, but the ploughs are divided into those in demesne and those held by the peasants. The question whether the *villani* alone held the men's ploughs or whether they were shared by all the peasants is discussed elsewhere.[34]

In the absence of evidence to the contrary it is to be assumed that the ploughs in question were drawn by teams of 8 oxen. There is no mention in the Dorset survey of the number of oxen to a plough-team, although oxen are mentioned in the case of some small manors. Eight small manors, each assessed at 1 virgate, are said to have land for 2 oxen,[35] and *Wintreburne* (nos. 387 and cxix), assessed at 1½ virgate, had land for 3

[33] Frampton (no. 121); Canford Magna (no. 243); Milton Abbas (nos. 94 and lxxiv); Sturminster Newton (no. 63); Cerne Abbas (nos. 76 and xxxix); Abbotsbury (nos. 109 and lviii); Loders (nos. 13 and ix); Stalbridge no. 42); Netherbury (no. 47); Handley (no. 125) and Broadwindsor (no. 505).

[34] See pp. 16–17.

[35] *Brige* (no. 348); *Brigam* (nos. 393 and cxxvi); *Brige* (no. 465); Rushton (no. 449); Tyneham (no. 473); Woolcombe (no. 474); Wool (no. 487); Worgret (no. 497).

oxen. Woodstreet (no. 508), assessed at 3 virgates, had land for 6 oxen. *Brige* or *Brigam* (nos. 348, 393 and cxxvi, 465) was divided into three manors of 1 virgate each, each of which had land for 2 oxen. But Lewell (no. 492), assessed at 3 virgates, had land for only 2 oxen, and Gillingham (no. 490), assessed at only ½ virgate, also had land for 2 oxen. Apart from these two cases the evidence suggests that a manor assessed at 1 hide would be likely to have land for 8 oxen or 1 plough.

The value of each manor is generally given twice; the first value being what it was worth at some time before 1086, the second what it was worth in 1086. In three cases the Exchequer text states that the earlier value relates to the time when the manor was received by the man who held it in 1086 (*quando recepit*). Exon. Domesday shows that this was the case in most entries, since it nearly always says that the manor was worth so much when its present owner received it. Sometimes Exon. departs from this practice. In the case of the manor of Puddletown Exon. in effect gives three values: *Ex tempore regis Edwardi hec mansio cum omnibus appendiciis suis reddidit per annum lxxiii libras et quando Aiulfus* (*recepit*) *reddebat tantundem.* In the cases of two manors belonging to the queen the previous values were the values in her lifetime; Cranborne (nos. 16 and xxii) and Ashmore (nos. 17 and xxiii) rendered respectively £24 and £15 *vivente regina.* Similarly Chaldon (nos. 408 and cxli) *valet per annum viii libras et quando Hugo recepit eam valebat x libras et in vita Hugonis reddidit xi libras.* For most of the manors of Cerne Abbey the previous value relates to the time *quando abbas recepit*, but at Renscombe (nos. 91 and liv) this was defined as *quando abbas W. recepit*, and at Littlebredy (nos. 85 and xlviii) the former value was that *tempore E. abbatis.*

Exon. Domesday reveals that some manors were being held at farm, such as Child Okeford (nos. 7 and i) by Fulcred, and Loders (nos. 13 and ix) by Roger. Both manors had belonged to Earl Harold and were held by the king in 1086. Woodsford (nos. 82 and xlv) was held by Bristuard at farm of Cerne Abbey. The Exchequer text omits these farmers, although it records that 6 men held Ringstead (no. 463) at farm of Brictuin. It is also plain that Osmund the baker's manor of Galton (no. 507) was held for rent by the four men there, who paid 12*s.* 6*d.*, since no 1086 value is recorded for the manor. Similarly Lyme (no. 36), belonging to the Bishop of Salisbury, was held by fishermen who paid 15*s. ad pisces*, but no 1086 value is recorded, and Ower (nos. 105 and lxxix) was held by 13 salt-workers who paid 20*s.* In all three cases the money paid by the tenants is the only recorded income from the manor, and they must have held the manors at a money rent. The value of the Count of Mortain's manor of Nyland (no. 150) was omitted because it was waste (*vasta est*) and no value is given for Odo fitz Eurebold's manor of Petersham (no. 375). The values of about one-fifth of the manors seem to have been based on a figure of £1 a hide, and in a few other cases the previous value had been based on this figure, but had changed. The tendency was for values to rise rather than fall.

The effect of the teamlands on this valuation has already been shown. Other considerations also seem to have affected the value. In the case of Puddletown (nos. 8 and ii), assessed at ½ hide and with land for 15 ploughs, the value of £73 must have taken into account the income derived from the third penny of the shire which was attached to this manor. Some of the manors which may be supposed to have been heads of hundreds were worth considerably more than one would expect, and it is possible that their values were affected by the profits from the hundred courts. At Sherborne (no. 37) the Bishop of Salisbury's demesne, consisting of 12 hides and 16 carucates which never paid geld, was worth £50. The bishop's demesne at Beaminster (no. 46) consisted of 6 hides and 2 carucates, and was worth £16. Loders (nos. 13 and ix), assessed at 18 hides, was worth £33, and Frampton (no. 121), assessed at 25½ hides, was worth £40. The value seems to have represented the amount at which the manor could be leased. At Wraxall (nos. 328 and c) there were 3 hides worth £3 and comparison with Exon. Domesday shows that 4 *villani* held this land for £3 rent. Similarly the 3 thegns with 3 hides at Cranborne (nos. 16 and xxii) paid £3. On the other hand, Brictuin, who held 4 hides worth £5 at Cerne Abbas (nos. 76 and xxxix), paid 30*s*.

It is difficult to compare earlier values with those of 1086, since there are several manors for which no previous value is recorded. In some cases it is legitimate to assume that the value had not changed, but in others this assumption would be misleading. No previous values are given for any of the estates of the New Minster, Winchester, Abbotsbury Abbey, Horton Abbey, Athelney Abbey, or the Countess of Boulogne. Only one or two of the manors of Milton Abbey, Tavistock Abbey, and Wilton Abbey have their previous values recorded, and previous values are given for only 4 of the Bishop of Salisbury's manors and 3 of the abbey of Glastonbury's manors. The previous value is given for the smaller of Serle of Burcy's manors, but not for the larger, and previous values are given for less than half the manors of William of Briouze. These fiefs have consequently been omitted from Table 2, except for those of the Countess of Boulogne and Tavistock Abbey which are supplied by Exon. Domesday.

TABLE 2

Comparative Values of Dorset Fiefs

Tenant-in-Chief	*Previous Value*			1086 *Value*			*Hides*	*Virgates*
	£	*s.*	*d.*	£	*s.*	*d.*		
Count of Mortain	180	15	8	181	4	6	191	2
	a 118	11	8					
	b 62	4	0					
Count Alan	23	0	0	23	0	0	15	
Earl Hugh	31	15	0	27	10	0	35	3
	a 26	5	0					
	b 5	10	0					
Roger de Beaumont	84	7	6	72	7	6	47	2
Roger de Courseulles	9	0	0	8	0	0	5	
Robert fitz Gerold	29	13	0	30	0	0	22	2
Edward of Salisbury	50	0	0	70	0	0	38	
Ernulf of Hesdin	9	10	6	12	10	6	15	3
	a 8	0	0					
	b 1	10	6					
Turstin fitz Rolf	8	15	0	10	0	0	11	1
	a 7	5	0					
	b 1	10	0					
William of Eu	72	15	0	89	7	0	90	3
William of Moyon	47	0	0	49	0	0	36	3
	a 40	10	0					
	b 6	10	0					
William of Falaise	12	0	0	8	0	0	13	2
William of Ecouis	14	0	0	13	0	0	11	
Walscin of Douai	8	0	0	6	0	0	10	
Waleran	36	5	0	37	15	0	38	
	a 25	0	0					
	b 11	5	0					
Walter de Claville	11	10	0	11	10	0	13	1
Baldwin	15	0	0	10	0	0	8	
Berenger Giffard	3	0	0	4	0	0	4	
Osbern Giffard	1	0	0	1	0	0	2	
Alvred of Epaignes	6	0	0	10	0	0	5	
Matthew de Moretania	15	0	0	15	0	0	14	3
Roger Arundel	44	17	6	52	17	6	65	2
	a 40	7	6					
	b 4	10	0					

TABLE 2 (*contd.*)

Tenant-in-Chief	*Previous Value*			*1086 Value*			*Hides*	*Virgates*
Aiulf the chamberlain	43	0	0	60	0	8	55	1½
	a 24	5	0					
	b 18	15	0					
Humphrey the chamberlain	12	0	0	13	10	0	10	1½
	a 7	10	0					
	b 4	10	0					
Hugh de Port	20	0	0	20	0	0	10	
Hugh de St. Quintin	2	5	0	2	15	0	4	2½
Wife of Hugh fitz Grip	115	10	6	110	15	6	116	3
	a 103	5	0					
	b 12	5	6					
Bishop of Bayeux	10	0	0	6	0	0	6	3
Bishop of Coutances	4	10	0	7	10	0	6	2
Bishop of Lisieux	18	8	0	19	0	0	26	
Cranborne Abbey	26	0	0	23	0	0	21	
Cerne Abbey	166	10	0	166	15	0	121	2
	a 119	15	0					
	b 46	15	0					
St. Stephen, Caen	52	0	0	52	0	0	33	2
Shaftesbury Abbey	115	10	0	146	0	0	167	1
	a 100	10	0					
	b 15	0	0					
Holy Trinity, Caen	9	0	0	14	0	0	10	
Canons of Coutances	10	0	0	15	0	0	8	
Abbey of Montevilliers	10	0	0	10	0	0	6	
*c*Tavistock Abbey	6	5	0	8	0	0	5	
*c*Countess of Boulogne	6	15	0	6	15	0		
	a 6	0	0					
	b	15	0					

a Previous value as given by Domesday. *b* Previous value deduced by assuming no change.
c Supplied from Exon. Domesday.

The Domesday survey does not give any pre-Conquest details for the peasantry in Dorset as it does for some other counties. In 1086 the peasants in Dorset consisted mainly of *villani* and bordars, with smaller numbers of cottars and cotsets, 33 *coliberti*, and over 1,000 *servi*. There were no sokemen or *liberi homines* as there were in the eastern counties, and no radknights as in some western counties, but 6 men (*homines*) held Ringstead (no. 463) at farm and there were 4 men (*homines*) paying 12*s*. 4*d*., apparently as rent, at Galton (no. 507). They may have been the same as the 4 free men (*liberi homines*) who held Galton T.R.E. Rent-paying tenants (*censores*) are recorded at Askerswell (nos. 119 and lxv) where there were 2 paying 15*s*., and at Allington (no. 253) where there were 9 paying 11*s*. Two French serjeants (*servientes francigeni*) are recorded at *Cerne* (no. 157) and 2 free Englishmen (*Angli liberi*) have 4 hides at Handley (no. 125). A smith (*faber*) is recorded at Melbury Osmond (no. 183), and two priests are recorded along with the peasants, one at Church Knowle (no. 235) and one at *Bleneford* (no. 455). Table 3 shows the numbers of all the various classes of peasants in Dorset in 1086, with the corresponding figures as calculated by Ellis[36] given in brackets.

In Dorset, as in some other counties, the *villani* are outnumbered by the bordars.[37] They are clearly distinguished from the cottager class, and were obviously more prosperous. Robert, Bishop of Hereford, in his description of the Domesday survey,[38] says that it was concerned both with the cottagers (*in tuguria tantum habitantibus*) and with those who had their homes and a share in the fields (*in domos et agros possidentibus*).

[36] H. Ellis, *Gen. Introd. to Dom. Bk.* ii. 419–514. The population totals for each county are currently being reckoned afresh in the Domesday Geography series, edited by Prof. Darby: see *Domesday Geog. of Eastern Eng.* (1952); *Domesday Geog. of Midland Eng.* (1954); *Domesday Geog. of SE. Eng.* (1962); and *Domesday Geog. of Northern Eng.* (1962). The SW. volume, covering Dorset, has not yet been published.

[37] In Cornw., Hants, Worcs., Essex, Norf., and Suff.: Ellis, op. cit. ii. 432, 441, 449–50, 469–70, 488–90, 504–6.

[38] *E.H.R.* xxii. 73–74.

TABLE 3

Peasantry in Dorset in 1086[a]

Class	(1)	(2)
Bordarii	2,947	(2,941)
Villani	2,636	(2,613)
Servi	1,161	(1,231)
Coscez	207	(209)
Cotarii	204	(188)
Coliberti	33	(33)
Censores (*gabulatores* in Exon.)	11	(11)
Homines	10	(4)
Ancille	3	(3)
Servientes Francigeni	2	(2)
Presbyteri	2	(5)[b]
Faber	1	(1)
TOTAL	7,217	(7,241)

[a] Column (1) lists the totals for each class as calculated by the author from the figures given in the Dorset Domesday survey, and column (2) the totals for the same classes as calculated by Sir Henry Ellis in his *General Introduction to Domesday Book* (1833), ii. 438.

[b] This number appears to include the 3 priests recorded at Hinton (no. 31), who were tenants of the king.

The latter must be the *villani*. As the more prosperous class, they are usually enumerated first.[39] Their exact status and the actual composition of the class as a whole are difficult to establish, but they were clearly not serfs. Although the word *villanus* in Domesday may conveniently be translated as 'villein', it had not by that date acquired the connotation of someone unfree that it had in later centuries. In 1086 it meant simply a man who lived in a vill, and was equivalent to the Anglo-Saxon word *tunesman*.[40] The class of *villani* must have included men who would have been described as geburs in pre-Conquest documents, but this is not to say that the two classes were coterminous. Men like the 4 *villani* holding 3 hides of land at Wraxall (nos. 328 and c) for rent could not have been classified as geburs, and among the *villani* of Domesday there must be included men who at one time had been free ceorls but had become economically dependent on a Norman lord. There is evidence that men whom pre-Conquest documents would have called geneats (and Domesday itself, in some instances, radknights) were sometimes included among the *villani*.[41] That some similar change had taken place in Dorset is suggested by a comparison of the Domesday description of Iwerne Minster (no. 131), belonging to Shaftesbury Abbey, and the description of the same manor preserved in a survey of the abbey's land about 1130. The survey states that the chaplain of Iwerne Minster had *de unoquoque genet i daiwenie ambram*. The Domesday description of the manor records only 29 *villani* and 20 bordars. The evidence of the later survey suggests that some of these men were, or had been, geneats.[42] In Dorset many manors were very small and were held by quite large groups of thegns in 1066, and it is plain that some of these thegns can have been hardly more prosperous in economic terms than the *villani*. In two instances it seems almost as if the pre-Conquest thegns or their heirs had survived as dependents of a Norman lord and were classed as *villani* in Domesday. Kingcombe (no. 247), assessed at 3¼ virgates, was held by 5 thegns T.R.E. In 1086 it belonged to Ernulf of Hesdin. He does not seem to have had any demesne there, and the only peasants were 5 *villani*, holding a plough. Another of Ernulf's manors, North Poorton (no. 249), assessed at ½ hide, was held by 7 thegns

[39] They do not always come first. At Beaminster (no. 46) there were *xix bordarii et ii villani et ii coscez*; at *Wai* (no. 163) *iii coscez cum uno villano habent unam carucam*; and at Spetisbury (no. 173) *ibi est unus bordarius et unus villanus*. But in general the *villani* precede the bordars, cotsets, and cottars.

[40] *V.C.H. Hunts.* i. 324.

[41] F. M. Stenton, *Anglo-Saxon Eng.* 471.

[42] B. M. Harl. MS. 61, ff. 45v–46.

T.R.E. In this manor, too, Ernulf does not seem to have had any demesne, and it was occupied by 7 *villani* with a plough. It is tempting to see here small, impoverished thegns, seeking the protection of a Norman lord, and being classified by the Domesday commissioners on the basis of their small holdings and not that of their wergild or social status.[43]

The Domesday survey of Middlesex gives details of the land held by the peasants,[44] but the Dorset survey is not so informative. Exon. Domesday, however, supplies a little information. At Winterborne Houghton (nos. 275 and lxxxv) a certain *villanus*, whom the Exchequer text does not mention, held ½ virgate, and at *Tarente* (nos. 400 and cxxxiii) a *villanus qui manet* held a virgate and ½ plough. At Burcombe (nos. 115 and lxii) there were 2 *villani qui tenent illam terram*, assessed at ½ hide. Tenements of a virgate and ½ virgate were common on the estates of Shaftesbury Abbey in the 12th century, and on the estates of Peterborough Abbey at the same period *villani* with a virgate were called *pleni villani* and *villani* with ½ virgate *dimidii villani* or *semi villani*.[45] At Swanage (nos. 515 and xxxviii), belonging to the Countess of Boulogne, a single *villanus* appears to have held the whole manor, assessed at 1 hide and ⅓ virgate, with a plough. The countess had no demesne in this manor in 1086.[46] Neither Exon. Domesday nor the Exchequer text has anything to say about such services as weekwork or ploughing. *Villani* paying money are mentioned only once, at Wraxall (nos. 328 and c) belonging to Roger Arundel. William held 3 hides at Wraxall of Roger Arundel which, according to Exon. Domesday, were held by 4 *villani* for £3 *de gablo*.[47] In view of the large amount of money involved it seems possible that the *villani* were holding the land at farm. Although this circumstance is rare, four cases are definitely recorded in Domesday, including two in the neighbouring county of Devon, at *Herstanhaia* and Lympstone.[48] In addition to these instances in Devon, two manors in Hampshire, Alverstoke and Millbrook, belonging to the abbey of Winchester, were held by the *villani* and may have been at farm, and in Surrey, Clandon, belonging to Chertsey Abbey, was held by the *villani* for a money rent.[49]

Information about the ploughs held by the *villani* is even scantier than that about their land. It is not certain whether the men's ploughs were held by the *villani* alone, or whether they were shared among all the peasants. The evidence on this point is vague and contradictory. The formula employed by Exon. Domesday would at first sight imply that only the *villani* had ploughs. A typical entry, for Abbotsbury (nos. 109 and lviii), runs: *habet abbas viii hidas et v carrucas in dominio et villani xxiii hidas et xvi carrucas. Ibi habet abbas xxxii villanos et xvi bordarios et xiiii servos*. This language seems to exclude the bordars from a share in the land and ploughs. But from other entries in Exon. it appears that the term *villani* was employed in two ways, both to designate the *villani* themselves, and to mean the whole group of peasants as opposed to the lord. At Cruxton (nos. 279 and lxxxix) *villani* (*habent*) *i hidam . . . et i carrucam*, but there were no *villani*, only 9 bordars and a *servus*. In this case it is obvious that *villani* means simply the men, and this is probably the meaning throughout.[50] The

43 On the likelihood that some such process had taken place, see F. M. Stenton, 'Eng. Families and the Norman Conquest', *Trans. R. H. S.*, 4th ser., xxvi. 7–8.

44 See *V.C.H. Mdx.* i. 92.

45 B. M. Harl. MS. 61, ff. 37–89 (Shaftesbury); *Chron. Petroburgense* (Camd. Soc. xlvii), 157–83 (Peterborough).

46 Count Eustace was credited with 1 hide and ⅓ virgate in demesne in *Aileveswode* hundred which must refer to Swanage, but in 1086 it is simply stated that King William never had geld from the manor: see pp. 136, 137.

47 The Exchequer text says merely that the land was worth £3 and that there were 4 *villani*.

48 *Dom. Bk.* (Rec. Com.), iv. 371, 425. The other cases are Oare (Kent) and Willesden (Mdx.): ibid. i, ff. 10, 127b. For a full discussion of the question, see R. S. Hoyt, 'The Farm of the Manor and the Community of the Vill', *Speculum*, xxx. 147–69; cf. R. Lennard, *Rural Eng.* 153–4.

49 *Dom. Bk.* (Rec. Com.), i, f. 41b; *V.C.H. Hants*, i. 442; *V.C.H. Suss.* i. 367–8; *V.C.H. Surr.* i. 290–1.

50 According to Maitland (*Dom. Bk. and Beyond*, 38–39) 'the term *villanus* may be used to cover the whole genus as well as to designate one of its three species'. Exon. once uses the word *rustici* in this general sense and once uses *rusticus* where it would normally use *villanus*: see pp. 76, 106.

Exchequer terminology is not helpful since it says merely that so many *villani* and so many bordars had so many ploughs, without indicating how the ploughs were divided. Two entries distinctly say that the ploughs were shared among all the peasants. At Burton Bradstock (nos. 2 and x) there were 41 *villani*, 30 bordars, 7 *coliberti*, and 74 cottars, and *inter omnes habent xxvii carucas*, and at *Wai* (no. 163) *iii coscez cum uno villano habent unam carucam*. On the other hand, two entries specifically assign the plough to the *villani* alone. At Corscombe (no. 488) there was *unus villanus cum i caruca et iiii bordariis et i servo*, and at Stoke Abbott (no. 45) *ibi est in dominio i caruca cum i servo et vi coscez. Ibi viii villani habent iiii carucas*. At Woolcombe (no. 262) the bordars but not the cottars seem to be sharing in the ploughs (*ii villani et viii bordarii cum i caruca et iii cotarii*). With this basic uncertainty it is obviously difficult to decide what fraction of a plough was held by the average *villanus*. Only the total number of ploughs is given and there is no guarantee that they were shared equally among the *villani* even if the share of the bordars and cottars could be satisfactorily established. In 19 cases the *villani* were either the only peasants or can be shown to have held all the ploughs. In 10 of these cases the proportion of *villani* to ploughs is exactly or approximately 2:1, so that it is possible that each *villanus* held about ½ plough. In 5 cases the proportion is exactly or approximately 4:1. There are 3 cases of a *villanus* with a whole team (nos. 182, 488, and 515) and at Gillingham (no. 250) there is the extremely rare case of a *villanus* with two teams of which there are only two other known examples, at *Haiugurge* (Suss.) and Keresforth (Yorks. W.R.).[51]

The bordars, cotsets, and cottars, who are enumerated after the *villani*, together form the cottager class, corresponding to the *kotsetlan* of the *Rectitudines Singularum Personarum*. The bordars are by far the most numerous, and usually take precedence over the cotsets, who in turn take precedence over the cottars.[52] Since the Domesday commissioners took the trouble to distinguish three classes of cottagers, there must have been some difference between them, but the nature of this difference is now unknown and there is evidence that the distinction was not clear-cut even in the 11th and 12th centuries. In the summary of the fief of Glastonbury Abbey in Exon. Domesday it is stated that the abbot had 72 bordars, whereas according to the Exchequer text he had 40 bordars and 32 cottars. The Exon. figure thus lumps the bordars and cottars together without distinction.[53] It is noticeable, also, that the Shaftesbury surveys of the 12th century record only cotsets, whereas in all but one case the Domesday account of the manors of that abbey mentions only bordars.[54] Round noted that in the accounts of Surrey and Sussex the cottager class were called bordars in some areas and cottars in others, the terms being mutually exclusive.[55] The Middlesex survey, on the other hand, which is the only one to record individual peasant holdings, suggests that there was a distinction between bordars and cottars based on the size of their holdings. Whereas most bordars in Middlesex had tenements of between 5 and 15 acres, the majority of cottars had no land at all or only their gardens. Those cottars who did have land had as a rule between 1 acre and 5 acres, only two having more than this. Only 54 out of 342 bordars had less than 5 acres, and only 9 had no land at all.[56] Whether this distinction holds good in Dorset is conjectural, since there are no details of individual holdings, but a distinction of this sort can be seen in the survey of

[51] *Dom. Bk.* (Rec. Com.), i, ff. 21b, 317; see also R. Lennard, 'The Economic Position of the Domesday *Villani*', *Econ. Jnl.* lvi. 260.

[52] It is unknown in Dorset for all 3 types to be found together in a single entry, but when bordars are found with cotsets or cottars they are enumerated first, and when cotsets are found with cottars the cotsets come first.

[53] See p. 148.

[54] On one occasion the Shaftesbury surveys do use the term 'bordar'. This is in the account of Melbury Abbas (B. M. Harl. MS. 61, f. 48v), which is the only Shaftesbury manor where cotsets are recorded in Domesday (no. 130).

[55] *V.C.H. Surr.* i. 292; *V.C.H. Suss.* i. 368.

[56] *V.C.H. Mdx.* i. 92.

Hinton St. Mary, belonging to Shaftesbury Abbey, in the later 12th century. There the *cotsettle*, with 5 acres each, are distinguished from the *cotarii*, who had only their houses and gardens.[57] The distinction between bordars and cotsets is, if anything, more problematical. It has been suggested that they were alternative names for the same group, bordar (from *borde*, meaning a wooden hut) being the French equivalent of the Anglo-Saxon *kotsetla* or cotset, but since bordars and cotsets occur together on two Dorset manors, this cannot be so.[58] Such information as there is about the holdings of the bordars comes from Exon. Domesday. At *Cerne* (nos. 108 and lxxxii) 7 bordars had a virgate and 5 acres, at *Waia* (nos. 380 and cxii) 6 bordars had ½ hide, and at Nutford (nos. 28 and xxxiii) there were 8 cotsets, two of whom held 8 acres,[59] while the third was apparently landless. There are no entries crediting the cottars with any land. In several cases the statement that the *villani* have so much land is followed by information about bordars or cotsets only. At *Wintreburne* (nos. 103 and lxxvii), for example, the *villani* are said to have a hide and a virgate, but there were in fact two bordars.[60] There is one striking entry concerning bordars (no. 480) where two of them held a ¼ virgate which they themselves had held freely T.R.E.: *Duo bordarii tenent quartam partem unius virgate terre. Valet xv denarios. Ipsi libere tenuerunt T.R.E.* The locality is not given, but it may have been part of Stourton Caundle which is the subject of the preceding entry. These two bordars do not appear to have been holding of any lord other than the king, and though their holding is very small it is not unique in this respect, since Alward, a thegn, held ⅓ virgate (perhaps part of Wilksworth) rendering 30*d.* (no. 446) as a manor. There is nothing to suggest that the two bordars were not holding as freely in 1086 as in 1066.

There is even less information about the rents and services of the bordars. Money rents are recorded twice. At Langton Herring (nos. 23 and xxix) there were eight bordars, one of whom paid 30*d.*, and at Lewell (no. 492) two bordars paid 20*d.* There is no reference to weekwork, ploughing, or any other services. The question of the bordars' share in the men's ploughs has already been discussed. On manors where there were no *villani* ploughs were held by bordars and sometimes cotsets, but never by cottars. At Frampton (no. 121) 24 bordars and 7 cottars had 14 ploughs, but whether the cottars shared the ploughs with the bordars or not cannot be determined.[61] At *Wintreburne* (no. 179) 7 cotsets had ½ plough. At Shilvinghampton (no. 216) there was land for 1 plough *que ibi est cum i coscet*, and at *Moleham* (no. 511) there was land for 1 plough *que ibi est cum i cotario*. It is hardly likely in these cases that each held a full team. Probably the ploughs belonged to the lord, and the bordars were merely in charge of them in the absence of *servi*. There are indications that bordars were sometimes attached to the demesne ploughs. At Worth Matravers (nos. 332 and civ) there was land for ½ plough *que ibi est cum iii bordariis*, and the corresponding Exon. entry shows that the plough belonged to the lord and not to the bordars; *ibi habet Rogerus dimidiam carrucam et iii bordarios*. At Creech (nos. 412 and cxlv) there was land for ½ plough *que ibi est cum iiii bordariis*, and the Exon. entry shows that this ½ plough was in demesne.

After the *villani* and bordars the largest group of peasants was that of the *servi*, of whom there were 1,161 in Dorset in 1086. Large numbers of *servi* were found in all the

[57] B. M. Harl. MS. 61, ff. 65v–66.

[58] H. P. R. Finberg, *Tavistock Abbey*, 61–62; see nos. 37, 46. The Peterborough survey records cotsets in some places and bordars in others, but both are recorded at Fiskerton (Lincs.), where there is *i plenus cotsetus et iii bordarii: Chron. Petroburgense*, 164.

[59] Four acres was the normal holding for a cotset on the estates of Shaftesbury Abbey in the 12th cent.

[60] For similar examples, see nos. 279 and lxxxix, 329 and ci, 376 and cviii, 401 and cxxxiv, 402 and cxxxv, 405 and cxxxviii, 410 and cxliii.

[61] For examples of bordars holding ploughs, see nos. 158, 169, 253, 272, 279 and lxxxix, 303, 338, 346, 376 and cviii, 401 and cxxxiv.

south-western counties, although this area was not unique in that respect. It is true to say, however, that in 1086 *servi* were most numerous in the area of the old West Saxon kingdom.[62] Apart from the male *servi* three female *ancille* were recorded at Crichel (no. 266).[63] It is probable that most of the *servi* recorded in Domesday were ploughmen. They are usually recorded in conjunction with the number of ploughs in demesne, and it is not uncommon to find a ratio of 2:1 between the *servi* and the demesne ploughs.[64] Where the number of *servi* falls short of the amount necessary to yield such a ratio, the deficiency can sometimes be supplied from some other class, such as the *bovarii* in Warwickshire, whose name indicates that they were ploughmen.[65] No *bovarii* are recorded in Dorset in 1086, but in one instance the *coliberti* seem to occupy a similar position. At Sturminster Newton (no. 63) there was in demesne land for 14 ploughs, although the entry does not say how many ploughs were actually there. There were only 15 *servi* but in addition there were 13 *coliberti*, whose number combined with that of the *servi* yields a ratio of 2:1 with the number of ploughs which could be in demesne. That the *coliberti* were sometimes linked with the demesne ploughs in the same way as the *servi* was demonstrated by Round in his introduction to the Somerset Domesday.[66] Their name suggests that the *coliberti* were freed *servi*. They occur only in the area of Wessex and western Mercia and appear in considerable numbers in some counties, though there were only 33 in Dorset. Apart from the 13 already mentioned at Sturminster Newton they were all on manors which had belonged to King Edward, 12 at Dorchester, 7 at Burton Bradstock, and 1 at Pimperne. At Dorchester and Pimperne they were grouped with the demesne ploughs and the *servi*, but at Burton Bradstock they were placed between the bordars and the cottars and the wording of the entry does not exclude them from a share in the men's ploughs.[67] In another instance a cotset seems to be associated with the *servi* and the demesne ploughs. At Uploders (no. 206) there was land for 2 ploughs *que ibi sunt cum i coscet et iii servis*.[68]

Comparison between Domesday and the surveys dating from the 12th century indicates a decrease in the number of *servi* after 1086. The earlier survey of the lands of Holy Trinity, Caen, records *servi* at Felstead (Essex) and Horstead (Norf.), but at Tarrant Launceston in Dorset, where there were 14 *servi* in 1086 (no. 141), no *servi* are recorded at all, and there has been a corresponding increase in the number of bordars.[69] In 1086 there was only one bordar but in the 12th century there were 13 bordars together with a smith and a shepherd. It has been suggested[70] that the successors of the *servi* were to be found among the *bovarii* and *bubulci* who figure so largely in the surveys. The Shaftesbury Abbey surveys[71] do not mention *servi* at all, with the possible exception of a *cliens qui servit in aula* at Cheselbourne.[72] There are, however, numerous references

[62] In 1086, according to Ellis (*Gen. Introd. to Dom. Bk.* ii), there were 995 *servi* in Norf., 905 in Suff., 1,768 in Essex, and 1,148 in Kent. But the largest figures occur in the SW.: over 3,000 in Devon, over 2,000 in both Som. and Glos., and over 1,000 in Cornw., Dors., Wilts., and Hants. Prof. Darby gives the figures for Norf., Suff., and Essex as 971, 917, and 1,788 respectively (*Domesday Geog. of Eastern Eng.* 169, 225), and for Kent as 1,160: *Domesday Geog. of SE. Eng.* 513.

[63] This is the only mention of *ancille* in the Dorset Domesday, but in the survey of the manors of Holy Trinity, Caen, dating from *temp.* Hen. I, 3 *ancille* are recorded at Tarrant Launceston, of whom 2 were dead and the third living (*harum ii sunt mortue alia vivit*): Bibliothèque Nationale, MS. Latina 5650, f. 27v.

[64] M. M. Postan, 'The Famulus', *Ec. H. R. Suppl.* ii. 6. In Dorset there were 312 manors on which *servi* were recorded, and on 66 of these (*c.* $\frac{1}{5}$) the ratio between them and the demesne ploughs was 2:1.

[65] *Ec. H. R. Suppl.* ii. 7–8.

[66] *V.C.H. Som.* i. 426.

[67] See nos. 2 and x: *Ibi sunt xli villani et xxx bordarii et vii coliberti et lxxxiiii cotarii. Inter omnes habent xxvii carucas.*

[68] For cotsets and cottars associated with demesne ploughs, see above.

[69] Bibliothèque Nationale, MS. Latina 5650, ff. 26v, 27v, 28v. For an analysis of this MS., see Jean Birdsall, 'The Eng. Manors of the Abbey of La Trinité at Caen', *Anniversary Essays . . . by Students of C. H. Haskins*, ed. C. H. Taylor, 25–44. The earlier survey, containing the account of Tarrant, seems to date from the reign of Hen. I.

[70] *Ec. H. R. Suppl.* ii. 8 sqq.

[71] These 2 12th-cent. surveys are preserved in the Shaftesbury Abbey cartulary: B.M. Harl. MS. 61, ff. 37–89. The earlier one dates from *c.* 1130, the later from *c.* 1175–80.

[72] Ibid. f. 45v.

to *bubulci*, who, as the context shows, were ploughmen. At Handley *bubulci qui tenent carucam habent singuli vi acras quietas pro suo servicio.* At Tisbury (Wilts.) there were 11 *bubulci*, to whom *datur cibus in natale Domini et in die Pasche et quando educant carros.* Each of the men held 4 acres and *tenet carucam et de ipsa arat suam terram.* At Cheselbourne the *bubulci* had 5 acres each (quit of all dues except geld), a piece of land, and a beast quit of herbage *pro utensilibus caruce quorum partem emunt de suo et partem accipiunt in nostram silvam.*[73] At Compton Abbas and Melbury Abbas the cotsets appear to have taken part in ploughing the demesne. On both manors the cotsets *ad carucas educendas habent dimidiam ambram et dimidiam multonem.*[74]

After describing the peasants Domesday gives an account of the non-arable appurtenances of the manor, such as meadow, pasture, and wood. Meadow (*pratum*) was an important adjunct, since, in the absence of root crops, hay was the staple diet of farm animals in wintertime.[75] Out of 515 manors recorded in the Dorset survey 418 had associated meadow, although only 63 manors had more than 25 acres. Occasionally the meadow lay at some distance from the manor to which it was attached. The Bishop of Salisbury had 130 acres of meadow attached to the manor of Sherborne (no. 37), 3 acres of which were in Somerset *iuxta Meleburne.* At Bingham's Melcombe (no. 30) 12 acres of meadow had been leased to Wlgar *Wit* T.R.E. and were held by William Belet in 1086, while at Rushton (nos. 407 and cxl) the wife of Hugh fitz Grip had subinfeudated the entire manor to two knights, retaining in demesne only 16 acres of meadow. Meadow was naturally located on or near rivers and streams, the largest concentrations lying along the valley of the Stour. Pasture (*pastura, pascua*), though less common than meadow, occurs in connexion with 366 manors and was spread over a larger area. One entry records an encroachment of arable land on pasture. At Swyre (no. 263) there was a piece of land which *prius erat pascualis modo seminabilis.* This land had been leased T.R.E. to Toxus the priest by a king's reeve, just as the meadow at Melcombe had been leased to Wlgar *Wit.* At Spetisbury (nos. 274 and lxxxiv) there was a piece of pasture 2½ furlongs long by 2 furlongs wide, and *in alio loco super aquam*[76] another piece 2½ furlongs long by 1½ furlong wide. A similar entry, concerning Tarrant Rawston (nos. 404 and cxxxvii), records a piece of pasture 3 furlongs by 2 furlongs and *in alio loco* another piece, measuring 8 furlongs. At Mapperton (no. 137) there were *inter pasturam et silvam xi quarentine longitudine et tantundem latitudine.* This may mean a piece of grassland with scattered clumps of trees, or it may refer to the use of woodland for grazing. Woods (*silva, nemus*) were used to pasture pigs[77] as well as to provide fuel and timber for building houses and barns.[78] At Stoke Wake in the 12th century Wulfric the priest had 10 pigs free of pannage in the Abbess of Shaftesbury's wood.[79] Wood which did not provide acorns and beechmast on which pigs could feed was called *silva infructuosa*, like the wood at Renscombe (nos. 91 and liv). According to Exon. Domesday, the wood at Nettlecombe (nos. 88 and li) *nullum fructum fert*, although the Exchequer text does not say that it was *infructuosa. Silva minuta* and *silva modica* are both recorded occasionally in the Dorset survey. What precisely these terms implied is now difficult

[73] B.M. Harl. MS. 61, ff. 45v, 55; cf. Iwerne Minster, Orchard, and Stoke Wake; ibid. ff. 47, 52, 52v.

[74] Ibid. ff. 48v, 49v–50.

[75] In the second survey of Shaftesbury Abbey's lands carting hay was a common obligation of virgaters and half-virgaters. At Iwerne Minster the virgaters carried ½ cart-load of hay from Combe, and at Fontmell Magna they had to find 20 mowers for the meadow *iuxta Sanctum Adwardum*: B.M. Harl. MS. 61, ff. 65, 67.

[76] This reference to pasture on or near water is similar to an entry in the earlier Shaftesbury survey which mentions *pascua de mareis* at Iwerne Minster: B.M. Harl. MS. 61, f. 46v.

[77] In some counties the Domesday survey gives the extent of woodland in terms of the number of pigs it could support: H. C. Darby, 'Domesday Woodland', *Ec. H. R.* N.S. iii. 23; cf. Laws of Ine, 44, 'a tree that can shelter 30 swine': *Laws of the Earliest Eng. Kings*, ed. and translated F. L. Attenborough, 51.

[78] Thatched with stubble (*stipula*). In the early 12th cent. the peasants of Cheselbourne reaped the stubble *ad domos cooperindos* (sic): B.M. Harl. MS. 61, f. 44v.

[79] Ibid. f. 52.

to determine, but they may both be translated as 'underwood'.[80] Marshland (*broca*) is recorded at Lytchett Matravers (no. 260) and a league of marshland at Wimborne Minster was attached to the manor of Canford Magna (no. 243). Heathland (*bruaria*) is recorded at Boveridge (no. 71) in Cranborne. The main concentrations of woodland in 1086 were in the areas of the later forests.[81] Although forests were not necessarily wooded areas, they frequently comprised large stretches of woodland. The only Dorset forest mentioned in Domesday is the forest of Wimborne, in which the king held the two best hides (*duas meliores hidas*) of Horton (no. 117) belonging to Horton Abbey. The wood (*boscus*) of *Hauocumbe* was attached to the manor of Burton Bradstock (nos. 2 and x), the third oak (*quercus*) being appurtenant to the manor of Frampton (no. 121).

Pasture and woodland were generally measured in leagues and furlongs (*leuge, quarentine*). At Handley (no. 125), for example, there was woodland 1 league in length and ½ league in width. It is difficult to see exactly what is being measured. The figures cannot in any case be more than a rough estimate of the extent of the wood or pasture, and cannot be taken as a reliable guide to the shape of the land in question. Other units of measurement sometimes used are perches (*pertice*) and virgates (*virgate*). At Poxwell (nos. 81 and xliv) there was *pastura viii quarentine et xxvi virgate longitudine et iii quarentine et xiiii pertice latitudine*, and at Symondsbury (nos. 92 and lv) there was *pastura v quarentine longitudine et una quarentina latitudine x virgatas minus*. The acre is sometimes used as a linear measurement. At Wootton Fitzpaine (no. 211) there was *vii quarentine et iiii acras* (sic) *pasture*. It is also not uncommon to find only one measurement given. At Hinton Martell (no. 31) there was *una leuga silve*, and at Little Puddle (nos. 14 and iii) *x quarentine pasture*. At Dewlish (no. 148) there was woodland *vi quarentine in longitudine et latitudine* and *pasture xxiii quarentine inter longitudinem et latitudinem*. It is uncertain what these phrases mean. They may be equivalent to the formula *pastura iii leuge longitudine et tantundem latitudine* (nos. 6 and xv), or they may represent an attempt to use the furlong as a square measure. A fresh difficulty is created by the fact that there is no indication how many furlongs there were in the league. Round considered that in Worcestershire there were four, since three furlongs was the largest measurement under the league. But at Shillingstone (no. 367) in Dorset there was pasture 42 furlongs long and 8 furlongs wide, and woodland 23 furlongs long and 9 furlongs wide. One is left with the problem of which is the larger; pasture 42 furlongs by 8 furlongs or pasture 4 leagues long and as much in width. This uncertainty makes any comparison of the relative sizes of stretches of pasture or woodland extremely difficult, and the situation is complicated by the fact that both pasture and woodland are sometimes measured in acres, especially in the case of underwood (*silva minuta*). It is impossible to say whether 140 acres of pasture (no. 223) is more or less than the amounts measured in leagues and furlongs.[82]

Among the other manorial assets mills were the most important. There were 276 mills in Dorset in 1086, attached to 178 manors. Some large concentrations are recorded; 12 at Dorchester (nos. 4 and xii), 12 at Sherborne (no. 37), 8 at Burton Bradstock (nos. 2 and x), and 8 at Wimborne Minster (nos. 3 and xi). In addition, 3 manors had 4 mills each, 10 manors had 3 mills each, and 30 manors had 2 mills each. Fractions of mills are sometimes recorded. There was half a mill at Worgret (nos. 84 and xlvii) belonging to Cerne Abbey. Worgret was a divided vill, and the other half of this mill belonged to the manor held by William of Briouze (no. 293). At Child Okeford (no.

[80] Prof. Darby so translates them at *Ec. H. R.* N.S. iii. 37, and in the Domesday Geography series.

[81] F. W. Morgan, 'Domesday Woodland in SW. Eng.' *Antiquity*, x. 316. The forests were Powerstock, Gillingham, Blackmore, and Cranborne Chase.

[82] The amount of meadow is almost always expressed in acres, but for meadow measured in furlongs, see nos. 110, 146, and 380.

152) the Count of Mortain had half of two mills (*medietas ii molinorum*) rendering 10*s.* Part of Child Okeford (nos. 7 and i) was held by the king, who held there two mills rendering 20*s.* of which, according to Exon. Domesday, *medietatem partu* (sic) *habet rex.* At Tarrant Crawford (no. 436) Alvric had a ¼ mill rendering 30*d.* Three quarters of a mill rendering 9*s.* were recorded at the unnamed manor (no. 494) belonging to William de Dalmar, which is presumably why Eyton identified this manor as part of Tarrant Crawford.[83] Both Alvric's manor of Tarrant Crawford and William de Dalmar's unnamed manor can with some confidence be assigned to the hundred of *Celeberge*[84] so that Eyton may well have been correct. One third of a mill is recorded at *Winburne* (nos. 388 and cxx) belonging to the wife of Hugh fitz Grip. It is possible that this was part of the mill recorded at Hervey the chamberlain's manor of Wimborne St. Giles (no. 499) where the entry reads *in molino ville xxii et dimidia* and then breaks off leaving a space. At Morden (no. 473) Ulvric had 11*d. de parte molini*, perhaps part of the mill at Morden (no. 172) held by the Count of Mortain. There was also ½ mill at Watercombe (no. 29) and another ½ mill at Ringstead (no. 359), each rendering 4*s.* The other halves cannot be traced. The mill of Stoborough (no. 201), belonging to the Count of Mortain, had ½ hide of land and 3 bordars attached to it. The mill at Povington (no. 242), belonging to Robert fitz Gerold, was claimed *ad opus regis.* The renders from mills varied considerably. At Sherborne, where there were 12 mills, four rendered jointly 18*s.* 6*d.*, three rendered jointly 30*d.*, three others 22*s.*, one 10*s.*, and one 5*s.* Where the composite render from a number of mills is given, it is not possible to deduce how much each one was worth since there is no guarantee that the money was divided equally. At *Waia* (nos. 380 and cxii) there were 3 mills which rendered 35*s.* and Exon. Domesday shows that while one of them rendered 10*s.* the other two rendered 25*s.* Of 131 mills for which individual values are given 45 rendered less than 5*s.*, 43 rendered from 5*s.* to 10*s.*, and 43 rendered 10*s.* and over. Renders in kind are mentioned once only, at Tarrant Keyneston (no. 60), where two mills rendered 30*s.* and 1,000 eels.

The largest numbers of mills were on the upper reaches of the Stour. Mills are sometimes mentioned in the 12th-century surveys of the land of Shaftesbury Abbey. At Compton Abbas, in the earlier survey, the abbess supplied the timber of the mill, the miller himself the mill-stones, and the *villani* transported the mill-stones to the mill.[85] At Bradford-on-Avon (Wilts.), in the same survey, the miller had timber from the wood yearly, the *villani* helped in the repair of the mill and the transportation of the mill-stones, and in return the miller did not receive toll from the lord's malt.[86] The mill at Compton was worth 4*s.* 2*d.* at the time of Domesday (no. 129) and according to the earlier survey, the miller still rendered 4*s.* 2*d.* in the 12th century, but this is the only such correspondence between Domesday and the Shaftesbury surveys.

Salt-pans and salt-workers are occasionally mentioned in Dorset, although the county was not an important centre of the salt industry. The Count of Mortain had 32 salt-pans (*saline*) at Studland (no. 209) which rendered 40*s.* and 12 at *Wai* (no. 163), and 16 salt-workers (*salinarii*) at Charmouth (no. 215). Glastonbury Abbey had 13 salt-workers rendering 13*s.* at Colway in Lyme Regis (no. 68), Milton Abbey had 13 rendering 20*s.* at Ower in Purbeck (nos. 105 and lxxix), and William Belet had 14 at Lyme (no. 504). The production of salt seems to have been confined to three areas, the Isle of Purbeck (Studland and Ower), the mouth of the Wey (*Wai*), and Lyme Regis

[83] R. W. Eyton, *Key to Domesday: Dorset*, 117–18.

[84] See p. 136.

[85] B.M. Harl. MS. 61, f. 49v.

[86] Ibid. f. 38: *habebit singulis annis i lignum in silva et auxilium de hominibus et carros ad fractum* (sic) *molendinum et molas adducendas.* At Bradford in the second survey the miller *debet habere i trunctum et i pomarium silvestrem unoquoque anno ad molendinum faciendum:* ibid. f. 75v. At Hinton at the same date the miller *debet habere . . . i quercum singulis annis ad reficiendum molendinum* (ibid. f. 65v), and at Tisbury *debent omnes reparare molendinum sua* (sic) *de bosco domine:* ibid. f. 71.

(Colway and Lyme). Later evidence records saltcotes in the same areas. Robert of Lincoln, in his charter founding the priory of Holme as a cell of Montacute, gave to it one tithe of salt from his saltcotes adjoining the manor of Langton Matravers, and Robert's son Alvred in confirming and extending his father's grant mentions a tithe of salt from his saltcotes in Purbeck.[87] In the second survey of Shaftesbury Abbey's lands (dating from the later 12th century) there is an account of Arne in Purbeck, which consisted of a hide of land devoted entirely to the production of salt.[88] Since all the places named are on the seaboard, it is evident that the salt was refined from sea water and not from brine-pits, and the account of Arne mentions the *plumba*, leaden vessels used to collect and boil the sea-water and isolate the salt.[89]

Fishermen (*piscatores*) are recorded in the Lyme Regis and Weymouth areas. The manor of Lyme, belonging to the Bishop of Salisbury (no. 36), was held by an unstated number of fishermen who paid 15*s.* to the monks *ad pisces*.[90] At *Brige* (no. 348), belonging to Aiulf the chamberlain, there were 2 fishermen, and 2 more in the same place belonging to Brictuin (no. 465). This manor lay in the neighbourhood of Weymouth.[91] These were obviously sea-fishermen, and it is plain that they cannot have been the total of fishermen in Dorset at this time. The second survey of Shaftesbury Abbey twice refers to the herrings of Wareham, and there must have been a fishing fleet to catch them.[92] The only reference to fishing in weirs is the statement that the 2 mills at Tarrant Keyneston (no. 60) rendered 1,000 eels.

Other manorial appurtenances occasionally recorded are vineyards, orchards, gardens, and honey. Two vineyards (*vinee*) are recorded, both belonging to Aiulf the chamberlain. At Durweston (no. 346) he had *ii acre vinee* and at Wootton Fitzpaine (no. 347) *ii arpenz vinee*. One orchard (*virgultum*) is recorded at the appropriately-named manor of Orchard (nos. 422 and clv) belonging to the wife of Hugh fitz Grip.[93] Gardens (*orti*) were more numerous. William of Eu had two gardens in Wareham attached to his manor of Lytchett Matravers (no. 260) and the Abbess of Shaftesbury had a garden in Shaftesbury itself. William of Moyon had a garden in Wareham attached to his manor of *Poleham* (nos. 276 and lxxxvi), which is recorded in Exon. Domesday but not in the Exchequer text. Hugh's wife had a garden at Turners Puddle (nos. 391 and cxxiv), which again is mentioned only by Exon. Domesday. Renders of honey (*mellis*) are recorded twice: 1 sester (*sextarium*) at Holworth (nos. 104 and lxxviii) and 4 sesters at Rushton (no. 292). Waste land is rare in Dorset. Nyland (no. 150), held by Drew of the Count of Mortain, was waste (*vasta est*), and according to Exon. Domesday part of Hurpston (nos. 414 and cxlvii) was laid waste (*hec terra omnino devastata est*). This manor belonged to the wife of Hugh fitz Grip, whose husband was apparently responsible for the wasting of the Dorset boroughs[94] and the diminution of the value of Bloxworth (nos. 79 and xlii) and Affpuddle (nos. 80 and xliii), belonging to Cerne Abbey. At Stourton Caundle (no. 363) Hugh *silvestris* had a little manor assessed at ½ hide, with land for ½ plough. He had there 2 bordars and 2 acres of meadow and *nil amplius*. It is not clear why he had no income from the manor.

Exon. Domesday's largest single addition to the Exchequer account is the information about the livestock, which is entirely omitted by the Exchequer scribes. Since the

[87] *Montacute Cartulary* (Som. Rec. Soc. viii), 160–2.

[88] B.M. Harl. MS. 61, ff. 60v–61.

[89] A. R. Bridbury, *Eng. and the Salt Trade in the Later Middle Ages*, 16–17. The author says (ibid. 19) that there were 32 salt-pans in Dorset in 1086, which must be the group at Studland, but he does not mention the 12 pans at *Wai*.

[90] Lyme was originally given to Sherborne for the taking of salt (see p. 41), but there are no salt-pans recorded in 1086. There was a house there rendering 6*d*.

[91] It is called *Bruge*(*s*) *iuxta Waymue* in 2 charters in the Montacute cartulary: see p. 56. There is a Bridge Farm in the area which may preserve the Domesday name: O.S. Map 25,000 SY 67 (1958).

[92] B.M. Harl. MS. 61, ff. 65, 67.

[93] This orchard is probably to be identified with the garden near Bradle, the tithe of which was given to Montacute Priory by Alvred of Lincoln (II): see p. 56.

[94] See p. 27.

greater part of the Dorset survey is missing from Exon. Domesday all the livestock figures need to be treated with some care and it is doubtful what conclusions can be based on them. It is, however, immediately clear that sheep were overwhelmingly important in the county's economy. There were 22,362 sheep recorded on the lands of the 12 landowners covered by Exon. (see Table 4),[95] or approximately 88 per cent. of the total livestock. Most of them were ewes (*oves*), which could provide both wool and milk, but *berbices*, male sheep kept for mutton, are recorded at Renscombe (nos. 91 and lv) and Mapperton (nos. 283 and xciii). The numbers of sheep are an indication of the importance of the wool trade even at this date.[96]

The largest flocks belonged to the king and were at Cranborne (nos. 16 and xxii), where there were 1,037 sheep, and Puddletown (nos. 8 and ii), where there were 1,600. It is difficult to generalize about distribution from the incomplete data, but there appear to have been more sheep on the western and southern slopes of the North Dorset downs and in the valley of the Piddle than elsewhere. About 3,000 sheep are recorded in this area.[97] Exon. Domesday, however, covers few manors in the north of Dorset, and Cranborne, with its 1,037 sheep, may have been the nucleus of an equally important sheep-farming area. Over 2,000 sheep were pastured in the coastal areas opposite Chesil Beach.[98] Sheep provided not only wool and mutton but cheese and milk, which was used much more than cow's milk. She-goats (*capre*), of which there were 811 in Dorset, were also kept for meat and milk. Four manors which kept goats kept cows also: Cranborne (nos. 16 and xxii); Ibberton (nos. 10 and v); Renscombe (nos. 91 and lv); and Farnham (nos. 396 and cxxix). Renscombe is the manor where only male sheep (*berbices*) were recorded. Only 58 cows (*vacce*) are recorded and it is unusual to find more than one or two on any single manor, although there were 4 at Ibberton, 4 at Holworth (nos. 104 and lxxviii), 5 at Winterborne Monkton (nos. 514 and xxxvii), 6 at *Wintreburne* (nos. 384 and cxvi), 10 at Cranborne, and 13 at Stafford (nos. 383 and cxv). *Animalia*, usually considered to mean cattle other than the plough-oxen, are more numerous, amounting to 520 in all. Nine oxen (*boves*) are recorded at Affpuddle (nos. 80 and xliii). The most numerous animals after the sheep were pigs (*porci*), presumably because they were easy to feed, foraging for themselves in the woods and feeding off acorns and beech mast. There were 1,613 pigs recorded in Exon. Domesday.

TABLE 4

Livestock Recorded in Exon. Domesday

	Sheep	*Pigs*	*Goats*	*Oxen*	*Horses*	*Cows*	*Mares*	*Asses*
The King	9,132	591	419	147	47	16		
Countess of Boulogne	100	16				5		
Cerne Abbey	2,632	196	68	15	2	6		
Abbotsbury Abbey	1,776	90	45	60	14			
Tavistock Abbey	260	20		9				
Milton Abbey	1,727	56	87	34	14	4		
William of Moyon	1,132	140	59	72	12			
Roger Arundel	872	120	48	29	2	4	13	
Serle of Burcy	443			10	1			
Wife of Hugh	4,096	357	80	122	15	23	12	1
Walter de Claville	192	27	8	31	6			
TOTAL	22,362	1,613	814	529	113	58	25	1

[95] No livestock are in fact recorded at Purse Caundle, the single manor belonging to Athelney Abbey, which was 1 of these 12.

[96] Eileen Power, *Medieval Eng. Wool Trade*, 31–32.

[97] There were 1,600 sheep at Puddletown, 393 at Waterston, 300 at Tolpuddle, 260 at Little Puddle, 115 at Burleston, 80 at Turners Puddle, and 12 at Affpuddle. On the western slopes of the downs there were 800 sheep at Burton Bradstock, 260 at Askerwell, 200 at Chilfrome, 158 at Powerstock, 150 at Compton Abbas, 108 at N. Poorton, and 93 at Loders.

[98] There were 600 sheep at Abbotsbury, 550 at Littlebredy, and 900 at Portland (which included Weymouth).

It is remarkable that out of 88 manors where pigs were kept, only 48 had associated woodland, and at Renscombe (nos. 91 and lv), where there were 12 pigs, the wood *nullum fructum fert*. In such cases they must have grazed on the pasture, or perhaps in the forests if they were near enough, or on the stubble of the fields. At Cheselbourne, in the 12th century, Wulfric the priest had *pascua suis porcis in stiplam cum porcis abbatisse*.[99] Cart or pack-horses (*runcini*) are recorded quite frequently, but in small numbers, usually only one or two to a manor. There were 122 in all. Mares (*eque*) are rare, being mentioned only three times, and numbering 25 in all. Roger Arundel had 12 unbroken mares (*indomite eque*) at Chelborough (nos. 324 and xcvi) and a mare at North Poorton (nos. 329 and ci), and at Turners Puddle (nos. 391 and cxxiv) the wife of Hugh fitz Grip had 12 mares with their foals (*eque cum suis pullis*). A single ass (*asinus*) is recorded at her manor of Frome Whitfield (nos. 377 and cix).

The four Dorset boroughs, Dorchester, Wareham, Bridport, and Shaftesbury, conform to the usual type of borough found in south-western England in 1086, small and not fully developed, but clearly distinguished from their agricultural surroundings. Of the boroughs three (Dorchester, Wareham, and Bridport) contributed to the *firma unius noctis*. Dorchester the borough was presumably connected with the group of manors headed by Dorchester (nos. 4 and xii) and Bridport with the group headed by Burton Bradstock (nos. 2 and x). Wareham was probably associated with Winfrith Newburgh (nos. 6 and xv), which is geographically nearest. A fourth group of royal manors, the Wimborne Minster group, seems to have had burgesses at its centre in 1086, although it was not at that time classed as a borough. A priest with land at Hinton Martell (no. 31) had 11 houses in Wimborne, and at Hinton also the church of Wimborne had 1½ hide and ½ virgate, and 8 burgesses. It is not impossible that the burgesses were at Hinton, but they may equally well have been at Wimborne.[1] The abbey of Horton (no. 117) had a chapel (*ecclesiola*) and the land of two houses (*terra duabus domibus*) at Wimborne. The two best hides of the manor of Horton lay in the forest of Wimborne, and it is possible that the chapel and the land were given to the abbey by the king in exchange for these two hides just as the church of Gillingham was given to Shaftesbury Abbey in exchange for a hide at Kingston (no. 134). Edward of Salisbury had two bordars and a house in Wimborne attached to his manor of Canford Magna (no. 243), and also a league of marshland. The fact that four persons had land in Wimborne provides one characteristic (though not invariable) feature of a borough, 'tenurial heterogeneity'.[2] This characteristic is exhibited in varying degrees by the four boroughs. In Dorchester in 1086 there were 88 houses standing and 100 destroyed, but the account does not state to whom they belonged. One house in Dorchester belonged to the abbey of Horton (no. 117) and the Bishop of Salisbury had one burgess and 10 acres of land in Dorchester attached to his manor of Charminster (no. 32). The same bishop had ½ acre of land in Bridport (no. 48), where in 1086 there were 100 houses standing and 20 ruined but still inhabited. Their owners are not specified. Shaftesbury was divided between the king and the Abbess of Shaftesbury. In 1066 the king had held 104 houses and the abbess 153 houses. In 1086 the king had 66 houses standing and 38 destroyed and the abbess 111 houses standing and 43 destroyed. She had there 151 burgesses, 20 empty *mansiones*, and a garden, which together were worth £3 5*s*. 0*d*. In Wareham T.R.E. there were 143 houses *in dominio regis*. In 1086 the king had 70 houses standing and 73 destroyed, the abbey of St. Wandrille had 45 houses standing and 17 destroyed, and *de partibus aliorum baronum* there were 20 houses standing and 60

[99] B.M. Harl. MS. 61, f. 44v.

[1] Ellis (*Gen. Introd. to Dom. Bk.* ii. 438) lists 8 burgesses in Wimborne who are presumably those mentioned in the Hinton entry.

[2] F. W. Maitland, *Dom. Bk. and Beyond*, 178.

destroyed. The abbey of St. Wandrille also held a church in Wareham (no. 124). A church and 5 houses in Wareham belonged to the abbey of Horton (no. 117). This church was probably that of St. Martin, which dates from the 11th century.[3] A house in Wareham was attached to the manor of Creech (no. 202), held by the Count of Mortain, and a house in Wareham belonged to the manor of Broadmayne (no. 223) held by Earl Hugh. Two burgesses and 12 acres belonging to the Bishop of Salisbury, and a burgess in Wareham, were attached to the manor of Povington (no. 242) held by Robert fitz Gerold. William of Eu had a bordar and two gardens in Wareham attached to his manor of Lytchett Matravers (no. 260) and William of Moyon had a garden in Wareham attached to his manor of *Poleham* (nos. 276 and lxxxvi). At Hurpston (nos. 413 and cxlvi), belonging to the wife of Hugh fitz Grip, there was a burgess rendering 8*d.* In view of the proximity of Hurpston to Wareham, it seems not unlikely that he was in Wareham.[4]

Although some burgesses are said to render money, there is nothing to throw light on their form of tenure, or the rate at which they paid rent. The burgess attached to Povington rendered 2*s.*, the one at Hurpston 8*d.* The Abbess of Shaftesbury had 65*s.* from 151 burgesses, 20 empty *mansiones*, and a garden. Assuming the empty *mansiones* to be unproductive and discounting the garden, the burgesses may have paid about 2*s.* each. The values of property in the boroughs are only incidentally mentioned. The church and five houses attached to Horton rendered 65*d.*, about 13*d.* a house. The house attached to Broadmayne rendered 5*d.* The Bishop of Salisbury had a house at Lyme rendering 6*d.*, and his ½ acre in Bridport rendered the same amount. William of Moyon's garden in Wareham rendered 3*d.*

Each of the four boroughs was assessed for geld. Bridport was assessed at 5 hides, Dorchester and Wareham at 10 hides each, and Shaftesbury at twenty. They all discharged this obligation by contributing to the support of the king's housecarls. Bridport rendered ½ mark of silver (6*s.* 8*d.*), Dorchester and Wareham 1 mark (13*s.* 4*d.*) each, and Shaftesbury 2 marks (26*s.* 8*d.*). The boroughs of Devon and the Wiltshire borough of Malmesbury did a similar service. In Devon the borough of Exeter paid geld only when London, York, and Winchester paid *et hoc erat dimidia marka argenti ad opus militum.* Exeter was assessed at five hides: *quando expeditio ibat per terram aut per marem serviebat hec civitas quantum v hide terre.*[5] Bridport, assessed at 5 hides, also rendered ½ mark *ad opus huscarlium.* The three other Devon boroughs—Barnstaple, Lydford, and Totnes—did jointly the same service as Exeter. Totnes paid geld when Exeter did, and then it rendered 3*s.* 4*d.*[6] At Malmesbury (Wilts.) *quando rex ibat in expeditionem vel terra vel mari habebat de hoc burgo aut xx solidos ad pascendos suos buzecarlos aut unum hominem ducebat secum pro honore v hidarum.* By analogy with the Dorset and Devon boroughs 20*s.* (1½ mark) was the amount one would expect a borough of 15 hides to pay.[7]

All four boroughs had moneyers in 1066 but none of these was said to be there in 1086. There had been one at Bridport, two each at Dorchester and Wareham, and three at Shaftesbury. Each rendered one mark of silver to the king and 20*s.* *quando moneta vertebatur*, that is when fresh dies were issued. The mints of Wareham and Shaftesbury are mentioned by name in Athelstan's mint Law[8] when there were two mints at each borough. Coins struck at Dorchester and Wareham under Athelstan have survived,[9]

[3] G. Baldwin Brown, *Arts in Early Eng.* (1925), ii. 484.

[4] For this burgess, see also M. Bateson, 'The Burgesses of Domesday and the Malmesbury Wall', *E.H.R.* xxi. 710.

[5] *Dom. Bk.* (Rec. Com.), i, f. 100.

[6] Ibid. f. 108b.

[7] *V.C.H. Wilts.* ii. 23.

[8] F. L. Attenborough, *Laws of the Earliest Eng. Kings*, 134. The 12th-cent. *Quadripartitus* version lists a mint at Dorchester.

[9] G. C. Brooke, *Eng. Coins from the 7th Cent. to the Present Day* (1955), 59.

and the Bridport mint is first recorded in the time of Aethelred II.[10] Although Domesday says only that the mints were there T.R.E. and does not say what the position was in 1086, coins from all four boroughs were struck in the reigns of William I and William II.[11]

It seems unlikely that at this date these little boroughs had courts of their own, but there is a possibility that Dorchester did have its own court. There was a hundred of Dorchester as well as a borough and a vill, and it seems quite likely that the hundred court met in the borough of Dorchester. The boroughs seem to have been extra-hundredal themselves, like the king's manors to which they were attached, and this fact probably contributed to the development of separate courts. Professor Tait observed that the hundred of Dorchester was later known as the hundred of St. George, to whom the parish church of Fordington was dedicated, Fordington being a suburb of Dorchester. He considered it possible that the hundred of Dorchester had split into two, one half covering the borough and the other half covering the geldable portion. It is possible that this division had taken place some time previously, and that consequently the borough of Dorchester had its own jurisdiction perhaps even before the Conquest.[12]

In all four boroughs a considerable number of houses had been destroyed after the Conquest. In Dorchester there were 172 houses T.R.E.; in 1086 there were 88 houses standing and 100 destroyed. In Wareham there were 143 houses T.R.E.; in 1086 the king had 70 houses standing and 73 destroyed, the abbey of St. Wandrille had 45 houses standing and 17 destroyed, and the other barons had 20 houses standing and 60 destroyed. In Shaftesbury T.R.E. the Abbess of Shaftesbury had 153 houses and the king had 104 houses; in 1086 the abbess had 111 houses standing and 43 destroyed and the king had 66 houses standing and 18 destroyed. In Bridport T.R.E. there were 120 houses. In 1086, according to the Exchequer text, there were 100 houses and 20 *sunt ita destitute quod qui in eis manent geldum solvere non valent*. The Exon. text implies that 20 houses must have been destroyed as well, by showing that the 20 impoverished houses were numbered among the 100 houses still standing: *xx ex his c domibus ita sunt adnichilate quod homines qui intus manent non habent unde reddent nullum*[13] *geldum*. There is no apparent reason for this destruction. The Chronicle does not record any disturbance in the area which could have led to such systematic wasting. Eyton's suggestion that it was caused by 'internal conflicts between the Anglican and Norman burgesses' may be the correct one,[14] but in view of his other depredations,[15] it is possible that the boroughs came into conflict with Hugh fitz Grip. In each account the devastation is said to have taken place *a tempore Hugonis vicecomitis usque nunc*.

II

King William had received in Dorset four groups of lands, the lands of King Edward, the lands of Earl Harold, the lands of Queen Maud, which had reverted to her husband on her death, and two manors which had belonged to Countess Goda, King Edward's sister. The lands of King Edward consisted of Portland and five large groups of manors. Portland (nos. 1 and vi) was not assessed in hides, and there is a blank space in the Exchequer entry where one would expect to find the number of teamlands. It rendered £65 blanched (*lxv libras albas*) a year, and did not pay geld. The five groups of manors consisted of Burton Bradstock, Bere Regis, *Colesberie* or *Colesbreia*, Shipton Gorge, Bradpole, and Chideock (nos. 2 and x); Wimborne Minster, Shapwick, Crichel, and *Opewinburne* or *Obpe Winborna* (nos. 3 and xi); Dorchester,

[10] Ibid. 70.
[11] Ibid. 83–85.
[12] J. Tait, *Medieval Eng. Boro.* 52–53.
[13] *nullum* is underlined in the Exon. text as if for erasure.
[14] Eyton, *Key to Domesday: Dorset*, 72.
[15] See pp. 23, 46.

Fordington, Sutton Poyntz, Gillingham, and *Frome* (nos. 4 and xii); Pimperne and Charlton Marshall (nos. 5 and xiv); and Winfrith Newburgh, Lulworth, *Wintreborne*, and Knowlton (nos. 6 and xv). None of them was assessed in hides, nor had they ever paid geld. The three groups headed respectively by Burton Bradstock, Dorchester, and Wimborne Minster each rendered one night's farm (*firma unius noctis*) and the two remaining groups headed by Pimperne and Winfrith Newburgh each rendered ½ night's farm (*dimidia firma unius noctis*). The night's farm was an ancient food-rent, dating from the time when the king continually travelled about with his court, and representing the supplies needed to support the king and his retinue for one day. It survived in 1086 largely in the area of the old West Saxon kingdom, and is found in Hampshire (where it is called the *firma unius diei*), Wiltshire, and Somerset as well as in Dorset, but traces of it also survive elsewhere. In Dorset it was not commuted to a money rent in 1086, but money values are given for the farm in the other three western counties. In Hampshire, the only county where the value was in any way standardized, the farm was worth £76 16*s.* 8*d.* T.R.E. and £104 12*s.* 2*d.* in 1086. No T.R.E. value is given for either Wiltshire or Somerset. In Somerset in 1086 two groups of manors rendered £106 0*s.* 10*d.*, a third group rendered £100 10*s.* 9½*d.*, and a fourth group £105 17*s.* 4½*d.* In Wiltshire in 1086 one manor paid £100 and another £110, while the remaining four manors liable to the night's farm were not valued in money.[16]

In Dorset the manors liable to the night's farm are grouped together in such a way that the only obvious reason for their association is that of size, although this is unlikely to have been the only consideration. Certainly they do not form compact geographical entities. Gillingham, in the northern tip of Dorset, is associated with Dorchester and its suburb of Fordington, in the south of the shire, and Bere Regis in the east is associated with Burton Bradstock, Chideock, and Shipton Gorge, which form a compact group in the west. If the number of teamlands can be taken as a rough guide to the comparative sizes of the manors, then the three groups rendering a full night's farm were approximately equal, if not in size, at least in agricultural capacity, having respectively 56 teamlands (Dorchester), 55 teamlands (Burton Bradstock), and 45 teamlands (Wimborne Minster). The two groups rendering ½ night's farm were about half the size, with 20 teamlands (Pimperne) and 24 teamlands (Winfrith Newburgh). Three of the four Dorset boroughs contributed to the night's farm in the manner already described, and some of the Dorset hundreds—Dorchester, Gillingham, Bere Regis, Pimperne, Winfrith Newburgh, and Knowlton—bear the names of royal manors, which must have been their heads.

Of the manors which had belonged to Earl Harold the most important was Puddletown (nos. 8 and ii). Since the third penny of the whole shire was attached to this manor it was clearly part of the official endowment of the earldom, and it was in the hands of Aiulf, Sheriff of Dorset, in 1086. With its adjuncts, consisting of 1½ hide in Purbeck and ½ hide in Mapperton, Puddletown was worth £73, and was beneficially hidated, being assessed at ½ hide, with land for 15 ploughs. It must also have been the head of the hundred of the same name. Of Earl Harold's other manors, Charborough (*Celeberge*) was also the head of a hundred, and Loders, assessed at 20 hides, was a hundred in itself.

The land of Queen Maud consisted of nearly 42 hides: 31 hides which had belonged to Beorhtric son of Aelfgar, and a further 18 hides which Hugh fitz Grip had held of her. According to Exon. Domesday Schelin held two of her manors, Witchampton (nos. 20

[16] For a full discussion of the night's farm and its commutation, see J. H. Round, *Feudal Eng.* 109–15; R. L. Poole, *Exch. in the 12th Cent.* 27–30; *Dialogus de Scaccario*, ed. C. Johnson, pp. xxxviii, 40–41.

and xxvi) and Edmondsham (nos. 18 and xxiv). Schelin also had held part of Hampreston (no. 443) of the queen, but in 1086 it was held by Torchil of the king. Another part of Hampreston (nos. 19 and xxv) was held of the queen by William Belet, according to Exon. Domesday. He also held 12 acres of meadow at Bingham's Melcombe (no. 30) which formerly had been leased to Wlgar *Wit*. Melcombe and Hinton Martell (no. 31) had formerly belonged to Countess Goda. Melcombe is said to have been taken by Earl Harold from Shaftesbury Abbey and the fact that the abbey had once held this manor is confirmed by the entry relating to the abbey's manor of Cheselbourne (no. 138) where it is stated that Earl Harold had seized the abbey's manors of Stour and Cheselbourne. King William had ordered them to be returned to the abbey in accordance with a writ of King Edward, but he himself still retained Melcombe. Since Goda was dead by 1056 it seems likely that Melcombe passed to Shaftesbury Abbey as a bequest, and that subsequently Harold committed the trespass. What became of Hinton in the interval between the death of Goda and the arrival of King William is unknown. Nearly half the manor was subinfeudated, mostly to ecclesiastics. A priest had held 1 hide of thegnland, which the king had in demesne in 1086. Another priest held 2½ hides T.R.E., of which he retained 1½ hide in 1086, the other hide being held by the Bishop of Lisieux. A third priest living in *Tarente* held 1⅓ hide, and Ulvric held 1 virgate of land. Lastly, 1½ hide and ½ virgate belonged to the church of Wimborne Minster, and were held by Maurice, Bishop of London. Attached to the manor of Melcombe were 3½ virgates in Buckland hundred which three free thegns had held T.R.E., and which, according to Domesday, Countess Goda had added to her manor. The Geld Roll for Buckland hundred gives a different account, attributing their acquisition to Robert de Oilly, who seems, from an entry in the Geld Roll for *Canendone* hundred, to have held Countess Goda's two manors at farm of the king.[17] Exon. Domesday records that Fulcred held the manor of Child Okeford (nos. 7 and i) *ad firmam de rege*. Child Okeford had belonged to Earl Harold, and Fulcred also held all the other manors of Earl Harold, with the exceptions of Loders (nos. 13 and ix) which was held at farm by Roger, and Puddletown which was held by Aiulf, Sheriff of Dorset, who also held the queen's manors of Frome St. Quintin (nos. 15 and xxi) and Wimborne (nos. 21 and xxvii). Fulcred appears in the Geld Roll for Uggescombe hundred, accounting for the geld on 1½ hide of Harold's land which can be identified as part of Fleet, and it seems likely that he held the other manors at farm also. Roger was perhaps Roger Arundel, a considerable landowner in the area, who had held the manor of Piddletrenthide (no. 69) before it passed to the New Minster at Winchester.

It is uncertain whether all King William's manors were exempt from geld or whether such exemption was confined to those of them which rendered the night's farm.[18] In the Geld Rolls the demesne of the king is exempt in the same way as the baronial demesnes, but in some cases, notably in the manors of Earl Harold, the *villani* had not paid geld either.[19] It is not clear whether these were defaults or whether the land in question was exempt. In the case of Ibberton in *Haltone* hundred there certainly seems to have been a default. It was a manor of 5 hides, 2½ hides in demesne and 2½ hides belonging to the *villani*. In *Haltone* hundred the king received £12 15*s*. on 45 hides. At 6*s*. on the hide he should have received £13 10*s*. and in fact the account concluded *restant xv solidi de terra Heroldi que est terra villanorum*, 15*s*. being the geld on 2½ hides. This certainly implies that the land was geldable and should have paid with the rest. Fleet (nos. 11 and vii), in Uggescombe hundred, is said to have paid geld in another

[17] See pp. 129, 146. Rob. de Oilly was Sheriff of Warws.

[18] See *V.C.H. Wilts*. ii. 176–7.

[19] Okeford, in *Ferendone* hundred; Charborough, in *Celeberge* (Charborough) hundred; Chaldon, in Winfrith hundred; and Loders, in Loders hundred: see pp. 136, 143, 146, 148.

hundred, though there is no record of this. Of the manors belonging to the queen two, Cranborne, in *Albretesberge* hundred, and Ashmore, in *Langeberge* hundred, had not paid geld. Hampreston, in *Canendone* hundred, had not paid geld. It was assessed at 2 hides and 1 virgate with 1 hide in demesne, and according to Exon. Domesday William Belet had held it of the queen. The Geld Roll for *Canendone* hundred states that *de ii hidis et i virga quas tenet i tagnus ad firmam de rege non habuit rex geldum*. The rest of the queen's manors appear to have paid geld in the usual way. The two manors which had belonged to Countess Goda, and which the king held in 1086, were certainly liable to geld. At Hinton there were 6 hides and 1 virgate in demesne, duly recorded as exempt in *Canendone* hundred, where the manor lay, and *de v hidis de terra Gode quam tenet Rotbertus de Oilleio ad firmam de rege habuit rex geldum post Pascha*. Hinton was assessed at 14 hides and 1 virgate so that 3 hides must have paid geld normally. The geld due from Melcombe was also withheld until after Easter, and the king had still not received it. The manor was assessed at 10 hides and lay in *Haltone* hundred, 3½ virgates in Buckland hundred being attached to it. The king's demesne consisted of 7 hides and 3 virgates, which were exempt, and Robert de Oilly *retinuit inde xv solidos usque post Pascha quos nundum habet rex*. In the Geld Roll for Buckland hundred it is further stated that *de dimidia hida et dimidia virga quas Rotbertus de Oilleio abstulit i tagno et posuit intra firmam regis in Melecoma non habuit rex geldum*. Thus no part of Melcombe had paid geld.

Alienations of royal land are occasionally recorded. A king's reeve had leased to Toxus a piece of land in Swyre (no. 263) *que nunquam geldavit T.R.E. sed erat in dominio et in firma regis*, and which in 1086 was held by William of Eu. The abbey of Cranborne held a piece of land in Gillingham (no. 70) which Hugh fitz Grip had given to the abbey, having taken it *de firma regis*. Half a hide attached to *Cerneli* (no. 212) *fuit de dominica firma Cerne T.R.E.* and an entry in the Geld Roll for Whitchurch hundred, which seems to refer to this land, says that it belonged to the king.[20] Apart from these pieces of land it seems likely that King Edward had already given Portland to the Old Minster at Winchester. A writ exists which purports to be a record of this grant, but it is of doubtful authenticity.[21] The grant, if genuine, may have been intended to take effect after the king's death, and it is noticeable that the king held Portland *in vita sua* or, as Exon. Domesday expresses it, *ea die qua ipse fuit vivus*, omitting the customary *et mortuus*. In any event the writ seems to reflect an actual grant, since in his charter to the Old Minster King Henry granted it Portland and its appurtenances as the gift of King Edward.[22] Soon to be alienated was Burton Bradstock, which in 1101 was given by King Henry to the abbey of St. Stephen, Caen, in exchange for the crown and other regalia which William I had left to that abbey.[23] Richard de Rivers (or Redvers) gave Loders to the abbey of Montebourg, with the king's permission, and its assessment was reduced from 20 hides to five.[24] Two of King Edward's manors, Winfrith Newburgh and Bradpole, were later held by serjeanty.

After King Edward the richest man in Dorset before the Conquest was Earl Harold, whose earldom of Wessex included Dorset. As well as the manors held in 1086 by King William, Harold had possessed Bincombe (no. 122), assessed at 8 hides, Waterston (nos. 334 and cvi), assessed at 10 hides, and Shillingstone (no. 367), assessed at 16 hides. He held in all 87½ hides, or about one-eighth of the land in Dorset held by

[20] See pp. 125, 126.

[21] This writ is printed in F. E. Harmer, *Anglo-Saxon Writs*, no. 112. For a discussion of it, see ibid. 385–7.

[22] This charter is printed in V. H. Galbraith, 'Royal Charters to Winchester', *E.H.R.* xxxv. 390 (no. xviii). In 1212 the Prior of Winchester held Portland *de antiquo fefemento regum Anglorum: Bk. of Fees*, 90.

[23] *Regesta Regum Anglo-Normannorum*, ed. C. Johnson and H. A. Cronne, ii, nos. 601, 1575.

[24] Ibid. no. 1018.

laymen excluding the king. He had taken four manors from Shaftesbury Abbey: Stour (no. 127), assessed at 17 hides, Cheselbourne (no. 138), assessed at 16 hides, Melcombe (no. 30), assessed at 10 hides, and a manor called *Pidele*.[25] He had also taken a manor belonging to a certain clerk (*quidam clericus*) and given it to Eadnoth the staller. This manor, Ilsington (no. 221), was held by Earl Hugh in 1086. Harold's mother, Countess Gytha, held two manors in Dorset T.R.E., Little Puddle (nos. 14 and iii) and Frampton (no. 121), assessed at 25½ hides, a total hidage of 30½ hides. To the manor of Frampton was attached the third share of the wood of *Hauocumbe*, belonging to Burton Bradstock.[26] Queen Edith, Earl Harold's sister and the widow of King Edward, had held the manor of Sherborne (no. 37), assessed at 43 hides. She presumably held it for life, since Bishop Aelfwold of Sherborne had held it before her, and in 1086 it belonged to the Bishop of Salisbury and the monks of Sherborne. Countess Goda had 24 hides in Dorset, consisting of the manors of Melcombe (no. 30) and Hinton (no. 31). She died before 1056 and on her death Melcombe appears to have passed to Shaftesbury Abbey.[27] Archbishop Stigand held one manor in Dorset, the large and valuable Sturminster Marshall (no. 232), assessed at 30 hides and worth £66.

The richest thegn in Dorset in 1086 was Beorhtric son of Aelfgar whose lands were given to Queen Maud and later formed the nucleus of the honor of Gloucester. Of Beorhtric's Dorset manors Cranborne, Ashmore, and Frome St. Quintin belonged to the king in 1086. The queen had given two other manors away, Tarrant Launceston (no. 141) to Holy Trinity, Caen, and Tyneham (no. 369) to Anschitil fitz Ameline. Boveridge, in Cranborne (no. 71), which belonged to the abbey of Cranborne in 1086, was held by Brictric T.R.E. who is probably Beorhtric son of Aelfgar. The latter may well be identified also with the T.R.E. holder of Dewlish (no. 148) which Count Alan held in 1086, since this manor was later part of the honor of Gloucester,[28] but whether he was the Brictric who held *Tarente* (no. 370) or the Brictric who preceded the Count of Mortain at Mappowder (no. 171) and Uploders (no. 206) is less certain. He certainly held 59 hides in Dorset T.R.E. and may have held 73 hides. Toli, whose name suggests that he was of Scandinavian origin, held 49½ hides in Dorset. He was a prosperous local thegn with 34 hides in Hampshire and land in Wiltshire and Devon, all of which was held by William of Eu in 1086. William's other predecessor was Aelfstan of Boscombe, whose land in 8 counties belonged to William in 1086. Most of Aelfstan's land lay in Wiltshire and Gloucestershire, but he was one of the larger landowners in Dorset where he held 34 hides. Ailvert (Aethelfrith) and Ailmar (Aelmer), the most important of Roger Arundel's predecessors, were quite wealthy thegns, with land in Somerset as well as Dorset which also passed to Roger. Aethelfrith has been identified as Ailferth *minister* who witnessed Edward the Confessor's grant to Bath Abbey in 1061.[29] He held 26½ hides in Dorset and Aelmer 25½ hides. They can be identified as the two men who held Piddletrenthide (no. 69), as two manors, of King Edward, since this manor was held by Roger Arundel before it passed to the New Minster, Winchester. It was assessed at 30 hides, and, assuming that it was roughly divided in half between the two men, they must have held in all about 40 hides apiece.

One of the Count of Mortain's predecessors was called Edmar. He held about 35 hides, consisting of the manors of Gussage All Saints (no. 192), *Blaneford* (no. 194), and some smaller manors, one of which, Wootton Fitzpaine (no. 211), appears to have been beneficially hidated.[30] Edmar is probably to be identified as the man of the same name

[25] See pp. 43, 83.

[26] See pp. 3, 65.

[27] See p. 29. For a full account of Goda's life and marriages, see J. H. Round, *Studies in Peerage and Family Hist.* 147–51.

[28] *Bk. of Fees*, 93 (1212).

[29] *V.C.H. Som.* 419; Eyton, *Domesday Studies: Som.* i. 155–6.

[30] It was assessed at 2 hides but had land for 7 ploughs.

whose manors in Devon and Somerset passed to the count. In the Devon survey he is called Edmer Atre, and in the Exon. Domesday for Somerset, *Edmeratorius*. He also held land in Cornwall.[31] Eadnoth the staller, whose lands passed to Hugh, Earl of Chester, held 25 hides in Dorset, and in King William's time had taken the manor of Burstock (no. 230), assessed at three hides, from a certain thegn. He is addressed in a writ of William relating to Bath Abbey.[32] He was killed in 1067, leading the militia against the sons of Harold. It was Harold from whom he had received the manor of Ilsington (no. 221). Two of his manors, South Perrott (no. 228) and Catsley (no. 229), he had bought from Bishop Aelfwold of Sherborne, on condition that at his death they should return to the church, but Earl Hugh held them in 1086. Two other manors held by Eadnoth had at one time belonged to Sherborne Abbey.[33] Eadnoth's son, Harding, also survived the Conquest, and became the ancestor of the Berkeleys.[34] He may be identical with Harding who held Bredy (Farm) (no. 317) which passed to Berenger Giffard. According to the Geld Roll for Godderthorn hundred, where Bredy (Farm) lay, Berenger's predecessor continued to hold of him at farm.[35] Wulfwynn, a wealthy English lady, with about 100 hides in six counties, held two manors in Dorset, Canford Magna and Kinson (nos. 243, 244), assessed jointly at 38 hides. Like the rest of her land, these two manors were held in 1086 by Edward of Salisbury. In the Middlesex survey she is called *Wlwene homo regis* and in the Buckinghamshire survey *Wlwen homo regis Edwardi*. In Buckinghamshire she is also called *Wlwene de Cresselai*, which appears to refer to her tenure of the manor of Creslow (Bucks.).[36]

The prevalence of names like Alvric and Alward makes identification uncertain, but it is at least likely that the Alvric who held five of the manors belonging to the wife of Hugh fitz Grip in 1086 is identical with the Alvric who T.R.E. had been the tenant of three of the manors which Hugh fitz Grip held of the queen. If this is the case he had 24½ hides. Alward Colin(c), who T.R.E. had held Langton Herring (nos. 23 and xxix), another of the manors held by Hugh fitz Grip of the queen, and who still held Thorncombe (no. 439) in 1086, was probably the man who held five manors belonging to the wife of Hugh fitz Grip in 1086 and also the manor of Little Waddon (no. 460) which Hugh gave to Brictuin. If so, he had 16 hides. It is unsafe to identify him with the Alward who held 14½ hides which passed to the Count of Mortain, or the Alward who held 15½ hides which passed to William of Moyon.

Bondi is a common Scandinavian name, but it occurs only twice in Dorset and it is probably safe to identify the man who held Broadwindsor (no. 505) with the man who held Compton Valence (no. 357), giving him a total of 30 hides. John, who held the two manors which passed to Matthew de Moretania (nos. 320 and 321), is probably to be identified with John the Dane (*danus*), a predecessor of Matthew in Gloucestershire and Somerset.[37] He had about 15 hides in Dorset. Godric held 12 hides as the predecessor of William of Moyon. Alfred the sheriff held Lulworth (no. 350), assessed at 8 hides, 3 virgates, which in 1086 was held by Aiulf the chamberlain, then Sheriff of Dorset. Since Alfred is a common Saxon name, it is unsafe to identify Alfred the sheriff with the pre-Conquest holders of Stour Provost (no. 231) and *Wintreburne* (no. 305), or with the man who held two manors belonging to the Count of Mortain in 1086.[38] Bricsi (Beorhtsige), *miles regis Edwardi*, held Wootton Fitzpaine (no. 347), assessed at

[31] *Dom. Bk.* (Rec. Com.), i, f. 104b; iv. 190, 191. Round (*V.C.H. Som.* i. 418) identifies him with Edmer *attile* or *atule*, who held land in Herts., Mdx., and Berks., which passed to the Count of Mortain. Feilitzen (*Pre-Conquest Personal Names of Dom. Bk.* 232 n.) regards this identification as no more than a possibility. Edmer *attile* was also called *teignus Heraldi comitis* and *teignus R.E.*: *Dom. Bk.* (Rec. Com.), i, ff. 129b, 136b, 146.

[32] *Regesta Regum Anglo-Normannorum*, i, no. 7.

[33] See p. 41.

[34] *V.C.H. Som.* i. 417–18; see also p. 57.

[35] See pp. 36, 131.

[36] *V.C.H. Wilts.* ii. 99.

[37] See p. 49.

[38] For a writ addressed to Alfred the sheriff, see F. E. Harmer, *Anglo-Saxon Writs*, no. 1.

12 hides, which Aiulf the chamberlain held in 1086. He also held Keevil (Wilts.) and about 20 hides in Somerset.[39] Ode the treasurer held ½ hide in Wimborne Minster (nos. 21 and xxvii). Round identified him with Odo of Winchester who held land in Hampshire, Berkshire, and Wiltshire, as a thegn in 1086.[40] Rainbald of Cirencester, who had the office if not the name of chancellor under Edward the Confessor, held Pulham (no. 146) in Dorset,[41] which he still held in 1086.

Wulfweard White, who held Pentridge (no. 67) and Silton (no. 271), had land in eleven counties. He may be identical with the Wulfweard who held Tarrant Crawford (no. 58), and Eyton identified Wlgar *Wit*, who T.R.E. held 12 acres of meadow at Bingham's Melcombe (no. 30), with Wulfweard White.[42] Other landowners with little land in Dorset but larger estates elsewhere were Saeweard, Alwi, and Wulfgifu. Saeweard, the predecessor of Baldwin at Iwerne Courtney (no. 316), held five manors in Somerset and five in Devon, all of which had passed to Baldwin. Alwi held Turnworth (no. 319) which in 1086 was held by Alvred of Epaignes. He was Alvred's predecessor in Wiltshire, Devon, and Somerset as well, and is called Alwi Banneson in Exon. Domesday. Wulfgifu, who held 11 hides in Dorset as the predecessor of the Countess of Boulogne, had 65 hides in Hampshire, where she was called Wulfgifu *Beteslau*.[43] In addition, she held 5 hides in Wiltshire and a manor in Somerset. Other women besides Wulfwynn and Wulfgifu held land in Dorset, although only in small amounts. Aelfrun held part of Afflington (no. 236), to which she gave her name.[44] Aethelflaed held 2 hides at Hethfelton (no. 294) and Leofrun held two manors, both in Stourton Caundle (nos. 363, 478), amounting to 1½ hide. Leofgifu held Blandford (no. 336) and Aelgifu held Morden (no. 337). The latter is probably to be identified with the woman of the same name who held Lyme Regis (no. 504) and Stourton Caundle (no. 219).

The relative rarity of the name Beorhtnod permits the identification of Britnod, who held Stafford (no. 155), with Bricnod, who held Melbury Bubb (no. 323), and Brisnod who held West Parley (no. 371).[45] Other rare names occur in Dorset. Sared (Saered) is found only in Dorset, where he and his brother held Blandford St. Mary (no. 185), and in Somerset, and Watman (Hwaetman), who held *Waia* (no. 364), occurs only in Dorset and Herefordshire. Burde, who held the little manor of Rushton (no. 292), is only found in Dorset. His name is apparently derived from the French *burdel* meaning mule. Her, who gave his name to Herston (nos. 333 and cv), is also peculiar to Dorset. Herston was a divided vill in 1086, part of it (no. 512) being held by Godfrey the scullion whose father held it T.R.E. His father's name is not given. Toxus the priest who held part of Swyre (no. 263) is not found anywhere else but Dorset. Aldebert (Ealdbeorht) and Wicnod (Wihtnoth), who held *Cerneli* (no. 212) and Milton on Stour (no. 272) respectively, were peculiar to Dorset. Bern (Beorn), who held part of Church Knowle (no. 312), has a name found otherwise only in East Anglia and Northamptonshire, and Turmund (Thormund) who held *Wintreburne* (no. 56) is otherwise only found in Somerset. Herling, who held Tarrant Keyneston (no. 60), is found only in Dorset and Berkshire, and Trawin, who held Lulworth (no. 199), Dachelin, who held Nyland (no. 251) in company with Edric and Alward, and Gerling, who held Turners Puddle (nos. 391 and cxxiv), are all peculiar to Dorset. Trasmund, who held Hill (no. 318), which passed to Osbern Giffard, is found elsewhere as Osbern's predecessor in Wiltshire, and also held Manston (no. 302), which passed to Waleran. He is not otherwise recorded. Herling, Trawin, Dachelin, Gerling, and Trasmund all bear names of Germanic origin, while Bern, Brune (Bruno, no. 149), Turmund, Her, Toli, Bondi,

[39] *V.C.H. Wilts.* ii. 66.
[40] *V.C.H. Hants*, i. 427.
[41] See p. 45.
[42] Eyton, *Key to Domesday: Dorset*, 112 n.
[43] i.e. Beslow (Salop): see *V.C.H. Hants*, i. 429.
[44] A. Fägersten, *Place-Names of Dorset*, 117.
[45] O. von Feilitzen, *Pre-Conquest Personal Names*, 196.

Askell (Anschil), and Azor are all of Scandinavian derivation. Askell (Anschil) occurs twice in Dorset (nos. 180, 490). Azor appears three times. One of his three manors, Ailwood (no. 482), had passed to Swain in 1086. Swain's three other manors had been held by his father T.R.E., and it is possible that he is to be identified with Swain son of Azor, who held land in Northamptonshire, and that Azor can be identified as Swain's father, the holder of some 20 hides in Dorset T.R.E.[46] The pre-Conquest holders of three manors are described as free men (*liberi homines*). Godwin who held *Cernel* (no. 147) is described as a *liber homo*. Four free men held the manor of Galton T.R.E. (no. 507) and may be identical with the 4 men holding it for rent in 1086. Three free men held Woodstreet (no. 508). Both Galton, assessed at 1 hide and ½ virgate, and Woodstreet, assessed at 3 virgates, had passed to Osmund the baker in 1086. *Cernel* was assessed at 3 hides and was held by Walter the deacon, an almsman of the king in 1086. Apart from these free men several manors were held by 'free thegns' T.R.E. A free thegn (*liber tainus*) held Hemsworth (no. 355). Three free thegns (*liberi taini*) held the 3½ virgates in Buckland hundred which were added to the manor of Melcombe. Mappowder (no. 431), which Bollo the priest held in 1086, was held T.R.E. by the same Bollo *cum aliis vii liberis tainis*. The thegn who held Church Knowle (no. 308) was free with his land (*liber erat cum hac terra*), which presumably means that he was not commended to any lord. Freedom to commend oneself to any lord is quite frequently mentioned, in a haphazard fashion which suggests that it was so common that it was not thought necessary to mention it in all cases. Five thegns who held three virgates attached to Rampisham (no. 55) could *quo volebant se vertere*. Alward, who held Little Windsor (nos. 282 and xcii), *potuit ire ad quemlibet dominum volebat*. Wulfgifu, the T.R.E. holder of the Countess of Boulogne's manors, *poterat ire cum terra sua quo volebat*.[47] Dodo who held Edmondsham (nos. 18 and xxiv), Saul who held Hampreston (nos. 19 and xxv), and the two thegns who held Witchampton (nos. 20 and xxvi) could all go with their land to any lord they liked. The men who held the manors which in 1086 were held by the wife of Hugh fitz Grip were all free to go to any lord, as appears from a note appended at the end of the account of her manors: *Omnes taini qui has terras tenebant poterant ire ad quem dominum volebant*. A similar statement is appended to the land of the king's serjeants: *Qui has terras tenebant T.R.E. poterant ire quo volebant*, and at the end of the account of the land of the Count of Mortain there is a note that *omnes qui has terras tenebant T.R.E. libere tenebant*. References to commendation are rare. The three thegns holding 3 hides at Cranborne of Beorhtric son of Aelfgar *non potuerant separari ab eo* and Alnod held Stourpaine *de Edwardo Lipe et non poterat separari a dominio suo*. Aelmer and Aethelfrith who held Piddletrenthide as two manors of King Edward *non poterant cum terra ista ire ad quemlibet dominum*. Aethelfrith also held Worth Matravers (no. 330) of King Edward *et non potuit separari a servicio regis*. Beorhtsige, who held Wootton Fitzpaine (no. 347), is described as *miles regis Edwardi*.

There are frequent references to land held in parage (*in paragio*, *pariter*), which consisted in the joint tenure of an estate by co-heirs. The merit of this system was that it prevented the fragmentation of manors which would otherwise have occurred in a society which did not recognize primogeniture. Sared and his brother held Blandford (no. 185) in parage and two brothers held Ranston (no. 241) in parage. Scirewold and Ulward, who held *Wai* (no. 162), and Edric, Dachelin, and Alward, who held Nyland (no. 251), are said to hold in parage. The necessity of such a system is obvious when the

[46] For these rare names, see Feilitzen, op cit. *passim*. For the identification of Swain as Swain son of Azor, see p. 52.

[47] See p. 114.

proportion of manors held by large numbers of unnamed thegns is taken into consideration. An extreme instance is the manor of *Poleham* (nos. 276 and lxxxvi), which was held by 21 thegns T.R.E., and which was assessed at 10 hides. The Exon. version shows that these thegns held in parage. If the manor had been divided between them the fragmentation would have produced a large number of tiny, uneconomic units. Even so, it is plain from such examples that many pre-Conquest thegns were scarcely more prosperous, in economic terms, than the *villani*. *Poleham* is unusual, but large groups of thegns are not exceptional. Twelve thegns held 7 hides in Purbeck and *poterant ire quo volebant*. Ten thegns held 3 hides in *Cerne* (no. 157). Four manors were each held by a group of 9 thegns,[48] two more were held by groups of 7 thegns,[49] and Stinsford (no. 358), assessed at 2½ hides, was held by 6 thegns. Kingcombe (no. 485), assessed at 1 hide and ¾ virgate, was held by 10 thegns *pro uno manerio* and they still held it in 1086. A certain amount of consolidation had taken place after the Conquest. There are cases where the lands of several thegns had been made into one holding for a single Norman lord. William of Ecouis held the land of 5 thegns in Stourton Caundle (no. 299), assessed at 5 hides, as one manor. Hugh de Lure held land in 3 places (*terras in tribus locis*) which had belonged to 11 thegns T.R.E. and which was assessed at 5 hides. William de Dalmar had the lands of 3 thegns, assessed at 3 hides, 3 virgates. Some manors had been held as two manors (*pro ii maneriis*) T.R.E. Piddlehinton (no. 168), which the abbey of Marmoutier held of the Count of Mortain in 1086, had been held T.R.E. by two thegns *pro ii maneriis*. Three thegns had held Wool (no. 208), which Bretel and Malger held of the Count of Mortain in 1086 *pro ii maneriis*. *Wintreburne* (no. 300), held by Walcher of Walscin of Douai in 1086, was held T.R.E. by Alward and Alwin *pro ii maneriis*. Roger Arundel's manor of North Poorton (nos. 329 and ci) was held T.R.E. by Alwin and Ulf *pro ii hidis* (sic). Comparison with Exon. Domesday shows that there were in fact two manors T.R.E., one of 1½ hide, held by Alwin, and one of ½ hide, held by Ulf. Stafford (nos. 383 and cxv) was held by 3 thegns in parage T.R.E. *pro ii maneriis*. At first sight this seems like a contradiction in terms, but Exon. Domesday shows that there were in fact 2 manors, one held by two thegns in parage and one held by Leving. At Hurpston (nos. 413 and cxlvi) the wife of Hugh had 3 hides which Alward held T.R.E. and ½ hide which Sawin held *pro manerio* T.R.E. Buckhorn Weston (no. 149) was held by Godric and Bruno in parage *pro ii maneriis*. Like the Stafford entry this seems to contradict itself. A similar position is revealed by the Exon. entry for Chilfrome (nos. 278 and lxxxviii) belonging to William of Moyon. The Exchequer text says that 3 thegns held the manor in parage T.R.E. Exon. Domesday repeats this, and adds *has iii mansiones clamat Willelmus pro ii*. This entry also suggests that whereas two or more manors might be given to one lord, and listed as a single manor in Domesday, they were still reckoned as two manors or more. Chilfrome was held by Dodoman and Niel (the Exchequer text says merely *duo homines*) of William of Moyon, and this is not the only manor of this sort to be held by more than one post-Conquest mesne tenant. Stafford was held by William and Hugh, and Wool by Bretel and Malger.

Some Englishmen can be shown to have survived the Conquest still in possession of at least some of their land, or to have received land which had belonged to other thegns T.R.E. Most of these men are numbered among the king's thegns in 1086, and are

[48] *Waia* (nos. 380 and cxii), assessed at 4 hides, E. Chaldon (nos. 408 and cxli), assessed at 5 hides, Martinstown (nos. 376 and cviii), assessed at 6 hides, and Rollington (nos. 331 and ciii), assessed at 2½ hides. According to Exon. Domesday the 9 thegns at Rollington still held the manor in 1086: see pp. 36, 99.

[49] Mappowder (no. 431) and Mapperton (no. 248). Mappowder was assessed at 5 hides, 3 virgates, and Mapperton at 3 hides, 3 virgates.

discussed elsewhere.[50] Some Englishmen appear as tenants of Norman lords in 1086,[51] and a few appear to have become economically dependent upon a Norman lord to the extent of being numbered among the *villani* in 1086.[52] Apart from these Regenbald was still in possession of his manor of Pulham (no. 146) in 1086, and Eadnoth the staller survived until his death in 1067 and in King William's time obtained Burstock (no. 230) from the thegn to whom it belonged T.R.E. Other thegns continued to hold their land, but as tenants of Norman lords. According to Exon. Domesday the 9 thegns who held Rollington (nos. 331 and ciii) T.R.E. still held it in 1086, although it had passed to Roger Arundel, and was subinfeudated to Robert Attlet. The Exchequer text does not mention the tenure of these 9 thegns. It is probable that the 4 men at Galton (no. 507) who rendered 12*s.* 4*d.* to Osmund the baker, to whom the manor belonged, were identical with the 4 free men who held the manor T.R.E. The Geld Rolls reveal other cases in which the English owners of a manor were still holding their land of a Norman. In Cullifordtree hundred a thegn *cuius ipsa terra fuit* held 1 hide and 1 virgate of William Belet. This land can be identified as part of Winterborne Belet or Cripton (no. 493), which 2 thegns held T.R.E. In Godderthorn hundred Berenger Giffard had a piece of land which his predecessor held of him at farm (*hanc tenet antecessor Berengerii de eo ad firmam*). Berenger held only one manor in Dorset, Bredy (Farm) (no. 317), which was held T.R.E. by Harding. It is possible that he is to be identified as Harding son of Eadnoth the staller, who held several manors in this area both before and after the Conquest. In Uggescombe hundred a thegn held 2½ hides of Aiulf the chamberlain. These 2½ hides were probably part of Aiulf's manor of Tatton (no. 345) held by a thegn of Cerne Abbey T.R.E., who may also have held it of Aiulf in 1084. Exon. Domesday reveals that the 3 thegns holding 3 hides of Cranborne (nos. 16 and xxii) of the king in 1086, held them of Beorhtric son of Aelfgar T.R.E. Brictuin, who held 4 hides of Cerne Abbas of the abbot in 1086, held it likewise T.R.E. Tenants with English names are quite common on ecclesiastical land in 1086. Chetel held Fifehead St. Quintin (no. 133) of Shaftesbury Abbey. Algar and Brictuin appear among the Bishop of Salisbury's tenants at Beaminster (no. 46). Chetel appears as a tenant of Glastonbury Abbey at Sturminster Newton (no. 63) and at Okeford Fitzpaine (no. 64), and Warmund held land at Buckland Newton (no. 65).[53] Two widows are mentioned in connexion with ecclesiastical land, one at Piddletrenthide (no. 69) and one at Atrim (nos. 116 and lxiii).

In contrast to the lay lands the possessions of the religious houses in Dorset suffered no major upset during the transition to Norman rule. Where the names of bishops or abbots are given, they are generally Norman, like Osmund de Seez, Bishop of Salisbury, Maurice, Bishop of London, and Geoffrey, Abbot of Tavistock. Various foreign ecclesiastics and religious houses had received small amounts of land. Odo, Bishop of Bayeux, the king's half-brother, had received Rampisham (no. 55) and Geoffrey, Bishop of Coutances, two small manors called *Wintreburne* (nos. 56, 57). The canons of Coutances also held a small manor called Winterborne Stickland (no. 142), the only land they had in England. Gilbert Maminot, Bishop of Lisieux, held four Dorset manors, amounting to 26 hides, and Maurice, Bishop of London, held ½ hide in *Odeham* (no. 62) and 1½ hide at Hinton Martell (no. 31) which belonged to the church of Wimborne. Another hide of land at Hinton, which had belonged to a priest T.R.E., was held in 1086 by the Bishop of Lisieux. The abbey of St. Stephen, Caen, had 35½ hides in Dorset, consisting of Frampton and Bincombe, which had belonged to Countess

[50] See pp. 51–53.

[51] See p. 49.

[52] See pp. 15–16.

[53] For a further discussion of ecclesiastical tenants and the question of thegnland, see pp. 39–40.

Gytha and Earl Harold respectively.[54] The sister house of Holy Trinity, Caen, held the manor of Tarrant Launceston (no. 141) which was the gift of Queen Maud.[55] The abbey of Montevilliers held Friar Waddon (no. 143), given to it by Hugh fitz Grip; the abbey of St. Wandrille held the churches of Bridport, Burton Bradstock, Whitchurch Canonicorum, and Wareham (nos. 123 and xviii, 124 and xx),[56] and the abbey of Marmoutier held Piddlehinton (no. 168) of the Count of Mortain.[57] According to the Geld Rolls the abbey of St. Leger, Préaux, held land in Dorset, and, although Domesday does not mention the fact, the land in question was probably the manor of Stour Provost (no. 231), held by Roger de Beaumont, whose father founded the two abbeys at Préaux.[58]

Of the losses sustained by the English houses some dated from before 1066. Earl Harold had taken four manors from Shaftesbury Abbey, two of which were restored by King William in accordance with a writ of King Edward. Queen Edith, Earl Harold's sister, had held Sherborne (no. 37) but Bishop Aelfwold (1045/6–1058) had held it previously, and it belonged to the Bishop of Salisbury in 1086. It is possible that Queen Edith had held the manor on a life-lease. One hide at Sherborne had been held by Alward of King Edward T.R.E. *sed prius erat de episcopatu.* In 1086 it had reverted to the bishopric. Sometimes the churches had lost lands because they had been leased to thegns whose estates had passed to Norman lords. Wulfweard White had held Pentridge (no. 66) of Glastonbury Abbey T.R.E., but in 1086 the manor was held by the king who had taken possession of most of Wulfweard's lands. Clifton and Trill (no. 225) had at one time belonged to the Bishop of Sherborne, but were held T.R.E. by Eadnoth the staller and passed to Hugh, Earl of Chester, with the rest of Eadnoth's lands.[59] Eadnoth had also bought South Perrott (no. 228) and Catsley (no. 229) from Bishop Aelfwold for his own lifetime, on condition that at his death they should revert to the church, but both these manors were held by Earl Hugh in 1086. Stock Gaylard (no. 269), which T.R.E. was held by Toli in pledge *de terra Scireburne*, had passed to William of Eu who received the rest of Toli's land. Attached to the manor of Silton, belonging to William of Falaise, was one hide which Wulfweard White had bought from the Bishop of Exeter. Some losses, usually involving smaller amounts of land, were due to deliberate seizure for which Hugh fitz Grip, the former sheriff, was largely responsible. From Abbotsbury Abbey he had taken a hide at Abbotsbury (nos. 109 and lviii) and a virgate at Portesham (nos. 112 and lxix), which his wife retained by force.[60] Tatton, which had belonged to Cerne Abbey T.R.E., was in 1086 held partly by Aiulf the chamberlain, then sheriff (no. 345), and partly by Hugh's wife (nos. 398 and cxxxi), and according to Exon. Domesday two other manors of this abbey, Bloxworth (nos. 79 and xlii) and Affpuddle (nos. 80 and xliii), had been devastated by Hugh. Farnham (no. 135), which T.R.E. belonged to Shaftesbury Abbey, was held in 1086 by Aiulf (no. 352) and Hugh's wife (nos. 396 and cxxix) and a virgate at Kingston (no. 134), belonging to the same abbey T.R.E., was held in 1086 by William of Briouze. Manasses held 3 virgates at Stalbridge (no. 42), belonging to Sherborne Abbey, which William the king's son had given him *sine consensu episcopi et monachorum*, and the two best hides of the manor of Horton (no. 117), belonging to Horton Abbey, had been taken into the king's forest of Wimborne.

The Exchequer text gives the hides in demesne on the ecclesiastical estates, though only rarely on lay estates, whereas Exon. Domesday regularly gives the hides in demesne and the hides held by the *villani* for both lay and ecclesiastical estates. It is

[54] *Regesta Regum Anglo-Normannorum*, i, no. 105.

[55] Ibid. no. 149.

[56] Ibid. no. 110.

[57] Piddlehinton had belonged to Countess Maud, Count Robert's wife, and was given by him to the abbey after her death: *Cal. Doc. France*, ed. Round, 435.

[58] See p. 141.

[59] For Clifton and Trill, see p. 41.

[60] *Adhuc uxor eius vi detinet.* The Abbotsbury entry has given rise to an error in *V.C.H. Dors.* ii. 49, where *vi* ('by force') is translated as 'six'.

noticeable that the term 'demesne' is used in three distinct senses, to designate the portion of a manor held by the lord (the home farm) as opposed to that held by the *villani*; the demesne (in this sense) with the *terra villanorum*, as opposed to the land subinfeudated to knights or thegns; and lastly, a whole manor which was or should have been held by the lord himself, and not by a tenant. The manor of Stockland (nos. 106 and lxxx) was held of Milton Abbey by Hervey fitz Ansger, but nevertheless was *de dominio monachorum ad victum et vestitum eorum*. Similarly the manor of Little Puddle (nos. 77 and xl), held of Cerne Abbey by William *de monasteriis*, was *de propria terra ecclesie*, and the 3 hides at Poxwell (nos. 81 and xliv), held by Hugh's wife of the same abbey, were *de dominica firma monachorum* T.R.E. The last case seems to imply an encroachment on the part of Hugh's wife. At *Cerneli* (no. 212) William held of the Count of Mortain ½ hide *que fuit de dominica firma CERNE T.R.E.*, which seems to be a similar use of 'demesne'. Hampreston (no. 443), which Torchil, a king's thegn, held in 1086, had been held by Schelin of the queen but *modo tenet rex in dominio*. It is probable that Schelin had held some of the queen's manors at farm[61] which in 1086 were in the king's hand, and the use of 'demesne' in this context is very unusual. It may be that Torchil held the manor at farm in 1086 or for some service.[62] Other ecclesiastical tenants include Wadard, who held Rampisham of the Bishop of Bayeux, as well as land in other counties of the same lord, and who is mentioned by name in the Bayeux Tapestry.[63] The two manors of the Bishop of Coutances were held by Osbern. Domesday does not mention any tenants on the land of Gilbert Maminot, Bishop of Lisieux, but the Geld Rolls name Hugh Maminot as his tenant in connexion with land which can be identified with Tarrant Crawford and Preston (nos. 58, 59), and the bishop's other two Dorset manors, Tarrant Keyneston and Coombe Keynes, passed to Hugh Maminot's daughter with the Wiltshire manor of Somerford Keynes.[64] The Bishop of Salisbury had subinfeudated several manors. Robert held Up Cerne (no. 34), the wife of Hugh fitz Grip held Bardolfeston (no. 51), and Otbold held Athelhampton (no. 52). *Cernel* (no. 50) was held by an unnamed woman, and it is worth noting that a manor of the same name (no. 153), belonging to the Count of Mortain, was also held by a woman (*quedam femina*). Hugh's wife held Woodyates (no. 65) of Glastonbury Abbey. John held Leftisford (no. 73) of Cranborne Abbey, and Chetel held Fifehead St. Quintin (no. 133) of Shaftesbury Abbey. Bollo the priest held Shilvinghampton (nos. 113 and lx) of Cerne Abbey, and a hide at Atrim (nos. 116 and lxiii), the other hide of which was held by a widow. Aiulf the sheriff held *Cerne* (nos. 108 and lxxxii) of the abbey of Milton, which T.R.E. was held by Edric, who could not be separated from the church with this land. Ulviet (Wulfgeat) held Colway (no. 68) of Glastonbury Abbey both T.R.E. and in 1086 and could not be separated from the church. According to Exon. Domesday Bristuin held Woodsford (nos. 82 and xlv) of Cerne Abbey at farm, although the Exchequer text does not mention his tenure. The Bishop of Salisbury's manor of Lyme Regis (no. 36) was held by fishermen (*piscatores*) who rendered 15*s*. *ad pisces*, and Ower (nos. 105 and lxxix), belonging to Milton Abbey, was held by salt-workers (*salinarii*) who rendered 20*s*. a year. Burcombe (nos. 115 and lxii) was held by the *villani* of Abbotsbury Abbey.

The enfeoffment of knights was frequent on the ecclesiastical estates, especially in the case of the richer houses, that is, Sherborne and Glastonbury. At Alton Pancras (no. 33), belonging to the Bishop of Salisbury, Edward and Pain held 2½ hides each and at Sherborne (no. 37) the knights of the bishop held 22½ hides and included

[61] See p. 119.

[62] For the king's thegns and their tenure, see p. 52.

[63] *Bayeux Tapestry*, ed. F. M. Stenton, 21.

[64] See pp. 60, 129.

Otbold, Sinod, Ingelbert, Ralph, Waleran, and the wife of Hugh. At Stalbridge (no. 42) Lambert held 2 hides, and at Beaminster (no. 46) the knights held 10 hides and a virgate. Two of them were obviously French (H. de Cartrai and Sinod) but the names Algar and Brictuin show that two others were English. At Netherbury (no. 47) Tezelin had 5 hides, 3 virgates, William and Godfrey 2 hides each, and Serle 1½ hide. Walter held Buckham (no. 54) and two knights, Walter and William, held Chardstock (no. 49). Three knights, Godfrey, Osmar, and Elfric, held Bowood (no. 53), which three thegns held T.R.E. Two of these knights also must have been English. Of the Glastonbury manors Okeford Fitzpaine was held by knights, namely the wife of Hugh, who held 4 hides, and Alvred of Epaignes and Chetel who held 2 hides each. Four thegns had held the manor T.R.E. At Sturminster Newton (no. 63) Waleran held 6 hides, Roger 1 hide, and Chetel 1 hide, and at Buckland Newton (no. 65) the wife of Hugh had 7 hides, 1½ virgate, and Warmund 2 hides. A knight and a widow held 3 hides at Piddletrenthide (no. 69) belonging to the New Minster, Winchester.

The meaning of the term 'thegnland' which occurs in connexion with some ecclesiastical land is obscure. It does not seem to have been held by military service, although a French knight (*miles francigenus*) held 2 hides of thegnland at Nettlecombe (nos. 88 and li). In some cases it seems to have been liable to some kind of service. At Cerne Abbas (nos. 76 and xxxix) Brictuin held 4 hides of land, which he also held T.R.E. *et non potuit recedere ab ecclesia*. Exon. Domesday records that the land was thegnland and that Brictuin rendered 30*s*. to the church *excepto servitio*. A similar entry is that of Cranborne (nos. 16 and xxii), where 3 thegns held 3 hides of land (not specifically said to be thegnland) for which they rendered £3 *excepto servitio*. Exon. Domesday adds that they held the same land T.R.E. of Beorhtric and *non poterant separari ab eo*. It is not altogether clear from these entries whether the thegns both performed service and rendered money, or rendered money instead of doing service. Other evidence favours the latter interpretation. Durnford (Wilts.) was held T.R.E. by 3 Englishmen, two of whom paid 5*s*. while the third *serviebat sicut tainus*.[65] At Winsford (Som.) there was ½ hide which 3 thegns held T.R.E. *et serviebant preposito manerii per consuetudinem absque omni firma donante*. If these thegns did not contribute to the farm because they performed some service, then presumably the Dorset thegns who paid money renders did not serve. The ½ hide attached to Winsford is entered twice, appearing again under the name of Robert de Odburville, who held it in 1086. According to the second entry the land was judged to be thegnland (*modo diratiocinata est in tainland*).[66] This second entry implies that the thegns rendered service in the capacity of foresters, and suggests that the thegnland was set aside for men serving in a ministerial capacity. But from other entries it is plain that the term could be used simply to describe land once held by thegns. At Loders (nos. 13 and ix) there were 2 hides of thegnland *que non ibi pertinent*, which 2 thegns held T.R.E. In the Geld Roll for Loders hundred (which consisted solely of the manor of Loders), it is stated that *ii hide quas tenuerunt tagni tempore regis Edwardi sunt addite huic mansioni*. There is no reason to suppose that these thegns owed either service or money to the manor of Loders. At Hinton a priest held a hide of thegnland T.R.E. *et poterat ire quo volebat*. This terminology does not suggest land owing a service to the holder of Hinton.[67] In 1086 the land was in the king's

[65] *Dom. Bk.* (Rec. Com.), i, f. 67b; *V.C.H. Wilts.* ii. 81. There is a similar entry in Dorset relating to Tatton (nos. 345, 398 and cxxxi). Part of Tatton had been held T.R.E. by a thegn of Cerne Abbey, who *non poterat ab ea separari*, while the other portion was held by 2 thegns of the same abbey for rent (*prestito*).

[66] *Dom. Bk.* (Rec. Com.), i, ff. 86b, 98b.

[67] The statement that a manor owed service is in itself ambiguous. It could mean service like that described in the Winsford entries, or it could mean the rent in money or kind derived from the manor. When the Som. Domesday states, in enumerating the manors in Som. taken from the abbey of Glastonbury, that the church had lost the service (*ecclesia servitium inde non habet, ecclesia servitium*

demesne. Most of the thegns holding land of the ecclesiastical tenants in 1086 are not said to hold thegnland, and they were presumably just men with a thegn's wergild. At Long Bredy (nos. 87 and l) an English thegn (*teignus anglicus*) had a hide of land worth £3. Six thegns held 8½ hides at Sherborne (no. 37) and 2 thegns held 2½ hides at Stoke Abbott (no. 45). The thegn who held part of Farnham (no. 352) of Shaftesbury Abbey T.R.E. *et non poterat ab ea separari* must have been commended to the church and may have owed some service like that of the 3 thegns at Winsford. He is probably identical with Alwin, who held the other part of Farnham (nos. 396 and cxxix) of the abbey T.R.E. *et non poterat ab ea separari*. Two free Englishmen (*angli liberi*) held 4 hides at Handley (no. 125) of Shaftesbury Abbey. Three thegns held Bowood (no. 53) T.R.E., which was held by the same number of knights in 1086, 2 of them, Osmar and Elfric, apparently being English.

There are a few references to churches in the Dorset survey. Bristuard the priest held the churches of Bere Regis and Dorchester, with the tithes and 1 hide and 20 acres of land (nos. 144 and xiii). The church of Gillingham was given to Shaftesbury Abbey in exchange for a hide of land at Kingston (no. 134) in which Corfe Castle was to be built.[68] The church of Winfrith Newburgh, with a virgate of land, and the churches of Puddletown, Chaldon, and Fleet, with 1½ hide of land, were held by Bollo the priest (nos. 145 and xvi, 145a and xix). The churches of Burton Bradstock, Bridport, and Whitchurch Canonicorum belonged to the abbey of St. Wandrille (nos. 123 and xviii) and so did the church of Wareham (nos. 124 and xx). Another church in Wareham, probably the 11th-century church of St. Martin,[69] and a chapel (*ecclesiola*) in Wimborne Minster belonged to Horton Abbey (no. 117). To Wimborne belonged 1½ hide and ½ virgate in Hinton (no. 31) which Bishop Maurice held in 1086. It is evident that this is not a comprehensive list of all the churches in Dorset in 1086. There must have been a Saxon church at Sherborne, and this is confirmed by the survival of a Saxon doorway in the west wall of the present building.[70] As their names suggest there must also have been Saxon churches at Yetminster (no. 35), Charminster (no. 32), Beaminster (no. 46), which belonged to the Bishop of Salisbury, Iwerne Minster (no. 131), belonging to Shaftesbury Abbey, and Sturminster (no. 232) belonging to Roger de Beaumont. Three priests are recorded at Hinton (no. 31), two of whom still held land in 1086. One lived at *Tarente*. There was a priest at Church Knowle (no. 235) and another at *Bleneford* (no. 455), both of them being enumerated in conjunction with the peasants. Bristuard the priest and Bollo the priest have already been mentioned and Godric the priest occurs among the king's thegns. Walter the deacon (*diaconus*) held *Cernel* (no. 147) as an almsman.

The most prosperous of the ecclesiastical landowners and after the king the wealthiest man in Dorset was the Bishop of Salisbury. The ancient see of Sherborne, founded by Ine in 705, and numbering Aldhelm and Asser among its bishops, had been restricted to the county of Dorset since the reign of Edward the Elder.[71] In 1058 Bishop Herman united the sees of Sherborne and Ramsbury and between 1075 and 1078 the episcopal seat was transferred to Salisbury.[72] This amalgamation of Sherborne and Ramsbury explains the size of Bishop Osmund's fief, which consisted of

perdit) this could be taken to mean the income from the manor, not any specific service: *Dom. Bk.* (Rec. Com.), i, f. 91. Abbotsbury Abbey was entitled to 6 a. of crops and 3 church-scots *de consuetudine* from Friar Waddon (no. 143) and this in turn could be described as service. In Som. Brictric and Ulward held Buckland (*Dom. Bk.* (Rec. Com.), i, f. 98b) as king's thegns. They had held the land of Bp. Peter *et reddebant ei x solidos*, but the king had had nothing since the bp.'s death. It is possible that they paid this sum instead of doing service, although the amount is rather large.

[68] *castellum WARHAM* in Domesday, but later evidence indicates that Corfe Castle is meant: see p. 83.

[69] G. Baldwin Brown, *Arts in Early Eng.* (1925), ii. 484.

[70] Ibid. 477–8.

[71] F. M. Stenton, *Anglo-Saxon Eng.* 433.

[72] W. Stubbs, *Registrum Sacrum Anglicanum*, 35. The transfer was sanctioned by the Council of London in 1075 and the removal took place between that date and Herman's death in 1078.

267 hides in Wiltshire, 8 hides in Somerset, and the two large manors of Sonning in Berkshire[73] (assessed at 60 hides T.R.E. but reduced to 24 hides in 1086) and Dunsden in Oxfordshire (assessed at 20 hides), with just under 100 hides in Dorset, where the monks of Sherborne held 119½ hides. In addition the bishop and the monks held between them about 40 carucates of land in Dorset which never paid geld. The original endowment of the Bishop of Sherborne seems to have been 300 hides. A letter from Bishop Aethelric to Aethelmaer, dating from the early 11th century, complains that he is not receiving ship-scot from 33 out of the 300 hides which his predecessors had for their diocese.[74] He itemized the deficit as 1 hide at *Bubbancumbe*, 2 hides at Alton Pancras, 7 hides at Up Cerne, 6 hides at Clifton, 5 hides at Hewish, 2 hides at Trill, 1 hide at *Wyllon*, 5 hides at *Buchaematune*, 3 hides at Dibberford, and 1 hide at *Peder*. Alton Pancras and Up Cerne (nos. 33, 34) were both held by the bishop in 1086. Clifton Maybank and Trill (no. 225) were held by Earl Hugh as the successor of Eadnoth the staller. Before the Conquest Eadnoth had bought two manors, Catsley and South Perrott (nos. 228, 229), of Bishop Aelfwold, on condition that at his death the manors should revert to the church; Earl Hugh, however, held them in 1086. It seems possible that South Perrott is the *Peder* of Bishop Aethelric's letter, but this has been disputed.[75] Dibberford lies in Dorset, but does not appear in the Dorset survey.[76]

Sherborne was originally a house of secular canons, but Bishop Wulfsige (992–1001) expelled the clerks and replaced them by monks.[77] A dubious charter of Aethelred II, dated 998,[78] confirms to the church the manors of Bradford Abbas, Over Compton, Oborne, Stalbridge, Stalbridge Weston, Thornford, and Lyme Regis, all of which, with the exception of Lyme, were *de victu monachorum Scireburne* in 1086. Lyme was held by the Bishop of Salisbury in 1086. It had never paid geld and was held by an unspecified number of fishermen who rendered 15*s*. for the fish (*ad pisces*). The bishop had a house there worth 6*d*. In a charter dated 774 Cynewulf, King of the West Saxons, gave Lyme to the church of Sherborne for a salt-pan.[79] Bradford Abbas and Stalbridge were given to the church by Aethelstan[80] and Oborne by Edgar.[81] Aethelstan's charters give the extent of Bradford as 10 hides and of Stalbridge Weston as 8 hides and these reckonings agree with the Domesday assessment of the manors, but in Aethelred's confirmation charter Bradford is reckoned as 7 hides and Stalbridge Weston as five. In Edgar's charter Oborne is reckoned as 5 hides, as in Domesday, but in the confirmation charter it is reckoned as ten. Eadred is supposed to have given 8 *cassati* in Thornford to Wulfsige II in 951, with a reversion to the church.[82] Thornford was reckoned as 15 *cassati* in the confirmation charter and in Domesday was assessed at 8 hides. Another charter of Aethelred II, dated 1014, gave 13 hides in Corscombe to Sherborne,[83] and in 1035 Cnut

[73] Potterne, Cannings, Ramsbury, and Salisbury (Wilts.), and Sonning (Berks.) were the endowment of the Bp. of Ramsbury.

[74] F. E. Harmer, *Anglo-Saxon Writs*, no. 63 (dated 1001/2–1009/12), where it is pointed out that the Bp. of Salisbury held 3 hundreds in Dorset, Yetminster, Beaminster, and Sherborne.

[75] For the alternative identifications of *Peder*, see Harmer, op. cit. 485. The Domesday form of the name S. Perrott is *Pedret*.

[76] Dibberford lay in Dorset in 1252, when it was held by Grece de Mucegros; there is no evidence that it belonged to the Bp. of Salisbury at that date: *Bk. of Fees*, 1267.

[77] Stenton, *Anglo-Saxon Eng.* 450.

[78] *Cod. Dipl.* no. 701. Stevenson seems to accept this charter (*E.H.R.* xxix. 689), but Miss Harmer (*Anglo-Saxon Writs*, 485) does not regard it as genuine.

[79] *Cart. Sax.* no. 224. Stenton accepts it as a genuine charter: *E.H.R.* xxxiii. 443 n. Although no salt-pans or salt-workers are recorded at the Bp. of Salisbury's manor of Lyme, there were 13 salt-workers at the manor of Colway (no. 68) held by the abbey of Glastonbury, and 14 salt-workers at the manor of Lyme held by William Belet (no. 504).

[80] *Cart. Sax.* nos. 695, 696. Stevenson appears to accept them as genuine (Asser, *Life of King Alfred*, ed. W. H. Stevenson, 148 n.). *Cart. Sax.* no. 695 calls Sherborne a *monasterium*, but this could mean a minster.

[81] A. J. Robertson, *Anglo-Saxon Charters*, no. 1; *Cart. Sax.* no. 1308.

[82] *Cart. Sax.* no. 894. The phrase *ad refectionem familie Sciréburnensis ecclesie* suggests a community, and Eadred styles himself *Occidentalium Saxonum rex*, whereas his normal style is *rex Anglorum*. Stevenson regards this charter as 'doubtful or spurious': *E.H.R.* xxix. 692 n.

[83] *Cod. Dipl.* no. 1309. Both Miss Harmer (*Anglo-Saxon Writs*, 553) and Miss Robertson (*Anglo-Saxon Charters*, 387) seem to accept it as genuine.

gave 16 *manse* in the same place to the monastery.[84] In 1086 Corscombe (no. 44) was assessed at 10 hides less a virgate.

The last five manors entered in the bishop's fief are preceded by the heading *Has terras que subterscribuntur habet episcopus pro excambio de Scipeleia*. He also held Chaddenwick in Mere (Wilts.) in exchange for *Scipeleia*. There is no indication where *Scipeleia* was or to whom the exchanged manors had belonged. The Dorset manors amount to over 20 hides and Chaddenwick is assessed at 5 hides, so *Scipeleia* should have been a sizeable manor. This consideration eliminates Shipley in Yorkshire, assessed at 3 carucates,[85] and Shipley in Derbyshire, assessed at 2 carucates.[86] William of Briouze held a manor called Shipley in Sussex, but the fact emerges only obliquely in the account of Fulking and this Shipley is omitted from the Sussex Domesday.[87] No other manor of this name occurs in Domesday and the exchange remains a mystery.

If Sherborne was the largest of the Dorset monasteries, the smallest was Horton, a poorly endowed little house with only the manor of Horton (no. 117) in Dorset and 3 hides in Devon, a total of 10 hides in all. It may conveniently be discussed here since in 1122 it was amalgamated with Sherborne and became a cell of that abbey.[88] It seems to have been founded between 1033, when Cnut gave 7 *manse* in Horton to his *minister* Bovi,[89] and 1061, when Edward the Confessor freed the monks of Horton from all duties except geld, the repair of fortifications, and the building of bridges.[90] According to William of Malmesbury Horton was founded by Ordwulf son of Ordgar, who also founded Tavistock Abbey, but he is last recorded in 1008.[91] It has been noted that Littleham (Devon), belonging to Horton Abbey in 1086, had been given by Edward to his *minister* Ordgar in 1042, and suggested that this Ordgar was a descendant of Ordwulf son of Ordgar and that the founder of Horton Abbey was a member of the same family.[92] William of Malmesbury stated that the land which Ordwulf left to Horton Abbey was seized by the Abbot of Tavistock, and in 1086 the abbey of Horton was claiming the manor of Antony (Cornw.) from Tavistock Abbey.[93]

The largest nunnery in Dorset, and indeed in the whole of England, was Shaftesbury, which possessed about 360 hides, including 172 hides in Wiltshire, 161 hides in Dorset, the manor of *Falcheham* (Suss.), and 10 hides in Somerset.[94] It was founded by King Alfred, whose daughter Aethelgifu was its first abbess.[95] Alfred left her a bequest of 100 hides[96] of which 40 hides were at Donhead St. Andrew (Wilts.) and Compton Abbas, 20 hides at Handley and Gussage St. Andrew, 10 at Tarrant, 15 at Iwerne Minster, and 15 at Fontmell Magna, all in Dorset. All these manors were in the possession of the abbey in 1086. Donhead St. Andrew was assessed at 40 hides, Compton Abbas at 10, and Iwerne Minster at 18, but the other hidages were the same as in Alfred's bequest. With the exception of Donhead St. Andrew these manors comprised the Domesday hundreds of *Sexpene* and Handley (later amalgamated under the name Sixpenny Handley). According to two charters preserved in the abbey's cartulary Mapperton (no. 137) was given by Edmund to Eadric the ealdorman in 943, when it was reckoned

84 *Cod. Dipl.* no. 1322.

85 *Dom. Bk.* (Rec. Com.), i, f. 318.

86 Ibid. f. 277b.

87 Ibid. f. 29b. Round suggested that Shipley (Suss.) was included in William of Briouze's manor of Thakeham, assessed at 20 hides and 3 virgates: *V.C.H. Suss.* i. 440 n.

88 *Regesta Regum Anglo-Normannorum*, ii, no. 1325.

89 *Cod. Dipl.* no. 1318. Miss Harmer (*Anglo-Saxon Writs*, 576) seems to accept it as genuine. Urk, who attests it, was the founder of Abbotsbury.

90 *Cod. Dipl.* no. 1341; Robertson, *Anglo-Saxon Charters*, no. cxx. Miss Robertson points out that this charter, which is incomplete, is almost identical with one granted by Aethelberht, King of Wessex, to Sherborne in 864.

91 Wm. of Malmesbury, *Gesta Pontificum Anglorum* (Rolls Ser.), 203.

92 H. P. R. Finberg, 'The House of Ordgar and the Foundation of Tavistock Abbey', *E.H.R.* lviii. 190–201.

93 *Dom. Bk.* (Rec. Com.), i, f. 121.

94 Kilmington (Som.) was given to the abbey by Serle of Burcy when his daughter became a nun there: *Dom. Bk.* (Rec. Com.), i, f. 98.

95 Asser, *Life of King Alfred*, 85.

96 *Cart. Sax.* no. 531; *Cod. Dipl.* no. 310; Robertson, *Anglo-Saxon Charters*, no. xiii.

as 11 *manse*,[97] and Hinton St. Mary (*Hamtune*) (no. 126) was given by Edmund to Wulfgar in 944, when it was reckoned as 5 *manse*.[98] Mapperton was assessed at 11 hides in 1086 and Hinton St. Mary at eight. Another charter of Edmund, dated 942, concerns the manor of Cheselbourne. According to this charter Edmund restored 7 *manse* of land at Cheselbourne to Wynflaed, a religious woman, with an additional grant of 8 *manse* in the same place.[99] According to Domesday Cheselbourne was one of the manors taken by Earl Harold from the abbey and restored by King William in accordance with a writ of King Edward. It was then assessed at 16 hides. Earl Harold had also taken another manor, *Pidele*, from the abbey, which was not returned and was held by the Count of Mortain in 1086. According to a charter in the abbey's cartulary Edgar in 966 restored to the church 10 *cassati* of land at *Uppidelen*, which had originally been given by Wynflaed, described as his grandmother (*ava*), whose charter had been lost through carelessness.[1] Of the four manors called *Pidele* held in 1086 by the Count of Mortain, only one, Piddlehinton (no. 168), assessed at 10 hides, is large enough to be identifiable with *Uppidelen*. It had been held T.R.E. by two thegns *pro ii maneriis*, and it is not said ever to have belonged to Shaftesbury Abbey. *Uppidelen* has in fact been identified as part of Piddletrenthide (no. 69),[2] held T.R.E. by Almar and Alverd of King Edward, which belonged in 1086 to the New Minster, Winchester. Neither *Pidele* (whether it be identified with Piddlehinton or Piddletrenthide) nor Melcombe (no. 30) was ever returned to the abbey, but half the hide in Farnham (no. 135), taken from the abbey by Aiulf and the wife of Hugh, was returned. Aiulf the chamberlain restored it to the abbey when his daughter became a nun there, and added the manor of Blandford (no. 336) for the soul of his wife. Drew of Montacute's daughter also became a nun at Shaftesbury, and on this occasion he gave to the abbey his manor of Nyland (no. 150).[3]

Apart from the two great houses of Sherborne and Shaftesbury the Dorset abbeys were quite small. Cerne Abbey was the foundation of Aethelmaer son of Aethelweard, patron of Aelfric the homilist. Aelfric was responsible for teaching at Cerne, and later became Abbot of Eynsham. Aethelmaer has been identified with the earl of the western provinces to whom Bishop Aethelric addressed his complaint about ship-scot mentioned above.[4] His foundation charter of 987[5] gave to the abbey Cerne Abbas itself, with 10 *manse* in Winterborne, the two manors of Littlebredy and Long Bredy, reckoned at 12 and 16 *manse* respectively, and 3 *manse* in Renscombe. Leofric the clerk of Poxwell gave Poxwell, and Aelfrith, a relative of Aethelmaer, gave 4 *cassati* at Puddle. Alfwold gave 5 *manse* at Bloxworth. All these manors belonged to the abbey in 1086. Winterbourne Abbas was still assessed at 10 hides, Littlebredy and Long Bredy were assessed at 11 and 9 hides respectively, and Renscombe at 5 hides, 1 virgate. Poxwell was a manor of 6 hides and Bloxworth of five and a half. Two manors called Puddle were

97 *Cart. Sax.* no. 781. Eadric *minister* attests nos. 763, 765, and 767, and no. 769 is a grant to Eadric *vassalus*, dated 941, of Beechingstoke (Wilts.) by Edmund, which Stevenson considered 'may be genuine': Asser, *Life of King Alfred*, 255. Eadric attests *Cart. Sax.* no. 775 (dated 942) as *dux*.

98 *Cart. Sax.* no. 793. For the identification of *Hamtune* with Hinton St. Mary, see A. Fägersten, *Place-Names of Dorset*, 41 and n.

99 *Cart. Sax.* no. 775. Two charters of Aethelred I are preserved, granting 7 *manse* of land at Cheselbourne to Earl Aelfstan: *Cart. Sax.* nos. 525, 526. One is printed in Robertson, *Anglo-Saxon Charters*, no. xii. Stevenson regarded no. 525 as doubtful or spurious: *E.H.R.* xxix. 692 n., 698 n. Cnut gave 16 hides at Cheselbourne to Agemund in 1019: *Cod. Dipl.* no. 730. These 3 charters and that of Edmund are discussed in Robertson, *Anglo-Saxon Charters*, 281–2.

1 *Cart. Sax.* no. 1186. The Wynflaed of this charter may be the same woman as the Wynflaed of Edmund's charter relating to Cheselbourne. The Wynflaed who received the grant of Cheselbourne has been identified with the woman who bequeathed Chinnock (Som.) to the abbey *c.* 950: D. Whitelock, *Anglo-Saxon Wills*, no. iii and nn.; cf. Robertson, *Anglo-Saxon Charters*, 379–80.

2 *Saxon Charters of Dorset* (Proc. Dorset Nat. Hist. and Arch. Soc. lix), 107.

3 *Regesta Regum Anglo-Normannorum*, ii. 346–7.

4 See p. 41. For the identification, see Robertson, *Anglo-Saxon Charters*, 386–7; Whitelock, *Anglo-Saxon Wills*, 144–5; Harmer, *Anglo-Saxon Writs*, 553.

5 *Cod. Dipl.* no. 656. Dr. Whitelock (*Anglo-Saxon Wills*, 145) seems to accept it as genuine.

held by the abbey in 1086, Affpuddle assessed at 9 hides, and Little Puddle assessed at two and a half. In all Cerne Abbey had 121½ hides in 1086, all in Dorset.

Milton Abbey had 120½ hides in Dorset and two manors in Glanvilles Wootton (nos. 284, 285) had also belonged to this abbey T.R.E. Its register was destroyed by fire in 1309, but there are in existence two versions of a charter attributed to Athelstan, one in Latin and the other in English.[6] If these documents represent a genuine charter of Athelstan, he gave to the church 26 hides at Milborne, 5 at Woolland, three at the mouth of the Frome 'on the island, two on sea and one on land, that is to say at Ower', 3 at Clyffe, 3½ at Lyscombe, 1 at Burleston, 1 at Little Puddle, 5 at Cattistock, 6 at Compton, 2 at Whitcombe, 5 at Osmington, and 6 at Holworth. In addition, he gave 30 hides at Sydling St. Nicholas for victuals, 2 hides at Chelmington and 6 at Hillfield, 10 hides at *Ercecombe* 'to timberlond', and a weir on the Avon at Twyneham, with 12 acres to support it. With the exception of Chelmington and Hillfield these lands all belonged to the abbey in 1086. Milborne was presumably Milton Abbas itself, assessed at 24 hides. Woolland in 1086 was still assessed at 5 hides and Ower at 3,[7] but the assessments of the other manors had changed from the earlier reckonings. Clyffe was assessed at 2 hides, Lyscombe at 3, Burleston (Puddle Burston) at 3, Little Puddle at 2, Cattistock at 10, Compton at 5, Whitcombe at 6, Osmington at 10, and Holworth at five. Sydling St. Nicholas was assessed at 29 hides. *Ercecombe* appears in Domesday as *Ertacomestoche* (nos. 106 and lxxx), and can be identified as Stockland (Devon), which lay in Dorset at that date. In 1086 it was worth £9 and *fuit semper de dominio monachorum ad victum et vestum eorum*. The abbey held 12 acres on the Avon in 1086 and there had once been a fishery there.[8] Since it is known that in 964 Edgar expelled the clerks from Milton Abbey and replaced them with monks under Abbot Cyneweard,[9] Athelstan's grant, if genuine, must have been made to a community of clerks.

Abbotsbury Abbey, with 75 hides in Dorset, was founded by Urk, who had been a housecarl of both Cnut and Edward the Confessor, and his wife Tole.[10] In 1024 Urk received 7 *manse* in Portesham from Cnut, and in 1044 5 *perticas* in Abbott's Wootton from Edward the Confessor.[11] Both these manors belonged to the abbey in 1086, when Portesham was assessed at 12 hides and Abbott's Wootton at two and a half. In a writ dating from between 1053 and 1058 Edward the Confessor commanded that his housecarl Urk should have his shore, with right of wreck. This is presumably a reference to Chesil Beach. A second writ of Edward, dating from between 1058 and 1066, gives permission to his *mann* Tole, Urks's widow, to bequeath her land to the abbey of Abbotsbury, which he takes under his protection.[12] One of the manors which the abbey derived from Tole must have been Tolpuddle, which bears her name.[13] William I issued two writs concerning the land and rights of the abbey, both addressed to Hugh fitz Grip, whose encroachments on the land of this and other abbeys have already been mentioned.[14]

[6] Robertson, *Anglo-Saxon Charters*, no. xxiii and nn. The Eng. version is printed in *Cart. Sax.* no. 738 and *Cod. Dipl.* no. 1119, and the Latin version in *Cart. Sax.* no. 739 and *Cod. Dipl.* no. 375.

[7] Ower could not be ploughed in 1086, and was held by salt-workers.

[8] *Dom. Bk.* (Rec. Com.), i, f. 43b.

[9] *Anglo-Saxon Chron.*, a revised translation ed. D. Whitelock and others, 76.

[10] *Regesta Regum Anglo-Normannorum*, i, no. 108. Urk's charter founding the guild of Abbotsbury is translated by D. Whitelock, in *Eng. Hist. Doc.* i, no. 139. The Latin text is printed in *Cod. Dipl.* no. 942. It is one of the few known examples of guild statutes, providing for the needs of the guildsmen and the minster. A charter of Tole to the abbey still exists, but in a very mutilated condition, which makes it impossible to read: O.S. *Facsimiles of Anglo-Saxon MSS. Pt. II* (1881), p. xv, and 'Earl of Ilchester', no. V. The original charter, with some others relating to Abbotsbury, is at County Hall, Dorchester.

[11] *Cod. Dipl.* nos. 741, 772. Both charters seem to be accepted as genuine by Miss Harmer: *Anglo-Saxon Writs*, 576.

[12] Printed in Harmer, op. cit. nos. 1–2.

[13] In 1212 the abbey held Abbotsbury, Portesham, Hilton, Tolpuddle, and Abbott's Wootton, *que data fuerant per Oro* (recte *Orc*) *et Tolam uxorem suam*: *Bk. of Fees*, 92.

[14] *Regesta Regum Anglo-Normannorum*, i, nos. 109, 203.

Cranborne Abbey was poorly endowed, having only 21 hides in Dorset and the same number in Wiltshire. Hugh fitz Grip gave to this abbey a piece of land in Gillingham, which he received from the king's farm, and 1 hide at Orchard (nos. 422 and clv) *pro anima sua*. The manor of Cranborne belonged to the king in 1086, having been one of the manors which passed to Queen Maud from Beorhtric son of Aelfgar.[15] When Robert fitz Hamon received the land which had once belonged to Beorhtric, he became the patron of Cranborne Abbey, and in 1102 made it a cell of Tewkesbury.[16]

Of the houses not situated in Dorset but holding land there, the most important was the abbey of Glastonbury, the richest house in England. The 52 hides held by the abbey in Dorset were only a fraction of its huge fief, totalling about 800 hides. The largest manors of the abbey in Dorset were Sturminster Newton and Buckland Newton. Each of these manors was the head of a hundred, and the two hundreds themselves were later amalgamated to form Buckland Newton hundred. Sturminster Newton had been bequeathed by Alfred to his younger son Aethelweard,[17] and according to a charter preserved in the Glastonbury cartulary it was given to the abbey by Edgar in 968.[18] Among the other religious houses with land in Dorset were the New Minster at Winchester (Hyde Abbey), with Piddletrenthide (no. 69) which had belonged to Roger Arundel; Athelney Abbey, which held Purse Caundle by an exchange with the Count of Mortain, who received Bishopston (Montacute) in return; Tavistock Abbey, with two small manors totalling 5 hides; and Wilton Abbey with Didlington and Philipston (*Winburne*).

The land of the king's almsmen follows the account of the bishops' and abbeys' land. Bristuard the priest held the churches of Dorchester and Bere Regis (nos. 144 and xiii) with their tithes and 1 hide, 20 acres, of land. Bollo the priest held the churches of Winfrith Newburgh, with a virgate of land, and the churches of Puddletown, Chaldon, and Fleet, with 1½ hide of land (nos. 145a and xvi, 145b and xix). He held land as a king's thegn as well, and was a tenant of Abbotsbury Abbey at Atrim. Walter the deacon (*diaconus*) held *Cernel* (no. 147), and Bernard held of him. But the most important of the king's almsmen was Rainbald (Regenbald) the priest, who held the manor of Pulham (no. 146). He is undoubtedly to be identified as Rainbald of Cirencester,[19] who held the post, if not the name, of chancellor under Edward the Confessor. He is called Rainbald *canceler* in the Herefordshire survey.[20] He had held Pulham T.R.E., assessed at 10 hides. William I confirmed his lands to him,[21] and in 1086 he held 67 hides in 5 counties, besides 8 carucates in Somerset. Some of this land had belonged to him T.R.E. and he had obtained some of it after the Conquest.[22]

III

In 1086 the greatest lay landowner in Dorset after the king was Robert, Count of Mortain, the king's half-brother, with 190 hides. His Dorset lands were a mere appendage of his vast estates in Cornwall, where he held virtually the whole county. He was probably the richest man in England apart from the king, with lands scattered in many areas, particularly the south-west, Yorkshire, Northamptonshire, and Sussex.

[15] There is a tradition that the abbeys of Tewkesbury and Cranborne were founded by Aelfweard, said to be the grandfather of Beorhtric: Dugdale, *Mon.* iv. 465; *V.C.H. Dors.* ii. 70.

[16] *Ann. Mon.* (Rolls Ser.), i. 44; D. Knowles and R. N. Hadcock, *Medieval Religious Houses*, 63.

[17] *Select Eng. Hist. Doc.* ed. F. E. Harmer, 17. For the identification, see A. Fägersten, *Place-Names of Dorset*, 47.

[18] *Cart. Sax.* no. 1214; *The Great Chartulary of Glastonbury, vol. iii* (Som. Rec. Soc. lxiv), 592.

[19] He is called Rainbald of Cirencester in the account of Berks.: *Dom. Bk.* (Rec. Com.), i, f. 63. In 1130 Alvred of Lincoln paid 60 silver marks to have the manor of Pulham *de honore Cirecestr'*: *Pipe R.* 1130 (Rec. Com.), 16.

[20] *Dom. Bk.* (Rec. Com.), i, f. 180b.

[21] *Regesta Regum Anglo-Normannorum*, i, no. 19.

[22] For a full account of Rainbald, see Round, *Feudal Eng.* 421–30.

In all, he held over 790 manors in 20 counties. One of his Dorset manors, Piddlehinton, had apparently belonged to his wife, Maud.[23] He derived his lands from a number of small thegns, but Edmar, who held his more important manors in Dorset, seems to have been a man of considerable wealth. He is probably identical with the Edmer who held land in Somerset and Devon which later passed to the count, and possibly identical with Edmer *attile* or *atule* who held land in Hertfordshire, Middlesex, and Berkshire which belonged to the Count of Mortain in 1086.[24] Count Alan, lord of Richmond in Yorkshire, held the 15-hide manor of Dewlish in Dorset. He held no other land in the area, and his possession of this solitary manor is rendered more inexplicable by the fact that it had formerly belonged to Beorhtric son of Aelfgar, whose lands generally passed to Queen Maud. Hugh, Earl of Chester, held 35 hides in Dorset in consequence of his acquisition of the lands of Eadnoth the staller, who had held all but two of the Dorset manors held by Earl Hugh in 1086. Aubrey de Couci, sometime Earl of Northumbria, had held Gussage St. Michael in Dorset which in 1086 was in the king's hand.[25] He had held several manors in Wiltshire and Gussage appears in the Wiltshire survey with the rest of his land. The Countess of Boulogne held 3 manors in Dorset, Winterborne Monkton, Bockhampton, and Swanage, all of which had been held by Wulfgifu T.R.E. The Geld Roll for *Aileveswode* hundred refers to the tenure by Count Eustace (of Boulogne) of a manor which can only be Swanage.[26]

The wife of Hugh fitz Grip held 116 hides in Dorset and 3 hides at Damerham (Hants), the latter as tenant of Glastonbury Abbey. Her name is not recorded in Domesday, but in an *inspeximus* of Philip IV, dated 1305, concerning the land of the abbey of Montevilliers, there is a charter by which *Hadwidis, filia Nicolai de Baschelvilla, uxor Hugonis de Varhan* (Wareham) *filii Griponis*, gave the manor of Waddon to the abbey. Friar Waddon (no. 143) belonged to this abbey in 1086 by the gift of Hugh fitz Grip. It seems likely that the charter is genuine, and that Hugh's wife was Hadwidis or Hawise de Baschelville.[27] Hugh fitz Grip, late Sheriff of Dorset, had held 18½ hides of the queen, which had reverted to the king. The Domesday survey itself supplies most of what is known about him, but two writs, both concerning the land of Abbotsbury Abbey, are addressed to him as sheriff.[28] Three Dorset abbeys, Shaftesbury, Abbotsbury, and Cerne, had suffered losses at his hands, and he seems to have been responsible for the devastation of the Dorset boroughs. He also appropriated a virgate of William of Moyon's manor of Winterborne Houghton (nos. 275 and lxxxv) and gave to Brictuin the manor of Little Waddon (no. 460) in exchange for a manor worth twice as much. He was dead by 1084, since Aiulf the chamberlain appears as sheriff both in the Geld Rolls and in Domesday. The wife of Hugh held 28 hides as a mesne tenant, 6 hides of the Bishop of Salisbury, 15 hides of Glastonbury Abbey (excluding Damerham), a piece of land in Purbeck of William of Briouze, and Ailwood (no. 482) of Swain.

Aiulf the chamberlain held just over 55 hides in Dorset, 6 in Wiltshire, and 10 in Berkshire. *Chirce* (no. 351) belonged to him as long as he was sheriff (*quamdiu erit vicecomes*) and Lulworth (no. 350) had belonged to Alfred, the Saxon sheriff. Aiulf's largest manor, Wootton Fitzpaine (no. 347), was held T.R.E. by Beorhtsige, a thegn of King Edward (*miles regis Edwardi*).[29] None of his other Saxon predecessors was a man of any importance. By 1091 Aiulf was Sheriff of Somerset, and held both offices in the

[23] See p. 130.

[24] See pp. 31–32.

[25] See p. 129. For Aubrey de Couci, see Stenton, *Anglo-Saxon Eng.* 606.

[26] See pp. 136, 137.

[27] *Gallia Christiana* (1874), xi, App. col. 329E; T. Bond, 'On the Barony of the Wife of Hugh fitz Grip', *Proc. Dorset Nat. Hist. and Antiq. Field Club*, xiv. 115–16.

[28] *Regesta Regum Anglo-Normannorum*, i, nos. 109, 203.

[29] Eyton (*Key to Domesday: Dorset*, 141–2) identified this manor as Marshwood, Fägersten (*Place-Names of Dorset*, 298) as Wootton Fitzpaine.

reign of Henry I, perhaps until about 1120.[30] He may have been alive in 1130, since he appears in the Pipe Roll for that year.[31] A daughter of his became a nun at Shaftesbury, whereupon he returned to that abbey the part of Farnham (no. 352) which he held in 1086 but which had belonged to the abbey T.R.E. Aiulf's brother, Humphrey the chamberlain, held just over 10 hides in Dorset. He held land in 8 counties, and seems to have been a protégé of Queen Maud. In Surrey he held the manor of Combe whose previous owner, a woman, placed herself under the queen's protection[32] and two of his manors in Gloucestershire had been given to him by the queen.[33] Queen Maud presumably gave him his two manors at Edmondsham (nos. 353, 354) since she had held the remaining portion of this vill herself (nos. 18 and xxiv). Eddeva, who held one of these two manors, is probably to be identified with the widow mentioned in the Geld Roll for *Albretesberge* hundred, who held a hide at farm of Humphrey the chamberlain which did not pay geld because *Aiulfus dicit reginam perdonasse pro anima Ricardi filii sui*. Humphrey seems to have held some official position in East Anglia under William Rufus, either as sheriff or as local justiciar.[34] William of Eu held 90 hides in Dorset. Over half of his entire fief (consisting of 336 hides in eight counties) lay in Wiltshire and Dorset. His lands were derived largely from Aelfstan of Boscombe, who held 36 hides in Dorset, and Toli, who, though less wealthy than Aelfstan, held a considerable amount of land in Dorset and the south-west. William's father, Count Robert, held land in Essex and Huntingdon, but the bulk of his fief lay in Sussex. The mother of William of Eu occurs once in the Dorset Geld Rolls, holding a manor which can only be Crichel (no. 266) which her son held in 1086.[35] Eyton suggested that William's mother was a relative of Ralph de Limesi, who had once held land in Dorset and Gloucestershire which belonged to William in 1086.[36] In Dorset Ralph de Limesi had held Blandford St. Mary (no. 261) and in Gloucestershire 34 carucates of the honor of Strigoil (later Chepstow) and several manors.[37] William of Eu was a rich and powerful baron but he did not retain his position long. In 1088 he took part in the rebellion against William Rufus, and in 1094 was involved in the plot against the king's life. In 1096 he was unable to clear himself of a charge of treason, and in consequence was blinded and mutilated, probably dying soon afterwards.[38] His steward, William de Aldrie, was involved in his downfall and hanged. He held land of William of Eu in Wiltshire, and in the Dorset Geld Rolls appears as the holder of a manor which is probably Blandford (no. 261).

Roger Arundel held a considerable amount of land in the south-west which later formed the honor of Powerstock. He had 65 hides in Dorset and $78\frac{1}{2}$ in Somerset, most of which he derived from two English thegns, Aethelfrith and Aelmer. He had at one time held the 30-hide manor of Piddletrenthide (no. 69) which in 1086 belonged to the New Minster, Winchester. Roger's surname appears to be a corruption of *l'hirondelle*, and has no connexion with Arundel in Sussex.[39] As Roger Derundel he witnessed a charter to the Bishop of Wells in 1068, but is otherwise unknown.[40] A much more famous figure was Roger de Beaumont,[41] who held $47\frac{1}{2}$ hides in Dorset and the manor of

[30] W. A. Morris, *Medieval Eng. Sheriff*, 47, n. 48 (reprinted from W. A. Morris, 'The Office of Sheriff in the Early Norman Period', *E.H.R.* xxxiii. 151, n.); *Regesta Regum Anglo-Normannorum*, ii, no. 1367 and n.

[31] *Pipe R.* 1130 (Rec. Com.), 14.

[32] *T.R.W. femina que hanc terram tenebat misit se cum ea in manu regine*: *Dom. Bk.* (Rec. Com.), i, f. 36b.

[33] Ibid. f. 170.

[34] *Regesta Regum Anglo-Normannorum*, i, p. xxv.

[35] See pp. 138, 139.

[36] Eyton, *Key to Domesday: Dorset*, 76; Eyton, *Domesday Studies: Som.* i. 64.

[37] *Dom. Bk.* (Rec. Com.), i, ff. 162, 166b–167.

[38] *Anglo-Saxon Chron.*, ed. D. Whitelock and others, 173; Ordericus Vitalis, *Hist. Eccl.*, ed. A. Le Prévost, iii. 411. According to the Chron. the accusation was brought by Geoffrey Bainard. Orderic says that the accuser was Earl Hugh, whose sister William had married. Le Prévost calls William the Count of Eu, but Dr. Whitelock rejects this.

[39] Eyton, *Domesday Studies: Som.* i. 62–63.

[40] *Regesta Regum Anglo-Normannorum*, i, no. 23.

[41] Name derived from Beaumont-le-Roger: Eure, arr. Bernay, cant. Beaumont.

Dorsington (Glos.), assessed at 10 hides. Eyton remarked that 'the appearance of this name on any page of Domesday is a marvel'[42] since Roger must have been of an advanced age in 1086. He was the son of Humphrey de Vieilles, who died before 1047.[43] Roger furnished 60 ships for the invasion of England, but was already too old to fight in the battle of Hastings, and was represented by his elder son Robert.[44] Nevertheless, Roger remained active throughout his long life. As late as 1090 he supported his son Robert in a quarrel with the Duke of Normandy[45] and about 1095 he entered the monastery of St. Pierre, Préaux, where he died as a monk, some years later (*post aliquot aunos* (sic) *conversionis suae bono fine quievit*).[46]

Some of the men holding smaller amounts of land in Dorset were powerful barons in neighbouring counties. Edward of Salisbury, who held two manors assessed at 38 hides in Dorset, was Sheriff of Wiltshire, where he held 193 hides. Much of his land in 8 counties, including his Dorset manors, had belonged to the English lady Wulfwynn. Waleran the huntsman (*venator*), who held 38 hides in Dorset, had extensive lands in Wiltshire also. One of his Domesday manors, Church Knowle (no. 308), was given to him by William fitz Osbern. Robert fitz Gerold held 22 hides in Dorset and 55 in Wiltshire. Ernulf of Hesdin, a Fleming from the Pas de Calais,[47] had land in Wiltshire and Gloucestershire, as well as his 15 hides in Dorset. William of Moyon,[48] Sheriff of Somerset, had 36 hides in Dorset, and 75 in Somerset, including the manor of Dunster, where he built his castle. Turstin fitz Rolf, another Somerset landowner, held 11 hides in Dorset. He is perhaps to be identified with Turstin son of Rollo, who is said to have borne the Norman banner at Hastings.[49] Two other Somerset barons, Serle of Burcy and William of Falaise, had 13 hides each in Dorset. William of Falaise was Serle's son-in-law, having married his daughter Geva.[50] Another of Serle's daughters was a nun at Shaftesbury.[51] Walter or Walscin of Douai, whose lands lay mainly in Devon, held 10 hides in Dorset, and Walter de Claville, who had 13 hides in Dorset, also held land in Devon. Unlike the foregoing barons, the bulk of the land of William of Briouze[52] lay at a distance, in Sussex, where he had over 400 hides. His 26 hides in Dorset were an insignificant part of his fief, later known as the honor of Bramber. A less important person was William of Ecouis,[53] who held 11 hides in Dorset, and also held land at Caerleon, then part of Herefordshire. Most of his land lay in East Anglia and Essex. Hugh de St. Quintin, who had 4½ hides in Dorset, held 3 manors in Essex, and was a tenant of Hugh de Port in Hampshire. Hugh de Boscherbert who held 11½ hides, is unknown outside Dorset, but appears also as a tenant of the wife of Hugh fitz Grip.

Some men who held isolated manors had received the estates of Englishmen whose lands were scattered over several shires. Baldwin of Exeter, Sheriff of Devon, held Iwerne Courtney (no. 316) as a result of his acquisition of the lands of Seward, who held this manor T.R.E. and appears as a predecessor of Baldwin in Devon and Somerset. It acquired its alternative name Shroton (i.e. sheriff's town) from Baldwin. The predecessor of Alvred of Epaignes[54] at Turnworth (no. 319) was Alwi, whose lands in Devon and Somerset had also passed to Alvred. Exon. Domesday for these two counties

42 Eyton, *Key to Domesday: Dorset*, 76.

43 D. C. Douglas, 'Companions of the Conqueror', *History*, xxviii. 136. Humphrey founded the 2 monasteries at Préaux, St. Pierre for monks and St. Leger for nuns: Ordericus Vitalis, *Hist. Eccl.* ii. 14.

44 *History*, xxviii. 136.

45 Ordericus Vitalis, *Hist. Eccl.* iii. 336–44.

46 Ibid. 426–7.

47 Hesdin: Pas de Calais, arr. Montreuil, cant. Hesdin. See *Cal. Doc. France*, ed. Round, 481–2.

48 Moyon: Manche, arr. St. Lô, cant. Tessy-sur-Vire.

49 Ordericus Vitalis, *Hist. Eccl.* ii. 147.

50 *Dom. Bk.* (Rec. Com.), i, f. 96b. For a discussion of the 2 families and their descendants, see H. Maxwell-Lyte, 'Burci, Falaise and Martin', *Proc. Som. Arch. Soc.* lxv. 1–27.

51 Her father gave Kilmington (Wilts.) to the abbey when she entered it: *Dom. Bk.* (Rec. Com.), i, f. 98.

52 Briouze: Orne, arr. Argentan, cant. Briouze.

53 Ecouis: Eure, arr. Les Andelys, cant. Fleury-sur-Andelle.

54 Epaignes: Eure, arr. Pont-Audemer, cant. Cormeilles.

gives his surname as Banneson. Trasmund, Osbern Giffard's predecessor at Hill (no. 318), had held one of his manors in Wiltshire also, and Matthew de Moretania's predecessor at Milborne St. Andrew and Owermoigne (nos. 320, 321) was John, who had previously held some of Matthew's land in Gloucestershire and Somerset. In the Exon. Domesday for Somerset he is called John the Dane. Strang the Dane held another of Matthew's Gloucestershire manors, and Torchil (another Danish name) appears as his predecessor in Somerset. The acquisition of the scattered land of an English thegn does not always account for the possession of these solitary manors. Hugh de Port's[55] manor of Compton Valence (no. 357) was held by Bundi, who does not appear as his predecessor elsewhere, and the manor of Corton (no. 238), belonging to Roger de Courseulles,[56] was held by two unnamed thegns T.R.E. Berenger Giffard's predecessor at Bredy (no.317), Harding, did not hold either of his two Wiltshire manors.

Subinfeudation had reached a considerable extent in 1086, especially on the larger estates. Both the Count of Mortain and the wife of Hugh fitz Grip had subinfeudated about two-thirds of their land in Dorset. Ernulf of Hesdin and Turstin fitz Rolf also had subinfeudated about two-thirds of their land, and William of Eu retained only about a quarter of his land in demesne. Earl Hugh and William of Briouze, whose chief possessions lay at some distance from Dorset, had subinfeudated all or virtually all their land, but William of Ecouis, whose land lay mainly in Norfolk, had retained all his Dorset manors in demesne. Roger Arundel and William of Moyon each held about half their land in Dorset in demesne. Roger de Beaumont, Robert fitz Gerold, and Aiulf the chamberlain[57] had retained the greater part of their land in demesne, and William of Falaise and Walter de Claville had so retained virtually all their Dorset manors. Some of this subinfeudated land was held by English tenants. Eddeva (Eadgifu) held Edmondsham (no. 354) of Humphrey the chamberlain, and Alwin (Aelfwine) held Stourton Caundle (no. 219) of the Count of Mortain. Beulf (Beowulf), who held Church Knowle (no. 308) of Waleran the huntsman, must have been English. It would appear from the Geld Rolls that other Englishmen had been holding land of Norman lords.[58] Most of the mesne tenants, however, were French. The Exchequer text does not as a rule mention their surnames, and Exon. Domesday, which usually does, only covers one-fifth of the manors in Dorset. In the case of lands not covered by Exon. Domesday it is sometimes possible to identify tenants in Dorset with men holding of the same lord in other counties. Vitalis, who held the single Dorset manor of Roger de Courseulles, is probably the same Vitalis who held land of Roger de Courseulles in Somerset. Urse, who held two manors in Dorset of Ernulf of Hesdin, held one of his Wiltshire manors too. Bernard, who held two Dorset manors of Turstin fitz Rolf, is probably to be identified with Bernard Pauncevolt, who held land of Turstin in Somerset and Gloucestershire, and was a tenant-in-chief in Hampshire and Wiltshire. Exon. Domesday for Somerset, Devon, and Cornwall supplies surnames for some of the tenants of the Count of Mortain, and some of the men holding land of the count in Dorset can tentatively be identified with men holding land of the count in these other South-western counties. Ansger, who held four Dorset manors of the count, may be identified with Ansger *Breto* or *Brito* who was a tenant of the count in Somerset and Devon. Malger, who held *Wintreburne* (no. 182) and part of Wool (no. 208) of the count, may be Malger de Cartrai, a tenant of the count in Somerset and Devon.[59] Hubert who held

[55] Port-en-Bessin: Calvados, arr. Bayeux, cant. Ryes.

[56] Courseulles-sur-Mer: Calvados, arr. Caen, cant. Creully.

[57] Domesday suggests that Aiulf retained nearly all his manors in demesne. The Geld Rolls, however, indicate that some of his land had been held by mesne tenants not mentioned in the Domesday survey.

[58] See pp. 35–36.

[59] A knight called H. de Cartrai held land at Beaminster (no. 46) of the Bp. of Salisbury.

three of the count's Dorset manors may be Hubert de St. Clare, who held land in Somerset of the count, and Alvred, who held the count's manor of Stanton St. Gabriel (no. 210) and part of Loders (no. 190), is almost certainly to be identified with Alvred *pincerna* who held land of the count in Somerset and Cornwall and in Dorset held $1\frac{1}{2}$ virgate at Purse Caundle (nos. 118 and lxiv) which the count gave to Athelney Abbey in exchange for Montacute.[60]

Exon. Domesday supplies surnames for some of the tenants of Roger Arundel, William of Moyon, and the wife of Hugh fitz Grip. Roger, who held Wyndlam (nos. 322 and xciv) of Roger Arundel, was Roger *de margella* and Robert, who held Blandford (nos. 326 and xcvii) and Rollington (nos. 331 and cii), was Robert Attlet. Godfrey, who held Todber (nos. 273 and lxxxiii) of William of Moyon, was Godfrey Maloret. Of the wife of Hugh's tenants, the William who held *Bere* (nos. 390 and cxxii) and Puncknowle (nos. 397 and cxxx) was William *de monasteriis* who also held land of Cerne Abbey; the William who held Morden (nos. 383 and cxvii), *Winburne* (nos. 388 and cxx), and Hampreston (nos. 389 and cxxi) was William de Creneto or Chernet; and the William holding Sturthill (nos. 394 and cxxvii) was William de Almereio, who as William de Dalmar held two manors as a king's serjeant.[61] Durand who held Wilkswood (nos. 423 and clvi) was Durand the carpenter, who also held land as a king's serjeant. Hugh who held Brenscombe (nos. 421 and cliv) was Hugh de Boscherbert, who held two manors in Dorset as a tenant-in-chief.[62] Roger who held Little Cheselbourne (nos. 378 and cx) was Roger Boissell, who appears as a tenant of Roger Arundel in the Exon. Domesday for Somerset. Walter, who held Turners Puddle (nos. 391 and cxxiv) and Swanage (nos. 417 and cl), was Walter Tonitruus. The Robert who held Creech (nos. 412 and cxlv) was Robert the corn-dealer (*frumentinus*), but Robert who held *Torne* (nos. 420 and cliii) was Hugh's nephew (*nepos Hugonis*) and Robert who held Hurpston (nos. 413 and cxlvi) was Robert the boy (*puer*). Ralph who held Ringstead (nos. 411 and cxliv) was Ralph the steward (*dapifer*).

The Geld Rolls sometimes mention surnames not given in Domesday. In Whitchurch hundred William *de estra* had one hide of the Count of Mortain, which can be identified as part of *Cerneli* (no. 212). Corscombe (no. 213) was held by the same William according to Domesday, so these two manors must have been held by William *de estra*.[63] Robert fitz Ivo, who appears as a tenant of the Count of Mortain in Exon. Domesday for Somerset, held land in *Celeberge* and Cullifordtree hundreds of the same count, probably to be identified as the manors of Morden (no. 172) and Stafford (no. 155). Ralph the clerk held land of the count in Dorchester hundred, which must be *Cerne* (no. 157) since this is the only manor in Dorset to be held of the count by a man called Ralph. William Malbeenc (*sic*) appears in the Geld Roll for Beaminster hundred holding a virgate of Earl Hugh, which can be identified as part of Catsley (no. 229). It is reasonable to assume that William Malbank held the other manors of Earl Hugh also, since he frequently appears as the earl's tenant. Clifton (no. 225) must have derived from him its later form of Clifton Maybank. He held all the count's manors in Dorset except one, Fifehead Magdalen (no. 220), which was held by Gilbert. In the hundred of Whitchurch it is stated that William 'the Goat' (*capru*) held $3\frac{1}{2}$ hides of Roger Arundel. A man called William held 3 hides of Roger Arundel at Wraxall (nos. 328 and c). He may therefore be identical with William 'the Goat', a tenant-in-chief in Somerset. In Combsditch hundred William *de monasteriis* is said to hold 3 virgates of William de Aldrie, which never paid geld. William de Aldrie does not appear as a tenant-in-chief

[60] See p. 8.
[61] See p. 54.
[62] See p. 48.
[63] Later evidence suggests that the William who held Knighton (no. 193) and Hooke (no. 207) was the same as William *de estra*, and that Drew who held Nyland (no. 150) and Toller (no. 214) was Drew of Montacute: see p. 60.

in Dorset. He was the steward of William of Eu, and the land in question may be the ½ hide at Blandford (no. 261) which did not pay geld, and which was held by William of William of Eu. It is true that the Geld Rolls mention 3 virgates, while the amount in Domesday is ½ hide, but it is difficult to see what other piece of land could be meant.

After the land of Hugh de Boscherbert is entered the land of nine men described in the index as *Hugo de Luri et alii franci*. Hugh de Lure held a manor of 5 hides (no. 362) in an unspecified locality (or rather localities, since it is called *terra in tribus locis*) which was held of him by a man called Ralph. Hugh de Lure was a tenant-in-chief in Northamptonshire where he held Weldon.[64] Hugh *silvestris* held ½ hide in Stourton Caundle (no. 363), but is otherwise unknown. Fulcred who held *Waia* and Moorbath (nos. 364, 365) had held all but two of the manors which had belonged to Earl Harold, and which in 1086 were held by King William. Richard de Rivers, who held Mosterton (no. 366), rose to prominence in the reign of Henry I, from whom he obtained Loders, which he gave to the abbey of Montebourg.[65] His son, Baldwin de Rivers, was made Earl of Devon by the Empress Maud, probably about 1141.[66] Schelin held the manor of Shilling Okeford, or Shillingstone (no. 367), to which he gave his name. It was the largest manor held by a *francus*, being assessed at 16 hides, and had belonged to Earl Harold. Schelin had held the manors of Edmondsham and Witchampton of the queen,[67] and had received from her also part of Hampreston (no. 443), which in 1086 was held by Torchil as a king's thegn.[68] In Somerset Schelin held Foddington, which according to Exon. he held at farm of the king.[69] Another protégé of Queen Maud was Anschitil fitz Ameline, who held Tyneham (no. 369) which he claimed to hold of the queen *sed post mortem eius regem non requisivit*. He seems to be identical with the man called Anschitil de Carisburgo in the Geld Roll for Hasilor hundred. David the interpreter (*interpres*) who held Poorton (no. 368) is not otherwise known, unless he is identical with the David who held Ash (no. 287) of William of Briouze. Poorton was held of him by Godeschal. Ralph of Cranborne held West Parley (no. 371), and may be identical with Ralph who held *Tarente* (no. 370). A man called Ralph held one hide of Cranborne Abbey at Wimborne (no. 72). Odo fitz Eurebold held four small manors, Farnham (no. 372), Milborne Stileham (no. 373), Rushton (no. 374), and Petersham (no. 375). Petersham was a divided vill, the other part being held by Iseldis (no. 424). This lady held only this one manor and is not known outside Dorset.

After the little manor of Iseldis are entered the lands of the king's thegns. They were Englishmen who had survived the Conquest either still in possession of some of their lands, or with the lands of other pre-Conquest thegns, and were the last representatives of the Saxon landowning class. The most prosperous thegns in Dorset in 1086 were Brictuin (Beorhtwine) and Swain. They may be the men addressed in a writ of William I concerning the lands of Abbotsbury Abbey, which is directed to Bishop Herman, Brihtwi, Scewine, and all the king's thegns of Dorset.[70] They each held about 20 hides. Brictuin held 11 small manors, totalling 19 hides and 8 acres, most of which he had also held T.R.E. His predecessor at Melbury Sampford (no. 441) is not named and Little Waddon (no. 460) was given to him by Hugh fitz Grip in exchange for a manor worth twice as much. The Count of Mortain is said to have held this manor in 1086, but it

[64] *Dom. Bk.* (Rec. Com.), i, f. 224b.

[65] *Regesta Regum Anglo-Normannorum*, ii, no. 825.

[66] Round, *Geoffrey de Mandeville*, 271.

[67] See pp. 28–29. It is possible that he continued to hold at least Edmondsham, since, according to a charter in the Montacute cartulary, his son Robert gave the tithe of Edmondsham and land in Shillingstone to Montacute: see p. 59.

[68] In 1194 Geoffrey Eskelling is entered in the Pipe Roll, rendering 15*s*. 9*d*. *de firma de Hamma Galfridi Eskelling*': *Pipe R.* 1194 (P.R.S. N.S. v), 20. Geoffrey is not mentioned again, and his connexion, if any, with Schelin is not known. The Domesday form of Hampreston was *Hame*.

[69] *Dom. Bk.* (Rec. Com.), i, f. 99; iv. 466. He can also be identified with the Schelin who held 5 hides in *Nategrave* (Glos.) as tenant of the church of Worcester: ibid. i, f. 165; see pp. 59–60.

[70] *Regesta Regum Anglo-Normannorum*, i, no. 108.

cannot be traced among his other manors. Two of Brictuin's manors were held of him by others. Stinsford (no. 464) was held by Aiulf and six men (*homines*) held Ringstead (no. 463) at farm. Brictuin is probably to be identified with the man called in the Geld Rolls Brictuin the reeve, since the land held by this man can be identified with some of Brictuin's Domesday manors. Swain held four manors, three of which were assessed at a total of 20 hides. The hidage of Milborne Stileham (no. 477) is not given. Three of his manors were held by his father T.R.E. and the fourth, Ailwood (no. 482), by a man called Azor. All four manors were subinfeudated in 1086. Hugh's wife held Ailwood, Osmund held Milborne, Ralph held Plumber (no. 453), and Robert held *Wintreburne* (no. 452). This suggests that Swain held land elsewhere. He may be identical with the Swain who held Stapleford (Wilts.) which his father had held T.R.E.[71] It is also possible that Azor, the T.R.E. holder of Ailwood, was in fact the father of Swain, which would identify him as Swain son of Azor, who held Stoke Bruern (Northants.) and 22 houses in Northampton.[72] In 1095 *Suegen filius Azor* contributed 20*s*. to the Worcester relief. A man called Swain had held *Colesborne* (Glos.) of the church of Worcester T.R.E. but does not appear to have held it in 1086.[73]

Some of the less prosperous thegns held lands which they had held T.R.E. as did Godmund at Milton on Stour (no. 425) and Saward at Stourton Caundle (no. 479). The ten thegns who held Kingcombe (no. 485) had held it T.R.E. as one manor, and the two bordars who held $\frac{1}{4}$ virgate (no. 480) in an unspecified locality had held it freely T.R.E.[74] Godwin the reeve held a virgate in *Wintreburne* (no. 450) and Alward the reeve held Wool (no. 486) both of which they had held T.R.E. Almar held one virgate in Wool, which had belonged T.R.E. to Alward, presumably Alward the reeve (no. 487). Alward Colinc held Thorncombe (no. 439) which he also held T.R.E. He had been the pre-Conquest holder of Langton Herring, which Hugh fitz Grip had held of the queen (nos. 23 and xxix), and had held several other manors which Hugh's wife held in 1086.[75] Thorncombe was the only manor which he had retained.

Some of the Englishmen who had retained or had been given lands evidently held them as a result of some service which they performed for the king. The number of huntsmen (*venatores*) recorded among the thegns of Dorset and neighbouring counties suggests that some of these men held their lands by serjeanty. Several men are called *venator* in the Geld Rolls, and can usually be identified with one or other of the king's thegns. Ulvric the huntsman held a hide in an unspecified locality (no. 454) which his father had held T.R.E. Ulvric the huntsman is mentioned in the Geld Roll for *Celeberge* hundred, holding land which can be identified with Morden (no. 437). According to Domesday it was held partly by Ulvric and partly by his brother's wife, who is probably the lady named Ulveva in the Geld Roll. The manor was held by Ulvric's father T.R.E. In *Canendone* hundred Ulvric the huntsman held land which can be identified with Ulvric's manor of Thornhill (no. 442), also held by his father T.R.E. Ulvric may be identified with the man of the same name who held a manor in Hampshire which his father held T.R.E.[76] Ulvric the huntsman also occurs as a king's thegn in Wiltshire.[77] In *Albretesberge* hundred Ulviet the huntsman had 1 hide, which is probably to be identified with the manor of Wimborne (no. 440) held by Ulviet. A man called Ulviet also held Blandford (no. 458), and may be identical with Ulviet the huntsman. Ulviet the huntsman held land in Hampshire and Wiltshire also as a king's thegn.[78] Alvric the

[71] *Dom. Bk.* (Rec. Com.), i, f. 74; *V.C.H. Wilts.* ii. 71.

[72] *Dom. Bk.* (Rec. Com.), i, ff. 219, 228; *V.C.H. Northants.* i. 292–3.

[73] *Hemingi Chartularium*, ed. T. Hearne (1723), i. 79–80, printed also in Round, *Feudal Eng.* 309; see also p. 59.

[74] See p. 18.

[75] See p. 32.

[76] *Dom. Bk.* (Rec. Com.), i, f. 50b.

[77] *V.C.H. Wilts.* ii. 174.

[78] *Dom. Bk.* (Rec. Com.), i, ff. 50b, 74.

huntsman held land in the hundreds of *Aileveswode* and Bere, which can be identified as the manors of Combe (no. 481) and Bovington (no. 483) both held by Alvric according to Domesday. He held both these manors himself T.R.E. Several other manors were held by Alvric in 1086, but whether this was the huntsman or not is uncertain. Alvric the huntsman held land in Wiltshire in 1086, and before the Conquest held 1½ hide at North Newton of the abbey of Wilton. In 1086 Richard Sturmid held this 1½ hide, and it is possible that the Alvric who held several other manors as Richard Sturmid's predecessor is identical with Alvric the huntsman.

Edwin the huntsman held land in the hundreds of *Langeberge*, Pimperne, Combsditch, and Uggescombe. His manors in these hundreds can be identified with *Bleneforde* (no. 438), Lazerton (no. 456), *Bleneford* (no. 455), and Shilvinghampton (no. 457). He may also be identical with the Edwin who held a virgate in Gillingham (no. 427). Unlike Ulvric, Ulviet, and Alvric, he did not hold any of this land T.R.E. Two of his manors had belonged to Alwi, one to Alwin, and one to Alward. He is probably to be identified with Edwin the huntsman who held Oakhanger (Hants), which Alwi held T.R.E., and Kingsclere (Hants). This last manor had been held T.R.E. by Edwin himself, of King Edward.[79] Godric, who held a virgate in Gillingham (no. 428), is probably the man called Godric the huntsman in the Geld Roll for Gillingham hundred. Edward the huntsman held ½ virgate in Gillingham (no. 490), and Ulwin, who held land in Gillingham (no. 429), was probably a huntsman also, although this is not certain. Godwin the huntsman held Walford (no. 448), which had belonged to Almar, and ½ virgate (no. 451) which had belonged to Godric. Edric, who held seven manors amounting to 8½ hides which had belonged to a thegn called Sawin T.R.E., can be identified with Edric the reeve mentioned in the Geld Rolls. Bollo the priest held two manors as a thegn, Mappowder (no. 431) which he and seven other free thegns had held T.R.E., and Chickerell (no. 432) which had belonged to Saulf. He held several churches as an almsman, and was a tenant of Cerne Abbey. Godric, who held Briantspuddle (no. 472) which had belonged to Azor, was not the huntsman, but can be identified with Godric the priest mentioned in the Geld Roll for Bere hundred.

Dodo held ½ hide of the queen in alms (no. 444) and the manor of Wilksworth (no. 445). The queen's manor of Edmondsham (nos. 18 and xxiv) had been held T.R.E. by a man called Dodo. Humphrey the chamberlain's manor of Edmondsham (no. 353) was also held by a man of this name T.R.E. and it seems likely that the same person is referred to in each case. A certain Dodo held a manor in Woolcombe (no. 474), assessed at 1 virgate. The other 3 virgates were held by Hugh Gosbert (no. 498) and were held T.R.E. by Dode *monachus*. It is uncertain whether Dodo the almsman of the queen is identical with Dode the monk, but this is quite possible. A man called Dodo had held Kington (no. 426) T.R.E., but in 1086 it was held by Chetel. Dodo is too common a name to identify him with either of the others.

The king's serjeants follow immediately upon the thegns. There are ten men in all under this heading. Hunger fitz Odin was the most important, with 21 hides, consisting of the manor of Broadwindsor (no. 505) and 1 hide in Little Windsor (no. 506). He may be identical with the son of Odo the chamberlain who claimed the manor of Chelborough (nos. 280 and xc), held by William of Moyon. Odin the chamberlain held Swindon (Wilts.). William Belet held 12 hides and 1 virgate. Although he is classed as a serjeant in Dorset, he was a tenant-in-chief in Hampshire, where he held Woodcott. He had given this manor in dower to Faderlin, who married his daughter.[80] William also held 12 acres of meadow at Hinton Martell (no. 31) and at one time held Hampreston

[79] Ibid. ff. 49b, 50b.

[80] Ibid. f. 48b.

(nos. 19 and xxv) of the queen, possibly at farm. William de Dalmar held two manors, Walditch (no. 501) and the land of three thegns (no. 494). The location of this land is unspecified, but it may be part of Tarrant Crawford.[81] He was a tenant of the wife of Hugh fitz Grip.[82] Hervey the chamberlain (*cubicularius*) is identified by Eyton as Hervey of Wilton, a *minister* in Wiltshire.[83] John, who held *Wintreburne* (no. 500), can be identified as John the usher (*hostiarius*) who is mentioned in the Geld Roll for Combsditch hundred. He held six manors in Somerset and two in Wiltshire. Osmund the baker (*pistor*) held Woodstreet (no. 507) and Galton (no. 508). Hugh Gosbert held four manors totalling 1 hide, 3 virgates. Durand the carpenter (*carpentarius*) held Afflington (no. 510) and *Moleham* (no. 511) and was a tenant of the wife of Hugh fitz Grip. Godfrey the scullion (*scutularius*) held a virgate in Herston (no. 512) which his father held T.R.E. Roger Arundel held ½ hide in Herston (no. 333) which Her held T.R.E. Her is not found outside Dorset and it is tempting to identify him with Godfrey's father. Apart from the men entered as king's serjeants, two serjeanties appear to have been provided for out of ecclesiastical land. Goscelm the cook (*cocus*) held 4 hides of land of the king at Sturminster Newton (no. 63) belonging to Glastonbury Abbey, and Manasses, who held 3 virgates at Stalbridge (no. 42) belonging to the Bishop of Salisbury *quas Willelmus filius regis tulit ab ecclesia sine consensu episcopi et monachorum*, is identified by the Geld Roll for Brownshall hundred as Manasses the cook.

Some of the serjeanties mentioned in Domesday can still be traced in the 13th century. In 1086 Osmund the baker held Galton. In 1212 Robert de Welles held 2 hides in Wool and 1 hide in Galton *a conquestu Anglie per servicium pistoris*.[84] In 1219 William de Welles, presumably his son, held 40*s*. of land in Wool *per serianteriam faciendi panem domini regis*[85] and still held it in 1244 *ut sit pistor domini regis*. Hunger fitz Odin's manor of Broadwindsor was held in 1212 by Thomas of Windsor *de conquestu et de dono Willelmi Bastardi regis Anglie per seriantiam* but the serjeanty is not specified. In 1219 the manor was held by John of Windsor, presumably Thomas's son, by the serjeanty *fundatoris scaccarii*, and was worth £15.[86] In 1244 Thomas, son of John, was *ponderator denariorum ad scaccarium domini regis de recepta apud Westmonasterium*.[87] The holder of the manor of Broadwindsor was in fact the pesour or *miles argentarius* of the *Dialogus de Scaccario*.[88]

Land held in 1086 by the king's thegns can sometimes be connected with later serjeanties. In the case of the baker serjeanty held by Robert de Welles, Galton was held in 1086 by Osmund the baker and Wool, the other manor involved, was held partly by Alward and partly by Almar, both king's thegns (nos. 486, 487). This seems to be an instance of an already existing serjeanty augmented by a grant of thegn's land. Edward the huntsman held ½ virgate in Gillingham (no. 490) as a thegn. In 1212 William de Hanton held ½ virgate in Gillingham hundred of the gift of Henry I *per servicium seriancie de luverez*,[89] a serjeanty connected with wolfhounds. This is possibly identical with Edward the huntsman's ½ virgate. Ulvric the huntsman in 1086 held Thorn Hill (no. 442) and Morden (no. 437) as a thegn. In 1212 Godfrey de Pourton held Thorn Hill, part of Church Knowle, and Morden, *et tenet terras istas per servicium unius haubergelli*.[90] In 1219 the same land was held *per servicium venandi*.[91]

[81] See p. 22.

[82] See p. 50.

[83] Eyton, *Domesday Studies: Som.* i. 149–50.

[84] *Bk. of Fees*, 89.

[85] Ibid. 260.

[86] Ibid. 94, 260, 1387; see also Round, *King's Sergeants*, 232–3.

[87] *Bk. of Fees*, 1387.

[88] *Dialogus de Scaccario*, ed. C. Johnson, pp. xxviii–xxix.

[89] *Bk. of Fees*, 91. William also held ¼ virgate of land *que solebat reddere manerio de Gillingeham ii solidos per annum* by the same serjeanty: ibid.

[90] Ibid. 88.

[91] Ibid. 260. In 1244 Roger de Langeford held the land *per seriantiam inveniendi unum hominem cum uno haubergello*, and in 1250 he had to find *unum servientem equitem armatum*: ibid. 1182, 1388.

Several chamberlains are mentioned in the Dorset survey but in most cases they cannot be connected with later serjeanties. It has been suggested that Aiulf the chamberlain was Robert Malet's deputy, since he held land in Lulworth, which was later connected with the deputy chamberlainship.[92] Lulworth, with the hundred of Winfrith and part of the hundred of Hasilor, was held in 1212 by Robert de Neuburgh, *per servicium camerarii*, and his ancestors' tenure by this service was said to go back to Henry I's time. In 1219 it was further defined as the service *dandi aquam domino regi in diebus Natalis, Pasche, Pentecoste*.[93] Robert was one of the co-heirs of Gerbert de Percy and Maud Arundel, who had held land in Lulworth at one time.[94] Maud in turn was the heir of Roger Arundel, who, however, held no land in Lulworth in 1086. Aiulf's manor of Lulworth was held T.R.E. by Alfred, the Saxon Sheriff of Dorset, and Aiulf was himself sheriff in 1086. Gerbert de Percy, Maud's husband, was also Sheriff of Dorset. It was possibly Gerbert who received the manor of Lulworth and transmitted it to Robert de Neuburgh with the land which Maud Arundel received as heir to Roger Arundel. Aiulf may have been alive in 1130, since he appears in the Pipe Roll for that year, but he was not sheriff at that time.[95]

Land held by a serjeant in 1086 was sometimes held by knight service later. William Belet was classed as a serjeant in the Dorset survey, but in 1212 Robert Belet, presumably a descendant of his, held his manors in Dorset as one knight's fee.[96] On the other hand, it is probable that though Matthew de Moretania was not classed as a serjeant in 1086, but entered as a baron as he was in Wiltshire and elsewhere, part (or all) of his lands was held by serjeanty as they were from the late 12th century by the Moyne family.[97] It was asserted that the serjeanty which William de Morville held at Bradpole in 1212 had existed *de conquestu Anglie*[98] but in 1086 Bradpole was among the group of royal manors headed by Dorchester (nos. 2 and xii). In 1212 also John Russell held Kingston Russell in Long Bredy *per serianciam essendi marescallus buteilerie domini regis ad Natale Domini et ad Pentecosten* and this serjeanty too is said to date from the time of William I, but the evidence of Domesday does not support this.[99]

The later history of the lands of the tenants-in-chief can sometimes be traced down to the 13th century. Roger de Beaumont's land passed to his son Robert, Count of Meulan, and thence to Waleran, Count of Meulan.[1] Waleran's son, Robert, resigned his lands to his daughter Mabel, wife of William de Rivers, Earl of Devon.[2] She and her husband were involved in a dispute in 1204 with William the Marshall over the ownership of Sturminster, which William the Marshall claimed had been given to him by Count Robert.[3] He was apparently successful, since in 1212 he was holding Sturminster of the Count of Meulan[4] and gave it the name of Sturminster Marshall.

Most of the manors of the wife of Hugh fitz Grip are later found in the possession of Alvred of Lincoln (not the Domesday tenant-in-chief) and his heirs. It is possible that Alvred was her second husband.[5] He seems to have been justiciar of Dorset in the reign of Henry I[6] and appears in the 1130 Pipe Roll paying 60 marks to have Regenbald's

[92] *Regesta Regum Anglo-Normannorum*, i, p. xxv. For this and other basin and towel serjeanties, see Round, *King's Sergeants*, 123–32.

[93] *Bk. of Fees*, 89, 260.

[94] See p. 57 and n.

[95] *Pipe R.* 1130 (Rec. Com.), 14.

[96] *Bk. of Fees*, 88.

[97] Ibid. 89; see *V.C.H. Wilts.* ii. 73.

[98] *Bk. of Fees*, 92.

[99] Ibid.

[1] G. H. White, 'The Career of Waleran, Count of Meulan and Earl of Worc.' *Trans. R. H. S.* N.S. xvii. 20; *Regesta Regum Anglo-Normannorum*, ii, no. 843.

[2] *Complete Peerage*, iv. 315 n.

[3] *Cur. Reg. R.* iii. 124.

[4] *Bk. of Fees*, 90.

[5] Eyton, *Key to Domesday: Dorset*, 78.

[6] *Regesta Regum Anglo-Normannorum*, ii, p. xviii and no. 754 (dated 1106); cf. precept of Henry to Richard de Rivers to give to the monks of St. Peter, Winchester, the land in the Isle of Wight as William II's writs ordered. If he did not, Alvred of Lincoln was to do it (*quod si non feceris Alveraldus de Lincol(nie) faciat ecclesie et episcopo habere*): ibid. no. 603 (dated 1101-Mich. 1102), calendared in V. H. Galbraith, 'Royal Charters to Winchester', *E.H.R.* xxxv. 390 (dated 1101–3).

manor, Pulham, for his lifetime.[7] He is presumably identical with Alvred of Lincoln who gave *Bruge*(*s*) near Weymouth (probably *Brigam*, held by the wife of Hugh in 1086) to Montacute Priory.[8] Robert of Lincoln, Alvred's son, founded the priory of Holme, as a cell of Montacute, and among his donations were 3 virgates in Worth Matravers (nos. 417 and cl), the tithes of Langton near Abbotsbury, that is, Langton Herring (nos. 406 and cxxxix), and the tithes of Okeford Fitzpaine (no. 64), which the wife of Hugh held of Glastonbury Abbey in 1086. He also gave one tribute of salt from the salt-cotes at Langton.[9] Robert's son, another Alvred of Lincoln, confirmed his father's grant, and added the church of Warmwell (nos. 410 and cxliii) and a garden near Bradle, which is probably the wife of Hugh's manor of Orchard (nos. 422 and clv).[10] Alvred returned a *carta* in 1166,[11] when among his knights were three who seem to have been kinsmen of men holding of the wife of Hugh in 1086: William *de monasteriis* was probably related to the man of the same name holding of the wife of Hugh; Alvred Tonarre was probably a kinsman of Walter Tonitruus, and Terry de Boscherbert (*Bosco Herberti*) of Hugh de Boscherbert. This Alvred of Lincoln was appointed Sheriff of Dorset in 1170 following the inquest of sheriffs.[12] His son and heir was Alvred of Lincoln (III) who in 1212 held Sturthill, Langton, Tatton, and Lyme, all held by the wife of Hugh in 1086, and part of Buckland Newton, which she held of the Abbot of Glastonbury.[13] The Glastonbury feodary furnishes a list of the possessions which the family of Lincoln held of that abbey,[14] which includes *Dontyssh* and *Hermyngswell* in Buckland, assessed at 7 hides, 1½ virgate, Damerham (Hants), assessed at 3 hides, Woodyates, assessed at 4 hides, Okeford Fitzpaine, assessed at 8 hides, land at Sturminster Newton, and Colway between Uplyme in Devon and Netherlyme in Dorset. In 1086 the wife of Hugh held of the abbey 7 hides, 1½ virgate, in Buckland, Damerham, Woodyates, and 4 hides in Okeford Fitzpaine. She held no land at Sturminster Newton, and Colway, now part of Lyme Regis, must be the manor of *Lym* (no. 68) held by Ulviet of Glastonbury Abbey. Alvred of Lincoln (IV) succeeded to the estates and died in 1264 without male heirs. His land passed to his 3 sisters and their heirs.[15] Robert fitz Paine, son of Margery of Lincoln, received Okeford, William de Goviz, son of Beatrice the second sister, received Turners Puddle, and the portion of the third sister, Aubrey, passed on her death to the heirs of her sisters, with the exception of Langton, which she gave to Ingram le Waleys, whence it derived the name Langton Wallis.[16]

Roger Arundel was probably the father of Robert de Arundel, who witnessed various charters of Henry I between 1122 and 1135 and was justice in eyre in the south-west in 1130.[17] Robert in turn was probably the father of Roger Arundel who appears in the Pipe Roll for 1161.[18] It appears that Robert also had a daughter Maud, who married Gerbert de Percy, Sheriff of Dorset.[19] Apparently she was her brother's heir since in 1165 Gerbert de Percy proferred 100 marks *pro terra Rogerii Arundel.*[20] In the following year he returned a *carta* as a tenant-in-chief in Dorset. One of his knights,

[7] *Pipe R.* 1130 (Rec. Com.), 16. Pulham belonged to Cirencester Abbey in 1212: *Bk. of Fees*, 94.

[8] *Montacute Cartulary* (Som. Rec. Soc. viii), 124, 168.

[9] Ibid. 160–1.

[10] Ibid. 161–2. According to this charter the salt-cotes lay in Purbeck. If so, Langton must be Langton Matravers, not Langton Herring (near Abbotsbury). In 1086 the wife of Hugh held a piece of land in Purbeck hundred of William of Briouze (no. 296), the other portion being held by a man named Richard. It is possible that all this land is Langton Matravers. In the 13th cent. one of the co-heirs of the last Alvred of Lincoln gave Langton to Ingram le Waleys, whence it became known as Langton Wallis (in Langton Matravers): see below.

[11] *Red Bk. Exch.* (Rolls Ser.), 214–16.

[12] *Gesta Regis Hen. II et Ric. I* (Rolls Ser.), ii, p. lxvii.

[13] *Bk. of Fees*, 93, 94.

[14] *A Feodary of Glastonbury Abbey* (Som. Rec. Soc. xxvi), 30–32.

[15] *Cal. Inq. p. m.* i, pp. 181–2.

[16] Ibid. ii, pp. 232–3; A. Fägersten, *Place-Names of Dorset*, 130 n.

[17] *Regesta Regum Anglo-Normannorum*, ii, p. xix, nos. 1324, 1347, 1915; *Pipe R.* 1130 (Rec. Com.), 13, 154, 155, 159. Robert Arundel is addressed in a writ dated 1129–30: *Regesta*, no. 166.

[18] *Pipe R.* 1161 (P.R.S. iv), 47.

[19] Hutchins, *Hist. Dors.* ii. 858–9.

[20] *Pipe R.* 1165 (P.R.S. viii), 65.

William de Margellis, may be a descendant of Roger *de margella*, who held land of Roger Arundel in 1086.[21] Gerbert does not appear in the Pipe Rolls after 1179. Between 1179 and 1184 the sheriff accounted for various sums *de exitu terre que fuit Mathildis de Arundel* at Lulworth.[22] On the death of Gerbert the land seems to have been divided between co-heirs.[23] In 1180 Roger de Poles proferred £100 *pro habenda medietatem de honore de Poostoche*, presumably Powerstock, held in 1086 by Roger Arundel.[24] Roger de Poles died at Acre in 1190 and his land passed to his brother, Robert.[25] In 1194 Robert de Poles and Robert Belet paid £30 scutage on the barony, Robert Belet having in the same year obtained custody of the land *que fuit Rogeri de Novo Burgo*.[26] By 1212 Robert de Novo Burgo or Newburgh, had given Powerstock to King John in exchange for the manor of *Herdecote* (Som.).[27] He was presumably the son of Roger de Newburgh (*Novo Burgo*) and a minor at the time when Robert Belet obtained custody of the land. This part of the barony continued in the possession of the Newburghs, but Robert de Poles's half passed to Robert fitz Payne, described as his brother in the Pipe Roll for 1189.[28] In 1236 Robert fitz Payne, presumably a son of the same name, held Worth, Rollington, and Blandford, all of which had belonged to Roger Arundel in 1086.[29] He married Margery de Lincoln, who held the manors in 1242–3[30] and their son Robert was heir, both to Roger Arundel's lands and also to some of Alvred of Lincoln's lands.

Robert fitz Gerold's heir was his nephew, William de Roumare, son of his brother Roger and Lucy, widow of Ivo Taillebois and later wife of Ranulf le Meschin, Earl of Chester. She held Bolingbroke and other lands in Lincolnshire.[31] The honor of Bolingbroke appears to have been composed of the lands of Lucy and those of Robert fitz Gerold.[32] In the reign of Henry I William de Roumare claimed the honor of Corfe (Mullen)[33] which he eventually received. When, however, William de Roumare (III) died without heirs, the Lincolnshire lands passed to the earls of Chester as the descendants of Lucy by her third marriage, but the manor of Corfe Mullen was given to Hubert de Burgh, who held it in 1212 *de dono regis Johannis*.[34]

Most of the Dorset manors held by Earl Hugh are later found as part of the honor of Chester, with the exceptions of Burstock and Catsley.[35] One manor, Little Mayne, passed to the Knights Hospitallers, in whose possession it is found in the 13th century.[36] Fifehead Magdalen (no. 220) was given to the canons of St. Augustine's, Bristol, by Robert fitz Harding, the gift being confirmed by Earl Ranulf.[37] This manor was held T.R.E. by Eadnoth the staller, whose son, Harding, survived the Conquest and became the ancestor of the Berkeleys. It is possible that Robert who gave Fifehead Magdalen to St. Augustine's was Harding's son and the grandson of Eadnoth.[38] The land of Edward of Salisbury passed to his son Walter, whose son Patrick was created Earl of

[21] *Red Bk. Exch.* (Rolls Ser.), 216–17.

[22] *Pipe R.* 1179 (P.R.S. xxviii), 71; 1180 (P.R.S. xxix), 111; 1181 (P.R.S. xxx), 9; 1182 (P.R.S. xxxi), 114; 1183 (P.R.S. xxxii), 32; 1184 (P.R.S. xxxiii), 127.

[23] According to the genealogy in Hutchins, *Hist. Dors.* ii. 858–9, Gerbert had 2 daughters. Sybil married first Maurice de Pole, and had by him Roger and Robert de Poles, and secondly Pain, by whom she had Robert fitz Payne. Gerbert's second daughter, Azilia, married Robert of Glastonbury and their daughter, Maud, was married to Robert de Newburgh; see also Sanders, *Eng. Baronies*, 72–73.

[24] *Pipe R.* 1180 (P.R.S. xxix), 94.

[25] *Gesta Regis Hen. II et Ric. I* (Rolls Ser.), ii. 149.

[26] *Pipe R.* 1194 (P.R.S. N.S. v), 190, 193.

[27] *Bk. of Fees*, 79; *Feud. Aids*, ii. 1–2.

[28] *Pipe R.* 1198 (P.R.S. N.S. ix), 128, 221.

[29] *Bk. of Fees*, 581.

[30] Ibid. 752.

[31] W. Farrer, *Honors and Kts.' Fees*, ii. 155. Lucy is sometimes supposed to have been the daughter of Earl Aelfgar of Mercia and sister to Edwin and Morcar: see *Complete Peerage*, vii, App. J., and *Eng. Hist. Doc.* ii. 989, where she is included among Aelfgar's children.

[32] Sanders, *Eng. Baronies*, 17–18.

[33] Ordericus Vitalis, *Hist. Eccl.* iv. 442. Le Prévost identified *Corvia* as Corby, but Corfe Mullen is a more likely identification.

[34] *Bk. of Fees*, 90. The lands of the Roumare family in Wilts., Dors., and Som. are fully discussed in F. A. Cazell, 'Norman and Wessex Charters of the Roumare Family', *A Medieval Miscellany for D. M. Stenton* (Pipe R. Soc. N.S. xxxvi), 77–88.

[35] Farrer, *Honors and Kts.' Fees*, ii. 284–6, 287.

[36] *Rot. Hund.* (Rec. Com.), i. 103.

[37] Dugdale, *Mon.* vi (1), 366.

[38] Farrer, op. cit. 286–7.

Salisbury by the empress.[39] Edward's manor of Canford (which may be presumed to include Kinson, since they were valued together in 1086) belonged to the fee of Salisbury in 1212.[40] The lands of Ernulf of Hesdin appear to have passed in the main to Patrick de Chaworth, his son-in-law.[41] In 1242–3 Patrick's descendant of the same name held 4½ knights' fees in Dorset,[42] which can be regarded as proof that he held some of Ernulf's manors, although none is named. At the same date, however, Ernulf's largest manor, Kington, belonged to the honor of the Earl of Salisbury.[43] It appears to have been part of the marriage portion of Earl Patrick's mother, Sybil, Patrick de Chaworth's daughter. In a note to the *carta* which Pain de Mundubleil, Patrick de Chaworth's grandson, submitted in 1166, it is stated that Patrick, Earl of Salisbury, then held 20 fees *de matrimonio matris suae*, presumably in the main manors which had belonged to Ernulf in Gloucestershire.[44]

The lands of Turstin fitz Rolf passed to Wynebald de Ballon[45] whose grandson, Henry of Neufmarché, returned a *carta* in 1166.[46] Henry's second son and eventual heir James died leaving two daughters between whom the barony was divided. Isabel married Ralph Russel and Hawise married twice, her second husband being Nicholas de Moels.[47] In 1242–3 Ralph Russel and Nicholas de Moels held 16½ knights' fees in Dorset.[48] One of Ralph Russel's manors was Allington,[49] which Turstin had held in 1086. It seems reasonable to assume that Waleran fitz William, who in 1130 rendered account for the dues of the New Forest,[50] was in some way related to Waleran the huntsman. Waleran fitz William is almost certain to be the father of Walter Waleram (*sic*) who accounted for the New Forest dues in 1156[51] and returned a *carta* in 1166.[52] Three of his knights, Julian de Manestone, John de Vifhida, and Thomas de Wintreburne, may reasonably be supposed to have derived their surnames from the manors of Manston, Fifehead Neville, and *Wintreburne*, which were held by Waleran the huntsman in 1086. Walter Waleran died in 1200–1, leaving as his heirs three daughters. Cecily married John de Monmouth, who in 1236 held Manston, Maiden Newton, and Sutton Waldron, which Waleran held in 1086.[53] Joan married William de Neville and in 1235–6 held Winterborne and Fifehead,[54] and in the same year Henry de Tore held 1 fee in Toller of Aubrey de Botreaux, the third sister.[55] John de Monmouth, son and heir of Cecily and her husband, died without issue, and Sutton Waldron passed to William de St. Martin, heir of Joan de Neville by her second husband.[56]

Of William of Moyon's eleven manors in Dorset nine can be traced in the possession of the family of Mohun in the 13th century. In 1235–6 Reynold de Mohun held Hammoon, Chelborough, Little Windsor, Mapperton, and Chilfrome, Steepleton Iwerne, which has been identified as the Domesday manor of *Werne* or *Iwerna* (nos. 281 and xci), and Cruxton, identified as the Domesday manor of *Frome* or *Froma* (nos. 279 and lxxxix).[57] Winterborne was part of the inheritance of Alice, Reynold's wife, and passed to his son John, when it was known as Winterborne Houghton.[58] John also held Todber.[59] Serle of Burcy's heir was his daughter Geva, who married first Martin and

[39] Round, *Geoffrey de Mandeville*, 271.

[40] *Bk. of Fees*, 90.

[41] *V.C.H. Wilts.* ii. 110.

[42] *Bk. of Fees*, 755 (Som. and Dors. return).

[43] Ibid. 753.

[44] *Red Bk. Exch.* (Rolls Ser.), 241, 298.

[45] Round, *Studies in Peerage*, 189 sqq.

[46] *Red Bk. Exch.* (Rolls Ser.), 296. None of Turstin's Dorset manors can be identified here.

[47] Sanders, *Eng. Baronies*, 68.

[48] *Bk. of Fees*, 751. No manors are mentioned by name.

[49] Ibid. 425.

[50] *Pipe R.* 1130 (Rec. Com.), 17.

[51] Ibid. 1156–8 (Rec. Com.), 56.

[52] *Red Bk. Exch.* (Rolls Ser.), 241–2.

[53] *Cur. Reg. R.* ix. 173; *Pipe R.* 1202 (P.R.S. N.S. xv), 126; *Bk. of Fees*, 425–6.

[54] *Bk. of Fees*, 425, 426.

[55] Ibid. 427. In the same year Walter Walerand held 1 fee in Toller: ibid. 426.

[56] *Ex. e Rot. Fin.* (Rec. Com.), ii. 41, 392; *Cal. Inq. p. m.* i, pp. 101, 166.

[57] *Bk. of Fees*, 424, 426. For the identifications, see A. Fägersten, *Place-Names of Dorset*, 57, 233.

[58] *Bk. of Fees*, 401 (partition of fees of William Briwerre).

[59] *Cal. Inq. p. m.* ii, pp. 178, 179.

then William of Falaise. Her lands passed to her children by her first marriage, and in 1212 William fitz Martin held the manor of Puddle Waterston which Serle had held in 1086.[60] The lands of William of Falaise passed to the family of Courcy as a result of his daughter Emma's marriage with William de Curcy.[61] In 1236 Silton and Milton on Stour, the two manors of William of Falaise in Dorset, were held by Margery de Rivers, daughter of Alice de Curcy and Warin fitz Gerold and widow of Baldwin de Rivers.[62] The Dorset lands of William of Briouze are less easy to trace but some at least of his Dorset manors can be identified in the possession of his heirs in the 13th and 14th centuries. In 1212 Henry de Glanville held 1 knight's fee in Buckland hundred *de honore de Bramele de conquestu Anglie*.[63] In 1303, in the same hundred, another Henry de Glanville held *Wolfrenewotton* of William *de Brewes*,[64] which identifies the manor with Glanvilles Wootton (nos. 284, 285). The same Henry de Glanville held, in 1303, *Grough* in the hundred of Rowbarrow and Hasilor.[65] This can be identified as the manor of Creech (no. 289), which William of Briouze held in 1086. In 1316 Henry de Glanville, John Mohun, Richard Joye, William of Stoke, and the Abbot of Cerne held *Wyrgered cum Westeporte, Byestewall et Wolleberg*.[66] Henry de Glanville can thus be shown to have some connexion with Worgret, one of the manors of William of Briouze in 1086 (no. 293). Baldwin of Exeter manor of Iwerne Courtney (no. 316) was held in 1212 by Hawise de Courtenay of the honor of Okehampton.[67] The Courtenays were the inheritors of most of the fief of Baldwin.[68] The three Dorset manors of the Countess of Boulogne passed to the Cluniac priory of Le Wast.[69] King John gave Winterborne and Bockhampton to Eustace le Moigne, who held them in 1212 of the abbey.[70] It was presumably from Eustace or his descendants that Winterborne acquired the name of Winterborne Monkton. Walter de Claville seems to have had a son, Robert, since in 1114 Henry I confirmed to the church of St. Mary, Tewkesbury, two hides in Purbeck of the fee of Robert de Claville,[71] which is probably to be identified with the manor of Church Knowle (no. 332), assessed at two hides and held by Walter in 1086. In 1195 Richard de Sifrewast renounced his claim to 30 acres of wood at Morden, belonging to Gillian de Claville, wife or William de Claville.[72] Morden (no. 314) belonged to Walter in 1086. The descendants of kinsmen of Walter de Claville evidently became tenants of the honor of Gloucester, since in 1285 William de Clavyle and John de Clavyle held Holme and West Morden in the hundred of Hasilor and Rushmore of the honor of Gloucester.[73] Both manors were held by Walter de Claville in 1086.

Schelin's manor of Shillingstone, or Shilling Okeford, passed to his son, Robert, who gave ½ hide and half the church of Okeford *Eskelin* to Montacute Priory. He also gave to the priory the tithe of Edmondsham, a manor which Schelin had held of the queen.[74] Schelin is to be identified with the man of the same name who held 5 hides in *Nategrave* (Glos.) as a tenant of the church of Worcester, since in 1095 Robert son of Skilin contributed 100*s*. to the Worcester relief.[75] It is too much of a coincidence that

[60] H. Maxwell-Lyte, 'Burci, Falaise and Martin', *Proc. Som. Arch. and Nat. Hist Soc.* lxv. 1–27; *Bk. of Fees*, 93.

[61] Hist. MSS. Com. *9th Rep. App. I*, 353. Emma witnessed a charter of her parents to Stogursey (*Stogursey Charters* (Som. Rec. Soc. lxi), no. 1) and an Emma de Falaise is mentioned in the Pipe Roll for 1130: *Pipe R.* 1130 (Rec. Com.), 22; see also Farrer, *Honors and Kts.' Fees*, i. 103–5.

[62] *Bk. of Fees*, 607.

[63] Ibid. 94.

[64] *Feud. Aids*, ii. 30.

[65] Ibid. 37.

[66] Ibid. 42.

[67] *Bk. of Fees*, 91.

[68] Sanders, *Eng. Baronies*, 69–70.

[69] Round, *Studies in Peerage*, 153.

[70] *Bk. of Fees*, 88.

[71] *Regesta Regum Anglo-Normannorum*, ii, no. 1069. The editors of *Regesta* identify the manor with Orchard, in Church Knowle, assessed at 1½ hide, ½ hide of which was held by the wife of Hugh, the other hide being given to Cranborne Abbey which became a cell of Tewkesbury. In view of the mention of Robert de Claville in the charter, it seems more likely to have been one of Walter de Claville's manors. The remainder of Orchard seems to have passed to Montacute Priory: see p. 56.

[72] *Fines sive Pedes Finium*, ed. J. Hunter, ii. 72.

[73] *Feud. Aids*, ii. 23–24. In 1242–3 Holme and Morden were part of the honor of Gloucester, but the names of the tenants at that date are not recorded: *Bk. of Fees*, 750.

[74] *Montacute Cartulary* (Som. Rec. Soc. viii), 162.

[75] *Hemingi Chartularium* ed. T. Hearne (1723), i. 79–80, printed also in Round, *Feudal Eng.* 309.

two men, both named Schelin, should each have a son named Robert. Moreover, a connexion can be established between the manor of Okeford and *Nategrave* at a later date. In 1166 John Eskeling held 4 fees of the honor of Gloucester,[76] and in 1201 John son of John Eskelling held 4 fees at Okeford and 1 fee at *Attegrave* of the honor of Gloucester.[77] Okeford continued to be part of the honor,[78] and some time during the 13th century passed to the family of Turberville who held it in 1303.[79]

Descendants of some of the tenants of the Count of Mortain can also be traced to the 13th century. The evidence of the Geld Rolls indicates that *Cerneli* and Corscombe were held in 1086 by William de Estra. A man called William de Lestra gave two-thirds of the tithes of Durweston (no. 193), held by William in 1086, to the priory of Montacute.[80] Richard del Estre, presumably a kinsman, returned a *carta* in 1166,[81] and in 1212 Richard *de atrio* held Durweston and Cerne (probably the *Cerneli* of Domesday).[82] He also held 2½ hides at Knighton (in Durweston) in *Hunesberge* hundred.[83] Durweston, which William held in 1086, lay in *Hunesberge* hundred, and was assessed at 2½ hides. William de Lestre, who may have been Richard's son, held 1 fee of Mortain at Hooke in 1235–6.[84] Hooke (no. 207) was held by William of the Count of Mortain in 1086. Drew, who held Nyland (no. 150) of the Count of Mortain in 1086, was Drew of Montacute, who gave the same manor to the abbey of Shaftesbury.[85] In 1166 Drew the younger returned a *carta* which names one of his knights as Thomas de Tolra, presumably Toller Whelme in Dorset, which Drew held of the Count of Mortain in 1086.[86] In 1212 William de Montacute held the hundred of Puddletown and his grandson of the same name held Toller and Puddle Loveford in 1235–6.[87]

According to the Geld Rolls Hugh Maminot held land of the Bishop of Lisieux, Gilbert Maminot, in 1086. Hugh's daughter married Ralph de Keynes and received as her marriage portion Tarrant in *Langeberge* hundred, Combe in Winfrith hundred, and Somerford (Glos.).[88] All three manors were held by the Bishop of Lisieux in 1086 and derived from Ralph the names Tarrant Keyneston, Coombe Keynes, and Somerford Keynes. A man called Ralph de Cahaines is mentioned in the Pipe Roll of 1130[89] and if he is identical with Hugh Maminot's son-in-law, then he was perhaps the father of Ralph de Keynes who returned a *carta* in 1166,[90] one of whose knights was William de Cumba. In 1212 William de Keynes held the three manors and his son, another William, succeeded him.[91]

76 *Red Bk. Exch.* (Rolls Ser.), 289.

77 *Pipe R.* 1201 (P.R.S. N.S. xiv), 33, 34.

78 *Bk. of Fees*, 750 (1242–3).

79 *Feud. Aids*, ii. 26 (1303); cf. the charter of Brian de Turberville, lord of *Acforde Eskelin*, in which he calls Robert son of Eskelin his ancestor: *Montacute Cartulary*, 163–4. The charter is dated 1298.

80 *Montacute Cartulary*, 125.

81 *Red Bk. Exch.* (Rolls Ser.), 231–2.

82 *Bk. of Fees*, 92.

83 Ibid. 87.

84 Ibid. 424.

85 *Regesta Regum Anglo-Normannorum*, ii. 347.

86 *Red Bk. Exch.* (Rolls Ser.), 228–9.

87 *Bk. of Fees*, 93, 426.

88 Ibid. 87.

89 *Pipe R.* 1130 (Rec. Com.), 16.

90 *Red Bk. Exch.* (Rolls Ser.), 218.

91 *Bk. of Fees*, 87, 424, 752.

NOTE

The following translation has been made from the texts printed in volume I of *Domesday Book seu Liber Censualis Willelmi Primi Regis Anglie* (1783) and in *Libri Censualis vocati Domesday Book: Additamenta ex codicibus antiquissimis*, ed. H. Ellis (Record Commission, 1816), both of which are referred to in the footnotes as 'the printed version'. These printed texts have been checked, in the case of the Exchequer text, against *Domesday Book, or the Great Survey of England . . . Fac-simile of the Part relating to Dorsetshire*, photozincographed at the Ordnance Survey office, 1862 (referred to in the footnotes as 'the facsimile'), and, in the case of Exon. Domesday (and the Geld Rolls), against a photocopy of the manuscript preserved in Exeter cathedral library (referred to in the footnotes as 'the MS.'). The text of the Dorset Domesday was first published in 1774 in volume 1 of John Hutchins's *History and Antiquities of Dorset*, together with the text of the Dorset Geld Rolls and two extracts from Exon. Domesday. Volume 4 of the second edition of Hutchins's work, which appeared in 1815, also contained a translation of the Dorset Domesday by the Revd. William Bawdwen.

In accordance with the practice of the *V.C.H.*, identifications of place-names in the Exchequer text of Domesday have been inserted in square brackets after the original forms. Where the Domesday place-name is that of a hamlet, farm, house, or similar site the name of the parish in which the site is or was situated has been added. The parish boundaries and spelling of place-names are taken from the Ordnance Survey 2½" sheets.

Quotations from the Latin text of both versions of the survey have been placed in round brackets and printed in italic type. Interpolations in the English translation are also indicated by round brackets. The expression 'T.R.E.' has been used throughout as a rendering of the phrases *t[empore] r[egis] E[dwardi]* or *tempore E[dwardi] regis* in the original texts.

In order to simplify cross-reference, each item in the Exchequer text (except the four borough entries at the beginning) has been given an arabic number. Each item in Exon. Domesday (with the same exception) has similarly been given a small roman number and is printed after the corresponding entry in the Exchequer text and marked by a vertical line. The arrangement of items throughout the translation is that of the Exchequer text, from which (as explained above at pp. 2–3, 5) Exon. differs in several places. The following key is designed to show the original order of the fiefs covered by Exon.

Exon. folios 25–28b	Dominicatus regis in Dorseta (nos. 1–14 and i–xii, xiv–xv)[a]
Exon. folios 29–30b	Terra regine Mathildis in Dorseta (nos. 15–21 and xxi–xxvii)
Exon. folios 31–32	Terre quas tenebant milites de regina in Dorseta (nos. 22–29 and xxviii–xxxv)
Exon. folio 33	Terra Boloniensis comitisse in Dorseta (nos. 513–15 and xxxvi–xxxviii)
Exon. folios 36–38b	Terra sancti Petri Cerneliensis ecclesie in Dorseta (nos. 76–92 and xxxix–lv)
Exon. folios 39–40b	Terra sancti Petri Abbodesberiensis ecclesie in Dorseta (nos. 109–16 and lvi–lxiii)
Exon. folio 41	Terra abbatis Adiliniensis in Dorseta (nos. 118 and lxiv)
Exon. folio 42	Terra abbatis Tavestochensis in Dorseta Gaufridi nomine (nos. 119–20 and lxv–lxvi)
Exon. folios 43–45	Terra sancti Petri Mideltonensis ecclesie in Dorseta (nos. 93–108 and lxvii–lxxxii)
Exon. folios 47–49b	Terra Willelmi de Moione in Dorseta (nos. 273–83 and lxxxiii–xciii)[b]
Exon. folios 50–52	Terra Rogerii Arundelli de Dorseta (nos. 322–33 and xciv–cv)
Exon. folio 53	Terram (*sic*) Serlonis de Burceio de Dorseta (nos. 334–5 and cvi–cvii)
Exon. folios 54–61b	Terra uxoris Hugonis (filii Gripi) in Dorseta (nos. 376–423 and cviii–clvi)
Exon. folios 62–62b	Terra Walterii de Clayilla in Dorseta (nos. 311–15 and clvii-clxi)

[a] Of the following entries, which are all inserted among the king's lands in Exon. Domesday, nos. xiii, xvi, and xix refer to land of the king's almsmen (Exchequer nos. 144, 145a, and 145b) and nos. xviii and xx to land of the abbey of St. Wandrille (Exchequer nos. 123 and 124). No. xvii, which describes land in *Wintreborna* held by Aiulf the sheriff, has no corresponding entry in the Exchequer text: see p. 101 n.

[b] William of Moyon's manor of Little Sutton in Sutton Veny (Wilts.) is entered on folio 47 before no. lxxxiii under the heading *Terra Willelmi de Moione in Wiltesira*: see *V.C.H. Wilts.* ii. 43–44.

[F. 75]

DORSETE

In DORECESTRE [Dorchester] T.R.E. there were 172 houses. They were assessed for all the king's service and paid geld for 10 hides, that is, 1 silver mark for the use of the housecarls excepting the customs which belong to the night's farm. There were 2 moneyers, each of them rendering to the king[1] 1 silver mark and 20*s*. when the coinage

[1] 'regi' interlined.

was changed. Now there are 88 houses and 100 were completely destroyed from the time of sheriff Hugh until now.

[Exon. f. 11b]

In Dorecestra there were 172 houses on the day when King Edward was alive and dead and they paid geld T.R.E. for 10 hides, that is, 1 silver mark for the use of the housecarls and they were assessed for all the king's service as 10 hides excepting the customs which belonged to the night's farm. And of these 172 houses there are 88[2] still standing and 100 were completely destroyed from the time of sheriff Hugh until now. And there were 2 moneyers T.R.E. each of whom rendered 1 silver mark to the king and 20*s.* when the coinage was changed.

In BRIDEPORT [Bridport] T.R.E. there were 120 houses and they were assessed for all the king's service and paid geld for 5 hides, that is, $\frac{1}{2}$ silver mark for the use of the king's housecarls excepting the customs which belonged to the farm of 1 night. There was 1 moneyer rendering to the king 1 silver mark and 20*s.* when the coinage was changed. Now there are 100 houses and 20 are so impoverished (*destitute*) that those who dwell in them are not prosperous enough to pay geld (*geldum solvere non valent*).

[Exon. f. 12]

In Brideport there were 120 houses on the day when King Edward was alive and dead and they paid geld T.R.E. for 5 hides, that is, $\frac{1}{2}$ silver mark for the use of the housecarls and they were assessed for all the king's service as 5 hides excepting the customs which belonged to the night's farm. And of these 120 houses there are 100 still standing and 20 of these 100 houses were so ravaged that[3] the men who dwell in them have nothing whence they may render geld (*xx ex his c domibus ita sunt adnichilate quod homines qui intus manent non habent unde reddent nullum*[4] *geldum*). And 20 houses[5] were completely destroyed from the time of sheriff Hugh until now. And there was 1 moneyer T.R.E. who rendered 1 silver mark to the king and 20*s.* when the coinage was changed.

In WARHAM [Wareham] T.R.E. there were 143 houses in the king's demesne. This vill (*villa*) was assessed for all the king's service and paid geld for 10 hides, that is, 1 silver mark for the king's housecarls excepting the customs which belonged to the farm of 1 night. There were 2 moneyers each rendering 1 silver mark to the king and 20*s.* when the coinage was changed. Now there are 70 houses and 73 were completely destroyed from the time of sheriff Hugh. In the part (belonging to) St. Wandrille (*de parte Sancti Wandregisili*) there are 45 houses standing[6] and 17 are[7] waste. In the parts (belonging to) the other barons (*de partibus aliorum baronum*) there are 20 houses standing[8] and 60 were destroyed.

[Exon. f. 12b]

In Warham there were 143 houses on the day when King Edward was alive and dead in the king's demesne, which paid geld. Of these 143 houses 70 are still standing and 73 were completely destroyed from the time of sheriff Hugh until now. In the part (belonging to) the Abbot of St. Wandrille (*de parte abbatis Sancti Wandregisili*) there are 45 (houses) standing and 17 destroyed. And in the parts

[2] 'viii' interlined.

[3] 'domibus ita sunt adnichilate quod' interlined. So the MS.; the printed version has 'na' for 'ita'.

[4] 'nullum' marked for omission.

[5] 'domus' interlined.

[6] 'stantes' interlined.

[7] 'sunt' interlined.

[8] 'stantes' interlined.

(belonging to) the other barons of the king (*de partibus aliorum baronum regis*) there are 20 houses standing and 60 completely destroyed. This vill paid geld T.R.E. for 10 hides, that is, 1 silver mark for the use of the housecarls and it was assessed for all the king's service as 10 hides excepting the customs which belonged to the night's farm. And there were 2 moneyers T.R.E. each of whom rendered 1 silver mark to the king and 20*s*. when the coinage was changed.

In the borough (*burgo*) of SCEPTESBERIE [Shaftesbury] T.R.E. there were 104 houses in the king's demesne. This vill was assessed for all the king's service and paid geld for 20 hides, that is, 2 silver marks for the king's housecarls. There were 3 moneyers each rendering 1 silver mark and 20*s*. when the coinage was changed. Now there are 66 houses and 38 houses were destroyed from the time of sheriff Hugh until now. In the part (belonging to) the abbess (of Shaftesbury) (*In parte abbatisse*) there were 153 houses T.R.E. Now there are 111 houses and 42 were utterly (*omnino*) destroyed. There the abbess has 151 burgesses (*burgenses*) and 20 vacant plots (*mansiones vacuas*) and 1 garden (*hortum*). It is worth 65*s*.

[Exon. f. 11]

In (the borough of) Saint Edward[9] there were 104 houses in the king's demesne which paid geld on the day of King Edward's death (*die obitu* (sic) *Edwardi regis*). Of these 104 houses there are 66 now standing in good repair (*in virtute*) and 38 were completely destroyed from the time of sheriff Hugh until now. And in the part (belonging to) the abbess (of Shaftesbury) (*in parte abbatisse*) there were 153 houses T.R.E. and there are 111 houses still standing and 42 were completely destroyed. This (vill) paid geld T.R.E. for 20 hides, that is, 2 silver marks for the use of the housecarls and it was always assessed for all the king's service as 20 hides. And there were T.R.E. 3 moneyers each of whom rendered 1 silver mark to the king and 20*s*. when the coinage was changed.

HERE ARE NOTED THE LANDHOLDERS IN DORSET

I. KING WILLIAM (*Rex Willelmus*)
II. THE BISHOP OF SALISBURY (*Episcopus Sarisberiensis*)
III. AND THE MONKS OF SHERBORNE (*et monachi Scireburn'*)
IIII. THE BISHOP OF BAYEUX (*Episcopus Baiocensis*)
V. THE BISHOP OF COUTANCES (*Episcopus Constantiensis*)
VI. THE BISHOP OF LISIEUX (*Episcopus Lisiacensis*)
VII. THE BISHOP OF LONDON (*Episcopus Lundoniensis*)
VIII. THE ABBEY OF GLASTONBURY (*Abbatia Glastingberie*)
IX. THE ABBEY OF WINCHESTER (*Abbatia Wintoniensis*)
X. THE ABBEY OF CRANBORNE (*Abbatia Creneburnensis*)
XI. THE ABBEY OF CERNE (*Abbatia de Cernel*)
XII. THE ABBEY OF MILTON (*Abbatia de Middeltune*)
XIII. THE ABBEY OF ABBOTSBURY (*Abbatia de Abedesberie*)
XIIII. THE ABBEY OF HORTON (*Abbatia de Hortune*)
XV. THE ABBEY OF ATHELNEY (*Abbatia de Adelingi*)
XVI. THE ABBEY OF TAVISTOCK (*Abbatia de Tavestoch*)
XVII. THE ABBEY OF CAEN (*Abbatia de Cadomis*)

[9] Shaftesbury was sometimes called after Edward the Martyr whose remains were transferred there from Wareham and buried in the abbey.

xviii. THE ABBEY OF ST. WANDRILLE (*Abbatia Sancti Wandregisili*)
xix. THE ABBESS OF SHAFTESBURY (*Abbatissa de Sceftesberie*)
xx. THE ABBESS OF WILTON (*Abbatissa de Wiltune*)
xxi. THE ABBESS OF CAEN (*Abbatissa de Cadom*)
xxii. THE ABBESS OF MONTEVILLIERS (*Abbatissa de Monasterio villari*)
xxiii. THE CANONS OF COUTANCES (*Canonici Constantienses*)
xxiiii. RAINBALD THE PRIEST[10] AND OTHER CLERKS (*clerici*)
xxv. COUNT ALAN (*Comes Alanus*)
xxvi. THE COUNT OF MORTAIN (*Comes Moritoniensis*)
xxvii EARL HUGH (*Comes Hugo*)
xxviii. ROGER DE BEAUMONT (*de Belmont*)
xxix. ROGER DE COURSEULLES (*de Curcelle*)
xxx. ROBERT FITZ GEROLD (*Girold*)
xxxi. EDWARD OF SALISBURY (*de Sarisberie*)
xxxii. ERNULF OF HESDIN (*de Hesding*)
xxxiii. TURSTIN FITZ ROLF
xxxiiii. WILLIAM OF EU (*de Ou*)
xxxv. WILLIAM OF FALAISE (*de Faleise*)
xxxvi. WILLIAM OF MOYON (*de Moiun*)
xxxvii. WILLIAM OF BRIOUZE (*de Braiose*)
xxxviii. WILLIAM OF ECOUIS (*de Scohies*)
xxxix. WALSCIN OF DOUAI (*de Dowai*)
xl. WALERAN THE HUNTSMAN (*venator*)
xli. WALTER DE CLAVILLE (*de Clavile*)
xlii. BALDWIN OF EXETER (*de Execestre*)
xliii. BERENGER GIFFARD (*Gifard*)
xliiii. OSBERN GIFFARD (*Gifard*)
xlv. MATTHEW DE MORETANIA (*Maci de Moretanie*)
xlvi. ROGER ARUNDEL
xlvii. SERLE OF BURCY
xlviii. AIULF THE SHERIFF (*vicecomes*)
xlix. HUMPHREY THE CHAMBERLAIN (*camerarius*)
l. HUGH DE PORT (*Hugo de Porth*)
li. HUGH DE ST. QUINTIN (*Hugo de Sancto Quintino*)
lii. HUGH DE BOSCHERBERT (*Hugo de Boscherberti*)
liii. HUGH DE LURE (*de Luri*) AND OTHER FRENCHMEN (*franci*)
liiii. THE WIFE OF HUGH FITZ GRIP (*uxor Hugonis filii Grip*)[11]
lv. ISELDIS
lvi. GUDMUND AND OTHER THEGNS (*taini*)
lvii. WILLIAM BELET[12] AND OTHER KING'S SERJEANTS (*servientes regis*)
lviii. THE COUNTESS OF BOULOGNE (*Comitissa Boloniensis*)

I. THE KING'S LAND

(1) The king holds the island which is called PORLAND [Portland]. King[13] Edward held (it) in his lifetime (*in vita sua*).[14] There the king has 3 ploughs in demesne and 5 serfs and there[15] 1 villein and 90 bordars have 23 ploughs. There (are) 8 acres of meadow. (There is) pasture 8 furlongs long and 8 wide. This manor with what belongs to it (*cum sibi pertinentibus*) renders £65 blanched (*lxv libras albas*).

(vi) The king has 1 island which is called Porlanda which King Edward held on the day when he was alive (*ea die qua ipse fuit vivus*). There the king has 3 ploughs in demesne and the villeins have there 23 ploughs. There the king has 1 villein and 90 bordars and 5 serfs and 3 pack-horses (*roncinos*) and 14 beasts (*animalia*) and 27 pigs (*porcos*) and 900 sheep (*oves*) and 8 acres of meadow and 8 furlongs of pasture in length and 8 in width. This renders £65[16] blanched (*libras candidos* (sic)) a year. This is from Portland and what belongs to it (*de hoc quod pertinet ei*).

(2) The king holds BRIDETONE [Burton Bradstock] and BERE [Bere Regis] and Colesberie [Colber Crib (House) in Sturminster Newton] and Sepetone [Shipton Gorge] and Bratepolle [Bradpole] and Cidihoc [Chideock]. King Edward held this in demesne. It is not known how many hides there are neither did it pay geld T.R.E. There is land for 55 ploughs. In demesne there are 8 ploughs and 20 serfs and 41 villeins and 30 bordars and 7 coliberts and 74 cottars. Among them all (*inter omnes*) they have 27 ploughs. There (are) 8 mills rendering £4 and 35*d.* and 111 acres of meadow. (There is) pasture 4 leagues long and as much in width. (There is) wood(land) 3 leagues long and 1 league wide. This manor with its appurtenances and customs renders

[10] 'presbyter' interlined.
[11] 'filii Grip' interlined.
[12] 'Belet' interlined.
[13] 'rex' interlined.
[14] The rest of this line in the text is left blank. For a comment, see p. 4.
[15] 'ibi' interlined.
[16] 'et v' interlined.

1 night's farm. The wood (*boscus*) of HAUOCUMBE [Haucomb[17]] belongs to Burton Bradstock just as (it did) T.R.E. (when) two-thirds of it were in the king's farm (*firma regis*). The third part or the third oak belonged to Earl Edwin[18] which now belongs to FRANTONE [Frampton], a manor (belonging to) St. Stephen, Caen (*Sancti Stefani Cadomensis*).

(x) The king has 1 manor which is called Bridetona and Bera and Colesbreia and Sepetona and Bratepolla and Cidiohoc. King Edward held these in demesne and it is not known how many hides there are because they did not pay geld T.R.E. and 55 ploughs can plough this land. There the king has 8 ploughs in demesne and the villeins 27 ploughs. There the king has 41 villeins and 30 bordars and 7 coliberts and 74[19] cottars and 20 serfs and 6 pack-horses and 9 beasts and 108 pigs and 800 sheep and 8 mills which render £4 3*s*. 11*d*. and 3 leagues of woodland in length and 1 in width and 111 acres of meadow and 4 leagues of pasture in length and 4 in width and these manors with their appurtenances and customs render one night's farm. The wood of Hauocumbe belongs to the above manor, that is Burton Bradstock, and T.R.E. two-thirds of this wood belonged to the king's farm (*adiacebant ad firmam regis*) so that no one had any part of this wood except Earl Godwin (*ita ut nullam partem aliquis huius bosci habuit excepto comite Goduino*) who had the third oak of this wood by reckoning (*per adnumerationem*) which now belongs to a manor of St. Stephen, Caen (*Sancti Stephani Cadomensis*), which is called Frantona.

(3) The king holds WINBORNE [Wimborne Minster] and Scapewic [Shapwick] and Chirce [Crichel, unidentified] and Opewinburne [All Hallows Farm, formerly Up Wimborne All Saints, in Wimborne St. Giles]. King Edward held (this) in demesne. It is not known how many hides there are because it did not pay geld T.R.E. There is land for 45 ploughs. In demesne there are 5 ploughs and 15 serfs and 63 villeins and 68 bordars and 7 cottars have 22 ploughs. There (are) 8 mills rendering 110*s*. and 150 acres of meadow. (There is) pasture 6 leagues long and 3 leagues wide. (There is) wood(land) 5 leagues long and 1 league wide. This manor with its[20] appurtenances renders 1 night's farm.

(xi) The king has 1 manor which is called Winborna and Escapewihc and Chirce and Obpe Winborna. King Edward held these in demesne and it is not known how many hides there are because they did not pay geld T.R.E. and 45 ploughs can plough this land. There the king has 5 ploughs in demesne and the villeins 22 ploughs. There the king has 63 villeins and 68 bordars and 15 serfs and 7 cottars and 3 pack-horses and 30 pigs and 250 sheep and 44 goats (*capras*) and 8 mills which render 110*s*. and 5 leagues of wood(land) in length and 1 in width and 150 acres of meadow and 6 leagues of pasture in length and 3 leagues in width. These manors with their appurtenances and customs render one night's farm.

(4) The king holds DORECESTRE [Dorchester] and Fortitone [Fordington in Dorchester All Saints and St. Peter] and Sutone [Sutton Poyntz in Preston] and Gelingeham [Gillingham] and Frome.[21] King Edward held (this). It is not known how many hides there are because it did not pay geld T.R.E. There is land for 56 ploughs. In demesne there are 7 ploughs and 20 serfs and 12 coliberts and 114 villeins and 89 bordars having 49 ploughs. There (are) 12 mills rendering £6 5*s*. and 160 acres of meadow. (There is) pasture 2 leagues long and 1 league wide. (There is) wood(land) 4 leagues long and 1 league wide. This manor with its appurtenances renders 1 night's farm.

(xii) The king has 1 manor which is called Dorecestra and Fortitona and Sutona and Gelingeham and Fromma. King Edward held these in demesne and it is not known how many hides there are because they did not pay geld T.R.E. Fifty-six ploughs can plough this land. There the king has 7 ploughs in demesne and the villeins 49 ploughs. There the king has 114 villeins and 89 bordars and 12 coliberts and 20 serfs and 5 pack-horses and 20 beasts and 72 pigs and 800 sheep and 40 goats and 12 mills which render £6 5*s*. and 4 leagues of wood(land) in length and 1 in width and 160 acres of meadow and 2 leagues of pasture in length and 1 in width. These manors with their appurtenances and customs render 1 night's farm.

(5) The king holds PINPRE [Pimperne] and Cerletone [Charlton Marshall]. King Edward held (this) in demesne. It is not known how many hides there are because it did not pay geld T.R.E. There is land for 20 ploughs. In demesne there are 4 ploughs and 5 serfs and 1 colibert and 18 villeins and 68 bordars with 14 ploughs. There are 2 mills rendering 40*s*. 6*d*. and 94 acres of meadow. (There is) pasture 2 leagues long and 2 leagues wide. (There is) wood(land) 1 league long and ½ league wide. This manor with its appurtenances renders ½ night's farm.

(xiv) The king has 1 manor which is called Pinpra and Cerletona. King Edward held these in demesne and it is not known how many hides there are because they did not pay geld T.R.E. Twenty ploughs can plough this land. There the king has 4 ploughs in demesne and the villeins 14 ploughs. There the king has 18 villeins and 68 bordars and 1 colibert and 5 serfs and 2 pack-horses and 16 beasts and 25 pigs and 400 sheep and 36 goats and 2 mills which render 40*s*. 6*d*. and 1 league of wood(land) in length and ½ (league) in width and 94 acres of meadow and 2 leagues of pasture in length and 2 in width. These manors with their appurtenances and customs render ½ night's farm.

(6) The king holds WINFRODE [Winfrith Newburgh] and Lulvorde [East and West Lulworth] and Wintreborne [unidentified][22] and Chenoltone [Knowlton[23] in Woodlands, site derelict]. King Edward held (this) in demesne. It is not known how

[17] R. W. Eyton (*Key to Domesday: Dorset*, 85) identifies this place as a region near Shipton Hill called Haucomb; A. Fägersten (*Place-Names of Dorset*, 260) identifies it with Hawcombe in Shipton Gorge parish, a site now lost.

[18] 'comitis' interlined.

[19] 'xxiiii' interlined.

[20] 'suis' interlined.

[21] Presumably some estate on or near the River Frome. Eyton (op. cit. 92) identifies it as the 3 modern parishes of Batcombe, Stockwood, and Hermitage; Fägersten has no comment to make on this identification.

[22] Eyton (op. cit. 97, 100) identifies this as Winterborne Zelston.

[23] The name survived as the name of the hundred of which Knowlton was the *caput*: see pp. 138–9.

many hides there are because it did not pay geld T.R.E. There is land for 24 ploughs. In demesne there are 4 ploughs and 8 serfs and 30 villeins and 30 bordars with 1 cottar having 16 ploughs. There (are) 4 mills rendering 50*s.* and 80 acres of meadow. (There is) pasture 3 leagues long and as much in width. (There is) wood(land) the same amount in length and width. This manor with its appurtenances and customs renders ½ night's farm.

xv) The king has 1 manor which is called Winfroda and Lulwrda and Wintreborna and Chenoltona. King Edward held these in demesne and it is not known how many hides there are for they did not pay geld T.R.E. Twenty-four ploughs can plough this land. There the king has 4 ploughs in demesne and the villeins 16 ploughs. There the king has 30 villeins and 30 bordars and 8 serfs and 1 cottar and 2 pack-horses and 50 pigs and 300 sheep and 6 goats and 4 mills which render 50*s.* and 3 leagues of wood(land) in length and 3 in width and 80 acres of meadow and 3 leagues of pasture in length and 3 in width. These manors with their appurtenances and customs render ½ night's farm.

EARL[24] HAROLD HELD THE FOLLOWING MANORS T.R.E.

(7) The king holds ACFORD [Child Okeford]. T.R.E. it paid geld for 5 hides. There is land for 6 ploughs. Of this there are in demesne 3 hides and there (are) 2 ploughs with 1 serf and 6 villeins and 8 bordars with 2 ploughs. There (are) 2 mills rendering 20*s.* and 40 acres of meadow and 2 furlongs of pasture. (There is) wood(land) 4 furlongs long and 1½ furlong wide. It was and is worth £10.

(i) The king has 1 manor which is called Acforda, which Earl Harold held on the day when King Edward was alive and dead, and it paid geld for 5 hides. Six ploughs can plough these. Thence the king has 3 hides and 2 ploughs in demesne and the villeins 2 hides and 2 ploughs. There the king has 6 villeins and 9 bordars and 1 serf and 1 pack-horse and 7 beasts and 10[25] pigs and 48 sheep and 2 mills which render 20*s.* a year, of which the king has half, and 4 furlongs of wood(land) in length and 1½ in width and 40 acres of meadow and 2 furlongs of pasture. This manor renders[26] £10 a year and when Fulcred received it at farm of the king, it rendered as much.

(8) The king holds PIRETONE [Puddletown]. T.R.E. it paid geld for ½ hide. There is land for 15 ploughs. In demesne there are 4 ploughs and 12 serfs and 14 villeins and 29 coscets with 10 ploughs. There (are) 2 mills rendering 32*s.* and 126 acres of meadow. (There is) pasture 1½ league long and 1 wide. (There is) wood(land) 2 furlongs long and as much in width. To this manor belong 1½ hide in PORBI [Purbeck] and ½ hide in MAPERTUNE [? Mapperton in Almer]. There is land for 1½ plough. To the manor of Puddletown also belongs the third penny of the whole shire of Dorset. It renders with all its appurtenances £73.

(ii) The king has 1 manor which is called Piretona which Earl Harold held T.R.E. and this paid geld for ½ hide. Fifteen ploughs can plough this. There the king has 4 ploughs and the villeins ten. There the king has 14[27] villeins and 29 cotsets and 12 serfs and 4 pack-horses and 17 beasts and 60 pigs and 1,600 sheep and 60 goats and 2 mills which render 32*s.* a year and 1 league and 8 furlongs of wood(land) in length and 1 league in width and in another place 2 furlongs of wood(land) in length and as much in width and 126 acres of meadow and 1½ league of pasture in length and 1 in width. And in Porbi the king has 1½ hides which lie in this manor of Puddletown. One plough can plough these, and in Mapertona the king has ½ hide which lies in the above-mentioned Puddletown, which ½ plough can plough. To this above-mentioned manor of Puddletown[28] also belongs the third penny of the whole[29] county of Dorset. From T.R.E. this manor with all its appurtenances rendered £73 a year and when Aiulf (received)[30] it, it rendered as much.

(9) The king holds CEREBERIE [Charborough (House) in Morden]. T.R.E. it paid geld for 5 hides. There is land for 3½ ploughs. Of this there are in demesne 3½ hides and there (is) 1 plough and 4 serfs and 5 villeins and 4 bordars with 1½ plough. There (is) wood(land) 2 furlongs long and 1 wide. It was and is worth £9.

(iv) The king has 1 manor which is called Cereberia which Earl Harold held on the day when King Edward was alive and dead, which paid geld for 5 hides. Three ploughs and ½ (plough) can plough these. There the king has in demesne 3½ hides and 1½[31] plough and the villeins have 1½ hide and 1½ plough. There the king has 5 villeins and 4 bordars and 4 serfs and 1 pack-horse and 13 pigs and 105 sheep and 2 furlongs of wood(land) in length and another in width. This manor is worth £9 a year and when that man[32] received (it) it was worth as much.

[f. 75b]

(10) The king holds ABRISTETONE [Ibberton]. T.R.E. it paid geld for 5 hides. There is land for 5 ploughs. Of this there are in demesne 2½ hides and there (are) 2 ploughs and 2 serfs and 10 villeins and 7 bordars with 3 ploughs. There (are) 11 acres of meadow and pasture 7 furlongs long and 3 furlongs wide. (There is) wood(land) 4 furlongs long and 2 furlongs wide. It was and is worth £10.

(v) The king has 1 manor which is called Abristentona which Earl Harold held on the day when King Edward was alive and dead. This paid geld T.R.E. for 5 hides. Five ploughs can plough these. Of these the king has 2½ hides and 2 ploughs in demesne and the villeins 2½ hides and 3 ploughs. There the king has 10 villeins and 7 bordars and 2 serfs and 2 pack-horses and 4 cows (*vacas* (sic)) and 10 pigs and 50 sheep and 50 goats and 4 furlongs of wood(land)[33] in length and 2 in width and 11 acres of meadow and 7 furlongs of pasture in length and 3 in width. This manor is worth £10 and when Fulcred received it, it was worth as much.

[24] 'comes' interlined.
[25] 'x' interlined.
[26] Originally 'valet'.
[27] 'ii' interlined.
[28] 'Piretone' interlined.
[29] 'omni' interlined.
[30] Supply 'recepit'.
[31] 'et dimidia' interlined.
[32] In Exon. Domesday this entry (for Charborough) immediately follows the entry for Little Puddle (nos. 14 and iii) which was held by Fulcred, to whom *ille* presumably refers.
[33] 'nemoris' interlined.

(11) The king holds FLETE [Fleet]. T.R.E. it paid geld for 5 hides. There is land for 5 ploughs. Of this there are in demesne 3½ hides and there (are) 2 ploughs and 2 serfs and 4 villeins and 7 bordars with 3 ploughs. There (are) 6 furlongs of pasture. It was and is worth £7.

(vii) The king has 1 manor which is called Fleta which Earl Harold held on the day when King Edward was alive and dead. This paid geld T.R.E. for 5 hides. Five ploughs can plough these. Thence the king has 3½ hides and 2 ploughs in demesne and the villeins 1½ hide and 3 ploughs. There he has 4 villeins and 7 bordars and 2 serfs and 1 pack-horse and 3 beasts and 4 pigs and 144 sheep and 6 furlongs of pasture. This manor renders £7 a year and when Fulcred received (it) it was worth as much.

(12) The king holds CALVEDONE [Chaldon Herring or East Chaldon]. T.R.E. it paid geld for 13 hides. There is land for 10 ploughs. Of this there are in demesne 6 hides and there (is) 1 plough and 4 serfs and 16 villeins and 15 cottars with 6 ploughs. There (is) a mill rendering 10*s.* and 20 acres of meadow. (There is) pasture 1 league long and ½ league wide. It was and is worth £13.

(viii) The king has 1 manor which is called Calvedona which Earl Harold held on the day when King Edward was alive and dead. This paid geld T.R.E. for 13 hides. Ten ploughs can plough these. Thence the king has 6 hides and 1 plough in demesne. And the villeins 7 hides and 6 ploughs. There the king has 16 villeins and 15 cottars and 4 serfs and 2 horses and 3 beasts and 500 sheep and 13 goats and 1 mill which renders 10*s.* and 20 acres of meadow and 1 league of pasture in length and ½ (league) in width. This manor renders £13 and when Fulcred received (it) it was worth as much.

(13) The king holds LODRES [Loders]. T.R.E. it paid geld for 18 hides. There is land for the same number of ploughs. Of this there are in demesne 8 hides and there (are) 3 ploughs and 9 serfs and 28 villeins and 24 bordars with 6 ploughs. There (are) 2 mills rendering 23*s.* 4*d.* There (are) 40 acres of meadow. (There is) underwood 3 furlongs long and 1 furlong wide. It was and is worth £33. In this manor there are 2 hides of thegnland (*tainland*) which do not belong there. T.R.E. 2 thegns held them. They are worth 30*s.*

(ix) The king has 1 manor which is called Lodres which Earl Harold held on the day when King Edward was alive and dead, and it paid geld for 18 hides. Eighteen ploughs can plough these. Thence the king has 8 hides and 3 ploughs in demesne and the villeins 10 hides and 6 ploughs. The king has there 28 villeins and 24 bordars and 9 serfs and 2 pack-horses and 16 pigs and 93 sheep and 2 mills which render 23*s.* 4*d.* and 3 furlongs of underwood in length and 1 in width and 40 acres of meadow. This renders £34 and when Roger received it at farm it rendered as much. With these 18 hides there are in this manor 2 hides of thegnland (*teglanda*) which do not belong to it and 2 thegns held them on the day when King Edward was alive and dead and they are worth 30*s.* a year.

[34] 'comitis' interlined.

(14) The king holds LITELPIDELE [Little Puddle in Piddlehinton]. Earl[34] Harold's mother held (it) T.R.E. and it paid geld for 5 hides. There is land for 3 ploughs. Of this there are in demesne 2½ hides and there (are) 2 ploughs and 8 serfs and 2 villeins and 3 bordars with ½ plough. There (are) 8 acres of meadow and 10 furlongs of pasture. It was worth 100*s.* Now (it is worth) £7.

(iii) The king has 1 manor which is called Litel Pidel which Earl Harold's mother held on the day when King Edward was alive and dead, which paid geld for 5 hides. Three ploughs can plough these. There the king has in demesne 2½ hides and the villeins have as many. There the king has in demesne 2 ploughs and the villeins ½ (plough). There are 2 villeins and 3 bordars and 8 serfs and 1 pack-horse and 100 sheep and 8 acres of meadow and 10 furlongs of pasture. This manor renders £7 a year and when Fulcred received (it) it was worth 100*s.*

QUEEN MAUD HELD THESE LANDS WRITTEN BELOW

(15) The king holds LITELFROME [Frome St. Quintin]. T.R.E. it paid geld for 13 hides. There is land for 8 ploughs. Of this there are in demesne 10½ hides and there (are) 3 ploughs and 6 serfs and 10 villeins and 3 bordars with 3 ploughs. There (is) a mill rendering 4*s.* and 10 acres of meadow. (There is) pasture 20 furlongs long and 2 furlongs wide. (There is) wood(land) 8 furlongs long and 6 furlongs wide. It was worth £12. Now (it is worth) £18.[35]

THE LAND OF QUEEN MAUD IN DORSET

(xxi) Queen Maud had 1 manor which is called Litelfroma, which Brictric held on the day when King Edward was alive and dead and it paid geld for 13 hides. Eight ploughs can plough these. And now King William holds (it) in demesne. Of these 13 hides the king holds 10½ hides and 3 ploughs in demesne and the villeins 2½ hides and 3 ploughs. There the king has 10 villeins and 3 bordars and 8 cottars and 6 serfs and 2 pack-horses and 19 beasts and 400 sheep and 50 goats and 1 mill which renders 4*s.* and 8 furlongs of wood(land) in length and 6 in width and 10 acres of meadow and 20 furlongs of pasture in length and 2 in width. This manor is worth £18 a year and when Aiulf received (it) it was worth £12.

(16) The king holds CRENEBURNE [Cranborne]. T.R.E. it paid geld for 10 hides. There is land for 10 ploughs. Of this there are in demesne 3½ hides and there are 2 ploughs and 10 serfs and 8 villeins and 12 bordars and 7 cottars with 8 ploughs. There (are) 4 mills rendering 18*s.* and 20 acres of meadow. (There is) pasture 2 leagues long and 1 furlong and 1 league wide. (There is) wood(land) 2 leagues long and 2 wide. It was worth £24. Now it renders £30. Of this land 3 thegns hold 3 hides and render £3 excepting service (*excepto servitio*).

(xxii) Queen Maud had 1 manor which is called Creneborna, which Brictric held on the day when King Edward was alive and dead, and this paid geld T.R.E. for 10 hides. Ten ploughs can plough these. Of these 10 hides 3 thegns held, and still hold, 3 hides of Brictric, and could not leave him, and each of them renders 20*s.* a year excepting service. Thence the king has 3½ hides and 2

[35] 'ii' interlined.

ploughs in demesne and the villeins 3½ hides and 8 ploughs. There the king has 8 villeins and 12 bordars and 7 cottars and 10 serfs and 4 pack-horses and 10 cows and 51 pigs and 1,037 sheep and 4 mills which render 18*s.* a year and 2½ leagues of wood(land) in length and 2 leagues in width and 20 acres of meadow and 2½ leagues of pasture in length and 1 league and 1 furlong in width and 40 goats. This manor rendered £24 in the queen's lifetime and now renders £30.

(17) The king holds AISEMARE [Ashmore]. T.R.E. it paid geld for 8 hides. There is land for 7 ploughs. Of this there are in demesne 4 hides and there (are) 3 ploughs and 8 serfs and 10 villeins and 6 bordars with 4 ploughs. There (are) 10 acres of meadow. (There is) pasture 10 furlongs long and 1 furlong wide. (There is) wood(land) 2 leagues long and 1 league wide. It was and is worth £15. Brictric held these 3 manors T.R.E.

(xxiii) Queen Maud had 1 manor which is called Aisemara which Brictric held on the day when King Edward was alive and dead. This paid geld T.R.E. for 8 hides. Seven ploughs can plough these. And now the king holds it in demesne. Thence the king has 4 hides and 3 ploughs in demesne and the villeins 4 hides and 4 ploughs. There the king has 10 villeins and 6 bordars and 8 serfs and 3 pack-horses and 10 beasts and 27 pigs and 826[36] sheep and 50 goats and 2 leagues of wood(land) in length and 1 league in width and 10 acres of meadow and 10 furlongs of pasture in length and 1 in width. This manor rendered £15 in the queen's lifetime and now renders as much.

(18) The king holds MEDESHAM [Edmondsham]. Dodo held (it) T.R.E. and it paid geld for 2 hides. There is land for 3 ploughs. Of this there is in demesne 1 hide and there (is) 1 plough with 1 serf and 8 bordars. There (is) a mill rendering 5*s.* and 2 acres of meadow. (There is) pasture 3 furlongs long and 1 furlong wide. (There is) wood(land) 5 furlongs long and 1½ furlong wide. It was and is worth £3.

(xxiv) Queen Maud had 1 manor which is called Medessan which Dodo held on the day when King Edward was alive and dead, and he could go with his land to any lord, and it paid geld for 2 hides. Three ploughs can plough these. Of these the king, who now holds this manor, has 1 hide and 1 plough in demesne, and 8 bordars and 1 serf and 8 beasts and 22 sheep and 1 mill which renders 5*s.* a year and 5 furlongs of wood(land) in length and 1½ in width and 2 acres of meadow and 3 furlongs of pasture[37] in length and 1[38] in width and it is worth 60*s.* a year and when Schelin, who used to hold this manor of the queen, received (it) it was worth the same amount.

(19) The king holds HAME [Hampreston]. Saul held (it) T.R.E. and it paid geld for 2 hides and 1 virgate of land. There is land for 2 ploughs. Of this there is in demesne 1 hide, and there (is) 1 plough and 2 serfs and 5 villeins and 4 bordars with 1 plough. There (are) 40 acres of meadow and pasture 1 league long and 5 furlongs wide and 2 acres of wood(land). It renders 50*s.*

(xxv) The king has 1 manor which is called Hama which William Belet held of the queen and (which) Saul held T.R.E. and he could go with his land to any lord, and it paid geld for 2 hides and 1 virgate and 2 ploughs can plough (it). There the king has 1 plough and the villeins 1 and the king has there in demesne 1½ hide less 6 acres and 2 villeins and 4 bordars and 2 serfs,[39] and the villeins have 3 virgates and 6 acres and (the king has) 1 pack-horse and 15 beasts and 11 pigs and 40 sheep and 2 acres of wood(land) and 40 acres (*aqros* (sic)) of meadow and 1 league of pasture in length and 5 furlongs in width and it renders 50*s.* a year.

(20) The king holds WICHEMETUNE [Witchampton]. Two thegns held (it) T.R.E. and it paid geld for 4⅔ hides. There is land for 4 ploughs. Of this there are in demesne 2 hides and 1⅔ virgate of land, and there (are) 2 ploughs and 2 serfs and 5 villeins and 15 bordars with 2 ploughs. There (is) a mill rendering 10*s.* and 16 acres of meadow. (There is) pasture 5 furlongs long and 3 furlongs wide. (There is) wood(land) 6 furlongs long and 2 furlongs wide. It was and is worth 100*s.*

(xxvi) The king has 1 manor which is called Wichamatuna which 2 thegns held T.R.E.[40] and these (men) could go with their land to any lord and it paid geld for 4⅔ hides. Four ploughs can plough these. Of these the king has 2 hides and 1⅔ virgate and 2 ploughs in demesne and the villeins 2 hides and 1 virgate and 2 ploughs. There the king has 5 villeins and 15 bordars and 2 serfs and 2 cows and 2 pigs and 40 sheep and 1 mill which renders 10*s.* a year and 6 furlongs of wood(land) in length and 2 furlongs in width and 16 acres of meadow and 5 furlongs of pasture in length and 3 furlongs in width. This manor renders 100*s.* a year and was worth as much formerly when Schelin[41] received (it) who[42] used to hold it of the queen (and) who never paid geld to the king on ⅔ hide in the manor which we mentioned above (*quam in hac mansione supra nominavimus*).

(21) The king holds WINBURNE [Wimborne Minster, part of]. Ode held (it) T.R.E. There is ½ hide and it never paid geld. There is land for 2 ploughs. In demesne there is 1 virgate and 1 plough and 2 serfs and 4 villeins and 7 bordars with 2 ploughs. There (are) 14 acres of meadow. (There is) wood(land) 1 furlong long and as much in width. It was and is worth £4. This land does not belong to the farm of Wimborne.

(xxvii) The king has 1 manor which lies in Winburne which Odo the treasurer (*thesaurarius*) held T.R.E. There is ½ hide and it never paid geld. Two ploughs can plough this. There the king has 1 virgate and 1 plough and the villeins the other virgate and 2 ploughs. There are 4 villeins and 7 bordars and 2 serfs and 2 beasts and 10 pigs and 127 sheep and 30 goats and 14 acres of meadow. This renders £4 a year and was worth

36 'et xxvi' interlined.

37 'pascue' interlined.

38 'i' interlined.

39 'et ii villanos et iiii bordarios et ii servos' interlined.

40 'tempore Edwardi regis' interlined.

41 The text reads here *quando et icelinus* with the 'et' interlined.

42 'qui' interlined.

as much when the sheriff received it and to this manor belongs a wood 1 furlong in length and another in width and this manor in no way belongs to (*nichil pertinet*) to the night's farm of Wimborne.

HUGH FITZ GRIP[43] *HELD THESE EIGHT*[44] *LANDS OF THE QUEEN WRITTEN BELOW* (*infra scriptas*[45])

(22) Alwin held WAIA [on the R. Wey, site unidentified][46] T.R.E. and it paid geld for 1½ hide. There is land for 1 plough. There are 2 bordars and 5 furlongs of pasture. It is worth 30*s*.

THE LANDS WHICH KNIGHTS HELD OF THE QUEEN[47] *IN DORSET*

(xxviii) Hugh held 1 manor of the queen which is called Waia which Alwin held on the day when King Edward was alive and dead, and it paid geld for 1½ hide. One plough can plough this. Now the king holds this land in demesne. There the king has 2 bordars and 5 furlongs of pasture and it is worth 30*s*. a year.

(23) The king holds LANGETONE [Langton Herring]. Alward held (it) T.R.E. and it paid geld for 1½ hide. There is land for 2 ploughs. There are 2 serfs and 8[48] bordars and 1 rendering 30*d*. There (are) 8 acres of meadow and pasture 5 furlongs long and 3 furlongs wide. It is worth 30*s*.

(xxix) Hugh held 1 manor of the queen which is called Languetona, which Alward Colin held on the day when King Edward was alive and dead, and it paid geld for 1½ hide. Two ploughs can plough this. Now the king has (it) in demesne. There the king has 7 bordars and 1 bordar who renders 30*d*. a year,[49] and 2 serfs and 8 acres of meadow and 5 furlongs of pasture in length and 3 in width and it is worth 30*s*. a year. This thegn could go with his land to any lord.[50]

(24) The king holds TARENTE [unidentified]. Alvric held (it) T.R.E. and it paid geld for 3½ hides. There is land for 4 ploughs. Of this there are in demesne 2 hides and there (are) ½ plough and 5 serfs and 6 villeins and 3 bordars with 2 ploughs. There (is) pasture 7 furlongs long and 2 furlongs wide. (There is) wood(land) 5 furlongs long and 3 furlongs wide. It was worth £4. Now (it is worth) 100*s*. To this manor belongs 1 virgate of land which Alvric had in pledge for ½ gold mark and it has not yet been redeemed (*necdum est redempta*).

(xxx) Hugh held 1 manor of the queen which is called Tarenta which Alvric held on the day when King Edward was alive and dead, and he could go with his land to any lord, and it paid geld for 3½ hides. Now the king has (it) in demesne. Four ploughs can plough these.[51] Of these the king has 2 hides and ½ plough in demesne and the villeins have 1½ hide and 2 ploughs. There the king has 6 villeins and 3 bordars and 5 serfs and 1 packhorse and 30 pigs and 290 sheep and 5 furlongs of wood(land)[52] in length and 3 in width and 7 furlongs of pasture in length and 2 in width and it renders 100*s*. a year (and) when Hugh received (it) it was worth £4. To this manor belongs 1 virgate of land which Alvric, Hugh's predecessor, had in pledge for ½ gold mark which still has not been redeemed (*quam adhuc non est redempta*).

(25) The king holds TARENTE [? Tarrant Gunville]. Alwin held (it) T.R.E. and it paid geld for ½ hide. There is land for 1 plough. There are 2 bordars. It is worth 10*s*.

(xxxi) Hugh held 1 manor of the queen which is called Tarenta which Alwin held on the day when King Edward was alive and dead and he could go with his land to any lord and now the king holds it in demesne, and it paid geld for ½ hide and 1 plough can plough (it). There the king has 2 bordars and it is worth 10*s*. a year.

(26) The king holds TARENTE [? Tarrant Rushton]. Two thegns held (it) T.R.E. and it paid geld for 3 hides and 1 virgate of land. There is land for 3 ploughs. Of this there are in demesne 2 hides and 3 virgates of land and there (is) 1 plough and 4 serfs and 2 villeins and 4 bordars—[*blank*].[53] There (is) a mill rendering 4*s*. and 13 acres of meadow. (There is) pasture 4 furlongs long and as much in width. It was worth £4. Now (it is worth) £3.

(xxxv) Hugh held 1 manor of the queen which is called Tarenta which 2 thegns held on the day when King Edward was alive and dead, and they could go with their land to any lord. Now the king has it in demesne. This paid geld for 3 hides and 1 virgate which 3 ploughs can plough. Of these the king has in demesne 2 hides and 3 virgates and 1 plough and the villeins have ½ hide. There the king has 2 villeins and 4 bordars and 4 serfs and 15 pigs and 60 sheep and 1 mill which is worth 4*s*.[54] and 13 acres of meadow and 4 furlongs of pasture in length and 4 in width and it renders 60*s*. a year and when Hugh received (it) it was worth £4.

(27) The king holds SCETRE [Shitterton in Bere Regis]. Ulviet held (it) T.R.E. and it paid geld for 5 hides. There is land for 4 ploughs. Of this there are in demesne 3½ hides and there (is) 1 plough and 5 serfs and 6 villeins and 3 bordars with 1 plough. There (are) 4 acres of meadow. (There is) pasture 2 furlongs long and 2 wide. (There is) wood(land) 3 furlongs long and 3 wide. It was worth £6. Now (it is worth) 100*s*.

(xxxii) Hugh held 1 manor of the queen which is called Scetra which Ulviet held on the day when King Edward was alive and dead, and he could go with his land to any lord. Now the king holds it in demesne. This paid geld for 5 hides, which 4 ploughs can plough. Of these the king has 3½ hides and 1 plough in demesne and the villeins have ½ (hide) and 1 plough and there the king has 6 villeins and 3 bordars and 5 serfs and 20 pigs and 120 sheep and 3 furlongs of wood(land) in length and 3 in width and 4 acres of meadow and 2 furlongs of pasture in length and 2 in width and it rendered 100*s*. a year and when Hugh received (it) it was worth £6.

[43] 'filius Grip' interlined. [44] 'octo' interlined.

[45] 'ri' of *scriptas* interlined.

[46] Presumably some estate on the River Wey, but it has not been possible to identify the numerous manors called *Wai* or *Waia*.

[47] 'na' of *regina* interlined. [48] 'i' interlined.

[49] 'et i bordarium qui reddit per annum xxx denarios interlined.

[50] 'ire cum terra sua ad quemlibet dominum' interlined.

[51] 'has' interlined. [52] 'nemoris' interlined.

[53] Space in the text. For a comment, see p. 4.

[54] 'valet iiii solidos' interlined.

28) The king holds NORTFORDE [Nutford (Farm) in Pimperne]. Alvric held (it) T.R.E. and it paid geld for 2½ hides. There is land for 2 ploughs. There are 2 serfs and 3 coscets and 8 acres of meadow. (There is) pasture 1 furlong long and 1 wide. It was and is worth 25*s*.

(xxxiii) Hugh held 1 manor of the queen[55] which is called Notforda which Alvric held on the day when King Edward was alive and dead, and he could go with his land to any lord he wished. Now the king holds it in demesne and it paid[56] geld for 2½ hides which 2 ploughs can plough.[57] Of these the king has in demesne 2½ hides and 1 plough, except for 8 acres which 2 coscets hold. There the king has 3[58] coscets and 2 serfs and 4 beasts and 80 sheep and 8 acres of meadow and 1 furlong of pasture[59] in length and 1 in width and now it renders 25*s*. and when Hugh received (it) it was worth as much.

(29) The king holds WATRECOME [Watercombe]. Alvric held (it) T.R.E. and it paid geld for 1 hide. There is land for 1 plough. There is 1 coscet and ½ mill rendering 4*s*. (There is) pasture 1 league in length and 1 furlong (in width).[60] It renders 15*s*. Those who held these lands T.R.E. could go to any lord they wished.

(xxxiv) Hugh held 1 manor of the queen which is called Watrecoma,[61] which Alvric held on the day when King Edward was alive and dead, and he could go with his land to any lord. Now the king holds it in demesne. This paid geld for 1 hide and 1 plough can plough (it). There the king has 1 coscet and ½ mill which renders 4*s*. a year and 1 league of pasture in length and 1 furlong in width, and it renders 15*s*. a year.

(30) The king holds MELCOME [Bingham's Melcombe in Melcombe Horsey]. Earl[62] Harold unlawfully (*iniuste*) took (it) from St. Mary of Shaftesbury. T.R.E. it paid geld for 10 hides. There is land for 10 ploughs. Of this there are in demesne 7½ hides and 1 virgate of land and there (are) 2 ploughs and 4 serfs and 9 villeins and 20 bordars with 7 ploughs. There (are) 5 acres of meadow and 1 league of wood(land). (There is) pasture 1 league long and 8 furlongs wide and 12 acres of meadow were leased (*prestite*) to Wlgar White,[63] which belonged to the same manor. Now William Belet holds (them). To this manor Goda added 3½ virgates of land which 3 free thegns held T.R.E. and which paid geld for that amount. There is land for 1 plough which is there with 3 villeins and 15 acres of meadow and 5 acres of wood(land). These 3½ virgates are in BOCHELANDE [Buckland] HUNDRED. The whole was and is worth £16. Countess Goda held (it).

[f. 76][64]

(31) The king holds HINETONE [Hinton Martell]. Countess[65] Goda held (it) T.R.E. and it paid geld for 14 hides and 1 virgate of land. There is land for 12 ploughs. Of this there are in demesne 6 hides and 1 virgate of land and there is 1 plough and 8 villeins and 14 bordars have 3 ploughs. There (is) a mill rendering 10*s*. and 37 acres of meadow. (There is) pasture 5 furlongs long and as much in width. (There is) wood(land) 1 league long and ½ league wide. It is worth £13 5*s*. Of this same land, a certain (*quidam*) priest held 1 hide of thegnland (*tainlande*) and could go with it where he would. Now it is in the king's demesne. Of the same land another priest held 2½ hides. The Bishop of Lisieux has 1 of these in demesne and it is worth 20*s*. The priest has the other 1½ hide of this manor and there he has 2 ploughs with 4 villeins and 2 bordars and a mill rendering 5*s*. and 11 acres of meadow and 1 furlong of wood(land) in length and ½ furlong in width and 11 houses in Winburne [Wimborne Minster]. The whole is worth 30*s*. This priest could go where he would with his land T.R.E. Of this same land another priest dwelling[66] in TARENTE [unidentified] holds 1⅓ hide and there he has 3 villeins and 4 bordars with 1 plough and 1 acre of meadow and 5 furlongs of pasture in length and 1 furlong in width. It is worth 30*s*. Of this same land Ulvric holds 1 virgate of land and it is worth 2*s*. Of this same land 1½ hide and ½ virgate of land belongs to the church of Wimborne Minster. Bishop Maurice[67] holds (it) and there he has 6 bordars and 8 burgesses and a mill rendering 5*s*. and 15 acres of meadow and ½ league of pasture in length and 4 furlongs in width. It is worth £6 7*s*. 6*d*.

[f. 75b (cont.)]

II. THE LAND OF THE BISHOP OF SALISBURY

(32) The Bishop of Salisbury holds CERMINSTRE [Charminster]. T.R.E. it paid geld for 10 hides. There is land for 8 ploughs. In demesne there are 2 ploughs and 4 serfs and 14 villeins and 12 bordars with 6 ploughs. There (is) a mill rendering 6*s*. and 15 acres of meadow. (There is) pasture 1 league long and 3 furlongs wide. (There is) wood(land) 2 furlongs long and 1 furlong wide. In Wareham 2 burgesses with 12 acres of land and in Dorchester 1 burgess with 10 acres of land belong to this manor. It was and is worth £16. Of this land 1 royal reeve (*prepositus regis*) holds 1 hide and there he has 1 plough with 3 bordars. In the same manor the bishop has as much land as 2 ploughs can plough. This never paid geld.

(33) The same bishop holds ALTONE [Alton Pancras]. T.R.E. it paid geld for 6 hides. There is land for 6 ploughs. Besides this he has land for 2 ploughs in demesne which never paid geld and there he has 2 ploughs and 4 serfs and 6 villeins and 10 bordars with 1 plough. There (is) a mill rendering 15*s*. and 7 acres of meadow. (There is) pasture 6 furlongs long and 2 furlongs wide. (There is) wood(land) 2 furlongs long and 1 furlong wide. Of this land Edward has 2½ hides and Pain 2½ hides. There are 3 ploughs and 1 villein and 5 bordars with 1 plough and pasture 4 furlongs long and 2 wide. The bishop's demesne is worth £13.[68] (The land) of the men is worth £4.

55 'de regina' interlined.
56 'di' of *reddidit* interlined.
57 'quas possunt arare ii carruce' interlined.
58 'i' interlined.
59 'r' of *prasti* (sic) interlined.
60 Supply 'latitudine'.
61 'que vocatur Watrecoma' interlined.
62 'comes' interlined.
63 'wit' interlined.
64 The entry for Hinton Martell was added on a separate leaf (f. 76) which contains no other entry.
65 'comitissa' interlined.
66 'manens' interlined.
67 Bishop of London.
68 'i' interlined.

(34) The same bishop holds OBCERNE ([Up Cerne]. T.R.E. it paid geld for 2½ hides. There is land for 4 ploughs. Of this 1½ hide is in demesne and there (are) 3 ploughs and 6 serfs and 4 villeins and 8 bordars with 1 plough. There (is) a mill rendering 15*s.* and 7 acres of meadow. (There is) pasture 1 league long and 3 furlongs wide. It is worth £10. Robert holds (it) of the bishop.

(35) The same bishop holds ETIMINSTRE [Yetminster]. T.R.E. it paid geld for 15 hides. There is land for 20 ploughs. Besides this he has land for 6 ploughs which never paid geld T.R.E. There are 4 ploughs in demesne and 6 serfs and 25 villeins and 25 bordars with 8 ploughs. There (is) a mill rendering 5*s.* and 30 acres of meadow and (there is) pasture 2 furlongs long and 1 furlong wide. (There is) wood(land) 1 league long and another in width. It was and is worth £22. Of this same land William holds 6 hides of the bishop and there he has 4 ploughs and 4 serfs and 6 villeins and 10 bordars with 2 ploughs, and a mill and 12 acres of meadow and wood(land)[69] 3 furlongs long and 1 furlong wide. It is worth £4. Those who held (it) T.R.E. could not be separated from the church.

(36) The same bishop holds LYM [Lyme Regis, part of]. There is land for 1 plough. It never paid geld. Fishermen hold (it) and render 15*s.* to the monks for the fish (*ad pisces*). There are 4 acres of meadow. There the bishop has 1 house rendering 6*d.*

[f. 77]
(37) The bishop himself holds SCIREBURNE [Sherborne]. Queen Edith held (it) and Bishop Alwold before her. T.R.E. it paid geld for 43 hides. There is land for 46 ploughs. Of this land the bishop holds 12 hides and there he has 25 villeins and 14 bordars with 12 ploughs. There (are) 130 acres of meadow, 3 acres of which are in Somerset near Meleburne [Milborne Port, Som.]. (There is) pasture 1 league long and 1 wide. (There is) wood(land) 2 leagues long and as much in width. Of the same land of this manor Otbold holds of the bishop 4 hides. Sinod 5½ hides. Ingelbert 5 hides. Waleran 3 hides. Ralph 3 hides. The wife of Hugh fitz Grip[70] 2 hides. In these 22½ hides there are 21 ploughs and 33 villeins and 15 bordars and 10 coscets and 4 serfs. There (are) 4 mills rendering 18*s.* Of the same land also 6 thegns hold 8½ hides and there they have 8 ploughs and 4 serfs and 17 villeins and 19 bordars and 3 mills rendering 30*d.* In this manor of Sherborne besides the aforesaid land the bishop has in demesne 16 carucates of land. This land was never reckoned (*divisa*) in hides, neither did it pay geld. There are in demesne 5 ploughs and 26 villeins and 26 bordars and 8 serfs with 9 ploughs. There (is) a mill rendering 10*s.* Of this exempt land (*quieta terra*) Sinod holds of the bishop 1 carucate of land, and Edward (holds) another. There are 2 ploughs and 2 serfs and 8 bordars.
III.[71] In this same Sherborne the monks of the same bishop hold 9½ carucates of land which were never reckoned in hides nor did they pay geld. There are in demesne 3½ ploughs and 4 serfs and 10 villeins and 10 bordars with 5 ploughs and 3 mills rendering 22*s.* and 20 acres of meadow. (There is) wood(land) 1 league long and 4 furlongs wide. Of this land of the monks Lanbert holds of them 1 carucate of land and there he has 1 plough and a mill rendering 5*s.* What the bishop has in demesne in this manor is worth £50. What the monks (have), £6 10*s.* What the knights of the bishop (have), £27. What the thegns (have), £6. Moreover Sinod holds of the bishop 1 hide in the same vill and there he has 1 plough and 2 serfs and 2 bordars. It is worth 12*s.* Alward held this[72] hide of King Edward, but it belonged to the bishopric previously.

(38) The same bishop holds WOCBURNE [Oborne]. T.R.E. it paid geld for 5 hides. There is land for 4 ploughs. Of this there are in demesne 2 hides and there (is) 1 plough and 2 serfs and 6 villeins and 5 bordars with 3 ploughs. There (are) 8 acres of meadow and 4 acres of underwood. It is worth £4.

(39) The same bishop holds TORNEFORD [Thornford]. T.R.E. it paid geld for 7 hides. There is land for 6 ploughs. Of this there are in demesne 3 hides and there (are) 2 ploughs with 1 serf and 7 villeins and 7 bordars with 4 ploughs. There (is) a mill rendering 12*s.* 6*d.* and 16 acres of meadow. (There is) wood(land) 10 furlongs long and 1 furlong wide. It is worth 100*s.*

(40) The same bishop holds BRADEFORD [Bradford Abbas]. T.R.E. it paid geld for 10 hides. There is land for 10 ploughs. Of this there is in demesne 1½ hide and there (are) 3 ploughs and 7 serfs and 8 villeins and 7 bordars with 7 ploughs. There (is) a mill rendering 15*s.* and 20 acres of meadow and 3 acres of underwood. It is worth £10.

(41) The same bishop (holds)[73] CONTONE [Over Compton]. T.R.E. it paid geld for 6 hides and 3 virgates of land. There is land for 8 ploughs. Of this there is in demesne 1 hide and 3 virgates of land, and there (are) 2 ploughs and 6 serfs and 13 villeins and 10 bordars with 6 ploughs. There (is) a mill rendering 10*s.* and 16 acres of meadow. (There is) wood(land) 2 furlongs long and wide. It is worth £6.

(42) The same bishop holds STAPLEBRIGE [Stalbridge]. T.R.E. it paid geld for 20 hides. There is land for 16 ploughs. Of this there are in demesne 6 hides and there (are) 2 ploughs with 1 serf and 19 villeins and 2 bordars with 11 ploughs. There (is) a mill rendering 15*s.* and 25 acres of meadow. (There is) pasture 4 furlongs long and 2 furlongs wide. (There is) wood(land) 1 league long and 3 furlongs wide.—[*Blank*][74] It is worth £12. Of the same land Lanbert holds 2 hides and there he has 1 plough with 6 bordars. It is worth 20*s.* Of the same land also Manasses holds 3 virgates which William the king's son took from the church without the consent of the bishop and the monks. There is 1 plough.

(43) The same bishop holds WESTONE [Stalbridge Weston in Stalbridge]. T.R.E. it paid geld for 8 hides. There is land for 6 ploughs. Of this there are

[69] The facsimile has *silva(m)*, the printed version *silva.*
[70] 'filii Grip' interlined.
[71] 'III' added in the margin at this point. For a comment, see p. 6.
[72] 'anc' of *Hanc* interlined.
[73] Supply 'tenet'.
[74] Space in the text. For a comment, see p. 5.

in demesne 5 hides and there (are) 2 ploughs with 1 serf and 7 villeins and 7 bordars with 3 ploughs. There (are) 12 acres of meadow. (There is) underwood 4 furlongs long and 1 furlong wide. It is worth £7.

(44) The same bishop holds CORSCUMBE [Corscombe]. T.R.E. it paid geld for 10 hides less 1 virgate. There is land for 9 ploughs. Of this there are in demesne 4 hides and 3 virgates[75] and there (are) 3 ploughs with 1 serf and 7 villeins and 7 coscets with 7 ploughs. There (is) a mill rendering 5*s.* and 10 acres of meadow. (There is) pasture 9 furlongs long and 4 furlongs wide. (There is) wood(land) 1 league long and 4 furlongs wide. It is worth £7.

(45) The same bishop holds STOCHE [Stoke Abbott]. T.R.E. it paid geld for 6½ hides. There is land for 7 ploughs. Besides this there are 2 carucates of land which were never reckoned in hides and there in demesne is 1 plough with 1 serf and 6 coscets. There 8 villeins have 4 ploughs and 2 thegns hold 2½ hides, and there they have 2 ploughs and 12 coscets and 5 serfs and a mill rendering 5*s.* (There is) pasture 5 furlongs long and 3 furlongs wide. (There is) underwood 3 furlongs long and 2 furlongs wide. The demesne is worth £6. What the thegns hold, 40*s.*

THESE NINE MANORS DESCRIBED ARE FOR THE PROVISION OF THE MONKS OF SHERBORNE

(46) The same bishop holds BEIMINSTRE [Beaminster]. T.R.E. it paid geld for 16 hides and 1 virgate of land. There is land for 20 ploughs. Besides this land he has in demesne 2 carucates of land which never paid geld and there he has 2 ploughs and a mill rendering 20*d.* Under the bishop there are 19 villeins and 20 bordars and 5 serfs and 33 acres of meadow. (There is) pasture 1 league long and ½ league wide. (There is) wood(land) 1½ league long and ½ league wide. Of this same land Algar holds 2 hides of the bishop. H. de Cartrai 2 hides less 1 virgate. Sinod 5 hides. Brictuin 1½ hide. There are 9 ploughs and 11 serfs and 19 bordars and 2 villeins and 2 coscets and 2 mills rendering 28*d.* and 40 acres of meadow. (There is) pasture 4 furlongs long and 2 furlongs wide and 32 acres of pasture as well. (There is) wood(land) 13 furlongs long and 9 furlongs wide. The bishop's demesne is worth £16. (The land) of the men, £7.

(47) The same bishop holds NIDERBERIE [Netherbury]. T.R.E. it paid geld for 20 hides. There is land for 20 ploughs. Besides this he has in demesne 2 carucates of land which never paid geld and there are 2 ploughs. There (are) 18 villeins and 22 bordars and 6 serfs with 8 ploughs. There (is) a mill rendering 10*s.* and 16 acres of meadow and 3 furlongs of pasture. (There is) wood(land) 9 furlongs long and 1 furlong wide. Of the same land Tezelin holds of the bishop 5 hides and 3 virgates of land. William 2 hides. Godfrey 2 hides. Serle 1½[76] hide. There are 10 ploughs and 12 villeins and 24 bordars and 5 serfs. There (is) a mill rendering 5*s.* and 21 acres of meadow and 3 furlongs of wood(land) in length and width. The bishop's demesne is worth £16. (The land) of the men, £8 10*s.*

(48) In BRIDEPORT [Bridport] the bishop has ½ acre rendering 6*d.*

(49) The same bishop holds CERDESTOCHE [Chardstock, Devon] and 2 knights (*milites*) Walter and William (hold it) of him. T.R.E. it paid geld for 12 hides. There is land for 20 ploughs. Of this there are in demesne 4 hides and there (are) 4 ploughs and 6 serfs and 45 villeins and 21 bordars with 17 ploughs. There (are) 2 mills rendering 20*s.* and 10 acres of meadow. (There is) pasture 3 leagues long and 1½ league wide. (There is) wood(land) 2 leagues in[77] length and width, and in another place 3 furlongs of underwood in length and 2 furlongs in width. The whole is worth £16.

THESE LANDS WHICH ARE LISTED BELOW THE BISHOP HAS IN EXCHANGE FOR SCIPELEIA [unidentified]

(50) In CERNEL [unidentified] the bishop has 1½ hide and 10 acres of land. Algar held (it) T.R.E. There is land for 1 plough. One woman has this there and she holds of the bishop with 4 bordars and 3 acres of meadow. (There is) pasture 2 furlongs long and 1 furlong wide. It is worth 20*s.*

(51) The same bishop holds PIDELE [Bardolfeston in Puddletown, now lost], and the wife of Hugh (holds it) of him. Agelric held (it) of King Edward and it paid geld for 4 hides. There is land for 3 ploughs. In demesne there is 1 (plough) and 3 bordars and 34 acres of meadow and 6 furlongs of pasture. It was worth £4. Now (it is worth) £3.

(52) The same bishop holds PIDELE [Athelhampton], and Otbold (holds it) of him. Agelric held (it) T.R.E. and it paid geld for 4 hides. There is land for 2 ploughs which are there with 1 villein and 5 bordars and 5 serfs. There (is) a mill rendering 67*d.* and 20 acres of meadow and 20 acres of pasture and 5 furlongs of wood(land). It was and is worth £3.

(53) The same bishop holds BOVEWODE [North and South Bowood in Netherbury] and 3 knights, Godfrey, Osmar,[78] and Aelfric, (hold it) of him. Three thegns held (it) T.R.E. and it paid geld for 6 hides. There is land for 6 ploughs. There are 5 ploughs and 3 serfs and 14 villeins and 18 bordars. There (are) 4½ acres of meadow and 10 acres of pasture and 12 acres of underwood. The whole is worth 70*s.*

(54) The same bishop holds BOCHENHAM [Buckham in Beaminster] and Walter (holds it) of him. Three thegns held (it) T.R.E. and it paid geld for 3 hides. There is land for 3 ploughs. Of this there are in demesne 2 hides and 1 virgate of land and there (is) 1 plough and 2 serfs and 3 villeins and 4 bordars with 2 ploughs. There (are) 4 acres of meadow and 30 acres of pasture. (There is) wood(land) 4 furlongs long and 2 furlongs wide. It is worth 30*s.* To this manor belongs 1 hide in WELLE [Wool]. There is land for 1 plough. There is 1 bordar. It is worth 40*d.* Osmar holds (it).

[75] 'et iii virgate' interlined.
[76] 'et dimidia' interlined.
[77] 'inter' interlined.
[78] The facsimile has *Osmar*, the printed version *Oswar*.

IIII. THE LAND OF THE BISHOP OF BAYEUX

(55) The Bishop of Bayeux holds RAMESHAM [Rampisham] and Wadard (holds it) of him. Lewin held (it) T.R.E. and it paid geld for 6 hides. There is land for 6 ploughs. Of this there are in demesne 3 hides and there (are) 2 ploughs with 1 serf and 10 villeins and 6 bordars with 3 ploughs. There (are) 12 acres of meadow. (There is) pasture 1½ league and 2 furlongs long and 1 league and 1 furlong wide. (There is) wood(land) 1 league and 2 furlongs long and 1 league and 1 furlong wide. It was worth £10. Now (it is worth) £6. With this manor hitherto Wadard held 3 virgates of land which 5 thegns held T.R.E. and they could go where they would.

V. THE LAND OF THE BISHOP OF COUTANCES

(56) The Bishop of Coutances holds WINTREBURNE [unidentified] and Osbern (holds it) of him. Turmund held (it) T.R.E. and it paid geld for 4½ hides. There is land for 4 ploughs. Of this there are in demesne 3 hides and 1 virgate of land and there (are) 2 ploughs and 2 serfs and 5 villeins and 3 bordars with 1 plough. There (is) a mill rendering 16*d.* and 8 furlongs of pasture. (There is) wood(land) 3½ furlongs long and 4 acres (*sic*)[79] and 2 wide. It was worth 60*s.* Now (it is worth) 100*s.*

(57) The same bishop holds WINTREBURNE [unidentified]. Two brothers held (it) T.R.E. and it paid geld for 2 hides. There is land for 2 ploughs. There is 1 plough and 3 serfs in demesne and 6 cottars. There (is) a mill rendering 15*d.* and 8 furlongs of pasture in length and 1 furlong in width. It was worth 30*s.* Now (it is worth) 50*s.* Osbern holds (it) of the bishop.

[f. 77b]

VI. THE LAND OF THE BISHOP OF LISIEUX

(58) The Bishop of Lisieux holds TARENTE [Tarrant Crawford]. Ulward held (it) T.R.E. and it paid geld for 5 hides. There is land for 3 ploughs. Of this 3 hides and 1 virgate of land are in demesne and there (are) 2 ploughs and 4 serfs and 2 villeins and 13 bordars with 1 plough. There (is) a mill rendering 5*s.* and 9 acres of meadow. (There is) pasture 5 furlongs long and 1 furlong wide. (There is) wood(land) 2 furlongs long and 2 wide. It was worth £4. Now (it is worth) 100*s.*

(59) The same bishop holds PRESTETUNE [Preston (Farm) in Tarrant Rushton]. Edward the clerk[80] held (it) T.R.E. and it paid geld for 1 hide. There is land for 1 plough. There is ½ acre of meadow and pasture 4 furlongs long and as much in width. It was and is worth 20*s.*

(60) The same bishop holds TARENTE [Tarrant Keyneston]. Herling held (it) T.R.E. and it paid geld for 10 hides and ⅓ of ½ hide. There is land for 8 ploughs. Of this there are in demesne 5½ hides and there (are) 3 ploughs and 6 serfs and 12 villeins and 14 bordars with 4 ploughs. There (are) 2 mills rendering 30*s.* and 1,000 eels (*anguillas*) and 76 acres of meadow and 22 furlongs of pasture in length and width. (There is) wood(land) 8 furlongs long and the same amount in width. It was and is worth £13.

(61) The same bishop holds CUME [Coombe Keynes]. Alvric held (it) T.R.E. and it paid geld for 10 hides. There is land for 7 ploughs. Of this there are in demesne 6 hides and 1 virgate of land and there (are) 2 ploughs and 4 serfs and 6 villeins and 9 bordars with 5 ploughs. There (are) 20 acres of meadow and 8 furlongs of pasture in length and the same amount in width. (There is) wood(land) 6 furlongs long and as much in width. It is worth £7.

VII. [THE LAND OF] THE BISHOP OF LONDON

(62) The Bishop of London, Maurice,[81] holds ½ hide in ODEHAM [unidentified]. Alvric Dod held (it) T.R.E. There is land for ½ plough but nevertheless there is 1 plough and 8 acres of meadow and wood(land) 1 furlong long and ½ furlong wide. It was and is worth 12*s.* 6*d.*

VIII. THE LAND OF ST. MARY, GLASTONBURY

(63) The church of St. Mary, Glastonbury, holds NEWENTONE [Sturminster Newton]. T.R.E. it paid geld for 22 hides. There is land for 35 ploughs. Besides this there is land for 14 ploughs in demesne there which never paid geld. There are 21 villeins and 18 bordars and 10 cottars and 13 coliberts and 15 serfs. There (are) 3 mills rendering 40*s.* and 66 acres of meadow. (There is) wood(land) 2½ leagues long and 1 league wide. It was worth £30. Now (it is worth) £25. Of the land of this manor Waleran holds 6 hides. Roger 1 hide. Chetel 1 hide. These 8 hides can be ploughed by 11 ploughs. They are worth £7. Of the same land Goscelm the cook[82] holds of the king 4 hides. There he has 2 ploughs and 2 serfs and 5 villeins and 6 bordars with 4 ploughs and a mill rendering 3*s.* 9*d.* and 16 acres of meadow. (There is) wood(land) ½ league long and 1 furlong wide. It was and is worth £4.

(64) The church itself holds ADFORD [Okeford Fitzpaine] and knights (hold it) of it. Four thegns held (it) T.R.E. and it paid geld for 8 hides. There is land for 16 ploughs. In demesne there are 4 ploughs and 10 serfs and 15 villeins and 15 bordars with 7 ploughs. There (is) a mill rendering 5*s.* and 21 acres of meadow. (There is) pasture 6 furlongs long and 3 furlongs wide. (There is) wood(land) 9 furlongs long and 6 furlongs wide. It was and is worth £12. The wife of Hugh has 4 hides. Alvred 2 hides. Chetel 2 hides.

(65) The church itself holds BOCHELANDE [Buckland Newton]. T.R.E. it paid geld for 15 hides. There is land for 24 ploughs. Besides this there is in demesne land for 8 ploughs which never paid geld. There (are) in demesne 4 ploughs and 4 serfs and 22 villeins and 22 bordars and 22 cottars with 8 ploughs. There

79 See p. 21.
80 'clericus' interlined.
81 'Mauricius' interlined.
82 'cocus' interlined.

(are) 20 acres of meadow. (There is) pasture 2 leagues long and ½ league wide and the same amount of wood(land). Of the same land of this manor the wife of Hugh holds of the abbot 7 hides and 1½ virgate of land, and Warmund 2 hides. There are in demesne 3 ploughs and 4 serfs and 3 villeins and 7 bordars with 1 plough and 3 acres of meadow and wood(land) 2 furlongs long and 1 furlong wide. The demesne of the church is worth £20. (The land) of the men, £6 10*s*.

(66) The church itself holds ODIETE [Woodyates in Pentridge] and the wife of Hugh (holds it) of the abbot. T.R.E. it paid geld for 4 hides. There is land for 4 ploughs. In demesne there are 3 hides and 1 virgate of land and there (is) 1 plough and 3 serfs and 2 villeins and 5 bordars. There (is) pasture 16½ furlongs in length and width. (There is) wood(land) 7 furlongs long and 5½ furlongs wide. It was worth £4. Now (it is worth) 40*s*.

(67) The church itself held PENTRIC [Pentridge] T.R.E. and it paid geld for 6 hides. There is land for 6 ploughs. Now the king holds (it) in demesne and he has there 1 plough and 4 serfs and 6 villeins and 6 bordars with 3 ploughs. There (is) pasture 8 furlongs long and 4 furlongs wide. (There is) wood(land) 1 league long and 3 furlongs wide. It is worth £6. Ulward, who held it T.R.E., could not be separated from the church.

(68) The church itself holds LYM [Colway in Lyme Regis, site lost].[83] T.R.E. it paid geld for 3 hides. There is land for 4 ploughs. Ulviet held and holds (it) of the abbot and there he has 2 ploughs and 9 villeins and 6 bordars and 4 acres of meadow. (There is) pasture 4 furlongs long and 2 furlongs wide, and 10 acres of wood(land). There (are) 13 salt-workers (*salinarii*) rendering 13*s*. The whole is worth 60*s*.

IX. THE LAND OF THE ABBEY OF ST. PETER, WINCHESTER

(69) The church of St. Peter, Winchester, holds PIDRIE [Piddletrenthide]. T.R.E. it paid geld for 30 hides. There is land for 17 ploughs. Of this there are in demesne 15 hides and 2½ virgates of land and there (are) 5 ploughs and 20 serfs and 20 villeins and 30 bordars with 8 ploughs. There (are) 3 mills rendering 60*s*. and 16 acres of meadow. (There is) pasture 2 leagues long and ½ league wide. Of the same land 1 knight and a certain widow hold 3 hides and there they have 2 ploughs. The demesne of the church is worth £28. The rest is worth 40*s*. Almar and Alverd held this manor T.R.E. as 2 manors (*pro ii maneriis*) of King Edward and they could not go with this land to any lord. Afterwards Roger Arundel[84] held (it) of King William.

X. THE LAND OF ST. MARY, CRANBORNE

(70) The church of St. Mary, Cranborne, holds INGELINGEHAM [land in Gillingham]. There is land for 2 ploughs. There are 5 bordars and 7 acres of meadow. It was worth 60*s*. Now (it is worth) 20*s*. Hugh received this land from the king's farm and gave (it) to this church.

(71) The church itself holds BOVEHRIC [Boveridge in Cranborne]. Brictric held (it) T.R.E. and it paid geld for 5 hides. There is land for 7 ploughs. Of this there are in demesne 2½ hides and there (are) 2 ploughs and 10 serfs and 5 villeins and 9 bordars with 3 ploughs. There (is) a mill rendering 6*s*. (There is) pasture 9½ furlongs in length and width. (There is) heathland (*bruaria*) 2 leagues (in) length and width. (There is) wood(land) 1 league long and ½ league wide. It was and is worth 100*s*. Of this land John holds 2½ virgates of land.

(72) The church itself holds WINBURNE [Monkton Up Wimborne]. T.R.E. it paid geld for 5 hides. There is land for 6 ploughs. Of this there is in demesne 1 hide and there (are) 2 ploughs and 7 serfs and 7 villeins and 7 bordars with 4 ploughs. There are 10 acres of meadow. (There is) pasture 1 league long and ½ league wide. (There is) wood(land) 4 furlongs long and 2 furlongs wide. Of the same land Ralph holds 1 hide. The whole (manor) was and is worth 100*s*.

(73) The church itself holds LEVETESFORD [Leftisford in Cranborne, now lost], and John (holds it) of the abbot. There is ½ hide and 2 ploughs with 4 villeins and 1 bordar and (there are) 4 acres of meadow. It is worth 15*s*.

(74) The church itself holds ½ hide in LANGEFORD [? Langford (Farm) in Stratton]. There is land for 1 plough. Two villeins have this there and (there are) 2 furlongs of pasture in length and width. (There is) wood(land) 1 furlong in length and width. It is worth 5*s*.

(75) The church itself holds TARENTE [Tarrant Monkton]. T.R.E. it paid geld for 10 hides. There is land for 8 ploughs. Of this there are in demesne 4½ hides and there (is) 1 plough and 4 serfs and 12 villeins and 12 bordars with 3 ploughs. There (is) a mill rendering 5*s*. and 35 acres of meadow. (There is) 1½ league of pasture in length and width. (There is) 10 furlongs of wood(land) in length and width. It was worth £12. Now (it is worth) £10.

XI. THE LAND OF ST. PETER OF CERNE

(76) The church of St. Peter, Cerne, holds CERNELI [Cerne Abbas]. T.R.E. it paid geld for 22 hides. There is land for 20 ploughs. Of this there are in demesne 3 hides and there (are) 3 ploughs and 5 serfs and 26 villeins and 32 bordars with 14 ploughs. There (is) a mill rendering 20*s*. and 20 acres of meadow. (There is) pasture 2 leagues long and 8 furlongs wide. (There is) wood(land) 1 league long and 8 furlongs wide. Of the same land Brictuin holds 4 hides of the abbot and there he has 4 ploughs. He held this likewise T.R.E. and he could not leave the church, nor can he. The demesne of the church was and is worth £21. (The land of) Brictuin (is worth) 100*s*.

[83] Now represented by Colway Lane Estate in Lyme Regis.

[84] 'Arundel' interlined.

THE LAND OF THE CHURCH OF ST. PETER OF CERNE IN DORSET

(xxxix) The abbot has 1 manor which is called Cernelium and it paid geld T.R.E. for 22 hides. Twenty ploughs can plough these. Of these the abbot has 3 hides and 3 ploughs in demesne and the villeins 15 hides and 14 ploughs. There the abbot has 26 villeins and 32 bordars and 5 serfs and 3 pack-horses and 6 beasts and 14 pigs and 500 sheep and 1 mill which renders 20*s*. and 1 league of wood(land) in length and 8 furlongs in width and 20 acres of meadow and 2 leagues of pasture in length and 8 furlongs in width. This manor renders £21 for the use of the church and when the abbot received it it was worth as much. Of these 22 hides a certain thegn called Brictuin holds 4 hides of thegnland (*taiglanda*) of the abbot and he could not leave the church on the day when King Edward was alive and dead, nor can he now. There Brictuin has 4 ploughs. And this land renders 100*s*. a year. And this thegn renders 30*s*. a year to the church, by which (it is) the less (*quo minus*) except service.

(77) The church itself holds LITELPIDRE [Little Puddle in Piddlehinton]. William (holds it) of the abbot. T.R.E. it paid geld for 3½ hides. There is land for 2 ploughs. In demesne there is 1 plough and 2 serfs and 1 villein and 3 bordars with ½ plough. There (are) 4 acres of meadow. (There is) pasture 2 furlongs long and 1 furlong wide. It was and is worth 50*s*.

(xl) The abbot has 1 manor which is called Litelpidra which paid geld T.R.E. for 3½ hides. Two ploughs can plough these. And now William *de monasterio* holds it of the abbot. And it is the church's own land (*et est de propria terra ecclesie*). Of this William has 3 hides and 1½ plough in demesne and the villeins ½ hide and ½ plough. There William has 1 villein and 4 bordars and 2 serfs and 2 cows and 160 sheep and 4 acres of meadow and 2 furlongs of pasture in length and 1 in width. This manor renders 50*s*. and when William received (it) it was worth as much.

(78) The church itself holds RETPOLE [Radipole in Weymouth]. T.R.E. it paid geld for 3 hides. There is land for 3 ploughs. Of this half is in demesne and there (is) 1 plough with 1 serf and 1 villein and 5 bordars having 2 ploughs. There (is) 10 acres of meadow and 5 furlongs of pasture. It is worth 40*s*.

(xli) The abbot has 1 manor which is called Retpola, which paid geld T.R.E. for 3 hides. Three ploughs can plough these. Thence the abbot has 1½ hide and 1 plough in demesne and the villeins 1½ hide and 2 ploughs. There he has 1 villein and 5 bordars and 1 serf and 1 pack-horse and 20 pigs and 100 sheep and 10 acres of meadow and 5 furlongs of pasture and it renders 40*s*. a year.

(79) The church itself holds BLOCHESHORDE [Bloxworth]. T.R.E. it paid geld for 5½ hides.[85] There is land for 6 ploughs. Of this there are in demesne 2 hides and there (are) 2 ploughs and 3 serfs and 13 villeins and 9 bordars and 7 cottars with 4½ ploughs. There (are) 8 acres of meadow and 8 acres of wood(land) and 8 furlongs of pasture in length and as much in width. It is worth £7 10*s*.

(xlii) The abbot has 1 manor which is called Blochesborda which paid geld T.R.E. for 5½ hides. Six ploughs can plough these. Thence the abbot has 2 hides and 2 ploughs in demesne and the villeins 3½ hides and 4½ ploughs. There the abbot has 13[86] villeins and 9[87] bordars and 7 cottars[88] and 3 serfs and 1 pack-horse and 17 pigs and 26 pigs (*sic*) and 8 acres of wood(land) and 8 acres of meadow and 8 furlongs of pasture in length and as much in width and it renders £7 10*s*. a year.

(80) The church itself holds AFFAPIDELE [Affpuddle]. T.R.E. it paid geld for 9 hides. There is land for 6 ploughs. Of this there are in demesne 4 hides and there (are) 2 ploughs and 3 serfs and 6 villeins and 4 bordars with 4 ploughs. There (are) 2 mills rendering 15*s*. and 55 acres of meadow. (There is) pasture 12 furlongs long and 6 furlongs wide. (There is) wood(land) 7 furlongs long and as much—[*blank*].[89]

(xliii) The abbot has 1 manor which is called Affapidela which paid geld for 9 hides T.R.E. Six ploughs can plough these. There the abbot has 4 hides and 2 ploughs in demesne[90] and the villeins 5 hides and 4 ploughs and there are[91] 6 villeins and 4 bordars and 5 cottars and 3 serfs. There the abbot has 9 oxen (*boves*) and 12 sheep and 1 pack-horse and 12 pigs and 2 mills which render 15*s*. a year and 7 furlongs of wood(land) in length and as much in width and 12 furlongs of pasture in length and 6 in width and 55 acres[92] of meadow. This manor renders £7 10*s*. a year,—[*blank*] and when the abbot received (them) the aforesaid 2 manors [? Bloxworth and Affpuddle] were worth 100*s*. more because they were devastated on account of Hugh fitz Grip (*et quando abbas recepit valebant c solidos plus predicte due mansiones quia pro Hugone filio Grip fuerunt depredati* (sic)).[93]

[f. 78]

(81) The church itself holds POCHESWELLE [Poxwell]. T.R.E. it paid geld for 6 hides. There is land for 7 ploughs. Of this there is in demesne 1½ hide and there (are) 2 ploughs with 1 serf and 4 villeins and 8 bordars with 3 ploughs. There (are) 15 acres of meadow. (There is) pasture 8 furlongs and 26 virgates long and 3 furlongs and 14 perches (*pertice*) wide. Of this same land the wife of Hugh holds 3 hides and there is 1 plough. This land belonged to the demesne farm of the monks and it is worth 40*s*. The church's demesne is worth £7.

(xliv) The abbot has 1 manor which is called Pocheswella which paid geld T.R.E. for 6 hides. Seven ploughs can plough these. Thence the abbot has 1½ hide and 2 ploughs in demesne and the villeins 1½ hide and 3 ploughs and the wife of

[85] 'et dimidia' interlined.

[86] 'ii' interlined.

[87] The MS. has *viiii*, the printed version *viii*.

[88] 'et vii cotarios' interlined.

[89] The text breaks off at this point, presumably because the Exchequer scribe could not understand the end of the parallel entry in Exon. Domesday: see n. 93 below.

[90] 'in dominio' interlined.

[91] 'ibi sunt' interlined.

[92] 'agros' interlined.

[93] There are traces of 2 or 3 words erased in the MS. before *et quando abbas*, but they cannot be made out and the sense of the sentence substituted for them is very confused.

Hugh fitz Grip has there 3 hides which belonged to the demesne farm of the monks on the day when King Edward was alive and dead. Now Roger Bissell holds them of the wife of Hugh and he has there 1 plough. He has there 4 villeins and 8 bordars and 1 serf and 1 pack-horse and 6 pigs and 200 sheep and 15 acres of meadow and 8 furlongs of pasture and 26 virgates in length and 3 furlongs and 14 perches in width. This vill is worth £7 for the use of the abbot and 40*s.* for the use of Roger Bissell.

(82) The church itself holds WERDESFORD [Woodsford]. T.R.E. it paid geld for 2½ hides. There is land for 2 ploughs which are there with 4 villeins and 3 bordars and 5 serfs. It is worth 30*s.*

(xlv) The abbot has 1 manor which is called Werdesfort which paid geld T.R.E. for 2½ hides. Two ploughs can plough these. Bristuin[94] has this (manor) at farm of the abbot and he has there 2 ploughs (and) 4 villeins and 3 bordars and 5 serfs and 4 pigs[95] and it renders 30*s.*

(83) The church itself holds 3 virgates of land in ELFATUNE [Hethfelton in East Stoke]. They were and are worth 5*s.*

(xlvi) The abbot has 3 virgates of land which is called[96] Aelfatune which were worth 5*s.* when the abbot received them and now render the same (amount).

(84) The church itself holds 1 hide of land in VERGROH [Worgret in Arne] and it paid geld for that amount T.R.E. There are 2 serfs and ½ mill and 8 acres of meadow. The whole is worth 15*s.*

(xlvii) The abbot has 1 hide which is called Vergroh which paid geld for 1 hide T.R.E. There are 2 serfs and 8 acres of meadow[97] and the abbot has there ½ mill and this land with the ½ mill renders 15*s.* a year.

(85) The church itself holds LITELBRIDE [Littlebredy]. T.R.E. it paid geld for 11 hides. There is land for 6 ploughs. Of this there are in demesne 5 hides and there (are) 2 ploughs and 5 serfs and 6 villeins and 5 bordars with 6 ploughs. There (are) 12 acres of meadow. (There is) pasture 1 league long and another in width. (There is) wood(land) 1 league long and 2 furlongs wide. It was and is worth £16.

(xlviii) The abbot has 1 manor which is called Litelbrida which paid geld T.R.E. for 11 hides. Six ploughs can plough these. Thence the abbot has 5 hides and 2 ploughs in demesne and the villeins 6 hides and 6 ploughs. The abbot has there 6 villeins and 5 bordars and 5 serfs and 12 pigs and 550 sheep and 1 league of wood(land) in length and 2 furlongs in width and 12 acres of meadow and 1 league of pasture in length and another in width. This manor renders £16 and it was worth as much[98] in the time of Abbot E.[99]

(86) The church itself holds WINTREBURNE [Winterbourne Abbas]. T.R.E. it paid geld for 10 hides. There is land for 10 ploughs. Of this there are in demesne 5 hides and there (are) 4 ploughs and 3 serfs and 10 villeins and 7 coscets with 3 ploughs. There (are) 20 acres of meadow. (There is) pasture 11 furlongs long and 10 furlongs wide. (There is) wood(land) 2 furlongs long and 1 furlong wide. It was and is worth £16.

(xlix) The abbot has 1 manor which is called Wintreborna and it paid geld T.R.E. for 10 hides and 10 ploughs can plough these each year. Of these the abbot has in demesne 5 hides and the villeins have 5 hides. There he has 4 ploughs in demesne and the villeins have 3 ploughs. The abbot has there 10 villeins and 7 coscets and 3 serfs and 12 pigs and 116 sheep and 18 goats and 2 furlongs of wood(land) in length and 1 furlong in width and 20 acres of meadow and 11 furlongs of pasture in length and 10 furlongs in width. This manor was worth £16 when the abbot received it and now it renders as much.[1]

(87) The church itself holds LANGEBRIDE [Long Bredy]. T.R.E. it paid geld for 9 hides. There is land for 9 ploughs. Of this there are in demesne 3 hides and there (are) 3 ploughs and 3 serfs and 7 villeins and 9 coscets with 5 ploughs and 1 thegn has 1 hide and there (is) 1 plough. There (is) a mill rendering 6*s.* and 11 acres of meadow. (There is) pasture 1 league long and as much in width. (There is) wood(land) ½ league long and 3 furlongs wide. The whole is worth £22.

(l) The abbot has 1 manor which is called Langebridia which paid geld T.R.E. for 9 hides. Of these the abbot has in demesne 3 hides and 3 ploughs and the villeins have 5 hides and 1 English thegn has 1 hide. The peasants (*rustici*) have 5 ploughs and the thegn has 1 plough. The abbot has 7 villeins and 9 coscets and 3 serfs and 1 pack-horse and 15[2] pigs and 353 sheep and 20 goats and 1 mill which renders 6*s.* a year and ½ league of wood(land) in length and 3 furlongs in width and 11 acres of meadow and 1 league of pasture in length and 1 league of pasture in width. This manor renders £16 for the use of the abbot and £3 for the use of the thegns (*sic*).

(88) The church itself holds NETELCOME [Nettlecombe in Powerstock]. T.R.E. it paid geld for 5 hides. There is land (for)—[*blank*].[3] Of this there is in demesne 1½ hide and ½ virgate of land, and there (is) 1 plough and 2 serfs and 5 villeins and 7 coscets with 2 ploughs. There (are) 10 acres of meadow. (There is) pasture 1 league long and 4 furlongs wide. (There is) wood(land) 1 league long and 8 furlongs wide. Of the same land 1 knight holds 2 hides.[4] It was worth £12. Now (it is worth) £8 to the abbot (and) 55*s.* to the knight.

(li) The abbot has 1 manor which is called Netelcoma and it paid geld T.R.E. for 5 hides. Of these the abbot has in demesne 1½ hide and ½ virgate and 1 plough and the villeins have 1 hide and 1½ virgate and 2½ ploughs, and 1 French knight has 2 hides of thegnland (*teinland*) which

[94] The MS. has *Bristuin(us)*, the printed version *Bristuan(us)*.

[95] 'iiii villanos et iii bordarios et v servos et iiii porcos et' interlined.

[96] 'vo' of *vocatur* interlined.

[97] 'et viii agri prati' interlined.

[98] 'tantundem' interlined.

[99] It has not been possible to trace Abbot E. of Cerne.

[1] 'reddit tantundem' interlined.

[2] 'v' interlined.

[3] Space in the text. For a comment, see p. 4.

[4] 'De eadem terra tenet unus miles ii hidas' added in the margin.

could not be separated from the church and 2 ploughs. The abbot has there 5 villeins and 7 coscets and 2 serfs and 25 sheep and 5 goats and 10 acres of meadow and 1 league of wood(land) in length and 8 furlongs in width, and this wood bears no fruit (*nullum fructum fert*) and 1 league of pasture in length and 4 furlongs in width. This manor renders £8 to the abbot and 55*s.* to the aforesaid knight and when the abbot received (it) it was worth 20*s.* more.

(89) The church itself holds MIDELTONE [West Milton in Powerstock]. T.R.E. it paid geld for 4 hides. There is land for 4 ploughs. Of this there are in demesne 2 hides and there (is) 1 plough and 2 serfs and 5 villeins and 13 bordars with 5 ploughs. There (is) a mill rendering 65*d.* and 16 acres of meadow. (There is) pasture 1 league long and 4 furlongs wide. (There is) wood(land) 3 furlongs long and 2 furlongs wide. It was worth £10. Now (it is worth) £9.

(lii) The abbot has 1 manor which is called Mideltona which paid geld for 4 hides on the day when King Edward was alive and dead. There the abbot has in demesne 2 hides and 1 plough and the villeins 2 hides and 3 ploughs. Four ploughs can plough these 4 hides. There the abbot has 5 villeins and 13 bordars and 2 serfs and 16 sheep and 5 goats and 1 mill which renders 5*s.* 5*d.* and 3 furlongs of wood(land) in length and 2 in width and 16 acres of meadow and 1 league of pasture in[5] length and 4 furlongs in width. This (manor) renders £9 and when he received (it) it was worth 20*s.* more.

(90) The church itself holds CAMERIC [Kimmeridge]. T.R.E. it paid geld for 5 hides. There is land for 4 ploughs. Of this there are in demesne 3 hides less 1½ virgate and there (are) 2 ploughs with 1 serf and 2 villeins and 8 bordars with 2 ploughs. There (are) 8 acres of meadow. (There is) pasture 6 furlongs long and 2 furlongs wide. It was and is worth £8.

(liii) The abbot has 1 manor which is called Cameric which paid geld T.R.E. for 5 hides. Four ploughs can plough these. Thence the abbot has 3 hides less 1½ virgate in demesne and 2 ploughs and the villeins 2 hides and 1½ virgate and 2 ploughs. There the abbot has 2 villeins and 8 bordars and 1 serf and 1 pack-horse and 2 cows and 16 pigs and 250 sheep and 18 acres of meadow and 6 furlongs of pasture in length and 2 in width and it renders £8 a year and when the abbot received (it) it was worth as much.

(91) The church itself holds ROMESCUMBE [Renscombe (Farm) in Worth Matravers]. T.R.E. it paid geld for 5 hides and 1 virgate of land. There is land for 6 ploughs. Of this there are in demesne 2 hides and 3 virgates of land and there (are) 2 ploughs and 3 serfs and 7 villeins and 7 bordars—[*blank*].[6] There (are) 12 acres of meadow. (There is) pasture 1 league long and 10 furlongs wide. (There is) wood(land) which does not bear fruit (*infructuosa*) 5 furlongs long and 1 furlong wide. It was and is worth £8.

(liv) The abbot has 1 manor which is called Romescumba which paid geld T.R.E. for 5 hides and 1 virgate. Six ploughs can plough these. Thence the abbot has 2 hides and 3 virgates and 2 ploughs in demesne and the villeins 3 hides and 1 virgate. There he has 7 villeins and 7 bordars and 3 serfs and 1 pack-horse and 2 cows and 12 pigs and 250 sheep (*berbices*) and 8 goats and 5 furlongs of wood(land), which does not bear fruit (*infructuosi*), in length and 1 in width and 12 acres of meadow and 1 league of pasture in length and 10 furlongs in width. This manor renders £8 and when Abbot W.[7] received (it) it was worth as much.

(92) The church itself holds SIMONDESBERGE [Symondsbury]. T.R.E. it paid geld for 19 hides. There is land for 20 ploughs. Of this there are in demesne 5 hides and there (are) 2 ploughs with 1 serf and 20 villeins and 10 bordars with 14 ploughs. There (are) 14 acres of meadow. (There is) pasture 5 furlongs long and 1 furlong, less 10 virgates, wide. (There is) woodland ½ league long and 1 furlong wide. It was and is worth £21.

(lv) The abbot has 1 manor which is called Simondesberga which paid geld T.R.E. for 19 hides. Twenty ploughs can plough these. Thence the abbot has 5 hides and 2 ploughs in demesne and the villeins 14 hides and 14 ploughs. There the abbot has 20 villeins and 10 bordars and 1 serf and 1 pack-horse and 100 sheep and 12 goats and ½ league of wood(land) in length and 1 furlong in width and 14 acres of meadow and 5 furlongs of pasture in length and 1 furlong in width, less 10 virgates. This (manor) renders £21 a year and when the abbot received (it) it was worth as much.[8]

XII. THE LAND OF THE ABBEY OF MILTON

(93) The church of Milton holds SIDELINCE [Sydling St. Nicholas]. T.R.E. it paid geld for 29 hides. There is land for 20 ploughs. Of this there are in demesne 6 hides and there (are) 2 ploughs and 6 serfs and 25 villeins and 10 bordars with 13 ploughs. There (are) 2 mills rendering 7*s.* 6*d.* and 12 acres of meadow. (There is) pasture 2½ leagues long and 6 furlongs wide. (There is) wood(land) 1 league long and as much in width. It is worth £25.

THE LAND OF THE CHURCH OF ST. PETER OF MILTON IN DORSET

(lxvii) The abbot has 1 manor which is called Sidelincea. This (manor) paid geld T.R.E. for 29 hides. Twenty ploughs can plough these. Of these the abbot has 6 hides and 2 ploughs in demesne and the villeins 23 hides and 13 ploughs. There the abbot has 25 villeins and 10 bordars and 6 serfs and 3 pack-horses and 10 beasts and 250 sheep and 2 mills which render 7*s.* 6*d.* a year and 1 league of wood(land) in length and as much in width and 12 acres of meadow and 2½ leagues of pasture in length and 6 furlongs in width. This manor is worth £25 a year.

[5] 'in' interlined.

[6] Space in the text. For a comment, see p. 4.

[7] A certain William, Abbot of Cerne, is said to have been present at the Council of Gloucester in 1085 by the compiler of the Chronicle of Lanercost: B.M. Cott. MS. Claud. D. vii, f. 53v, cited in Dugdale, *Mon.* ii. 623.

[8] 'tantundem' interlined.

(94) The church itself holds MIDELTUNE [Milton Abbas], and it is the chief (manor) of the abbey (*caput abbatie*). T.R.E. it paid geld for 24 hides. There is land for 18 ploughs. Of this there are in demesne 10 hides less 1 virgate and there (are) 2 ploughs and 6 serfs and 26 villeins and 20 bordars with 13 ploughs. There (is) a mill rendering 15*s.* and 40 acres of meadow. (There is) pasture 3 leagues long and 1 league wide. It is worth £20.

(lxxiv) The abbot has 1 manor which is called Miteltona and it is the chief (manor) of the abbey. It paid geld T.R.E. for 24 hides. Eighteen ploughs can plough this land. Of these the abbot has 10 hides less 1 virgate and 2 ploughs in demesne. And the villeins (have) 14 hides and 1 virgate and 13 ploughs. There the abbot has 27 villeins and 20 bordars and 6 serfs and 2 pack-horses and 20 pigs and 450 sheep and 50 goats and 1 mill which renders 15*s.* and 40 acres of meadow and 3 leagues of pasture in length and 1 league in width. This manor is worth £20 a year.

(95) The church itself holds CONTONE [Compton Abbas (West) or West Compton]. T.R.E. it paid geld for 5 hides. There is land for 3 ploughs. Of this there are in demesne 3 hides and there (is) 1 plough and 3 serfs and 6 villeins and 5 bordars. There (are) 10 acres of meadow and pasture 1 league long and 2 furlongs wide. It is worth £4.

(lxviii) The abbot has 1 manor which is called Contona. This (manor) paid geld T.R.E. for 5 hides. Three ploughs can plough these hides. Of these the abbot has 3 hides and 1 plough in demesne and the villeins 2 hides and 2 ploughs. There the abbot has 6 villeins and 5 bordars and 3 serfs and 1 pack-horse and 150 sheep and 10 acres of meadow and 1 league of pasture in length and 2 furlongs in width. This manor is worth £4 a year.

(96) The church itself holds STOCHE [Cattistock]. T.R.E. it paid geld for 10 hides. There is land for 6 ploughs. Of this there are in demesne 3 hides and there (is) 1 plough and 6 serfs and 12 villeins and 5 bordars with 5 ploughs. There (is) a mill rendering 15*d.* and 18 acres of meadow. (There is) pasture 1 league long and 2 furlongs wide. (There is) wood(land) 6 furlongs long and 4 furlongs wide. It is worth £6.

(lxix) The abbot has 1 manor which is called Estocha. This (manor) paid geld T.R.E. for 10 hides. Six ploughs can plough these. Of these the abbot has 3 hides and 1 plough in demesne. And the villeins (have) 7 hides and 5 ploughs. There the abbot has 12 villeins and 5 bordars and 6 serfs and 2 pack-horses and 14 pigs and 150 sheep and 1 mill which renders 15*d.* and 6 furlongs of wood(land) in length and 4 in width and 18 acres of meadow and 1 league of pasture in length and 2 furlongs in width. This manor is worth £6 a year.

(97) The church itself holds PIDELE [Burleston]. T.R.E. it paid geld for 3 hides. There is land for 2 ploughs. Of this there are in demesne 2½ hides and there (are) 2 ploughs and 4 serfs and 5 bordars. There (is) a mill rendering 40*d.* and 16 acres of meadow. It is worth 40*s.*

(lxx) The abbot has 1 manor which is called Pidela which paid geld for 3 hides on the day when King Edward was alive and dead. Two ploughs can plough these. There the abbot has 2½ hides and 2 ploughs in demesne and the villeins ½ hide. There the abbot has 5 bordars and 4 serfs and 1 pack-horse and 3 beasts and 115 sheep and 1 mill which renders 40*d.* a year and 16 acres of meadow. This manor is worth 40*s.* a year.

(98) The church itself holds CLIVE [Clyffe (Farm) in Tincleton]. T.R.E. it paid geld for 2 hides. There is land for 2 ploughs. There are 5 villeins. It is worth 20*s.*

(lxxi) The abbot has another manor which is called Clive which paid geld for 2 hides on the day when King Edward was alive and dead. Two ploughs can plough these. The villeins hold these and there are 5 villeins. This manor is worth 20*s.* a year.

(99) The church itself holds OSMENTONE [Osmington]. T.R.E. it paid geld for 10 hides. There is land for 10 ploughs. Of this there are in demesne 4 hides and there (are) 2 ploughs and 3 serfs and 16 villeins and 7 bordars with 6 ploughs. There (is) a mill rendering 5*s.* and 5 acres of meadow and 1 league of pasture. It is worth £8.

(lxxii) The abbot has 1 manor which is called Osmentona which paid geld T.R.E. for 10 hides. Ten ploughs can plough these. Thence the abbot has 4 hides and 2 ploughs in demesne and the villeins 6 hides and 6 ploughs. There the abbot has 16 villeins and 7 bordars and 3 serfs and 2 pack-horses and 3 pigs and 127 sheep and 1 mill which is worth 5*s.* a year and 5 acres of meadow and 1 league of pasture and it is worth £8 a year.

(100) The church itself holds WIDECOME [Whitcombe]. T.R.E. it paid geld for 6 hides. There is land for 6 ploughs. Of this there are in demesne 4 hides and there (is) 1 plough and 2 serfs and 7 villeins and 5 bordars with 3 ploughs. There (are) 5 acres of meadow and pasture 13 furlongs long and 2 furlongs wide. It is worth £4 10*s.*

(lxxiii) The abbot has 1 manor which is called Widecoma which paid geld T.R.E. for 6 hides. Six ploughs can plough these. Thence the abbot has 4 hides and 1 plough in demesne and the villeins 2 hides and 3 ploughs. There the abbot has 7 villeins and 5 bordars and 2 serfs and 1 pack-horse and 86 sheep and 5 acres of meadow and 13 furlongs of pasture in length and 2 furlongs in width and it is worth £4 10*s.* a year.

(101) The church itself holds LISCOME [Lyscombe (Farm) in Cheselbourne]. T.R.E. it paid geld for 3 hides. There is land for 2 ploughs. Of this there are in demesne 2 hides and there (is) 1 plough and 2 serfs and 3 villeins and 5 bordars with 1 plough. There (is) pasture 6 furlongs long and 3 furlongs wide. It is worth 40*s.*

(lxxv) The abbot has 1 manor which is called Liscoma which paid geld T.R.E. for 3 hides. Two ploughs can (plough) these. Of these the abbot has 2 hides and 1 plough in demesne and the villeins 1 hide and 1 plough. There the abbot has 3 villeins and 5 bordars and 2 serfs and 1 cow and 3 pigs and 50 sheep and 6 furlongs of pasture in length and 3 in width. This manor is worth 40*s.* a year.

(102) The church itself holds WINLANDE [Woolland]. T.R.E. it paid geld for 5 hides. There is land for 4 ploughs. Of this there are in demesne 2 hides and there (is) 1 plough and 3 serfs and 5 villeins and 5 bordars with 2 ploughs. There (are) 8 acres of meadow. (There is) wood(land) 7 furlongs long and 4 furlongs wide. It is worth 60*s*.

(lxxvi) The abbot has 1 manor which is called Winlanda which paid geld T.R.E. for 5 hides. Four ploughs can plough these. Of these the abbot has 2 hides and 1 plough in demesne and the villeins 3 hides and 2 ploughs. There the abbot has 5 villeins and 5 bordars and 3 serfs and 1 pack-horse and 8 pigs and 60 sheep and 16 goats and 7 furlongs of wood(land) in length and 4 in width and 8 acres of meadow. This (manor) is worth 60*s*. a year.

(103) The church itself holds WINTREBURNE [unidentified]. T.R.E. it paid geld for 2 hides and 1 virgate of land. There is land for 1½ plough. Of this there is in demesne 1 hide and there (is) 1 plough with 1 serf and 2 bordars. There (are) 6 acres of meadow and 10 acres of pasture. It is worth 25*s*.

(lxxvii) The abbot has 1 manor which is called Wintreborna which paid geld T.R.E. for 2 hides and 1 virgate and it can be ploughed with 1½ plough. Thence the abbot has 1 hide and 1 plough in demesne and the villeins 1 hide and 1 virgate. There the abbot has 2 bordars and 1 serf and 6 acres of meadow and 10 acres of pasture. This (manor) is worth 25*s*. a year.

(104) The church itself holds HOLVERDE [Holworth in Owermoigne]. T.R.E. it paid geld for 5 hides. There is land for 5 ploughs. Of this there are in demesne 3 hides and there (are) 2 ploughs and 4 serfs and 4 villeins and 5 coscets with 2 ploughs. There (are) 3 acres of meadow and pasture 5 furlongs long and the same in width. It is worth £3 and a sester (*sextarium*) of honey.

(lxxviii) The abbot has 1 manor which is called Holverda. This (manor) paid geld for 5 hides on the day when King Edward was alive and dead. Five ploughs can plough these. Of these the abbot has in demesne 3 hides and 2 ploughs and the villeins 2 hides and 2 ploughs. There the abbot has 4 villeins and 5 coscets and 4 serfs and 1 pack-horse and 4 cows and 224 sheep and 3 acres of meadow and 5 furlongs of pasture in length and the same in width and it is worth 60*s*. and 1 sester of honey a year.

(105) The church itself holds ORA [Ower (Farm) in Corfe Castle]. T.R.E. it paid geld for 3 hides. There are no ploughs but 13 salt-workers render 20*s*.

(lxxix) The abbot has 1 manor which is called Ora and it paid geld for 3 hides T.R.E. In these there is no plough, neither can it be ploughed. But there are 13 salt-workers and they render 20*s*. a year.

(106) The church itself holds ERTACOMESTOCHE [Stockland, Devon] and Hervey (holds it) of the abbot. T.R.E. it paid geld for 10 hides. There is land for 16 ploughs. Of this there are in demesne 4 hides and there (are) 2 ploughs and 4 serfs and 40 villeins have 20 ploughs. There (are) 3 mills rendering 37*d*. and 23 acres of meadow. (There is) wood(land) 13 furlongs long and 12 wide. It is worth £9. This manor always belonged to the monks' demesne for their food and clothing.

(lxxx) The abbot has 1 manor which is called Ertacomestoca. This (manor) paid geld for 10 hides T.R.E. which 16 ploughs can plough. Of these the abbot has in demesne 4 hides and 2 ploughs and the villeins 6 hides and 20 ploughs. There the abbot has 40 villeins and 4 serfs and 4 beasts and 7 pigs and 20 goats and 3 mills which render 37*d*. a year and 13 furlongs of wood(land) in length and 12 in width and 23 acres of meadow and it is worth £9 a year. Hervey fitz Ansger holds this manor of the abbot and this manor was always for the food and clothing of the monks and always[9] belonged to the demesne farm T.R.E.

(107) The church itself holds PIDRE [Little Puddle in Piddlehinton]. T.R.E. it paid geld for 2 hides. There is land for 1 plough which is there and 12 acres of meadow and 2 acres of wood(land). (There is) pasture 1 league long and 3 furlongs wide. It is worth 10*s*.

(lxxxi) The abbot has 1 manor which is called Pidra. This (manor) paid geld for 2 hides T.R.E. which 1 plough can plough. There the abbot has 1 plough and 5 beasts and 2 acres of wood(land) and 12 acres of meadow and 1 league of pasture in length and 3 furlongs in width and it is worth 10*s*. a year. This (manor) belongs to the demesne farm of the abbot.

(108) The church itself holds CERNE [unidentified] and Aiulf (holds it) of the abbot. T.R.E. it paid geld for 1½ hide. There is land for 2 ploughs. Of this there is in demesne 1 hide and 1 virgate less 5 acres[10] and there (is) 1 plough. There are 5 bordars and a mill rendering 20*d*. and 13 acres of meadow and 19 acres of pasture. It was worth 10*s*. Now (it is worth) 25*s*. He who held (it) T.R.E. could not be separated from the church.

(lxxxii) The abbot has 1 manor which is called Cerna which Edric held T.R.E. and he could not be separated from the service of the church. This (manor) paid geld for 1½ hide. Two ploughs can plough this. Now Aiulf holds it of the abbot. Of these (*sic*) Aiulf has in demesne 1 hide and 1 virgate less 5 acres[11] and 1 plough and the bordars have 1 virgate and 5 acres. There Aiulf has 7 bordars and 1 mill which renders 25*d*.[12] a year and 12 beasts and 2 pigs and 65 sheep and 13 acres of meadow and 19 acres of pasture and it is worth 25*s*. a year (and) when Aiulf received (it) it was worth 10*s*.

XIII. THE LAND OF THE ABBEY OF ABBOTSBURY

(109) The church of Abbotsbury holds ABEDESBERIE [Abbotsbury]. T.R.E. it paid geld for 21 hides. There is land for 16 ploughs. Of this there are in demesne 8 hides and there (are) 5 ploughs and 14

[9] 'semper' interlined.

[10] 'v acras minus' added at the end of the line.

[11] 'v agros minus' interlined.

[12] 'v' interlined.

serfs and 32 villeins and 16 bordars with 16 ploughs. There (are) 2 mills rendering 16*s.* 3*d.* and 36 acres of meadow. (There is) pasture 27 furlongs long and 1 league and 3 furlongs wide. (There are) 8 furlongs of wood(land). It is worth £26. To this manor belongs 1 hide. T.R.E. it was for the food of the monks. Hugh unlawfully took this and kept (it) and his wife still retains (it) by force.

THE LAND OF THE CHURCH OF ST. PETER OF ABBOTSBURY IN DORSET

(lviii) The abbot has 1 manor which is called Abbatesberia which paid geld T.R.E. for 21 hides. Sixteen ploughs can plough these. Thence the abbot has 8 hides and 5 ploughs in demesne and the villeins 23 hides and 16[13] ploughs. There the abbot has 32[14] villeins and 16 bordars and 14 serfs and 4 pack-horses and 23 beasts and 30 pigs and 600 sheep and 2 mills which render 16*s.* 3*d.* and 8 furlongs of wood(land) and 36 acres of meadow and 27 furlongs of pasture in length and 1 league and 3 furlongs in width. This manor is worth £26 a year and in this manor lies 1 hide of land which on the day of King Edward's death was for the food of the monks and Hugh fitz Grip unlawfully took it and his wife still retains (it) by force.[15]

[f. 78b]

(110) The church itself holds PIDELE [Tolpuddle]. T.R.E. it paid geld for 18 hides. There is land for 12 ploughs. Of this there are in demesne 8 hides and there (are) 3 ploughs and 4 serfs and 16 villeins and 14 coscets with 5 ploughs. There (are) 2 mills rendering 20*s.* and 6 furlongs of meadow and 18 furlongs of pasture. It is worth £12.

(lvi) The abbot has 1 manor which is called Pidela which paid geld T.R.E. for 18 hides. Twelve ploughs can plough these. Of these the abbot has in demesne 8 hides and the villeins ten. There the abbot has 3 ploughs and the villeins five. There the abbot has 16 villeins and 14 cotsets and 4 serfs and 2 pack-horses and 10 beasts and 20 pigs and 300 sheep and 2 mills which render 20*s.* a year and 6 furlongs of meadow and 18 furlongs of pasture and this (manor) is worth £12 a year.

(111) The church itself holds ELTONE [Hilton]. T.R.E. it paid geld for 18 hides. There is land for 10 ploughs. Of this there are in demesne 9 hides and 1 virgate of land and there (are) 3 ploughs and 8 serfs and 17 villeins and 12 bordars with 7 ploughs. There (is) a mill rendering 20*d.* and 10 acres of meadow. (There is) pasture 1 league long and ½ league wide. (There are) 3 furlongs of wood(land). It is worth £15.

(lvii) The abbot has 1 manor which is called Heltona which paid geld T.R.E. for 18 hides. Ten ploughs can plough these. Of these the abbot has 9 hides and 1 virgate and 3 ploughs in demesne and the villeins 9 hides less 1 virgate and 7 ploughs. There the abbot has 17 villeins and 12 bordars and 8 serfs and 3 pack-horses and 8 beasts and 20 pigs and 406 sheep and 25 goats and 1 mill which renders 20*d.* and 3 furlongs of wood(land) and 10 acres of meadow and 1 league of pasture in length and ½ (league) in width. This manor is worth £15 a year.

(112) The church itself holds PORTESHAM [Portesham]. T.R.E. it paid geld for 12 hides. There is land for 9 ploughs. Of this there are in demesne 5 hides and there (are) 4 ploughs and 12 serfs and 12 villeins and 10 bordars with 5 ploughs. There is a mill rendering 10*s.* and 24 acres of meadow. (There is) pasture 1 league long and 2 furlongs wide. It is worth £12. To this manor belongs 1 virgate which Hugh fitz Grip[16] unlawfully took and which his wife still holds by force.[17] This was for the food of the monks T.R.E.

(lix) The abbot has 1 manor which is called Portesham which paid geld T.R.E. for 12 hides. Nine ploughs can plough these. Thence the abbot has 5 hides and 4 ploughs in demesne and the villeins 7 hides and 5 ploughs. There the abbot has 12 villeins and 10 bordars and 12 serfs and 3 pack-horses and 13 beasts and 20 pigs and 250 sheep and 1 mill which renders 10*s.* and 24 acres of meadow and 1 league of pasture in length and 2 furlongs in width. This (manor) is worth £12 a year. And to this manor belongs 1 virgate of land which on the day of King Edward's death was for the food of the monks and Hugh fitz Grip unlawfully took it and his wife still retains it by force.

(113) The church itself holds SEVEMETONE [Shilvinghampton in Portesham]. T.R.E. it paid geld for 5 virgates of land. There is land for 1 plough which is there with 1 serf and 1 bordar. There (are) 6 acres of meadow and 3 furlongs of pasture. It is worth 15*s.* 6*d.*

(lx) The abbot has 1 manor which is called Sefemetona which paid geld T.R.E. for 5 virgates which 1 plough can plough. And now Bollo the priest holds it of the abbot and he cannot withdraw from the church with this land. There Bollo has 1 plough in demesne. And he has there 1 bordar and 1 serf and 100 sheep and 6 acres of meadow and 3 furlongs of pasture. This (manor) is worth 15*s.* 6*d.* a year.

(114) The church itself holds WIDETONE [Abbott's Wootton (Farms, Higher and Lower) in Whitchurch Canonicorum]. T.R.E. it paid geld for 2½ hides. There is land for 4 ploughs. Of this there is 1 hide in demesne and there (are) 2 ploughs and 4 serfs and 4 villeins with 2 ploughs. There (are) 5 acres of meadow and 3 furlongs of pasture and 3 furlongs of wood(land). It is worth 40*s.*

(lxi) The abbot has 1 manor which is called Widetona which paid geld T.R.E. for 2½ hides. Four ploughs can plough these. Thence the abbot has 1 hide and 2 ploughs in demesne and the villeins 1½ hide and 2 ploughs. There the abbot has 4 villeins and 4 serfs and 1 pack-horse and 4 beasts and 100 sheep and 20 goats and 3 furlongs of wood(land) and 5 acres of meadow and 3 furlongs of pasture. This (manor) is worth 40*s.* a year.

(115) The church itself holds ½ hide in BOURTONE [Burcombe (Farm) in North Poorton]. There is

[13] 'v' interlined.

[14] 'x' interlined.

[15] 'et in ista mansione pertinet i hida terre que die obitus regis Edwardi erat in victum monachorum et Hugo filius Gripponis iniuste sibi accepit et adhuc uxor sua vi detinet' interlined.

[16] 'filius Grip' interlined.

[17] 'vi' interlined.

land for 1 plough. Two villeins have this (plough) there and (there are) 3 furlongs of wood(land). It is worth 10*s*.

(lxii) The abbot has ½ hide of land in Bourtona and it can be ploughed by 1 plough. There the abbot has 2 villeins who hold this land and they have there 1 plough. There he has 3 furlongs of wood(land). This is worth 10*s*. a year.

(116) The church itself holds Atrem [Atrim in Netherbury] and Bollo and 1 widow[18] (hold it) of the abbot. T.R.E. it paid geld for 2 hides. There is land for 2 ploughs which are there, and (there are) 2 serfs and 1 villein and 3 bordars. There (are) 5 acres of meadow and 3 furlongs of wood(land). It is worth 20*s*.

(lxiii) The abbot has 1 manor which is called Atrum which paid geld T.R.E. for 2 hides. Two ploughs can plough these. And now Bollo the priest holds 1 of these 2 hides and a certain widow woman holds the other hide. There Bollo has 1 plough and the above-mentioned widow woman has another plough. There the widow has 1 villein and Bollo has there 3 bordars and 2 serfs and 1 pack-horse and 2 beasts and 20 sheep and 3 furlongs of wood(land) and 5 acres of meadow. This (manor) is worth 20*s*. a year. And these (tenants) cannot be separated from the church with this land.

XIIII. THE LAND OF THE ABBEY OF HORTON

(117) The church of Horton holds Hortune [Horton]. T.R.E. it paid geld for 7 hides. There is land for 7 ploughs. Of this there are in demesne 2 hides and there (are) 2 ploughs and 3 serfs and 4 villeins and 10 bordars with 1 plough. There (are) 2 mills rendering 15*s*. and 6 acres of meadow. (There is) pasture 2 leagues (in) length and width. (There is) wood(land) 1 league long and ½ league wide. It is worth £4. The king holds the best 2 hides of these 7 in the forest of Wimborne. To this church belong 1 chapel (*ecclesiola*) in Wimborne Minster and the land of 2 houses and in Wareham 1 church and 5 houses rendering 65*d*. and in Dorchester 1 house.

XV. THE LAND OF THE ABBEY OF ATHELNEY

(118) The church of Athelney holds Candel [Purse Caundle].[19] T.R.E. it paid geld for 4 hides and 1½ virgate of land. There is land for 4 ploughs. Of this there are in demesne 4 hides and there (is) 1 plough and 2 villeins and 14 bordars with 2 ploughs. There (are) 14 acres of meadow. (There is) wood(land) 3 furlongs long and 2 furlongs wide. Of this land Alvred holds 1½ virgate of land. The whole (manor) is worth 67*s*. 6*d*.

THE LAND OF THE ABBEY OF ATHELNEY IN DORSET

(lxiv) The abbot has 1 manor which is called Candel which 7 thegns held T.R.E. and they could go to any lord, which paid geld for 4 hides and 1½ virgate. Four ploughs can plough these. Of these the abbot has in demesne 4 hides and 1 plough and the villeins 1½ virgate and 2 ploughs. There the abbot has 2 villeins and 14 bordars and 3 furlongs of wood(land) in length and 2 in width and 14 acres of meadow and it is worth 60*s*. a year for the abbot's use and for the use of Alvred the butler (*pincerne*), who holds 1½ virgate of these 4 hides of the abbot, it is worth 7*s*. 6*d*.

XVI. THE LAND OF THE ABBEY OF TAVISTOCK

(119) The church of Tavistock holds Oscherwille [Askerswell]. T.R.E. it paid geld for 3 hides. There is land for 6 ploughs. Of this there is in demesne 1 hide and there (are) 2 ploughs and 4 serfs and 7 villeins and 17 bordars with 4 ploughs. There (are) 2 mills rendering 7*s*. and 9 acres of meadow. (There is) pasture 15 furlongs long and 2 furlongs wide and 2 *censores*[20] rendering 15*s*. It is worth £6.

THE LAND OF THE ABBOT OF TAVISTOCK, NAMED GEOFFREY, IN DORSET

(lxv) Abbot Geoffrey has 1 (manor) which is called Oscherwilla which paid geld for 3 hides on the day when King Edward was alive and dead. Six ploughs can plough these. Thence the abbot has in demesne 1 hide and 2 ploughs and the villeins 2 hides and 4 ploughs. There the abbot has 7 villeins and 17 bordars and 4 serfs and 2 mills which render 7*s*. and 9 beasts and 13 pigs and 260 sheep and 9 acres of meadow and 15 furlongs of pasture in length and 2 furlongs in width. In the same manor there are 2 *gablatores*[21] who render 15*s*. a year. This (manor) is worth £6 and when he received (it), 100*s*.

(120) The church itself holds Powrtone [North Poorton]. T.R.E. it paid geld for 2 hides. There is land for 2 ploughs. Of this there is 1 hide in demesne and there (is) 1 plough and 5 villeins and 3 bordars and 2 acres of meadow and 16 acres of wood(land). (There is) pasture 8 furlongs long and 2 furlongs wide. It was worth 25*s*. Now (it is worth) 40*s*.

(lxvi) Abbot Geoffrey has 1 manor which is called Powrtona which paid geld T.R.E. for 2 hides. Two ploughs can plough these. Thence the abbot has 1 hide and 1 plough and the villeins 1 hide and 1 plough. There the abbot has 5 villeins and 3 bordars and 7 pigs and 16 acres of underwood (*nemusculi*) and 2 acres of meadow and 8 furlongs of pasture in length and 2 in width. This (manor) is worth 40*s*. a year and when the abbot received (it) it was worth 25*s*.

XVII. THE LAND OF ST. STEPHEN OF CAEN

(121) The church of St. Stephen, Caen, holds Frantone [Frampton]. Gytha held (it) T.R.E. and it paid geld for 25½ hides. There is land for the same number of ploughs. Of this there are in demesne 9½ hides and there (are) 7 ploughs and 27 serfs and 24 bordars and 7 cottars with 14 ploughs. There (are) 2 mills rendering 20*s*. and 67 acres of meadow. (There is) pasture 1½ league long and ½ league wide.

[18] 'et una vidua' interlined.

[19] This manor was given to the abbey by the Count of Mortain in exchange for the manor of Montacute (Bishopston) (Som.): *Dom. Bk.* (Rec. Com.), i, f. 93.

[20] Rent-paying tenants.

[21] Rent-paying tenants.

(There is) wood(land) 8 furlongs long and 3 furlongs wide. To this manor are attached 2 hides which Queen[22] Maud gave to St. Stephen. The whole (manor) was worth, and renders, £40.

(122) The church itself holds BEINCOME [Bincombe]. Earl[23] Harold held (it) T.R.E. and it paid geld for 8 hides. There is land for 6 ploughs. Of this there are in demesne 5 hides and there (are) 2 ploughs and 3 serfs and 2 villeins and 10 bordars with 1 plough. There (are) 20 acres of meadow and 2 leagues of pasture. It was worth, and renders, £12.

XVIII. [THE LAND OF THE ABBEY OF ST. WANDRILLE][24]

(123) The church of St. Wandrille holds the church of Bridetone [Burton Bradstock] and of Brideport [Bridport] and of Witcerce [Whitchurch Canonicorum]. Four hides belong to them. They render £7.

> (xviii) The Abbot of St. Wandrille has the church of Bridetona and the church of Brideport and the church of Witcercie. Four hides of land belong to them and they render £7 a year.

(124) The church itself holds 1 church in WARHAM [Wareham] of the king, to which belongs 1 hide, and there is 1 plough with 2 bordars. It is worth 70*s.* with what belongs to it.

> (xx) The Abbot of St. Wandrille has 1 church in Warham which he holds of King William, to which belongs 1 hide of land which can be ploughed with 1 plough, which is in that land. There he has 2 bordars. This church with what belongs to it is worth 70*s.* a year.

XIX. THE LAND OF THE ABBEY OF SHAFTESBURY

(125) The church of St. Mary, Shaftesbury, holds HANLEGE [Sixpenny Handley]. T.R.E. it paid geld for 20 hides. There is land for 20 ploughs. Of this there are in demesne 4 hides less 1 virgate and there (are) 4½ ploughs and 4 serfs and 30 villeins and 15 bordars with 12 ploughs. There (are) 7 acres of meadow and wood(land) 1 league long and ½ league wide. It was and is worth £12. Of this land 2 free Englishmen hold 4 hides and they have there 3 ploughs.

(126) The church itself holds HAINTONE [Hinton St. Mary]. T.R.E. it paid geld for 8 hides. There is land for 9 ploughs. Of this there are in demesne 3 hides and there (are) 3 ploughs and 3 serfs and 16 villeins and 9 bordars with 6 ploughs. There (is) a mill rendering 10*s.* and 30 acres of meadow. (There is) 1 furlong of wood(land) in length and as much in width, and the same amount of pasture. It was worth £8. Now (it is worth) £10.

(127) The church itself holds STURE [East and West Stour]. T.R.E. it paid geld for 17 hides. There is land for 10 ploughs. Of this there are in demesne 10 hides less 1½ virgate and there (are) 2 ploughs and 25 villeins and 18 bordars with 5 ploughs. There (are) 3 mills rendering 30*s.* and 10 acres of meadow. (There is) pasture 8 furlongs long and 6 furlongs wide. It was worth £8. Now (it is worth) £10.

(128) The church itself holds FONTEMALE [Fontmell Magna]. T.R.E. it paid geld for 15 hides. There is land for 16 ploughs. Of this there are in demesne 3 hides and 1 virgate of land and there (are) 2 ploughs and 3 serfs and 45 villeins and 20 bordars with 14 ploughs. There (are) 3 mills rendering 11*s.* 7*d.* and 8 acres of meadow and 4 furlongs of pasture and 8 furlongs and 2 acres of wood(land). It was worth £10. Now (it is worth) £15.

(129) The church itself holds CUNTONE [Compton Abbas]. T.R.E. it paid geld for 10 hides. There is land for 10 ploughs. Of this there are in demesne 4 hides and 1 virgate of land and there (are) 2 ploughs. There (are) 18 villeins and 14 bordars with 8 ploughs. There (is) a mill rendering 1*d.* and 3 acres of meadow. (There is) pasture ½ league long and 2 furlongs wide. It is worth £10.

(130) The church itself holds MELEBERIE [Melbury Abbas]. T.R.E. it paid geld for 10 hides. There is land for 12 ploughs. Of this there are in demesne 3 hides and there (are) 6 ploughs and 27 villeins and 20 coscets with 6 ploughs. There (are) 4 mills rendering 15*s.* 3*d.* (There is) pasture ½ league long and 2 furlongs wide. (There is) wood(land) 8 furlongs long and 2 furlongs wide. It was worth £9. Now (it is worth) £13.

(131) The church itself holds EUNEMINSTRE [Iwerne Minster]. T.R.E. it paid geld for 18 hides. There is land for 16 ploughs. Of this there are in demesne 5½ hides and there (are) 2 ploughs and 29 villeins and 21 bordars with 14 ploughs. There (are) 3 mills rendering 17*s.* and 18 acres of meadow. In Iwerne Minster (there is) wood(land) 1 league long and ½ (league) wide.[25] (There is) pasture 10 furlongs long and 2 furlongs wide. It was worth £10. Now (it is worth) £14.

(132) The church itself holds TARENTE [Tarrant Hinton]. T.R.E. it paid geld for 10 hides. There is land for 8 ploughs. Of this there are in demesne 2½ hides and there (are) 2 ploughs and 3 serfs and 18 villeins and 14 bordars with 6 ploughs. There (are) 18 acres of meadow. (There is) pasture 1 league long and ½ league wide. (There is) wood(land) 50 perches long and 40 wide. It was worth £6. Now (it is worth) £10.

(133) The church itself holds FIFHIDE [Lower Fifehead or Fifehead St. Quintin in Fifehead Neville]. T.R.E. it paid geld for 5 hides. There is land for 4 ploughs. Of this there are in demesne 3½ hides and there (are) 2 ploughs and 2 serfs and 4 villeins and 3 bordars with 2 ploughs. There (is) a mill rendering 5*s.* and 6 acres of meadow. (There is) wood(land) 4 furlongs long and 3 furlongs wide. It is worth £3. Chetel holds (it) of the abbess.

(134) The church itself holds CHINGESTONE [Kingston in Corfe Castle]. T.R.E. it paid geld for 16

[22] 'regina' interlined as well as occurring in the text.
[23] 'comes' interlined.
[24] The scribe entered the number of this fief, but omitted the heading.
[25] This sentence was added at the foot of the following entry.

hides. There is land for 20 ploughs. Of this there are in demesne 3 hides and 3 virgates of land and there (are) 2 ploughs and 2 serfs and 22 villeins and 16 bordars with 18 ploughs. There (are) 12 acres of meadow. (There is) pasture 1 league long and as much in width. It was worth £16. Now (it is worth) £23. The king has 1 hide of the manor of Kingston in which he built the castle of WARHAM [Corfe Castle][26] and (in exchange) for this he gave to St. Mary the church of GELINGEHAM [Gillingham] with what belongs to it, which is worth 40*s*. Of the same manor William of Briouze has 1 virgate of land which the church held T.R.E.[27]

(135) The church itself holds 1 hide in FERNEHAM [Farnham] which Aiulf and the wife of Hugh fitz Grip hold of it.

(136) The church itself holds STOCHE [Stoke Wake]. T.R.E. it paid geld for 5 hides. There is land for 4 ploughs. Of this there are in demesne 3 hides and 1 virgate of land and there (are) 2 ploughs and 4 serfs and 7 villeins and 4 bordars with 2 ploughs. There (is) a mill rendering 12*d*. and 15 acres of meadow. (There is) pasture 6 furlongs long and 1 furlong wide. (There is) wood(land) 12 furlongs long and 4 furlongs wide. It was and is worth £4.

(137) The church itself holds MAPLEDRETONE [Mapperton in Almer]. T.R.E. it paid geld for 11 hides. There is land for 4 ploughs. Of this there are in demesne 7 hides and 1 virgate of land and there (are) 2 ploughs with 1 serf and 6 villeins and 4 bordars with 2 ploughs. There (are) 7 acres of meadow. (There are) 11 furlongs in length and as much in width of pasture and wood(land). It was worth 30*s*. Now (it is worth) 100*s*.

(138) The church itself holds CESEBURNE [Cheselbourne]. T.R.E. it paid geld for 16 hides. There is land (for)—[*blank*].[28] Of this there are in demesne 2 hides and 3 virgates of land and there (are) 3 ploughs and 5 serfs and 21 villeins and 10 bordars with 8 ploughs. There (is) a mill rendering 15*s*. and 10 acres of meadow. (There is) pasture 1½ league long and 1 league wide. It was and is worth £16. Earl[29] Harold took this manor and STURE [East and West Stour] from St. Mary T.R.E. but King William restored them because a writ with the seal of King Edward was found in the church itself ordering that they should be returned to the church with MELECOME [Bingham's Melcombe in Melcombe Horsey][30] which the king still holds. Earl[31] Harold himself also took from the church PIDELE [unidentified]. The Count of Mortain holds (it).

[f. 79]

XX. THE LAND OF THE ABBEY OF WILTON

(139) The church of St. Mary, Wilton, holds DEDILINTONE [Didlington (Farm) in Chalbury]. T.R.E. it paid geld for 6 hides. There is land for 5 ploughs. Of this there are in demesne 2 hides and 3 virgates of land and there (are) 2 ploughs and 4 serfs and 7 villeins and 12 bordars with 2 ploughs. There (is) a mill rendering 12*s*. 6*d*. and 36 acres of meadow. (There is) pasture ½ league long and as much in width. (There is) wood(land) 1 league long and ½ league wide. It is worth £7.

(140) The church itself holds WINBURNE [Philipston in Wimborne St. Giles, site lost].[32] T.R.E. it paid geld for 3½ hides. There is land for 2 ploughs. It is all in demesne except for 1 virgate and there (is) 1 plough and 2 serfs with 1 villein and 6 bordars. There (is) a mill rendering 7*s*. 6*d*. and 7 acres of meadow. (There are) 4 furlongs of pasture in length and width. (There is) wood(land) 3 furlongs long and 1 furlong wide. It was worth 40*s*. Now (it is worth) 30*s*.

XXI. THE LAND OF HOLY TRINITY, CAEN

(141) The church of Holy Trinity, Caen, holds TARENTE [Tarrant Launceston]. Brictric held (it) T.R.E. and it paid geld for 10 hides. There is land for 8 ploughs. Of this there are in demesne 4 hides less 4 acres and there (are) 2 ploughs and 14 serfs and 9 villeins and 1 bordar with 4 ploughs. There (are) 38 acres of meadow. (There are) 33 furlongs of pasture in length and width. (There is) 15 furlongs of wood(land) in length and width. It was worth £11. Now (it is worth) £14.

XXII. THE LAND OF THE CANONS OF THE CHURCH OF COUTANCES

(142) The canons of Coutances hold WINTREBURNE [Winterborne Stickland]. T.R.E. it paid geld for 8 hides. There is land for 9 ploughs. Of this there are in demesne 3 hides and 3 virgates of land, and there (are) 4 ploughs and 5 serfs and 12 villeins and 20 bordars with 4 ploughs. There (is) a mill rendering 12*s*. 6*d*. (There is) pasture 26 furlongs long and 3 furlongs wide. (There is) wood(land) 5 furlongs long and 4 furlongs wide. It was worth £10. Now (it is worth) £15.

XXIII. THE LAND OF ST. MARY MONTEVILLIERS

(143) The church of St. Mary Villiers holds WADONE [Friar Waddon in Portesham]. Three thegns held (it) T.R.E. and it paid geld for 6 hides. There is land for 5 ploughs. Of this there are in demesne 5½ hides and there (are) 3 ploughs and 4 serfs and 2 villeins and 7 bordars with 2 ploughs. There (are) 20 acres of meadow and 15 furlongs of pasture. It was and is worth £10. Hugh fitz Grip[33] gave this land to the same church. Of this the church of Abbotsbury had 6 acres of crops and 3 church-scots by custom T.R.E. but Hugh never gave (this).

26 That this was Corfe Castle is shown by the fact that in 1212 the abbess held the advowson of Gillingham church *in escambium pro terra ubi castellum de Corf positum est*: *Bk. of Fees*, 91.

27 The conclusion of no. 134 and the whole of no. 135 were added at the foot of the column (after no. 138).

28 Space in the text. For a comment, see p. 5.

29 'comes' interlined.

30 See no. 30.

31 'comes' interlined.

32 See Eyton, *Key to Domesday: Dorset*, 119–20, for this identification. The manor of Philipston was held by the abbess in 1235–6: *Bk. of Fees*, 426. Her *carta* of 1166 mentions a certain Philip de Winburne from whom the name possibly derived: *Red Bk. Exch.* (Rolls Ser.), 239.

33 'filius Grip' interlined.

XXIIII. THE LAND OF THE KING'S ALMSMEN

(144) Bristuard the priest holds the churches of Dorecestre [Dorchester] and BERE [Bere Regis] and the tithes. One hide and 20 acres of land belong there. It is worth £4.

(xiii) Bristuard the priest has the church of Dorecestre and the church of Bere and 1 hide of land and 20 acres of land and the tithes belonging to them and they are worth £4 a year.

(145a) Bollo the priest has the church of WINFRODE [Winfrith Newburgh] with 1 virgate of land. There is ½ plough. It is worth 10*s.*

(xvi) Bollo the priest has the church of Winfrode and he has there 1 virgate of land and he has there ½ plough and it is worth 10*s.* a year.

(145b) Bollo the priest has the church of PITRETONE [Puddletown] and Calvedone [Chaldon Herring or East Chaldon] and Flote [Fleet]. To these belongs 1½ hide. It renders 67*s.* 6*d.*

(xix) Bollo the priest has the church of Pidretone and the church of Calvedone and the church of Flote. To these belongs 1½ hide of land and they render 67*s.* 6*d.*

(146) Rainbald the priest holds POLEHAM [Pulham] of the king. He himself held (it) T.R.E. and it paid geld for 10 hides. There is land for 10 ploughs. Of this there are in demesne 4 hides—[*blank*][34] and 2 serfs and 9 villeins and 5 bordars with 4 ploughs. There (are) 8 furlongs of meadow in length and width and 2 leagues of wood(land) in length and width. It is worth 110*s.*

(147) Walter the deacon holds CERNEL [unidentified] of the king, and Bernard (holds it) of him. Godwin, a free man,[35] held it T.R.E. and it paid geld for 3 hides. There is land for 5 ploughs. In demesne there are 2 ploughs and 3 serfs and 8 villeins and 6 bordars with 2 ploughs. There (is) a mill rendering 10*s.* and 3 acres of meadow and 7 furlongs of pasture in length and 6 furlongs in width. It was worth 100*s.* Now (it is worth) £6.

XXV. THE LAND OF COUNT ALAN

(148) Count Alan holds DEVENIS [Dewlish] of the king. Brictric held (it) T.R.E. and it paid geld for 15 hides. There is land for 15 ploughs. Of this there are in demesne 5 hides and there (are) 3 ploughs and 13 serfs and 19 villeins and 6 bordars with 6 ploughs. There (are) 15 acres of meadow. (There is) pasture 23 furlongs in length and width. (There is) wood(land) 6 furlongs in length and width. It was and is worth £23.

XXVI. THE LAND OF THE COUNT OF MORTAIN

(149) The Count of Mortain holds WESTONE [Buckhorn Weston] and Haimo (holds it) of him. Godric and Bruno held (it) in parage[36] T.R.E. as 2 manors and it paid geld for 7 hides. There is land for 6 ploughs. In demesne there are 2 ploughs and 5 serfs and 14 villeins and 7 bordars with 1½ plough. There (are) 40 acres of meadow and (there is) wood(land) ½ league long and as much in width. It was worth £4. Now (it is worth) £7.

(150) The same count holds 2 hides in ILAND [Higher and Lower Nyland in Kington Magna] and Drew (holds it) of him. There is land for 1 plough. It is waste.

(151) The count himself holds HANFORD [Hanford]. Alward held (it) T.R.E. and it paid geld for 4 hides. There is land for 3 ploughs. In demesne there are 2 ploughs and 4 serfs and 2 villeins and 2 bordars with 1 plough. There (are) 2 mills rendering 16*s.* and 35 acres of meadow and 15 acres of wood(land). (There is) pasture 1 league long and 1 furlong wide. It was and is worth 100*s.*

(152) The count himself holds ACFORD [Child Okeford]. Alwin held (it) T.R.E. and it paid geld for 5 hides. There is land for 6 ploughs. In demesne there are 2 ploughs with 1 serf and 6 villeins and 17 bordars with 5 ploughs. There (is) half of two mills rendering 10*s.* and 40 acres of meadow and the same amount of pasture. (There is) wood(land) 2 furlongs and ½ league long and 1½ furlong wide. It was and is worth £7.

(153) The same count holds 1½ hide in CERNEL [unidentified] and a certain woman (holds it) of him. Brungar held (it) T.R.E. There is land for 1 plough which is there and 3 acres of meadow. (There is) pasture 2 furlongs long and 1 furlong wide. It is worth 10*s.*

(154) The same count holds FROME [Bhompston Farm in Stinsford] and William (holds it) of him. Alward held (it) T.R.E. and it paid geld for 4 hides. There is land for 3 ploughs. In demesne there are 2 (ploughs) and 15 acres of meadow. (There is) pasture 4 furlongs long and 2 furlongs wide. It was worth 40*s.* Now (it is worth) 60*s.*

(155) Robert holds STANFORD [West Stafford] of the count. Britnod held (it) T.R.E. and it paid geld for 3 hides. There is land for 2 ploughs. There is 1 villein and 3 bordars with ½ plough. There (is) a mill worth 4*s.* and 30 acres of meadow. (There is) pasture 1 league long and 3 furlongs wide. It is worth 20*s.*

(156) Ansger holds CERNE [unidentified] of the count. Two thegns held (it) freely[37] T.R.E. and it paid geld for 3 hides. There is land for 2 ploughs, which are there in demesne, and 2 villeins and 6 bordars. There is a mill worth 5*s.* and 4 acres of meadow. (There is) pasture 5 furlongs long and 3 furlongs wide. It was and is worth £3.

(157) Ralph holds CERNE [unidentified] of the count. Ten thegns held (it) in parage[38] T.R.E. and it paid geld for 3 hides. There is land for 2 ploughs. In demesne there is 1 (plough) and 2 villeins and 2 bordars and 2 French serjeants (*servientes francigeni*) with 1 plough. There (are) 3 acres of meadow.

[34] Space in the text. For a comment, see p. 5.

[35] 'liber homo' interlined.

[36] 'in paragio' interlined.

[37] 'libere' interlined.

[38] 'in paragio' interlined.

(There is) pasture 5 furlongs long and 3 wide. It is worth 40*s*.

(158) The count himself holds 2½ hides in CERNE [unidentified]. Six thegns held (it) in parage[39] T.R.E. There is land for 2 ploughs. There (are) 2 bordars with 1 plough and a mill rendering 40*d*. and 3 acres of meadow. (There is) pasture 3 furlongs long and 2 furlongs wide. It is worth 50*s*.

(159) Ansger holds CERNE [unidentified] of the count. Brictuin held (it) T.R.E. and it paid geld for 2 hides. There is land for 1 plough. It is worth 15*s*.

(160) Bretel holds 1 hide in FROME [Bhompston Farm in Stinsford] of the count. There is land for 1 plough. There are 5 acres of meadow and 30 acres of pasture. It is worth 12*s*.

(161) Robert holds 1 hide in[40] WINTREBURNE [unidentified] of the count. Alvred held (it) T.R.E. There is land for 1 plough which is there with 3 villeins. It was and is worth 10*s*.

(162) Dodeman holds WAI [unidentified] of the count. Scirewold and Ulward held (it) in parage[41] T.R.E. and it paid geld for 2 hides. There is land for 1½ plough. In demesne there is 1 plough with 1 serf and 2 bordars. There (are) 2 mills rendering 20*s*. and 12 acres of meadow. (There is) pasture 5 furlongs long and 2 wide. It was and is worth 40*s*.

(163) Amun holds WAI [unidentified] of the count. Nine thegns held (it) freely[42] T.R.E. and it paid geld for 4 hides. There is land for 4 ploughs. In demesne there is 1 plough and 3 coscets with 1 villein have 1 plough. There (are) 2 mills rendering 32*s*. and 12 salt-pans (*saline*) and 9 acres of meadow and 9 furlongs of pasture. It is worth £4.

(164) Robert holds WAI [unidentified] of the count. Eight thegns held (it) freely[43] T.R.E. and it paid geld for 4 hides less 1 virgate. There is land for 3 ploughs. There are 2 bordars and 7 acres of meadow. (There is) pasture 7 furlongs long and 4 furlongs wide. It is worth 40*s*.

(165) Bretel holds HALEGEWELLE [Holwell in Radipole] of the count. Alwin held (it) T.R.E. and it paid geld for 2 hides. There is land for 1½ plough. There are 12 acres of meadow and pasture 7 furlongs long and 1 furlong wide. It is worth 10*s*.

(166) Robert holds WINTREBURNE [unidentified] of the count. Alvred held (it) T.R.E. and it paid geld for 3 hides. There is land for 2 ploughs. In demesne there is 1 plough and 2 serfs and 1 villein and 3 bordars. There (are) 10 acres of meadow and pasture 5 furlongs long and 3 furlongs wide. It was worth 40*s*. Now (it is worth) 30*s*.

(167) Robert holds WINTREBURNE [unidentified] of the count. Two thegns held (it) in parage[44] T.R.E. and it paid geld for 2½ hides. There is land for 1½ ploughs, which are there with 2 villeins and 2 serfs. There (are) 2 acres of meadow. (There is) pasture 5 furlongs long and 1 furlong wide. It was and is worth 40*s*.

(168) The abbey of Marmoutier holds PIDELE [Piddlehinton] of the count. Two thegns held (it) T.R.E. as 2 manors and it paid geld for 10 hides. There is land for 7 ploughs. Of this there are in demesne 5 hides and there (are) 2 ploughs and 3 serfs and 13 villeins and 8 bordars with 3 ploughs. There (are) 33 acres of meadow and 15 furlongs of pasture. It is worth £10.

(169) Humphrey holds PIDELE [unidentified] of the count. One thegn held (it) freely[45] T.R.E. and it paid geld for 1½ hide. There is land for 1 plough. There are 4 bordars with ½ plough. There (is) a mill rendering 40*d*. and 4 acres of meadow and 5 furlongs of pasture. It was worth 30*s*. Now (it is worth) 40*s*.

[f. 79b]

(170) Humphrey holds PIDELE [unidentified] of the count. Two thegns held (it) freely[46] T.R.E. and it paid geld for 2½ hides. There is land for 2 ploughs. There is 1 plough with 1 serf and 7 bordars. There (is) a mill rendering 40*d*. and 1½ acre of meadow. (There is) pasture 3 furlongs long and 1½ furlong wide. It is worth 50*s*.

(171) The count himself holds MAPLEDRE [Mappowder]. Brictric held (it) T.R.E. and it paid geld for 3½ virgates and 7 acres of land. There is land for 1 plough. There is 1 serf and 12 acres of meadow. (There is) wood(land) 2 furlongs long and 1 furlong wide. It was worth 20*s*. Now (it is worth) 12*s*.

(172) Robert holds MORDONE [Morden] of the count. Two thegns held (it) T.R.E. and it paid geld for 1 hide. There is land for 1 plough. There are 2 villeins and a mill rendering 6*s*. 3*d*. and 5 acres of meadow and ½ league of pasture. It was worth 20*s*. Now (it is worth) 15*s*.

(173) The count himself holds SPESTEBERIE [Spetisbury]. Three thegns held (it) T.R.E. and it paid geld for 1½ hide. There is land for ½ plough. There is 1 bordar and 1 villein and 16 acres of meadow and 34 acres of pasture. Of this land the count has 1 virgate of land and 3 acres and Robert (has) 3 virgates and 6 acres. The whole (manor) is worth 18*s*.

(174) Ansger holds SIDELINCE [Sydling St. Nicholas] of the count. Edmar held (it) T.R.E. and it paid geld for 5 hides. There is land for 4 ploughs. In demesne there (are) 2 ploughs and 5 serfs and 4 villeins and 4 bordars with 1 plough. There (is) a mill rendering 5*s*. and 12 acres of meadow. (There is) pasture 1 league long and 4 furlongs wide. It was and is worth £4.

(175) Amund holds SIDELINCE [Sydling St. Nicholas] of the count. Swain held (it) T.R.E. and it paid geld for 1 hide. There is land for 1 plough. There are 4 furlongs of pasture in length and 2 furlongs in width. It is worth 10*s*.

[39] 'in paragio' interlined.
[40] 'IN' interlined.
[41] 'in paragio' interlined.
[42] 'libere' interlined.
[43] 'libere' interlined.
[44] 'in paragio' interlined.
[45] 'libere' interlined.
[46] 'libere' interlined.

(176) Bretel holds LITELTONE [Littleton in Langton Long Blandford] of the count. Ulviet held (it) T.R.E. and it paid geld for 5 hides. There is land for 3 ploughs. In demesne there is 1 plough and 6 bordars and 6 serfs. There (is) a mill rendering 7*s*. 6*d*. and 20 acres of meadow and 30 acres of pasture. It was worth £4. Now (it is worth) 40*s*.

(177) Bretel holds BLENEFORD [unidentified] of the count. Alward held (it) T.R.E. and it paid geld for 1½ hide. There is land for 1 plough. It renders 12*s*. It was worth 20*s*.

(178) Robert holds WINTREBURNE [unidentified] of the count. Godwin held (it) T.R.E. and it paid geld for 2 hides. There is land for 1 plough which is there with 3 bordars and 3 furlongs of pasture. It is worth 20*s*.

(179) Robert holds WINTREBURNE [unidentified] of the count. Alward held (it) T.R.E. and it paid geld for 3 hides. There is land for 2 ploughs. There are 7 coscets with ½ plough and 2 furlongs of wood(land) and pasture 3 furlongs long and 1 furlong wide. It is worth 30*s*.

(180) Robert himself holds WINBURNE [unidentified] of the count. Aschil held (it) T.R.E. and it paid geld for 3 hides. There is land for 2 ploughs. In demesne there is 1 plough with 1 serf and 5 bordars. There (is) a mill rendering 2*s*. and 2½ acres of meadow. (There is) pasture 1 league long and 4 furlongs wide. (There is) wood(land) 6 furlongs long and 2 furlongs wide. It was and is worth £3.

(181) Hubert holds WINTREBURNE [unidentified] of the count. Two thegns held (it) in parage[47] T.R.E. and it paid geld for 5 hides. There is land for 3 ploughs. In demesne there (are) 2 ploughs and 2 villeins and 4 bordars with ½ plough. There (are) 20 acres of meadow. (There is) pasture 2 furlongs long and 1 wide. (There is) wood(land) 3 furlongs long and 2 furlongs wide. It was worth £4. Now (it is worth) 40*s*.

(182) Malger holds 2 hides in[48] WINTREBURNE [unidentified] of the count. Three thegns held (it) T.R.E. There is land for 1 plough which is there with 1 villein. There (are) 3 furlongs of pasture. It is worth 30*s*.

(183) Dodeman holds MELESBERIE [Melbury Osmond][49] of the count. Three thegns held (it) in parage[50] T.R.E. and it paid geld for 2½ hides. There is land for 2 ploughs. There is 1 smith and 2 bordars and 2 serfs and 9 acres of meadow. (There is) wood(land) 8 furlongs long and 2 furlongs wide. It is worth 20*s*.

(184) Dodeman holds WINTREBURNE [unidentified] of the count. Alric held (it) T.R.E. and it paid geld for 1½ hide. There is land for 1 plough. There is 1 bordar with 1 serf and 6 acres of meadow and 2½ furlongs of pasture. It is worth 15*s*. In the same vill the count has 5½ virgates of land. There is land for 1 plough. There are 13 acres of meadow and 1½ furlong of pasture. It was and is worth 14*s*.

(185) Dodeman holds BLANEFORD [Blandford St. Mary] of the count.[51] Sared and his brother held (it) in parage[52] T.R.E. and it paid geld for 1½ hide. There is land for ½ plough. There are 3 bordars and 2 serfs and 9 acres of meadow and 5 furlongs of pasture. It is worth 15*s*.

(186) The count himself has 2 hides in MANITONE [Mannington in Holt]. There is land for 1 plough. Alvric held (it). There are 3 villeins and 2 bordars with 1 plough. (There is) pasture 1 league long and ½ league wide. (There is) wood(land) ½ league in length and width. It is worth 20*s*.

(187) Hubert holds HEMEDESWORDE [East and West Hemsworth in Witchampton] of the count. One thegn held (it) T.R.E. and it paid geld for 1 hide. There is land for 1½ ploughs which are there with 1 serf and 3 bordars. (There are) 3 furlongs of pasture in length and width and as much wood(land). It is worth 25*s*.

(188) Hubert holds WICHEMETUNE [Witchampton] of the count. One thegn held (it) T.R.E. and it paid geld for 2 hides. There is land for 1½ plough. There is 1 villein and 3 bordars with 1 plough and a mill rendering 5*s*. and 8 acres of meadow. (There is) pasture 2 furlongs long and 1 furlong wide. (There is) wood(land) 1 furlong long and 8 acres wide. It was and is worth 25*s*. Hubert has there 1⅓ virgate of land on which he never paid geld.

(189) Girard holds 1 hide at LODRE [Matravers, formerly Loders Lutton, in Loders] of the count. Ulviet held (it) T.R.E. There is land for 1 plough which is there with 5 bordars. There (is) a mill rendering 3*s*. and 4 acres of meadow and 26 acres of pasture. It is worth 25*s*.

(190) The count himself holds 1 hide at LODRE [Matravers, formerly Loders Lutton, in Loders]. Alvric held (it) T.R.E. There is land for 1 plough. There are 6 bordars with 1 serf and 2 acres of meadow and 30 acres of pasture. It is worth 25*s*. Alvred holds half this hide of the count.

(191) Ansger holds 2 hides in CHENOLTUNE [Knowlton in Woodlands, site derelict] of the count. Ailmer held (it) T.R.E. and it paid geld.[53] There is land for 1 plough which is there with 1 serf and 1 bordar. There is a mill rendering 12*s*. 6*d*. It was and is worth 25*s*.

(192) The count himself holds GESSIC [Gussage All Saints]. Edmer held (it) T.R.E. and it paid geld for 15 hides. There is land for 12 ploughs. In demesne there are 3 ploughs and 9 serfs and 8 villeins and 18 bordars with 5 ploughs. There (is) a mill rendering 25*s*. and 60 acres of meadow. (There is) pasture 2

[47] 'in paragio' interlined.

[48] 'IN' and 'ii hidas' interlined in the facsimile; the printed version has *IN*.

[49] Presumably the manor given by William of Mortain to Montacute Priory, whence the name. For this identification, see Fägersten, *Place-Names of Dorset*, 226.

[50] 'in paragio' interlined.

[51] 'de comite' interlined.

[52] 'in paragio' interlined.

[53] 'et geldabat' interlined.

leagues long and 1 league wide and as much wood-(land). It was and is worth £15.

(193) William holds DERVINESTONE [Knighton House in Durweston] of the count. Five thegns held (it) T.R.E. and it paid geld for 2½ hides. There is land for 2 ploughs which are there in demesne and 2 serfs and 2 villeins and 5 bordars with 1 plough. There (are) 8 acres of meadow and 7 furlongs of pasture and 1 furlong of underwood in length and width. It is worth 50*s.*

(194) The count himself holds BLANEFORD [? Blandford Forum]. Edmer held (it) T.R.E. and it paid geld for 10 hides. There is land for 6 ploughs. In demesne there are 3 ploughs and 8 serfs and 7 villeins and 9 bordars with 2 ploughs. There (is) a mill rendering 20*s.* and 20 acres of meadow. (There is) pasture 9 furlongs long and 3 furlongs wide. (There are) 5½ furlongs of wood(land). It was worth £10. Now (it is worth) £11.

(195) The count himself holds BROCHEMTUNE [Brockhampton Green in Buckland Newton]. Godric held (it) and it paid geld for 1½ hide. There is land for 1 plough which is there and 10 acres of meadow and pasture 2 furlongs long and 1 furlong wide. It is worth 20*s.*

(196) The count himself holds WINTREBURNE [unidentified]. Alvred and 2 others held (it) T.R.E. and it paid geld for 1 hide and 1 virgate of land. There is land for 1 plough. There are 3 bordars and pasture 4 furlongs long and 2 furlongs wide. (There is) wood(land) 2 furlongs long and 2 wide. It is worth 20*s.* Dodeman holds 2 virgates of this land.

(197) The count himself holds BEASTEWELLE [Bestwall (Farm) in Wareham Lady St. Mary]. Edmar held (it) T.R.E. and it paid geld for 3 hides. There is land for 1½ plough. In demesne there is 1 plough and 4 serfs and 4 cottars and 1 villein with ½ plough. (There are) 20 acres of meadow and 20 acres of pasture. (There is) wood(land) 2 furlongs long and 1 furlong wide. It was worth 30*s.* Now (it is worth) 60*s.*

(198) The count himself holds LOLOWORDE [East and West Lulworth]. Alsi held (it) T.R.E. and it paid geld for 3½ hides. There is land for 2 ploughs. In demesne there is 1 plough with 1 serf and 4 bordars—[*blank*].[54] There (are) 2 acres of meadow. (There is) pasture 3 furlongs long and 1 furlong wide. It was worth 60*s.* Now (it is worth) 30*s.*

(199) The count himself holds LOLOWORDE [East and West Lulworth]. Trawin held (it) T.R.E. and it paid geld for 2 hides. There is land for 1½ plough. In demesne there is 1 plough and 2 bordars and 2 acres of meadow. (There is) pasture 2 furlongs long and 2 wide. It was worth 40*s.* Now (it is worth) 20*s.*

(200) The count himself holds STOCHES [Stock Gaylard (House) in Lydlinch]. Edmer held (it) T.R.E. and it paid geld for 2 hides. There is land for 2 ploughs which are there in demesne and 2 serfs and 2 villeins and 3 bordars with 1 plough. There (is) a mill rendering 15*s.* and 20 acres of meadow. (There is) pasture 5 furlongs long and as much in width. It was and is worth 50*s.*

(201) The count himself has 1 mill in STANBERGE [Stoborough in Arne] with ½ hide and 3 bordars. The whole (manor) is worth 40*s.*

(202) Bretel holds CRIST [East Creech in Church Knowle] of the count. Sirewald held (it) T.R.E. and it paid geld for 2 hides. There is land for 1 plough which is there with 1 villein and 1 bordar and 4 acres of meadow. (There is) pasture 6 furlongs long and as much in width and 1 house in Wareham. It was worth 20*s.* Now (it is worth) 40*s.*

(203) Bretel holds TIGEHAM [Tyneham] of the count. Six thegns held (it) T.R.E. and it paid geld for 3½ hides. There is land for 3 ploughs. There are 3 villeins and 4 bordars and 2 acres of meadow. (There is) pasture 5 furlongs long and 2 furlongs wide. It was and is worth 47*s.*

(204) Robert holds MORTUNE [Moreton] of the count. Six thegns held (it) T.R.E. and it paid geld for 3 hides. There is land for 3 ploughs. Six villeins with 3 coscets have these (ploughs) there. There (is) a mill rendering 3*s.* and 30 acres of meadow. (There is) pasture 1 league long and as much in width. It was and is worth £4.

(205) Robert holds WARMWELLE [Warmwell] of the count. Lewin held (it) T.R.E. and it paid geld for 1 hide. There is land for 1 plough. There are 3 bordars and 9 furlongs of pasture in length and 1 furlong in width. It is worth 16*s.*

(206) The count himself holds LODRE [Uploders in Loders]. Brictric held (it) T.R.E. and it paid geld for 1½ hide. There is land for 2 ploughs which are there with 1 coscet and 3 serfs and 15 acres of meadow and 6 furlongs of pasture in length and 1 furlong in width. It was and is worth 47*s.* 6*d.*

(207) William holds LAHOC [Hooke] of the count. Alvric held (it) T.R.E. and it paid geld for 2 hides. There is land for 3 ploughs. In demesne there are 2 ploughs with 1 serf and 4 villeins and 3 bordars with 1 plough. There (is) a mill rendering 6*s.* and 6 acres of meadow and 5 furlongs of pasture and 4 furlongs of wood(land). It was and is worth 40*s.*

(208) Bretel and Malger hold WELLE [Wool] of the count. Three thegns held (it) T.R.E. as 2 manors[55] and it paid geld for 1 hide and 3 virgates of land. There is land for 1½ plough. There (are) 2 villeins and 6 coscets. There (are) 4 acres of meadow. (There is) pasture 5 furlongs long and 2 furlongs wide. It was and is worth 23*s.*

(209) Haimo holds STOLLANT [Studland] of the count. Almar held (it) T.R.E. and it paid geld for 3½ hides. There is land for 4 ploughs. In demesne there are 2 ploughs and 6 serfs and 5 villeins and 13 bordars.
[f. 80]
(There is) pasture 1 league long and as much in width. (There is) wood(land) 2 furlongs long and 1

[54] Space in the text. For a comment, see p. 5.

[55] 'pro ii maneriis' interlined.

furlong wide. There are 32 salt-pans rendering 40*s*. The whole (manor) is worth £8.

(210) Alvred holds ½ hide in STANTONE [St. Gabriel's House in Stanton St. Gabriel] of the count. Edwi held (it) T.R.E. There is land for 6 ploughs. In demesne there are 2½ ploughs and 5 serfs and 3 villeins and 8 bordars with 3½ ploughs. There (are) 24 acres of meadow and 2½ leagues of pasture and 2 furlongs of wood(land). It was and is worth 60*s*.

(211) Bretel holds WODETONE [Wootton Fitzpaine] of the count. Edmer held (it) T.R.E. and it paid geld for 2 hides. There is land for 7 ploughs. In demesne there are 2 ploughs and 2 serfs and 12 villeins and 9 bordars with 5 ploughs. There (is) a mill rendering 15*d*. and 6 acres of meadow and 7 furlongs and 4 acres of pasture and 1 league and 5 furlongs of wood(land). It is worth 100*s*.

(212) William holds CERNELI [? Catherston Leweston][56] of the count. Aldebert held (it) T.R.E. and it paid geld for 3 hides. There is land for 4 ploughs. In demesne there are 2 ploughs and 5 serfs and 6 villeins and 2 bordars with 2 ploughs. There (is) a mill rendering 3*d*. and 8 acres of meadow. (There is) pasture 10 furlongs long and 1 furlong wide. (There is) wood(land) 2 furlongs long and 2 wide. It was and is worth 60*s*. In the same vill William holds ½ hide which belonged to the demesne farm of Cerne T.R.E.

(213) The same William holds CORIESCUMBE [Corscombe] of the count. Lewin held (it) T.R.E. and it paid geld for 1 hide. There is land for 1½ ploughs which are there with 1 villein and 7 bordars and 2 serfs. There (is) pasture 1 furlong long and ½ furlong wide and as much wood(land). It was and is worth 15*s*.

(214) Drew holds TOLRE [Toller Whelme in Corscombe] of the count. Almar held (it) T.R.E. and it paid geld for 3 hides. There is land for 3 ploughs. In demesne there is 1 plough with 6 bordars. There (is) ½ acre of meadow. (There is) pasture 5 furlongs long and 2 furlongs wide. It was worth 20*s*. Now (it is worth) 40*s*.

(215) Robert holds CERNEMUDE [Charmouth] of the count. Algar held (it) T.R.E. and it paid geld for 3 hides. There is land for 3 ploughs. In demesne there are 2 ploughs and 3 serfs and 3 villeins with 2 ploughs. There (are) 16 salt-workers and 16 acres of meadow. (There is) pasture 3 furlongs long and 1 furlong wide. (There is) wood(land) 7 furlongs long and 1 furlong wide. It is worth 60*s*.

(216) The count himself holds SCILFEMETUNE [Shilvinghampton in Portesham]. Three thegns held (it) in parage[57] T.R.E. and it paid geld for 1 hide and 1 virgate. There is land for 1 plough which is there with 1 coscet. There (is) pasture 2 furlongs long and 2 wide. It was and is worth 15*s*.

(217) Bretel holds WODETONE [Wootton Fitzpaine] of the count. Ulfret held (it) T.R.E. and it paid geld for ½ hide. There is land for 1 plough. There are 2 villeins with ½ plough and 5 acres of meadow and 4 acres of wood(land). It is worth 5*s*.

(218) The count himself holds CANDEL [Stourton Caundle]. Alstan held (it) T.R.E. and it paid geld for 1 hide. There is land for 1 plough. There are 3 bordars and 2 serfs and 6 acres of meadow and 8 acres of underwood. It was worth 20*s*. Now (it is worth) 10*s*.

(219) Alwin holds CANDEL [Stourton Caundle] of the count. Alveva held (it) T.R.E. and it paid geld for 3 hides. There is land for 3 ploughs which are there with 1 serf and 2 villeins and 5 bordars. There (are) 3 acres of meadow and wood(land) 4 furlongs long and as much in width. It was and is worth 40*s*. All who had these lands T.R.E. held (them) freely.

XXVII. THE LAND OF EARL HUGH

(220) Earl Hugh holds FIFHIDE [Fifehead Magdalen] and Gilbert (holds it) of him. Alnod held (it) T.R.E. and it paid geld for 5 hides. There is land for 5 ploughs. In demesne there are 3 ploughs and 6 serfs[58] and 4 villeins and 4 bordars with 2 ploughs. There (are) 2 mills rendering 22*s*. 6*d*. and 30 acres of meadow. (There is) wood(land) 4 furlongs long and 2 furlongs wide. It was and is worth £7.

(221) William holds ELSANGTONE [Ilsington in Puddletown] of the earl. Elnod held (it) T.R.E. through Earl[59] Harold, who took it from a certain clerk. Then it paid geld for 2 hides. There is land for 1½ plough which is there and (there is) a mill and 8 acres of meadow and 5 furlongs of pasture and 3 furlongs of wood(land). It was and is worth 20*s*.

(222) William holds TINCLADENE [Tincleton] of the earl. Ednod held (it) T.R.E. and it paid geld for 2 hides. There is land for 2 ploughs. In demesne there is 1 plough with 1 serf and 1 villein and 4 bordars. There (are) 5 acres of meadow and 5 furlongs of pasture and 2 furlongs of wood(land). It is worth 20*s*.

(223) William holds MAINE [Broadmayne] of the earl. Ednod held (it) T.R.E. and it paid geld for 3 hides. There is land for 2 ploughs. In demesne there is 1 plough and 3 serfs and 6 villeins and 2 bordars with 1 plough. There (are) 3 acres of meadow and 140[60] acres of pasture. (There is) 1 house in Wareham rendering 5*d*. It was and is worth 40*s*.

(224) William holds MAINE [Little Mayne (Farm) in West Knighton] of the earl. Edric held (it) T.R.E. and it paid geld for 2 hides. There is land for 1½ plough. In demesne there is 1 plough with 1 serf and 4 bordars. There (are) 3 acres of meadow. (There is) pasture 8 furlongs long and 1 furlong wide. It is worth 40*s*.

(225) William holds CLISTONE [Clifton Maybank] of the earl. Ednod held (it) T.R.E. and it paid geld for 6 hides. There is land for 4 ploughs. In demesne there are 3 ploughs and 3 villeins and 14 bordars with 2 ploughs. There (is) a mill rendering 10*s*. and 12 acres of meadow. (There is) wood(land) 8 furlongs

[56] See Eyton, op. cit. 141–2.
[57] 'in paragio' interlined.
[58] 'et vi servi' interlined.
[59] 'comitem' interlined.
[60] 'c' interlined.

long and 4 furlongs wide. It was and is worth £6. To this manor of Clifton are attached 3 hides in TRELLE [Trill (Farm) in Beer Hackett] which 3 thegns held in parage T.R.E. and it paid geld for 3 hides. There is land for 2 ploughs. There are 3 villeins and 4 bordars with 1 plough and a mill rendering 50*d.* and 8 acres of meadow. (There is) wood(land) 6 furlongs long and 2 furlongs wide. It was and is worth £3.

(226) William holds WARMEMOILLE [Warmwell] of the earl. Two thegns held (it) T.R.E. and it paid geld for 2 hides and 1 virgate of land. Besides this there is 1 virgate of land which never paid geld. There is land for 2 ploughs. In demesne there is 1 plough with 1 serf and 2 villeins and 7 bordars with ½ plough. There (is) a mill rendering 5*s.* (There is) pasture 9 furlongs long and 2 furlongs wide. It is worth 50*s.*

(227) The same William holds 1 hide and 1 virgate of land in TINGEHAM [Tyneham] of the earl. Alnod held (it) T.R.E. There is land for 1 plough. There are 3 villeins and 1 acre of meadow and 6 acres of wood(land) and 4 furlongs of pasture. It was and is worth 20*s.*

(228) The same William holds PEDRET [South Perrott] of the earl. Alnod held (it) T.R.E. and it paid geld for 5 hides. There is land for 5 ploughs. In demesne there are 2 ploughs and 3 serfs and 6 villeins and 14 bordars with 3 ploughs. There (is) a mill rendering 2*s.* and 12 acres of meadow. (There is) pasture 14 furlongs long and 3 furlongs wide. (There is) wood(land) 7 furlongs long and 5 furlongs wide. It was worth 100*s.* Now (it is worth) £6. Alnod bought this manor from Bishop Alwold for his lifetime only on the condition that after his death it should be restored to the church.

(229) The same (William) holds CATESCLIVE [Catsley (Farm) in Corscombe] of the earl. Alnod held (it) T.R.E. and it paid geld for 1 hide. There is land for 1½ plough. There is 1 virgate of land the geld on which was concealed T.R.W. (*de qua celatum est geldum*).[61] There is 1 villein and 3 bordars with 1 serf and 12 acres of meadow. (There is) pasture 4 furlongs long and as much in width. (There is) wood(land) 1 furlong long and 1 furlong wide. It was worth 5*s.* Now (it is worth) 10*s.* and this land also Alnod bought from Bishop Alwold on that condition that after his death it should return to the church.

(230) The same William holds BUREWINESTOCH [Burstock]. One thegn held (it) T.R.E. and Alnod took (it) from him T.R.W. and it paid geld for 3 hides. There is land for 3 ploughs. In demesne there are 1½ plough and 3 serfs and 4 villeins and 5 bordars with 1½ plough. There (are) 8 acres of meadow and pasture 2 furlongs long and 2 furlongs wide. It was worth 20*s.* Now (it is worth) 40*s.*

XXVIII. THE LAND OF ROGER DE BEAUMONT

(231) Roger de Beaumont holds STUR [Stour Provost] of the king. Alvred held (it) T.R.E. and it paid geld for 7 hides. There is land for 9 ploughs. Of this there are in demesne 4½ hides and there (are) 2 ploughs and 6 serfs and 12 villeins and 12 bordars with 3 ploughs. There (is) a mill rendering 100*d.* and 20 acres of meadow. (There is) wood(land) 1½ league long and ½ league wide. It was worth £9. Now (it is worth) £8.

(232) The same Roger holds STURMINSTRE [Sturminster Marshall]. Archbishop[62] Stigand held (it) T.R.E. and it paid geld for 30 hides. There is land for 25 ploughs. Of this there are in demesne 12½ hides and there (are) 3 ploughs and 8 serfs and 64 villeins and 26 bordars with 15 ploughs. There (are) 2 mills rendering 28*s.* and 124 acres of meadow. (There is) pasture 3 leagues long and 1½ league wide. (There is) wood(land) 1 league long and ½ league wide. It used to be worth £66 when he received (it). Now (it is worth) £55.

(233) The same Roger holds CRIZ [East Creech in Church Knowle]. Colebrand held (it) T.R.E. and it paid geld for 2 hides. There is land for 2 ploughs which are there with 2 villeins and 4 serfs. There (are) 4 acres of meadow. (There is) pasture 6 furlongs long and as much in width. (There is) wood(land) 6 furlongs long and 3 furlongs wide. It was and is worth 40*s.*

(234) The same Roger holds STIPLE [Steeple]. Lewin held (it) T.R.E. and it paid geld for 2½ hides. There is land for 3 ploughs. In demesne there is 1 plough and 2 serfs and 1 villein and 3 bordars with 1 plough. There (are) 4 acres of meadow and 3 acres of wood(land). (There is) pasture 3 furlongs long and 1 furlong wide. It was and is worth 50*s.*

(235) The same Roger holds GLOLE [Church Knowle]. Three thegns held (it) in parage[63] T.R.E. and it paid geld for 3½ hides. There is land for 3 ploughs. There is a priest and 1 villein and 1 bordar with 1 plough. There (are) 3 acres of meadow and pasture 3 furlongs long and 1 furlong wide. It was and is worth 40*s.*

(236) The same Roger holds ALVRONETONE [Afflington (Farm) in Corfe Castle]. Alveron held (it) T.R.E. and it paid geld for 2 hides. There is land for 2 ploughs which are there with 2 villeins and 2 bordars. There (are) 2½ acres of meadow and 2 acres of wood(land). (There is) pasture 4 furlongs long and 1 furlong wide. It was and is worth 50*s.*

(237) The same Roger holds ALVRETONE [part of the above]. Leodmar held (it) T.R.E. and it paid geld for ½ hide and 4 acres of land. There is land for 1 plough. There are 2 villeins. It is worth 7*s.* 6*d.*

XXIX. THE LAND OF ROGER DE COURSEULLES

(238) Roger de Courseulles holds CORFETONE [Corton (Farm) in Portesham] of the king. Two thegns held (it) in parage T.R.E. and it paid geld for 5 hides. There is land for 4 ploughs. In demesne there are 2 ploughs and 12 bordars and 15 acres of meadow. (There is) pasture 1 league long and ½

[61] This sentence was added in the margin.
[62] 'archiepiscopus' interlined.
[63] 'in paragio' interlined.

league wide. It was worth £9. Now (it is worth) £7. Vitalis holds (it) of Roger.

[f. 80b]

XXX. THE LAND OF ROBERT FITZ GEROLD

(239) Robert fitz Gerold holds CORF [Corfe Mullen] of the king. Wada and Egelric held (it) T.R.E. and it paid geld for 10 hides. There is land for 10 ploughs. Of this there are in demesne 7½ hides and there is 1 plough and 4 serfs and 12 villeins and 12 bordars with 5 ploughs. There (is) a mill rendering 20*s*. and 102 acres of meadow. (There is) pasture 2 leagues in[64] length and width. (There is) wood(land) 2 leagues long and 1 league wide. It was and is worth £15.

(240) The same Robert holds LEGE [Leigh in Colehill]. Two thegns held (it) T.R.E. and it paid geld for 1 hide. There is land for 1 plough. Three villeins have this (plough) there. There (are) 2 acres of meadow. (There is) wood(land) 1 furlong long and 5 virgates wide. It was worth 13*s*. Now (it is worth) 20*s*.

(241) Robert holds IWERNE [Ranston in Iwerne Courtney][65] of Robert. Two brothers held (it) in parage[66] T.R.E. and it paid geld for 3 hides. There is land for 2½ ploughs. In demesne there is 1 plough and 6 villeins and 3 bordars with 1 plough. There (is) a mill rendering 3*s*. and 10 acres of meadow. (There is) pasture 3 furlongs long and 1 furlong wide. (There is) wood(land) 5 furlongs long and 3 furlongs wide. It was and is worth £3.

(242) Robert himself holds POVINTONE [Povington in Tyneham, site derelict]. Almar held (it) T.R.E. and it paid geld for 8½ hides. There is land for 6 ploughs. In demesne there are 3 ploughs and 8 serfs and 4 villeins and 5 bordars with 3 ploughs. There (is) a mill rendering 25*s*. and 8 acres of meadow and 6 acres of wood(land). (There is) pasture 6 furlongs long and as much in width. In Wareham (there is) 1 burgess rendering 2*s*.[67] It was and is worth £11. The mill of this manor is claimed for the king's use.

XXXI. THE LAND OF EDWARD OF SALISBURY

(243) Edward of Salisbury holds CHENEFORD [Canford Magna] of the king. Ulwen held (it) T.R.E. and it paid geld for 25 hides. There is land for 18 ploughs. Of this there are in demesne 11½ hides and there (are) 3 ploughs and 9 serfs and 35 villeins and 40 bordars with 15 ploughs. There (are) 2 mills rendering 15*s*. and 118 acres of meadow. (There is) pasture 2 leagues in length and width. (There is) wood(land) 1 league long and ½ league wide. At Winburne [Wimborne Minster] (there are) 3 bordars and 1 house belonging to this manor and there (is) 1 league of marshland (*broce*).

(244) The same Edward holds CHINESTANESTONE [Kinson, Hants, now part of Bournemouth]. Ulwen held (it) T.R.E. and it paid geld for 13 hides. There is land for 9 ploughs. Of this there are in demesne 5 hides and 1 virgate of land and there (are) 2 ploughs and 7 serfs and 18 villeins and 14 coscets and 4 cottars with 7 ploughs. There (is) a mill rendering 5*s*. and 1 acre of wood(land) and 95 acres of meadow. (There is) pasture 3 leagues long and 2 leagues wide less 3 furlongs. These 2 manors used to be worth £50 when he received (them). Now (they are worth) £70.

XXXII. THE LAND OF ERNULF OF HESDIN

(245) Ernulf holds CHINTONE [Kington Magna] of the king. Edric held (it) T.R.E. and it paid geld for 6 hides and 1 virgate of land.[68] There is land for 5 ploughs. Of this there are in demesne 4 hides and 3 virgates of land and there (are) 2 ploughs and 6 serfs and 6 villeins and 1 bordar with 2 ploughs. There (are) 20 acres of meadow and 1 furlong of wood(land). It was and is worth £4. Urse holds of Ernulf.

(246) Urse holds MELESBERIE [Melbury Osmond] of Ernulf. Three thegns held (it) in parage[69] T.R.E. and it paid geld for 4½ hides. There is land for 4 ploughs. In demesne there are 3 ploughs with 1 villein and 7 bordars with ½ plough. There (are) 12 acres of meadow. (There is) wood(land) 8 furlongs long and 4 furlongs wide. It was worth 40*s*. Now (it is worth) £4.

(247) Ernulf himself holds CHIMEDECOME [Higher and Lower Kingcombe in Toller Porcorum]. Five thegns held (it) T.R.E. and it paid geld for 3¼ virgates of land. There is land for 1 plough. Five villeins have this (plough) there and there (are) 3 acres of meadow and pasture 8 furlongs long and 2 furlongs wide. It is worth 10*s*.

(248) Ernulf himself holds MAPERETONE [Mapperton]. Seven thegns held (it) T.R.E. and it paid geld for 3 hides and 3 virgates of land. There is land for 3½ ploughs. In demesne there are 2 ploughs and 3 villeins and 10 bordars with 1½ plough. There (are) 8 acres of meadow. (There is) pasture 1 league long and 4 furlongs wide. (There is) wood(land) 5 furlongs long and 4 furlongs wide. It was worth 40*s*. Now (it is worth) 60*s*.

(249)[70] The same Ernulf holds POVERTONE [North Poorton]. Seven thegns held (it) T.R.E. and it paid geld for ½ hide. There is land for 1 plough. Seven villeins have this (plough) there and (there are) 2 furlongs of pasture in length and width. It is worth 20*s*. 6*d*.

XXXIII. THE LAND OF TURSTIN FITZ ROLF

(250) Turstin fitz Rolf holds GELINGHAM [Gillingham] of the king and Bernard (holds it) of him. Alwold held (it) T.R.E. and it paid geld for 3½ hides. There is land for 4 ploughs. In demesne there are 2 ploughs and 8 serfs and 1 villein with 2 ploughs.

64 'in' interlined.
65 See Fägersten, op. cit. 11–12 and n., for this identification.
66 'in paragio' interlined.
67 This sentence was added in the margin.
68 'et una virgata terre' added in the margin.
69 'in paragio' interlined.
70 This entry was added at the foot of the column.

There (are) 12 acres of meadow. It was and is worth 60*s*.

(251) Ranulf holds INLANDE [Higher and Lower Nyland in Kington Magna] of Turstin. Edric, Dachelin, and Alward held (it) in parage[71] T.R.E. and it paid geld for 2 hides. There is land for 2 ploughs. In demesne there is 1 plough with 1 serf and 2 villeins and 2 bordars with ½ plough. There (are) 8 acres of meadow. It was and is worth 20*s*.

(252) Bernard holds 1 hide in the same vill of Turstin. Dode held (it) T.R.E. There is 1 plough and it is worth 10*s*. It was worth 5*s*.

(253) Turstin himself holds ADELINGTONE [Allington]. Brictui held (it) T.R.E. and it paid geld for 3 hides. There is land for 3 ploughs. In demesne there are 2 ploughs and 12 bordars with ½ plough and 9 *censores* paying 11*s*. There (is) a mill rendering 15*s*. and 10 acres of meadow and 6 acres of wood(land). (There is) pasture 7½ furlongs long and 1 furlong wide. It was worth £3. Now (it is worth) £4.

(254) Ranulf holds STOCHES [Stoke Wallis in Whitchurch Canonicorum, site lost][72] of Turstin. Ulviet held (it) T.R.E. and it paid geld for 1 hide. There is land for 1 plough which is there with 1 serf and 5 bordars. There (are) 10 acres of meadow and 16 acres of wood(land). It is worth 20*s*.

(255) Ranulf holds STOCHES [Thurstanshay in Whitchurch Canonicorum, site lost] of Turstin. Brictuin held (it) T.R.E. and it paid geld for 3 virgates of land. There is land for 1 plough which is there and 4 acres of meadow and 16 acres of wood(land). It is worth 10*s*.

XXXIIII. THE LAND OF WILLIAM OF EU

(256) William of Eu holds TORENTONE [Thorton (Farm) in Marnhull] of the king and William (holds it) of him. Alestan held (it) T.R.E. and it paid geld for 2 hides. There is land for 3 ploughs. In demesne there are 2 ploughs and 4 serfs and 3 villeins and 6 bordars with 1 plough. There (are) 10 acres of meadow. (There is) wood(land) 3 furlongs long and 2 furlongs wide. It was and is worth 40*s*.

(257) The same William holds BRADEFORD [Bradford Peverell] of William. Tol held (it) T.R.E. and it paid geld for 17 hides. There is land for 8 ploughs. In demesne there are 2 ploughs and 4 serfs and 10 villeins and 13 bordars with 5 ploughs. There (are) 2 mills rendering 20*s*. and 30 acres of meadow. (There is) pasture 10 furlongs long and 4 furlongs wide. It was and is worth £12.

(258) William holds 1 hide in HIWES [unidentified] of William. There is land for ½ plough. It is worth 20*s*.

(259) Hugh holds MAPLEDRE [Mappowder] of William. Ulward and Almar held (it) T.R.E. and it paid geld for 3 virgates of land. There is land for 1 plough. There (are) 4 acres of meadow and 5 acres of wood(land). It was worth 15*s*. Now (it is worth) 7*s*.

(260) The same Hugh holds LICHET [Lytchett Matravers] of William. Tholi held (it) T.R.E. and it paid geld for 12 hides. There is land for 8 ploughs. In demesne there are 2 ploughs and 3 serfs and 16 villeins and 11 coscets with 5 ploughs. There (are) 40 acres of meadow. (There are) 11 furlongs of pasture. (There is) wood(land) ½ league in[73] length and width. (There is) 1 league of marshland in length and width. In Wareham (there are) 2 gardens (*ortos*) and 1 bordar. It was worth £9. Now (it is worth) £10.

(261) William holds BLENEFORD [Blandford St. Mary] of William. Tou held (it) T.R.E. and it paid geld for 3½ hides. There is land for 2 ploughs. In demesne there is 1 plough and 3 serfs and 3 bordars. There (are) 12 acres of meadow and 56 acres of pasture. It was and is worth 40*s*. In the vill itself William holds ½ hide which Tou had in pledge and it was redeemed, (but) which Ralph de Limesi took with that other land. Afterwards the king did not have geld from it. It was worth 3*s*.

(262) Hugh holds WELLECOME [Woolcombe in Melbury Bubb] of William. Brismar held (it) T.R.E. and it paid geld for 5 hides. There is land for 4 ploughs. In demesne there is 1 plough and 2 serfs and 2 villeins and 8 bordars with 1 plough and 3 cottars. There[74] (are) 8 acres of meadow. (There is) pasture 8 furlongs long and 2 furlongs wide. (There is) wood(land) 2 furlongs long and 1 furlong wide. It was and is worth 50*s*.

(263) William holds SUERE [Swyre] of William. Tol held (it) T.R.E. and it paid geld for 9 hides. There is land for 7 ploughs. In demesne there are 3 ploughs and 5 serfs and 5 villeins and 11 bordars with 3 ploughs. There (is) a mill rendering 16*s*. and 30 acres of meadow. (There is) pasture 7 furlongs long and 1 furlong wide. It was and is worth £9. In that vill William holds a certain piece of land which never paid geld T.R.E. but was in the demesne and farm of the king. A certain royal reeve let this (land) to Toxus[75] the priest. Later he took it back into the king's hand. Toxus was given seizin of it again by King Edward (*per regem Edwardum iterum fuit saisitus*), as he says, and thus he held it in the life and death of King Edward and in the time of Harold. Formerly it was for grazing, now it is good for seed (*prius erat pascualis modo seminabilis*).

(264) William himself holds WENFROT [Wynford Eagle] in demesne. Alestan held (it) T.R.E. and it paid geld for 14[76] hides. There is land for 11 ploughs. In demesne there are 6 hides of this land and there (are) 3 ploughs and 2 serfs and 13 villeins and 18 bordars with 8 ploughs. There (is) a mill rendering 10*s*. and 8 acres of meadow. (There is) pasture 2 leagues long and 1 league and 4 furlongs wide.

[71] 'in paragio' interlined.

[72] For the identification of *Stoches* in this and the following entry, see Fägersten, op. cit. 297–8.

[73] 'inter' interlined.

[74] 'Ibi' interlined.

[75] The facsimile has *Toxo* with 'p(resbytero)' interlined, the printed version *Toxos*. For a discussion of this name, see O. von Feilitzen, *Pre-Conquest Personal Names of Dom. Bk.* 338.

[76] 'ii' interlined.

(There is) wood(land) 5 furlongs long and 3 furlongs wide. It was worth £12. Now (it is worth) £19.

(265) Ansfrid holds Frome [Frome Vauchurch] of William. Alestan held (it) T.R.E. and it paid geld for 6 hides. There is land for 3 ploughs. In demesne there is 1 plough and 2 serfs and 4 villeins and 8 bordars with 2 ploughs. There (is) a mill rendering 10*s*. and 10 acres of meadow. (There is) pasture 6 furlongs long and 2 furlongs wide. (There is) wood(land) 2 furlongs long and 1 furlong wide. It used to be worth £3. Now (it is worth) £4.

(266) William himself holds Circel [Long Crichel and Moor Crichel]. Alestan held (it) T.R.E. and it paid geld for 12 hides. There is land for 9 ploughs. Of this there are in demesne 7½ hides and there (are) 2 ploughs and 8 serfs and 3 female slaves (*ancille*) and 13 villeins and 7 bordars with 4 ploughs. There (are) 2 acres of meadow. (There is) pasture 20 furlongs long and 3 furlongs wide. (There is) wood(land) 3 furlongs long and 2 furlongs wide. It was worth £10. Now (it is worth) £15.

(267) William holds Terente [unidentified] of William. Toul held (it) T.R.E. and it paid geld for 3½ hides. There is land for 3 ploughs. In demesne there is 1 plough and 2 serfs and 4 villeins and 2 bordars with 1½ plough. There (is) pasture 5 furlongs long and 3 furlongs wide. (There is) wood(land) 8 furlongs long and 4 furlongs wide. It was worth 20*s*. Now (it is worth) £4.

(268) Ansfrid holds Aleurde [East and West Elworth in Portesham] of William. Alestan held (it) T.R.E. and it paid geld for 2 hides. There is land for 2 ploughs. In demesne there is 1 plough with 1 serf and 3 villeins
[f. 82]
and 4 bordars with 1 plough. There (are) 8 acres of meadow and pasture 3 furlongs long and 2 furlongs wide. It was and is worth 60*s*.

(269) Hugh holds Stoches [Stock Gaylard (House) in Lydlinch] of William.[77] Toul held (it) T.R.E. and it paid geld for 1 hide. There is land for 3 ploughs. Eight villeins and 3 bordars have these (ploughs) there. There (are) 8 acres of meadow. (There is) wood(land) 10 furlongs long and 4 furlongs wide. It was and is worth 50*s*. Toul held this land in pledge of the land of Scireburne [Sherborne] T.R.E.

(270) The same Hugh holds Candel [Stourton Caundle] of William. Toul held (it) T.R.E. and it paid geld for 3½ hides. There is land for 3 ploughs. In demesne there is 1 plough and 2 serfs and 4 villeins and 2 bordars with 1 plough. There (are) 7 acres of meadow and pasture 4 furlongs long and 1 furlong wide. It was and is worth 60*s*.

XXXV. THE LAND OF WILLIAM OF FALAISE

(271) William of Falaise holds Seltone [Silton] of the king. Ulward White[78] held (it) T.R.E. and it paid geld for 8 hides. There is land for 8 ploughs. In demesne there are 2 ploughs and 6 serfs and 8 villeins and 10 bordars with 4 ploughs. There (are) 3 mills rendering 5*s*. and 20 acres of meadow. (There is) wood(land) 1 league long and ½ league wide. It was worth £11. Now (it is worth) £6. With this land the same William holds 1 hide and ½ virgate of land. There is land for 1 plough. Three villeins have this (plough) there and it is worth 10*s*. Ulward held this land in pledge T.R.E. from a certain reeve of his. With the land itself the same William still holds 1 hide. There is land for 1 plough which is there in demesne and it is worth 20*s*. Ulward bought this hide from the Bishop of Exeter T.R.E. but it did not belong to the manor itself.

(272) With the same aforesaid land the same William holds 3 hides in Miltetone [Milton on Stour in Gillingham] and Roger (holds it) of him. Wicnod held (it) T.R.E. There is land for 1½ plough. There are 5 bordars with 1 plough and a mill rendering 15*d*. and 8 acres of meadow and wood(land) 8 furlongs long and 2 furlongs wide. It was and is worth 20*s*.

XXXVI. THE LAND OF WILLIAM OF MOYON

(273) William of Moyon holds Todeberie [Todber] of the king and Geoffrey (holds it) of him. Godric held (it) T.R.E. and it paid geld for 2 hides. There is land for 2 ploughs which are there in demesne and a mill rendering 10*s*. and 12 acres of meadow. (There is) wood(land) ½ league long and 1 furlong wide. It was worth £3. Now (it is worth) £4.[79]

THE LAND OF WILLIAM OF MOYON IN DORSET

(lxxxiii) William has 1 manor which is called Todeberia which Godric held on the day when King Edward was alive and dead. This (manor) paid geld for 2 hides T.R.E. Two ploughs can plough these. And now Geoffrey Maloret holds it of William. Geoffrey has there 2 ploughs and 1 pack-horse and 8 beasts and 12 pigs and 100 sheep and 1 mill which renders 10*s*. a year and ½ league of wood(land) in length and 1 furlong in width and 12 acres of meadow. This (manor) is worth £4 and when William received (it) it was worth 60*s*.

(274) William himself holds Spehtesberie [Spetisbury]. Agelward and Godric held (it) as 2 manors T.R.E. and it paid geld for 7 hides and 1 virgate of land and 6 acres. There is land for 6 ploughs. In demesne there are 4 ploughs and 6 serfs and 10 villeins and 12 bordars with 3 ploughs. There (is) a mill rendering 12*s*. 6*d*. and 50 acres of meadow and pasture 5½ furlongs long and 2 furlongs wide and in another place on the water (*super aquam*) pasture 2½ furlongs long and 1½ furlong wide. It was worth 100*s*. Now (it is worth) £7 10*s*.

(lxxxiv) William of Moyon has 1 manor which is called Spestesberia which 1 thegn (called) Alward held on the day when King Edward was alive and dead. This (manor) paid geld for 5 hides and 1 virgate and 6 acres. Four ploughs and ½ (plough) can plough these. In the same vill William has 1 manor which Godric held on the day when King Edward was alive and dead, which paid geld for 2 hides. One plough and ½ (plough) can plough these. William holds these 2 manors as one. There William has in demesne 3 hides and 1

[77] 'de Willelmo' interlined.
[78] 'wit' interlined.
[79] 'ii' interlined.

virgate and 10 acres and 4 ploughs and the villeins have 4 hides less 4 acres and 3 ploughs. There are 10 villeins and 12 bordars and 6 serfs and 2 pack-horses and 5 beasts and 30 pigs and 166 sheep and 1 mill which renders 12*s.* 6*d.* and 50 acres of meadow and 5½ furlongs of pasture in length and 2 in width and in another place 2½ furlongs of pasture in length and 1½ furlong in width. This manor is worth £7 10*s.* a year and when he received (it) it was worth 100*s.*

(275) Ogisus holds WINTREBURNE [Winterborne Houghton] of William. Alward held (it) T.R.E. and it paid geld for 2½ hides. There is land for 2 ploughs. There are 4 bordars with 1 serf and 2 acres of meadow and 6 furlongs of pasture and 13 acres of underwood. It was worth 50*s.* Now (it is worth) 40*s.*

(lxxxv) William has 1 manor which is called Wintreborna which Alward held in parage on the day when King Edward was alive and dead. This (manor) paid geld T.R.E. for 2½ hides and of these 2½ hides, Hugh de Boscherbert holds 1 virgate unlawfully of the wife of Hugh fitz Grip, and it can be ploughed with 2 ploughs, and now Ogisus holds it of William. Thence Ogisus has in demesne 2 hides and ½ virgate and a certain villein has ½ virgate. Ogisus has there 4 bordars and 1 serf and 4 beasts and 4 pigs and 10 sheep and 13 acres of underwood and 6 furlongs of pasture and 2 acres of meadow. This (manor) is worth 40*s.* and when William received it it was worth 50*s.*

[f. 81b][80]

(276) The same William of Moyon holds POLEHAM [? Hazelbury Bryan]. Twenty-one thegns held (it) T.R.E. and it paid geld for 10 hides. There is land for 8 ploughs. In demesne there are 3 ploughs and 6 serfs and 14 villeins and 25 bordars with 7 ploughs. There (is) a mill rendering 40*d.* and 32 acres of meadow. (There is) wood(land) 2 leagues long and 8 furlongs wide. It was worth £10. Now (it is worth) £8.

(lxxxvi) William of Moyon has 1 manor which is called Poleham which 21 thegns held in parage on the day when King Edward was alive and dead, and they could go to any lord. This (manor) paid geld T.R.E. for 10 hides. Eight ploughs can plough these. Thence William has 4 hides and 1 virgate and 6 acres in demesne and 3 ploughs and the villeins (have) 5½ hides and 4 acres and 7 ploughs. There William has 14 villeins and 25 bordars and 1 garden in Wareham which renders 3*d.*[81] and 6 serfs and 2 pack-horses and 6 beasts and 25 pigs and 170 sheep and 15 goats and 1 mill which renders 3*s.* 4*d.* and 2 leagues of wood(land) in length and 8 furlongs in width and 32 acres of meadow. This (manor) is worth £8 and when William received (it) it was worth £10.

(277) The same William holds HAME [Hammoon]. Godric held (it) T.R.E. and it paid geld for 5 hides. There is land for 4 ploughs. In demesne there are 2 ploughs and 4 serfs and 6 villeins and 5 bordars with 2 ploughs. There (is) a mill rendering 7*s.* 6*d.* and 50 acres of meadow and 3 furlongs of pasture in length and 1 furlong in width. It was worth 60*s.* Now (it is worth) 100*s.*

(lxxxvii) William has 1 manor which is called Ham which a certain thegn who is called Godric held on the day when King Edward was alive and dead. This (manor) paid geld for 5 hides. Four ploughs can plough these. And now Torstin holds it of William. Thence Torstin has 3 hides and 8 acres and 2 ploughs in demesne and the villeins (have) 2 hides less 12 acres and 2 ploughs. There Torstin has 6 villeins and 5 bordars and 4 serfs and 2 pack-horses and 14 beasts and 24 pigs and 67 sheep and 1 mill which renders 7*s.* 6*d.* and 50 acres of meadow and 3 furlongs of pasture in length and 1 furlong in width. This (manor) is worth 100*s.* and when William received (it) it was worth 60*s.*

(278) The same William holds FROME [Chilfrome]. Three thegns held (it) in parage[82] T.R.E. and it paid geld for 10 hides. There is land for 6 ploughs. In demesne there are 4 ploughs and 4 serfs and 4 villeins and 7 bordars. There (is) a mill (rendering) 3*s.* and 20 acres of meadow and 9 acres of wood(land). (There is) pasture 17 furlongs long and as much in width. It was and is worth £6. Two men hold (it) of William.

(lxxxviii) William has 1 manor which is called Froma which 3 thegns (held)[83] in parage[84] on the day when King Edward was alive and dead. William claims these 3 manors as two. They paid geld for 10 hides. Now Dodoman holds 5 hides of William. Dodoman has these 5 hides in demesne except for 1 virgate and 4 acres and 2 ploughs and 2 villeins and 1 bordar and 2 cottars and 2 serfs and 7 pigs and 60 sheep and 7 goats and 18*d.* from 1 mill and 4½ acres of wood(land) and 10 acres of meadow and 8½ furlongs of pasture in length and the same amount in width. This (manor) is worth 60*s.* and when he received (it it was worth) as much. Of these aforesaid 10 hides, Niel holds 5 hides of William. Three ploughs can plough these. There Niel has in demesne 5 hides less 1 virgate and 2 ploughs and the villeins (have) 1 virgate. There are 2 villeins and 6 bordars and 2 serfs and 5 beasts and 7 pigs and 140 sheep and 7 goats[85] and 18*d.* from 1 mill and 4½ acres of wood(land) and 10 acres of meadow and 8½ furlongs of pasture in length and the same amount in width. This manor is worth £3 and when he received (it it was worth) the same amount.

(279) Robert holds FROME [Cruxton in Maiden Newton][86] of William. Alward held (it) T.R.E. and it paid geld for 4 hides. There is land for 2 ploughs which are there in demesne with 1 serf and 9 bordars. There (is) a mill rendering 10*s.* and 7 acres of meadow and 7 furlongs of pasture in length and 5 furlongs in width. It was worth £4. Now (it is worth) £3.

(lxxxix) William has 1 manor which is called Froma which Ailward held on the day when King Edward was alive and dead which paid geld for 4 hides. Two ploughs can plough these. Now

[80] Nos. 276–83 were added on a separate leaf (f. 81b).

[81] 'et i ortum in Warham qui reddit iii denarios' interlined.

[82] 'in paragio' interlined.

[83] Supply 'tenuerunt'.

[84] 'pariter' interlined.

[85] 'et vii capre' interlined.

[86] See pp. 133–4.

Robert holds (it) of William. Thence Robert has in demesne 3 hides and 8 acres and 2 ploughs and the villeins have 1 hide less 8 acres and 1 plough. There are 9 bordars and 1 serf and 1 pack-horse and 6 pigs and 80 sheep and 1 mill which renders 10*s.* and 7 acres of meadow and 7 furlongs of pasture in length and 5 in width. This (manor) is worth 60*s.* and when he received (it) it was worth £4.

(280) Ranulf holds CELBERGE [Chelborough] of William. Godric held (it) T.R.E. and it paid geld for 3 hides. There is land for 3 ploughs. In demesne there is 1 plough and 1 villein and 5 bordars with 1 plough. There (are) 10 acres of meadow and 7 furlongs of pasture in length and 3 furlongs in width. It was and is worth £3. The son of Odo the chamberlain claims these 3 hides.

(xc) William has 1 manor which is called Celberga which Godric held on the day when King Edward was alive and dead which gave geld for 3 hides. Three ploughs can plough these. Now Ranulf holds (it) of William. Thence Ranulf has in demesne 2½ hides and 1 plough and the villeins (have) ½ hide and 1 plough. There is 1 villein and 5 bordars and 6 pigs and 1 league of wood(land) in length and ½ (league) in width and 10 acres of meadow and 7 furlongs of pasture in length and 3 in width. This (manor) is worth £3 and when he received (it it was worth) as much. The son of Odo the chamberlain claims these 3 hides. The king ordered that he should have right (*ut inde rectum habeat*). There is 1 hide of these 3 which did not give geld.

(281) Geoffrey holds WERNE [Steepleton Iwerne in Iwerne Stepleton] of William. Godwin held (it) T.R.E. and it paid geld for 3 hides. There is land for 3 ploughs. In demesne there are 2 ploughs and 2 serfs and 6 villeins and 6 bordars with 1 plough. There (are) 8 furlongs of wood(land) and 10 furlongs of pasture in length and 3 furlongs in width. It was and is worth £4.

(xci) William has 1 manor which is called Iwerna which Godwin held on the day when King Edward was alive and dead. This (manor) paid geld for 3 hides T.R.E. Three ploughs can plough these.[87] And now Geoffrey holds it of William. Thence Geoffrey has 1½ hide and 2 ploughs in demesne and the villeins (have) 1½ hide and 1 plough. There Geoffrey has 6 villeins and 6 bordars and 2 serfs and 1 pack-horse and 6 beasts and 282 sheep and 8 furlongs of wood(land) and 10 furlongs of pasture in length and 3 in width. This (manor) is worth £4 and when William received (it) it was worth as much.

(282) The same William holds WINDRESORIE [Little Windsor in Broadwindsor]. Alward held (it) T.R.E. and it paid geld for 4 hides. There is land for 3 ploughs. In demesne there are 2 ploughs and 2 serfs and 9 villeins and 2 bordars with 1 plough. There (are) 30 acres of meadow and 8 furlongs of pasture in length and 6 furlongs in width and 6 furlongs of wood(land) in length and 3 furlongs in width. It is worth 60*s.*

(xcii) William has 1 manor which is called Windresoria which Aelward held T.R.E. and he could go to any lord he wished and it paid geld for 4 hides which 3 ploughs can plough. Of these William has 3 hides and 1 virgate and 2 ploughs and the villeins (have) ½ hide and 1 virgate and 1 plough. There William has 9 villeins and 2 bordars and 2 serfs and 1 pack-horse and 10 beasts and 3 pigs and 10 sheep and 6 furlongs of wood(land) in length and 3 in width and 30 acres of meadow and 8 furlongs of pasture in length and 6 in width and it is worth 60*s.* and when he received (it) it was worth 40*s.*

(283) The same William holds MALPERETONE [Mapperton]. Elmer held (it) T.R.E. and it paid geld for 5 hides and 1 virgate of land. There is land for 4 ploughs. In demesne there are 3 ploughs and 6 serfs and 6 villeins and 7 bordars with 1 plough. There (is) a mill rendering 5*s.* and 8 acres of meadow and 12 acres of pasture. (There is) wood(land) 6 furlongs in length and 4 furlongs in width. It is worth 70*s.*

(xciii) William has 1 manor which is called Malperretona which Elmer held on the day when King Edward was alive and dead and he could go to any lord and it paid geld for 5 hides and 1 virgate which 4 ploughs can plough. Of these William has 3 hides and 3 ploughs in demesne and the villeins (have) 2 hides and 1 virgate and 1 plough. There William has 6 villeins and 7 bordars and 6 serfs and 2 pack-horses and 14 beasts and 16 pigs and 47 sheep (*berbices*) and 30 goats and 1 mill which renders 5*s.* and 6 furlongs of wood(land) in length and 4 in width and 8 acres of meadow and 12 acres of pasture and it is worth 70*s.* and it was worth 60*s.* when he received (it).

[f. 82 (cont.)]

XXXVII. THE LAND OF WILLIAM OF BRIOUZE

(284) William of Briouze holds WIDETONE [Glanvilles Wootton] of the king and Ralph (holds it) of him. The Abbot of Milton held (it) T.R.E. and it paid geld for 3 hides. There is land for 3 ploughs. In demesne there is 1 plough with 1 serf and 3 villeins and 4 bordars with 1 plough. There (are) 16 acres of meadow and 4 acres of pasture. (There is) wood(land) 5 furlongs long and 4 furlongs wide. It was and is worth £3.

(285) Ralph holds 2 hides in the same vill of William. There is land for 1 plough. There are 2 serfs and 1 bordar and 6 acres of meadow and 2 acres of pasture. (There is) wood(land) 5 furlongs long and 2 furlongs wide. It was worth 30*s.* Now (it is worth) 40*s.*

(286) William himself holds ½ hide in HOLTONE [West Holton in Wareham St. Martin]. There is land for ½ plough. It is worth 10*s.*

(287) David holds AISSE [Ash in Stourpaine] of William. Two thegns held (it) T.R.E. and it paid geld for 2½[88] hides. There is land for 2 ploughs.

[87] 'Has possunt arare iii carruce' added in the margin.

[88] 'et dimidia' interlined.

There is 1 plough and 3[89] serfs and 3 coscets and 10 acres of meadow and pasture 10 furlongs long and 2 furlongs wide. It was and is worth 40*s*.

(288) Richard holds CUNELIZ [Kimmeridge] of William. Brictwold held (it) T.R.E. and it paid geld for 1½ hide. There is land for 1½ plough. In demesne there is 1 plough and 4 acres of meadow. (There is) pasture 2 furlongs long and 1 furlong wide. It was and is worth 30*s*.

(289) The same William holds ½ hide in CRIC [East Creech in Church Knowle] and Walter (holds it) of him. Ednod held (it) T.R.E. There are 2 bordars and 3 acres of meadow and 3 acres of wood(land) and pasture 7 furlongs long and 4 furlongs wide. It was and is worth 10*s*.

(290) The same Walter holds 3½ virgates of land in ALVRETONE [Afflington (Farm) in Corfe Castle] of William. There is land for 1 plough which is there with 2 bordars and 1 acre of meadow and 1 furlong of pasture. It was and is worth 16*s*.

(291) The same Walter holds 1 hide in CHENOLLE [Church Knowle] of William. There is land for 1 plough. There is 1 acre of meadow. (There is) pasture 4 furlongs in length and 2 furlongs in width. It is worth 20*s*. Sawin held (it) T.R.E.

(292) The same W. holds 1½ hide in RISTONE [Rushton in East Stoke]. There is land for 1 plough which is there and a mill and 20 acres of meadow and 1 league of pasture. It renders 30*s*. and 4 sesters of honey. Burde held (it).[90]

(293) The same Walter holds 1 hide and 3 virgates of land in WEREGROTE [Worgret in Arne] of William. Brictuin held (it) T.R.E. There is land for 1½ plough. There is 1 villein and 1 bordar and ½ mill rendering 10*s*. The whole (manor) renders 28*s*.

(294) Robert holds 2 hides of land in HAFELTONE [Hethfelton in East Stoke] of William. Aedelflete held (it) T.R.E. There is land for 1 plough. There are 2 villeins with 1 serf and 10 acres of meadow. (There is) pasture 1 league long and ½ league wide. It was and is worth 10*s*.

(295) Richard holds ½ hide in METMORE [Smedmore (House) in Kimmeridge] of William. There is land for ½ plough. There is 1 villein and 1 serf and 3 acres of meadow. It is worth 10*s*.

(296) Richard holds of William 7 hides less ½ virgate in PORBICHE [Purbeck] HUNDRED [? Langton Matravers].[91] Twelve thegns held (it) T.R.E. and could go where they would. There is land for 7 ploughs. In demesne there are 2 ploughs and 4 villeins and 2 bordars. It is worth 70*s*. The wife of Hugh fitz Grip[92] holds part of this land [? Langton Wallis in Corfe Castle][93] and there she has 2 ploughs and 4 villeins and 5 bordars and pasture 1 league long and 6 furlongs wide. It is worth £4.

[89] The facsimile has *iii*, the printed version *iiii*.
[90] 'Burde tenuit' added in the margin.
[91] See p. 56 n.
[92] 'filii Grip' interlined.

(297) Humphrey holds ORGARESTONE [Woolgarston in Corfe Castle] of William. Five thegns held (it) T.R.E. and it paid geld for 2 hides less 4 acres. There is land for 2 ploughs. There are 6 villeins and 8 acres of meadow. (There is) pasture ½ league long and 1 furlong wide. It is worth 40*s*.

XXXVIII. THE LAND OF WILLIAM OF ECOUIS

(298) William of Ecouis holds CHENISTETONE [West Knighton] of the king. Two thegns held (it) in parage T.R.E. and it paid geld for 6 hides. There is land for 4 ploughs. In demesne there are 2 ploughs and 6 serfs and 5 villeins and 5 bordars—[*blank*][94] with 1 plough. There (are) 2 mills rendering 12*s*. and 20 acres of meadow and 20 acres of wood(land) and 250 acres of pasture. It was worth £7. Now (it is worth) £6.

(299) The same William holds the land of 5 thegns in CANDELLE [Stourton Caundle] as 1 manor. There are 5 hides. Of this there are in demesne 3½ hides and there (are) 2 ploughs and 3 serfs and 7 villeins and 3 bordars with 3 ploughs. There (is) a mill rendering 9*s*. and 10 acres of meadow and 12 acres of wood(land). (There is) pasture 6 furlongs long and 3 furlongs wide. It was and is worth £7.

XXXIX. THE LAND OF WALSCIN OF DOUAI

(300) Walscin of Douai holds WINTREBURNE [unidentified] of the king and Walcher (holds it) of him. Alward and Alwin[95] held (it) T.R.E. as 2 manors and it paid geld for 6 hides. There is land for 4 ploughs. In demesne there are 2 ploughs and 3 serfs and 5 villeins and 3 bordars with ½ plough. There (are) 12 acres of meadow and 8 acres of wood(land). (There is) pasture 4 furlongs long and 3 furlongs wide. It was worth £6. Now (it is worth) £4.

(301) Wimer holds CANDELLE [Stourton Caundle] of Walscin. Alsi held (it) T.R.E. and it paid geld for 3 hides. There is land for 3 ploughs. In demesne there are 2 ploughs and 2 serfs and 2 villeins and 2 bordars with 1 plough. There (is) a mill rendering 3*s*. and 10 acres of meadow and 3 acres of underwood. It was and is worth 40*s*.

XL. THE LAND OF WALERAN

(302) Waleran holds MANESTONE [Manston] of the king and Warenger (holds it) of him. Trasmund held (it) T.R.E. and it paid geld for 5 hides. There is land for 8 ploughs. In demesne there are 2 ploughs and 3 serfs and 10 villeins and 6 bordars with 2 ploughs. There (are) 2 mills rendering 12*s*. and 25 acres of meadow. (There is) wood(land) 4 furlongs long and 1 furlong wide. It was worth £6. Now (it is worth) 100*s*.

(303) Ranulf holds CHINTONE [Little Kington (Farm) in Kington Magna] of Waleran. Leviet held (it) T.R.E. and it paid geld for 3 hides. There is land for 2 ploughs. In demesne there is 1½ plough and 2

[93] See p. 56 n.
[94] There is a small space here in the facsimile but not in the printed version. For a comment, see p. 5.
[95] 'et Alwin' interlined.

serfs and 7 bordars with ½ plough. There (are) 8 acres of meadow and 4 acres of pasture. It was worth 30*s*. Now (it is worth) 50*s*.

(304) Waleran himself holds SUDTONE [Sutton Waldron]. Godmund held (it) T.R.E. and it paid geld for 8 hides. There is land for 6 ploughs. In demesne there is 1 plough with 1 serf and 11 villeins and 12 bordars with 3 ploughs. There (is) a mill rendering 7*s*. 6*d*. and 6 acres of meadow and 40 acres of wood(land). It was and is worth £8.

(305) Urse holds WINTREBURNE [unidentified] of Waleran. Alvred held (it) T.R.E. and it paid geld for 4 hides. There is land for 2 ploughs which are there and 3 serfs and 6 villeins and 80 acres of pasture and 35 acres of meadow. (There is) wood(land) 9 furlongs long and 1 furlong wide. It was and is worth 40*s*.

(306) Azelin holds DODESBERIE [Dudsbury in West Parley] of Waleran. Godwin held (it) T.R.E. and it paid geld for 1 hide. There is land for 1 plough which is there with 4 bordars and 7 acres of meadow and 6 acres of wood(land). (There is) pasture ½ league long and 5 furlongs wide. It was and is worth 20*s*.

(307) Ingelram holds FIFHIDE [Fifehead Neville] of Waleran. One thegn held (it) T.R.E. and it paid geld for 5 hides. There is land for 3 ploughs which are there with 4 bordars and 4 serfs. There (is) a mill rendering 40*d*. and 15 acres of meadow. (There is) wood(land) 8 furlongs long and 4 furlongs wide. It is worth £4.

(308) Beulf holds CNOLLE [Church Knowle] of Waleran. One thegn held (it) T.R.E. and he was free with this land, and it paid geld for 1 hide. There is land for 1 plough which is there with 3 serfs. There (is) pasture 2 furlongs long and as much in width. (There is) wood(land) 1 furlong long and as much in width. It is worth 25*s*. Waleran held this of Earl William. Now, as he says, he holds of the king.

[f. 82b]
(309) Waleran himself holds NEWETONE [Maiden Newton]. Alward held (it) T.R.E. and it paid geld for 6 hides. There is land for 7 ploughs. Of this there is ½ hide in demesne and there are 2 ploughs and 5 serfs and 7 villeins and 14 bordars with 5 ploughs. There (are) 2 mills rendering 20*s*. and 18 acres of meadow. (There is) pasture 14 furlongs long and 7 furlongs wide. (There is) wood(land) 5 furlongs long and 3 furlongs wide. It is worth £10.

(310) Ogier holds TOLRE [Toller Porcorum] of Waleran. Alward held (it) T.R.E. and it paid geld for 5 hides. There is land for 4 ploughs. In demesne there are 2 ploughs and 3 serfs and 4 villeins and 5 bordars with 1 plough. There (is) a mill rendering 30*d*. and 15 acres of meadow. (There is) pasture 12 furlongs long and 10 furlongs wide. (There is) wood(land) 5 furlongs long and 3 furlongs wide. It was worth £3. Now (it is worth) £4.

XLI. THE LAND OF WALTER DE CLAVILLE

(311) Walter de Claville holds ALVERONETUNE [Afflington (Farm) in Corfe Castle] of the king. Brictric held (it) T.R.E. and it paid geld for 2 hides and 1½ virgate of land. There is land for 2½ ploughs. In demesne there are 2 ploughs with 1 serf and 1 bordar. There (are) 3 acres of meadow and 4 acres of underwood. (There are) 4 furlongs of pasture in length and width. It was and is worth 50*s*.

> *THE LAND OF WALTER DE CLAVILLE IN DORSET*
> (clvii) Walter has 1 manor which is called Alfrunetona which Brictric held on the day when King Edward was alive and dead and it paid geld for 2 hides and 1½ virgate. Two ploughs and ½ (plough) can plough these. There Walter has 2 ploughs and 1 bordar and 1 serf and 2 pack-horses and 10 beasts and 8[96] pigs and 50 sheep and 4 acres of underwood and 3 acres of meadow and 4 furlongs of pasture in length and width. This (manor) is worth 50*s*. a year and when Walter received it it was worth as much.

(312) The same (Walter) holds CNOLLE [Church Knowle]. Bern held (it) T.R.E. and it paid geld for 2 hides. There is land for 2 ploughs. In demesne there is 1 plough with 1 serf and 2 villeins and 3 acres of meadow and 3 furlongs of pasture in length and as much in width. It was and is worth 40*s*.

> (clviii) Walter has 1 manor which is called Canolla which 1 thegn (called) Beorn held and it paid geld for 2 hides. Two ploughs can plough these. Of these Walter has in demesne 1 hide and 1 virgate and 1 plough and the villeins (have) 3 virgates. There Walter has 2 villeins and 1 serf and 1 pack-horse and 11 beasts and 57 sheep and 3 acres of meadow and 3 furlongs of pasture in length and as much in width. This (manor) is worth 40*s*. a year and when Walter received it it was worth as much.

(313) The same (Walter) holds HOLNE [East Holme]. Eldred held (it) T.R.E. and it paid geld for 2 hides and 1 virgate of land. There is land for 2 ploughs. In demesne there is 1 plough and 4 villeins and 10 acres of meadow and 3 acres of wood(land). (There is) pasture 6 furlongs long and as much in width. It was and is worth 20*s*.

> (clix) Walter has 1 manor which is called Holna which 1 thegn (called) Aldred held T.R.E. and it paid geld for 2 hides and 1 virgate. Two ploughs can plough these. Of these Walter has in demesne ½ hide and 1 plough and the villeins (have) 1½ hide and 1 virgate. There Walter has 4 villeins and 1 pack-horse and 2 beasts and 3 acres of wood(land) and 10 acres of meadow and 6 furlongs of pasture in length and 6 in width. This (manor) is worth 20*s*. a year and when Walter received (it) it was worth as much.

(314) The same (Walter) holds CUME [Coombe Keynes]. Two thegns held (it) T.R.E. and it paid geld for 3 hides. There is land for 3 ploughs. In demesne there is 1 plough and 2 serfs and 2 villeins and 1 bordar with 1½ plough. There (are) 2 acres of

[96] 'i' interlined.

meadow and 2 furlongs of pasture in length and width. It was and is worth 60*s*.

(clx) Walter has 1 manor which is called Cume which 2 thegns held in parage on the day when King Edward was alive and dead and it paid geld for 3 hides. Three ploughs can plough these. Of these Walter has in demesne 2 hides and 1 plough and the villeins (have) 1 hide and 1½ plough. There Walter has 2 villeins and 1 bordar and 2 serfs and 2 pack-horses and 5 beasts and 5 pigs and 2 acres of meadow and 2 furlongs of pasture[97] in length and width. This (manor) is worth £3 a year and when Walter received it it was worth as much.

(315) The same (Walter) holds MORDUNE [Morden]. Four thegns held (it) T.R.E. and it paid geld for 3 hides and 2½ virgates of land. There is land for 3 ploughs. In demesne there is 1 plough and 8 villeins and 10 bordars with 2 ploughs. There (is) a mill rendering 45*d*. and 14 acres of meadow and 3 leagues of pasture in length and width. (There is) wood(land) 2 furlongs long and 1 furlong wide. It was and is worth 60*s*.

(clxi) Walter has 1 manor which is called Mordona which 4 thegns held in parage T.R.E. and it paid geld for 3½ hides and ½ virgate. Three ploughs can plough these. Of these Walter has in demesne 1½ virgate and 1 plough and the villeins have 3 hides and 1 virgate and 2 ploughs. There Walter has[98] 8 villeins and 10 bordars and 14 pigs and 85 sheep and 1 mill which renders 45*d*. a year and 5 goats and 2 furlongs of wood(land) in length (and) 1 in width and 14 acres of meadow and 3 leagues of pasture in length and width and this (manor) is worth £3 a year and when Walter received (it) it was worth as much.

[f. 81][99]

XLII. THE LAND OF BALDWIN

(316) Baldwin the sheriff[1] holds WERNE [Iwerne Courtney or Shroton] of the king. Seward held (it) T.R.E. and it paid geld for 8 hides. There is land for 8 ploughs. In demesne there are 3 ploughs and 4 serfs and 4 villeins and 9 bordars with 4 ploughs. There (are) 2 mills rendering 12*s*. and 30 acres of meadow. (There is) pasture 9 furlongs long and 6 furlongs wide. It was worth £15. Now (it is worth) £10.

[f. 82b (cont.)]

XLIII. THE LAND OF BERENGER GIFFARD

(317) Berenger Giffard[2] holds BRIDIE [Bredy (Farm) in Burton Bradstock] of the king. Harding held (it) T.R.E. and it paid geld for 4 hides. There is land for 3 ploughs. In demesne there is 1 plough and 2 serfs and 5 villeins and 7 bordars with 2 ploughs. There (is) a mill rendering 10*s*. and 15 acres of meadow and pasture 3 furlongs long and 1 wide. It was worth £3. Now (it is worth) £4.

XLIIII. THE LAND OF OSBERN GIFFARD

(318) Osbern Giffard[3] holds HILLE [Hill (Farm) in Iwerne Minster] of the king. Trasmund held (it) T.R.E. and it paid geld for 2 hides. There is land for 1 plough which is there in demesne and 20 acres of meadow and 20 acres of pasture. It was and is worth 20*s*.

XLV. THE LAND OF ALVRED OF EPAIGNES

(319) Alvred of Epaignes holds TORNEWORDE [Turnworth] of the king. Alwi held (it) T.R.E. and it paid geld for 5 hides. There is land for 6 ploughs. In demesne there are 4 ploughs and 4 serfs and 7 villeins and 8 bordars with 1 plough. There (are) 10 acres of meadow and 10 furlongs of pasture in length and 4 in[4] width. (There is) wood(land) 10 furlongs in length and 5 furlongs in width. It was worth £6. Now (it is worth) £10.

XLVI. THE LAND OF MATTHEW DE MORETANIA

(320) Matthew de Moretania holds MELEBURNE [Milborne St. Andrew] of the king. John held (it) T.R.E. and it paid geld for 5 hides. There is land for 4 ploughs. In demesne there are 2 ploughs with 1 villein and 9 bordars. There (is) a mill rendering 32*d*. and 5 acres of meadow and 6 furlongs of underwood. It was and is worth 100*s*.

(321) The same (Matthew) holds OGRE [Owermoigne]. John held (it) T.R.E. and it paid geld for 10 hides less 1 virgate. There is land for 8 ploughs. In demesne there are 2 ploughs and 6 serfs and 7 villeins and 6 coscets with 5 ploughs. There (is) a mill rendering 6*s*. and 20 acres of meadow and 1 league of pasture in length and ½ league in width. It was and is worth £10.

XLVII. THE LAND OF ROGER ARUNDEL

(322) Roger Arundel holds WINDELHAM [Wyndlam (Farm) in Gillingham] of the king. Alnod held (it) T.R.E. and it paid geld for 2 hides. There is land for 1½ plough. In demesne there is 1 plough with 1 serf. There (are) 3 acres of meadow and 4 furlongs of wood(land). It was worth 30*s*. Now (it is worth) 20*s*. Roger holds (it) of Roger.

THE LAND OF ROGER ARUNDEL IN DORSET

(xciv) Roger Arundel has 1 manor which is called Windelham which Alnod held on the day when King Edward was alive and dead. This (man) could go to any lord. This (manor) paid geld T.R.E. for 2 hides. One plough and ½ (plough) could plough these. And now Roger *de margella* holds it of Roger. There Roger (has) 1 plough and 1 serf and 4 beasts and 8 pigs and 4 furlongs of wood(land) and 3 acres of meadow and when Roger received it it was worth 30*s*. and now it is worth 20*s*.

97 'pascue' interlined.
98 'habet' interlined.
99 No. 316 was entered on a separate leaf (f. 81).
1 'vicecomes' interlined.
2 'Gifard' interlined.
3 'Gifard' interlined.
4 'IN' interlined in the facsimile; the printed version has 'In'.

(323) Roger himself holds MELEBERIE [Melbury Bubb]. Bricnod held (it) T.R.E. and it paid geld for 6 hides. There is land for 4 ploughs. There are 4 villeins and 7 bordars and 4 serfs with 2 ploughs. There (is) a mill rendering 5*s*. and 12 acres of meadow and 3 furlongs of pasture. (There is) wood(land) 10 furlongs long and 4 furlongs wide. It was and is worth £4.

(xcv) Roger Arundel has 1 manor which is called Meleberia which Brisnod held on the day when King Edward was alive and dead. This (manor) paid geld T.R.E. for 6 hides. Four ploughs can plough these. Thence Roger has 3 hides and 1 virgate and the villeins (have) 2 hides and 3 virgates and 2 ploughs. There Roger has 4 villeins and 7 bordars and 4 serfs and 3[5] beasts and 15 pigs and 1 mill which renders 5*s*. and 12 acres of meadow and 10 furlongs of wood(land) in length and 4 in width and 3 furlongs of pasture. This manor is worth £4 and when Roger received it it was worth as much.

(324) He himself holds CELBERGE [Chelborough]. Alvert held (it) T.R.E. and it paid geld for 5 hides. There is land for 2 ploughs. In demesne there is 1 plough with 1 serf and 4 villeins and 7 bordars with 1 plough. There (are) 2 acres of meadow and 1 furlong of pasture in length and 1 in width. (There is) wood(land) 4 furlongs long and 2 furlongs wide. It was and is worth 50*s*.

(xcvi) Roger has 1 manor which is called Celberga which Ailvert held on the day when King Edward was alive and dead (and) which paid geld for 5 hides. Two ploughs can plough these.[6] There Roger has in demesne 3 hides and 1 plough and the villeins (have) 2 hides[7] and 1 plough and (he has) 4 villeins and 7 bordars and 1 serf and 12 unbroken mares (*indomitas equas*) and 5 beasts and 5 pigs and 4 furlongs of wood(land) in length and 2 furlongs in width and 2 acres of meadow and 1 furlong of pasture in length and 1 in width. This (manor) is worth 50*s*. and when he received (it) it was worth the same amount.

(325) Robert holds BLENEFORD [Langton Long Blandford] of Roger. Ailvert held (it) T.R.E. and it paid geld for 5 hides. There is land for 4 ploughs. In demesne there are 3 ploughs and 4 serfs and 1 villein and 2 bordars. There (are) 4 acres of meadow and 6 furlongs of pasture in length and 4 furlongs in width. It was and is worth £4.

(xcvii) Roger Arundel has 1 manor which is called Blaeneford which Agelferd held T.R.E. and it paid geld for 5 hides. Four ploughs can plough these. Robert Attlet[8] holds this of Roger Arundel. Of these 5 hides Robert has 4 hides in demesne and 3 ploughs. There Robert has 1 villein and 2 bordars and 4 serfs and 12 pigs and 140 sheep and 4 acres of meadow and 6 furlongs of pasture in length and 4 furlongs in width. This manor is worth £4 a year and when he received it it was worth as much.

(326) Roger himself holds BESSINTONE [West Bexington in Puncknowle]. Ailmar held (it) T.R.E. and it paid geld for 9½ hides. There is land for 7 ploughs. In demesne there are 2 ploughs and 8 serfs and 4 villeins and 8 bordars with 4 ploughs. There (are) 4 acres of meadow and 8 furlongs of pasture in length and 1 furlong in width. It was worth £4. Now (it is worth) £6.

(xcviii) Roger Arundel has 1 manor which is called Bessintona which Ailmar held on the day when King Edward was alive and dead (and) which paid geld for 9½ hides. Seven ploughs can plough these. Thence Roger has in demesne 4 hides and ½ virgate and 2 ploughs and the villeins (have) 5 hides less 1 virgate and 4 ploughs. There are 4 villeins and 8 bordars and 8 serfs and 2 cows and 5 pigs and 136 sheep and 4 acres of meadow and 8 furlongs of pasture in length and 1 in width. This manor is worth £6 and when he received (it it was worth) £4.

(327) Hugh holds POVRESTOCH [Powerstock] of Roger. Ailmar held (it) T.R.E. and it paid geld for 6 hides. There is land for 6 ploughs. In demesne there are 2½ ploughs and 5 serfs and 5 villeins and 9 bordars with 2½ ploughs. There (are) 2 mills rendering 3*s*. and 13 acres of meadow and 15 furlongs of pasture in length and 2 furlongs in width. (There is) wood(land) 11 furlongs long and 2½ furlongs wide. It was worth £4. Now (it is worth) £6.

(xcix) Roger has 1 manor which is called Povrestoca which Ailmar held on the day when King Edward was alive and dead (and) which paid geld for 6 hides. Now Hugh holds it of Roger. Six ploughs can plough these. Thence Hugh has in demesne 3 hides and 2½ ploughs and the villeins (have) 3 hides and 2½ ploughs. There are 5 villeins and 9 bordars and 5 serfs and 2 pack-horses and 4 beasts and 13 pigs and 158 sheep and 16 goats and 2 mills which render 3*s*. and 11 furlongs of wood(land) in length and 2½ furlongs in width and 13 acres of meadow and 15 furlongs of pasture in length and 2 in width. This (manor) is worth £6 and when he received (it it was worth) £4.

(328) Ralph holds BROCHESHALE [Wraxall] of Roger. Ailmar held (it) T.R.E. and it paid geld for 10 hides. There is land for 8 ploughs. In demesne there are 2 ploughs and 4 serfs and 4 villeins and 14 bordars with 2 ploughs. There (is) a mill rendering 5*s*. and 5 acres of meadow and 8 furlongs of pasture in length and 2½ furlongs in width. (There is) wood(land) 8 furlongs long and 3 furlongs wide. It is worth 100*s*. In the same vill William holds 3 hides of Roger. There are 4 villeins. They are worth £3 and 1 knight holds 1 hide of Roger and it is worth 20*s*. In all the manor is worth £9. When he received (it) it was worth £4.

(c) Roger has 1 manor which is called Brochessala which Ailmar held on the day when King Edward was alive and dead (and) which paid geld for 10 hides. Eight ploughs can plough these. Of this manor Ralph holds 6 hides of Roger. Ralph has 3½ hides of these 6 in demesne and 2 ploughs and the villeins (have) 2½ hides and 2 ploughs. There are 4 villeins and 14 bordars and 4 serfs and 2 cows and 17 pigs and 60 sheep and 1 mill which renders 5*s*. and 8 furlongs of wood(land) in length and 3 furlongs in width and 5 acres of meadow and 8 furlongs of pasture in length and

[5] 'villanos et vii bordarios et iiii servos et iii' added in the margins.

[6] 'Has possunt arare ii carruce' interlined.

[7] 'hidas' interlined.

[8] 'Attlet' interlined.

$2\frac{1}{2}$ furlongs in width. This (manor) is worth 100*s*. In the same manor William has 3 hides of Roger. Four villeins have these 3 hides for £3 rent (*de gablo*). In the same vill Roger gave 1 hide to a certain knight from which he has 20*s*. This manor is now worth £9. When he received (it) it was worth £4.

(329) Wido holds POVERTONE [North Poorton] of Roger. Alwin and Ulf held (it) for 2 hides.[9] There is land for 2 ploughs. In demesne there is 1 plough and there are 9 coscets and 6 acres of meadow and 15 furlongs of pasture in length and width. It is worth 30*s*.

(ci) Roger has 1 manor which is called Povertona which Alwin held on the day when King Edward was alive and dead and it paid geld for $1\frac{1}{2}$ hide. Roger has there also $\frac{1}{2}$ hide which Ulf held and now Wido holds these 2 hides of Roger, and 2 ploughs can plough these. Of these Wido has in demesne 1 hide and 1 virgate and the villeins have 3 virgates. There Wido has 1 plough and 9 coscets and 1 mare and 13 beasts and 32 pigs and 108 sheep and 15 acres of wood(land) and 32 goats and 6 acres of meadow and 15 furlongs of pasture in length and width. This manor was worth 20*s*. when Roger received it and now it is worth 30*s*. a year.

(330) Roger himself holds ORDE [Worth Matravers]. Ailvert held (it) of the king[10] T.R.E. and it paid geld for $16\frac{1}{2}$ hides and $\frac{1}{2}$ virgate. There is land for 12 ploughs. In demesne there are 4 ploughs and 8 serfs and 9 villeins and 8 bordars with 9 ploughs. There (is) a mill rendering 7*s*. 6*d*. and 15 acres of meadow and 15 furlongs of pasture[11] in length and in width and 7 furlongs of wood(land) in length and width. It was and is worth £16 7*s*. 6*d*.

(cii) Roger has 1 manor which is called Orda which Ailvert held on the day when King Edward was alive and dead, and he could not withdraw from the king's service. This (manor) paid geld for $16\frac{1}{2}$ hides and $\frac{1}{2}$ virgate. Twelve ploughs can plough these. Of these Roger has in demesne $3\frac{1}{2}$ hides and $\frac{1}{2}$ virgate and 4 ploughs and the villeins (have) 13 hides and 9 ploughs. There Roger has 9 villeins and 8 bordars and 8 serfs and 13 pigs and 250 sheep and 1 mill which renders 7*s*. 6*d*. a year and 7 furlongs of wood(land) in length and the same amount in width and 15 acres of meadow and 15 furlongs of pasture in length and in width and it is worth £16 7*s*. 6*d*. a year and when he received (it) it was worth the same amount.

(331) Robert holds RAGINTONE [Rollington (Farm) in Corfe Castle] of Roger. Nine thegns held (it) freely[12] T.R.E. and it paid geld for $2\frac{1}{2}$ hides less[13] $\frac{1}{4}$ virgate. There is land for 2 ploughs. There (are) 4 acres of meadow and 14 furlongs of pasture in length and width. It is worth 40*s*.

(ciii) Roger has 1 manor which is called Ragintona. Nine thegns held it on the day when King Edward was alive and dead and they could go to any lord. Now Robert Attlet holds (it) of Roger. This (manor) paid geld for $2\frac{1}{2}$ hides less $\frac{1}{4}$ virgate, which 2 ploughs can plough. These thegns[14] still have these $2\frac{1}{2}$ hides less $\frac{1}{4}$ virgate in demesne and 4 acres of meadow and 14 furlongs of pasture in length and in width and it is worth 40*s*. a year.

(332) Roger himself holds WRDE [Worth Matravers]. Alward held (it) T.R.E. and it paid geld for $\frac{1}{2}$ hide. There is land for $\frac{1}{2}$ plough which is there with 3 bordars. It is worth 10*s*.

(civ) Roger has 1 manor which is called Urda which Alward held on the day when King Edward was alive and dead, and he could go to any lord. This (manor) paid geld for $\frac{1}{2}$ hide which $\frac{1}{2}$ plough can plough. There Roger has $\frac{1}{2}$ plough and 3 bordars and it is worth 10*s*. a year.

(333) Roger himself holds HERESTONE [Herston in Swanage]. Her held (it) T.R.E. and it paid geld for $\frac{2}{3}$ hide. There is land for $\frac{1}{2}$ plough. There (are) $2\frac{1}{2}$ acres of meadow. It is worth 10*s*.

(cv) Roger has 1 manor which is called Herestona which Her held on the day when King Edward was alive and dead, and he could go to any lord. This (manor) paid geld for $\frac{2}{3}$ hide which $\frac{1}{2}$ plough can plough. There Roger has $2\frac{1}{2}$ acres[15] of meadow and it is worth 10*s*. a year.

XLVIII. THE LAND OF SERLE OF BURCY

(334) Serle of Burcy holds PIDERE [Waterston in Puddletown] of the king. Earl[16] Harold held (it) T.R.E. and it paid geld for 10 hides. There is land for 6 ploughs. In demesne there are 3 ploughs and 2 serfs and 12 villeins and 12 bordars with 3 ploughs. There (is) a mill rendering 3*s*. and 40 acres of meadow and 20 acres of wood(land). (There is) pasture 16 furlongs long and 4 furlongs wide. It is worth £10.

THE LAND OF SERLE OF BURCY IN DORSET

(cvi) Serle has 1 manor in Pidra which Earl[17] Harold held T.R.E. and it paid geld for 10 hides and can be ploughed by 6 ploughs, and he has 6 hides and 1 virgate in demesne and he has 3 ploughs and his villeins have 3 hides[18] and 3 virgates and they have 3 ploughs and there are in that land 12 villeins and 12 bordars and 2 serfs and 1 pack-horse and 10 beasts and 393 sheep and 1 mill which renders 3*s*. and 20 acres of wood-(land) and 40 acres of meadow and 16 furlongs of pasture in length and 4 in width, and it is worth £10.

(335) The same (Serle) holds WITECLIVE [Whitecliff (Farm) in Swanage]. Alward held (it) T.R.E. and it paid geld for 3 hides. There is land for 3 ploughs. In demesne there are 2 ploughs and 2 serfs and 1 villein and 4 bordars. There (are) 6 furlongs of pasture in length and 1 furlong in width. It was and is worth 60*s*.

[9] At this point the text should probably be emended to read *Alwinus et Ulf tenuerunt pro ii maneriis T.R.E. et geldabat pro ii hidas*. See p. 4.

[10] 'de rege' interlined.

[11] 'pasture' interlined.

[12] 'libere' added in the margin.

[13] 'minus' added in the margin.

[14] 'illi tagni' interlined.

[15] 'agros' interlined.

[16] 'comes' interlined.

[17] 'comes' interlined.

[18] 'hidas' interlined.

(cvii) Serle of Burcy has 1 manor which is called Witecliva which Alward held on the day when King Edward was alive and dead, and he could go to any lord he wished. This (manor) paid geld for 3 hides. Three ploughs can plough these. Of these Serle has in demesne 2½ hides[19] and 2 ploughs and the villeins (have) ½ hide. There Serle has 1 villein and 4 bordars and 2 serfs and 50 sheep and 6 furlongs of pasture in length and 1 in width and it is worth 60*s*. a year. When he himself received (it) it was worth as much.

XLIX. THE LAND OF AIULF THE CHAMBERLAIN

(336) Aiulf holds BLANEFORDE [Blandford St. Mary] of the king. Leveva held (it) T.R.E. and it paid geld for 1½ hide. There is land for 1 plough which is there and 5 acres of meadow and 2 furlongs of pasture. It was worth 20*s*. Now (it is worth) 30*s*.

(337) Aiulf himself holds MORDUNE [Morden]. Ailveva held (it) T.R.E. and it paid geld for 3 virgates of land. There is land for ½ plough. It is worth 25*s*.

(338) Aiulf himself holds HAME [Hampreston]. Five thegns held (it) T.R.E. and it paid geld for 6 hides. There is land for 5 ploughs. In demesne there are 2 ploughs and 4 serfs and 6 bordars with 2 ploughs. There (are) 20 acres of meadow and 8 furlongs of pasture in length and the same amount in width and 4 furlongs of wood(land) in length and the same amount in width. It is worth £4 10*s*.

(339) Aiulf himself holds SELAVESTUNE [unidentified]. Two thegns held (it) T.R.E. and it paid geld for 4 hides and 1½ virgate of land. There is land for 3 ploughs. In demesne there are 2 ploughs and 2 serfs and 5 villeins and 1 bordar with 1 plough. There (are) 30 acres of meadow and 4 furlongs of pasture in length and 2 furlongs in width. It is worth 60*s*.

(340) The same Aiulf holds TERENTE [? Tarrant Gunville]. One free man held (it) T.R.E. and it paid geld for 2 hides. There is land for 1 plough which is there in demesne and 3 villeins and 2 bordars and 2 serfs. There (are) 15 acres of pasture and as much wood(land). It is worth 40*s*.

(341) The same Aiulf holds STIBEMETUNE [Stubhampton in Tarrant Gunville]. One thegn held (it) T.R.E. and it paid geld for 1 hide. There is land for 1 plough which is there in demesne and 4 serfs. There (are) 3 acres of pasture and 25 acres of wood(land). It is worth 20*s*.

[f. 83]
(342) The same Aiulf holds CEOTEL [Chettle] and Airard (holds it) of him. One thegn held (it) T.R.E. and it paid geld for 1 hide. There is land for 1 plough. There are 12 acres of pasture. It is worth 20*s*.

(343) Aiulf himself holds FERNHAM [Farnham]. One thegn held (it) T.R.E. and it paid geld for 2 hides[20] which are there with 1 serf and 4 bordars. There (are) 10 acres of pasture and 3 furlongs of wood(land) in length and 2 furlongs in width. It is worth 30*s*.

(344) The same Aiulf holds BRADELEGE [Bradle (Farm) in Church Knowle]. One thegn held (it) T.R.E. and it paid geld for 4 hides. There is land for 2 ploughs. In demesne there is 1 plough and 2 serfs and 1 villein and 2 bordars with ½ plough. There (is) 1 acre of meadow and 2 furlongs of pasture and 1 furlong of wood(land) in length and ½ (furlong) in width. It was worth 40*s*. Now (it is worth) 60*s*.

(345) Aiulf himself holds TATETUN [Tatton in Portesham]. One thegn held (it) T.R.E. of the church of Cerne and could not withdraw from it and it paid geld for 3 hides. There is land for 2 ploughs. In demesne there is 1 plough and 2 serfs and 1 villein and 4 bordars. There (are) 4 acres of meadow and 2 furlongs of pasture in length and width. It is worth 75*s*.

(346) Aiulf himself holds DERWINESTONE [Durweston]. Three thegns held (it) T.R.E. and it paid geld for 4½ hides. There is land for 3 ploughs. In demesne there are 2 ploughs and 4 serfs and 8 bordars with 1 plough. There (are) 2 acres of vineyards (*vinee*) and 15 acres of meadow and 3 furlongs of pasture in length and 1 furlong in width. (There is) wood(land) 3 furlongs long and 2 furlongs wide. It was worth 60*s*. Now (it is worth) £4 10*s*.

(347) Aiulf himself holds ODETUN [Wootton Fitzpaine]. Bricsi, a knight of King Edward (*miles regis Edwardi*), held (it) and it paid geld for 12 hides. There is land for 16 ploughs. Of this there are in demesne 4 carucates and there (are) 3 ploughs and 6 serfs and 12 villeins and 11 bordars with 9 ploughs. There (are) 2 mills rendering 15*s*. and 2 acres (*arpenz*) of vineyards and 50 acres of meadow and 40 acres of wood(land) and 1 league of pasture in length and as much in width. It was worth £10. Now (it is worth) £20.

(348) The same Aiulf holds 1 virgate of land at BRIGE [Bridge in Weymouth, site lost]. Saward held (it) T.R.E. There is land for 2 oxen. There are 2 fishermen and it renders 5*s*.

(349) The same Aiulf holds 1½ hide in HAFELTONE [Hethfelton in East Stoke]. Azor held (it) T.R.E. There is land for 1 plough which is there in demesne and 5 acres of meadow and 6 furlongs of pasture. It was worth 5*s*. Now (it is worth) 40*s*.

(350) Aiulf himself holds LULVORDE [East and West Lulworth]. Alfred the sheriff[21] held (it) T.R.E. and it paid geld for 8 hides and 3 virgates of land. There is land for 5 ploughs. In demesne there are 3 ploughs and 3 serfs and 3 villeins and 8 bordars with 1 plough. There (are) 12 acres of meadow and 6 furlongs of pasture in length and as much in width. It was worth £6. Now (it is worth) £7.

(351) Aiulf himself holds CHIRCE [? part of Long

[19] 'hidas' interlined.

[20] The teamlands have been omitted from this entry which should probably be emended to read *Terra est ii carucarum que ibi sunt cum uno servo* etc.

[21] 'vicecomes' interlined.

Crichel]. Alvric held (it) T.R.E. and it paid geld for 4 hides. There is land for 3 ploughs. In demesne there are 2 ploughs and 2 serfs and 4 villeins and 7 bordars with ½ plough. There (is) a mill rendering 20*s.* and 18 acres of meadow and 4 furlongs of pasture in length and 1 furlong in width and 6 furlongs of wood(land) in length and 1 furlong in width. It was worth 40*s.* Now (it is worth) 65*s.* 8*d.* Aiulf holds this of the king as long as he shall be sheriff (*quamdiu erit vicecomes*).

(352) The same Aiulf holds FERNHAM [Farnham] which 1 thegn held T.R.E. of the church of Shaftesbury and he could not withdraw from it and it paid geld for ½ hide. There is land for ½ plough. There is 1 furlong of pasture in length and ½ (furlong) in width and 2 furlongs of wood(land) in length and 1 furlong in width. It is worth 30*s.*[22]

L. THE LAND OF HUMPHREY THE CHAMBERLAIN

(353) Humphrey holds AMEDESHAM [Edmondsham] of the king. Dodo held (it) T.R.E. and it paid geld for 1½ hide. There is land for 1½ ploughs which are there with 1 villein and 2 bordars and 1 serf. There (is) a mill rendering 30*d.* and 1½ acre of meadow and 8 furlongs of pasture in length and 3 furlongs in width and 5 furlongs of wood(land) in length and 1½ furlong in width. It is worth 60*s.*

(354) The same (Humphrey) holds MEDESHAM [Edmondsham]. T.R.E. it paid geld for 1½[23] hide. There is land for 1 plough which is there. It is worth 30*s.* Eddeva holds (it) of Humphrey.

(355) The same (Humphrey) holds HEMEDESWRDE [East and West Hemsworth in Witchampton]. One free thegn held (it) T.R.E. and it paid geld for 1 hide. There is land for 1 plough which is there with 1 serf and 3 bordars. There (are) 2 acres of meadow and 2 furlongs of pasture in length and 1 furlong in width. It was and is worth 60*s.*

(356) The same (Humphrey) holds STURE [Stourpaine]. Alward held (it) T.R.E. and it paid geld for 6 hides and 1½ virgate of land. There is land for 4 ploughs. In demesne there are 2 ploughs with 1 serf and 6 villeins and 7 bordars with 1½ plough. There (is) a mill rendering 3*s.* and 40 acres of meadow and 8 furlongs of pasture in length and 5 furlongs in width. It was worth £4 10*s.* Now (it is worth) £6.

LI. THE LAND OF HUGH DE PORT

(357)[24] Hugh de Port[25] holds CONTONE [Compton Valence] of the king. Bundi held (it) T.R.E. and it paid geld for 10 hides. There is land for 8 ploughs. In demesne there are 3[26] ploughs and 3 serfs and 10 villeins and 12 bordars with 3 ploughs. There (are) 32 acres of meadow. (There is) pasture 18 furlongs long and 1 league wide. It was and is worth £20.

LII. THE LAND OF HUGH DE ST. QUINTIN

(358) Hugh de St. Quintin holds STITEFORD [Stinsford] of the king. Six thegns held (it) in parage T.R.E. and it paid geld for 2 hides and 2½ virgates of land. There is land for 2 ploughs which are there in demesne and 3 villeins and 2 bordars with 1 plough. There (are) 23 acres of meadow and 2 furlongs of pasture in length and 1 furlong in width. It was and is worth 15*s.*

(359) The same (Hugh) holds RINGESTEDE [Ringstead in Osmington, site derelict]. Four thegns held (it) in parage[27] T.R.E. and it paid geld for 2 hides. There is land for 2 ploughs which are there in demesne with 6 bordars. There (is) ½ mill rendering 4*s.* and 8 acres of meadow and 12 furlongs of pasture in length and 1 furlong in width. It was worth 30*s.* Now (it is worth) 40*s.*

LIII. [THE LAND OF HUGH DE BOSCHERBERT][28]

(360) Hugh de Boscherbert holds CERNEL [unidentified] of the king. Godwin held (it) T.R.E. and it paid geld for 1½ hide. There is land for 1 plough which is there in demesne with 1 serf and 2 villeins and 1 bordar. There (are) 1½ acre of meadow and 3 furlongs of pasture in length and 1 in width. It was worth 25*s.* Now (it is worth) 20*s.*

(361) The same Hugh holds 1 manor which 2 brothers held T.R.E. and it paid geld for 10 hides. There is land for 8 ploughs. In demesne there are 2 ploughs and 6 serfs and 9 villeins and 5 bordars with 4 ploughs. There (is) a mill rendering 30*d.* and 12 acres of meadow. (There is) pasture 1 league and 4 furlongs long and 1 league wide. It was worth £6. Now (it is worth) £9.

LIIII. [THE LAND OF HUGH DE LURE AND OTHER FRENCHMEN]

(362) Hugh de Lure holds of the king land in 3 places which 11 thegns held and it paid geld for 5 hides. There is land for 4 ploughs. Ralph holds (it) of Hugh. In demesne there is ½ plough and 12 villeins with 3½ ploughs. There (are) 10 acres of meadow and 5 furlongs of pasture in length and 2 furlongs in width. It was and is worth £4.

(363) Hugh *silvestris* holds ½ hide of land in CANDEL [Stourton Caundle]. Leverone held (it) T.R.E. There is land for ½ plough. There are 2 bordars and 2 acres of meadow. Nothing more (*Nil amplius*).

(364) Fulcred holds WAIA [unidentified] of the king.[29] Wateman held (it) T.R.E. and it paid geld for 2½ hides. There is land for 2 ploughs. In demesne there is 1 plough and 3 serfs and 1 villein

[22] The surviving portion of Exon. Domesday does not cover the lands of Aiulf the sheriff in Dorset, but in the part concerning the king's lands occurs the following entry which has no parallel in the Exchequer text: Aiulf the sheriff has 1 virgate of land in *Wintreborna* [unidentified] of reeveland (*de revelanda*) and it renders 5*s.* a year.

[23] 'et dimidia' interlined.

[24] Hugh de Port's manor was added at the foot of the folio (after no. 375).

[25] 'de Porth' interlined.

[26] The facsimile has *iii*, the printed version *ii*.

[27] 'in paragio' interlined.

[28] The scribe entered the number of this and the following fief, but omitted the headings.

[29] 'de rege' interlined.

and 2 bordars. There (are) 4 acres of meadow and 7 furlongs of pasture. It is worth 30*s*.

(365) Fulcred holds MORDAAT [Moorbath in Symondsbury]. Alric held (it) T.R.E. and it paid geld for 2 hides. There is land for 2 ploughs which are there in demesne and 3 villeins and 4 bordars. There (are) 11 acres of meadow and 50 acres of pasture and 30 acres of wood(land). It is worth 30*s*.

(366) Richard de Redvers holds MORTESTORNE [Mosterton]. Almer held (it) T.R.E. and it paid geld for 6 hides. There is land for 5 ploughs. In demesne there are 2 ploughs and 5 serfs and 8 villeins and 5 bordars with 3 ploughs. There (is) a mill rendering 7*s*. 6*d*. and 30 acres of meadow. (There is) wood(land) 1 league long and ½ league wide. It was and is worth £12.

(367) Schelin holds ALFORD [Shillingstone]. Earl[30] Harold held (it) T.R.E. and it paid geld for 16 hides. There is land for 16 ploughs. In demesne there are 3 ploughs and 5 serfs and 15 villeins and 26 bordars with 8 ploughs. There (is) a mill rendering 23*s*. 6*d*. and 183 acres of meadow. (There is) pasture 42 furlongs long and 8 furlongs wide. (There is) wood(land) 23 furlongs long and 9 furlongs wide. It was worth £16. Now (it is worth) £19.

(368) David the interpreter holds POURTONE [North Poorton]. Eight thegns held (it) T.R.E. and it paid geld for 1 hide and 2½ virgates of land. There is land for 2 ploughs which are there with 8 villeins. There (is) a mill and 4 acres of wood(land) and 2 furlongs of pasture in length and ½ furlong in width. It was and is worth 30*s*. Godescal holds (it) of David.

(369) Anschitil fitz Ameline[31] holds TINGEHAM [Tyneham]. Brictric held (it) T.R.E. and it paid geld for 3 hides. There is land for 3 ploughs. In demesne there are 2 ploughs and 9 serfs and 4 villeins with 1 plough. There (are) 4 acres of meadow and 8 furlongs of pasture in length and 4 furlongs in width. It was worth £3. Now (it is worth) £4. Anschitil held this land of the queen, as he says, but after her death he did not seek it of the king (*regem non requisivit*).

(370) Ralph holds TARENTE [unidentified]. Brictric held (it) T.R.E. and it paid geld for 2 hides. There is land for 1½ plough. In demesne there is 1 plough and 2 serfs and 2 villeins and 2 coscets with ½ plough. There (are) 3 acres of meadow and 7 furlongs of pasture in length and 1½ furlong in width. (There is) wood(land) 1 furlong long and 4 acres wide. It was and is worth 40*s*.

(371) Ralph of Cranborne holds PERLAI [West Parley]. Brisnod held (it) T.R.E. and it paid geld for 2 hides. There is land for 2 ploughs which are there and 5 villeins and 4 bordars and 2 serfs and 15 acres of meadow. (There is) pasture 1 league long and 7 furlongs wide. (There is) wood(land) 4 furlongs long and 1 furlong wide. It was and is worth 30*s*.

(372) Odo fitz Eurebold holds FERNHAM [Farnham]. Ulviet held (it) T.R.E. and it paid geld for 2 hides. There is land for 2 ploughs which are there in demesne and 4 serfs and 3 bordars. (There are) 10 acres of pasture in length and width. (There is) wood(land) 3 furlongs long and 2 furlongs wide. It is worth 40*s*.

(373) The same (Odo) holds MELEBURNE [Milborne Stileham]. Dodo held (it) T.R.E. and it paid geld for 2 hides. There is land for 1 plough which is there in demesne and 4 acres of meadow and 2 furlongs of pasture. It was worth 44*s*. Now (it is worth) 30*s*.

(374) The son of Eurebold holds 3 virgates of land in RISTONE [Rushton in East Stoke]. There is land for 1 plough which is there with 4 villeins and 1 acre of meadow and 4 acres of wood(land) and 1 league of pasture in length and width. It is worth 10*s*.

(375) The same (man) holds PETRISHESHAM [Petersham (Farm) in Holt]. Saward held (it) T.R.E. and it paid geld for 3 virgates of land. There is land for 1 plough which is there and 6 acres of meadow.

[f. 83b]

LV. THE LAND OF THE WIFE OF HUGH FITZ GRIP

(376) The wife of Hugh fitz Grip[32] holds WINTREBURNE [Martinstown in Winterborne St. Martin] of the king. Nine thegns held (it) in parage[33] T.R.E. and it paid geld for 6 hides. There is land for 6 ploughs. In demesne there are 3 hides of this land and there (are) 2 ploughs and 5 serfs and 17 bordars with 2 ploughs. There (is) a mill rendering 16*d*. and 13 acres of meadow. (There is) pasture 9 furlongs long and 8 furlongs wide. It was worth £10. Now (it is worth) £6.

THE LAND OF THE WIFE OF HUGH FITZ GRIP[34] IN DORSET

(cviii) The wife of Hugh has 1 manor which is called Wintreborna which 9 thegns held in parage of King Edward on the day when King Edward was alive and dead and these thegns could go with their lands to any lord. This manor paid geld for 6 hides T.R.E. Six ploughs can plough these. Thence the lady has in demesne 3 hides and 2 ploughs and the villeins have 3 hides and 2 ploughs. The lady has there 17 bordars and 5 serfs and 1 pack-horse and 8 pigs and 380 sheep and 1 mill which renders 16*d*. a year and 13 acres of meadow and 9 furlongs of pasture[35] in length and 8 in width and it is worth £6 a year and when Hugh received (it) it was worth £10.

(377) William holds FROME [Frome Whitfield in Stinsford] of her. Godric held (it) T.R.E. and it paid geld for 4 hides. There is land for 3 ploughs. In demesne there are 2 ploughs with 1 serf and 8 bordars and 4 cottars. There (is) a mill rendering 5*s*. and 30 acres of meadow. (There is) pasture 4 furlongs long and 2 furlongs wide. It was worth 40*s*. Now (it is worth) £4.

[30] 'comes' interlined.
[31] 'filius Ameline' interlined.
[32] 'filii Grip' interlined.
[33] 'in paragio' interlined.
[34] 'filii Gripi' interlined.
[35] 'pascue' interlined.

(cix) The wife of Hugh has 1 manor which is called Froma which Godric held on the day when King Edward was alive and dead and now William holds it of the wife of Hugh and it paid geld T.R.E. for 4 hides. Three ploughs can plough these. William holds these 4 hides[36] in demesne. There William has 2 ploughs and 8 bordars and 4 cottars[37] and 1 serf and 1 pack-horse and 15 beasts and 30 pigs and 250 sheep and 1 ass (*asinum*) and 1 mill which renders 5*s.* a year and 30 acres of meadow and 4 furlongs of pasture in length and 2 in width. This manor is worth £4 a year and when Hugh received (it) it was worth 40*s.*

(378) Roger holds CEOSELBURNE [Little Cheselbourne or Cheselbourne Ford in Puddletown, now lost] of the same (woman). Elgar and Alstan held (it) T.R.E. and it paid geld for 2 hides. There is land for 2 ploughs. In demesne there is 1 plough and 6 bordars. There (is) a mill rendering 30*d.* and 5 acres of meadow and 1 furlong of pasture. It was worth 50*s.* Now (it is worth) 25*s.* Hugh held this land of the Abbot of Abbotsbury, as his men say, but the abbot denies it.

(cx) The wife of Hugh has 1 manor which is called Ceoselburna. Two thegns, Alfgar and Alstan, held it T.R.E. and they could go to any lord with their land. Hugh fitz Grip[38] held this land of the Abbot of Abbotsbury, as his men say, but the abbot utterly denies this. This land paid geld for 2 hides. Two ploughs can plough these. Roger Boissell holds this land of the wife of Hugh. There Roger has 1 plough and 6 bordars and 50 sheep and 1 mill which renders 30*d.* a year and 5 acres of meadow and 1 furlong of pasture and this (manor) was worth 50*s.* when Hugh received it. Now it is worth 25*s.*

(379) The woman herself holds BOCHELAND [Buckland Ripers in Radipole]. Four thegns held (it) in parage[39] T.R.E. and it paid geld for 4 hides. There is land for 3 ploughs. In demesne there are 2 ploughs with 1 serf and 2 villeins and 5 bordars with 1 plough. There (is) a mill rendering 20*s.* and 10 acres of meadow. (There is) pasture 15 furlongs long and 1 furlong wide. It was and is worth 100*s.*

(cxi) The wife of Hugh fitz Grip has 1 manor which is called Bochelant which 4 thegns held in parage on the day when King Edward was alive and dead. They could go with their lands to any lord and (the manor) paid geld T.R.E. for 4 hides. Four ploughs can plough these. Thence the wife of Hugh has 3 hides and 1 virgate and 2 ploughs in demesne and the villeins (have) 3 virgates and 1 plough. There the wife of Hugh has 2 villeins and 5 bordars and 1 serf and 1 pack-horse and 4 pigs and 200 sheep and 1 mill which renders 20*s.* a year and 10 acres of meadow and 15 furlongs of pasture in length and 1 in width and it is worth 100*s.* a year and when Hugh received (it) it was worth as much.

(380) She herself holds WAIA [on the R. Wey, site unidentified]. Nine thegns held (it) in pargae[40] T.R.E. and it paid geld for 4 hides and 1 virgate of land. There is land for 4 ploughs. In demesne there are 2 ploughs and 3 serfs and 6 bordars. There (are) 3 mills rendering 35*s.* and meadow 9 furlongs long and 1 furlong wide. (There is) pasture 3 furlongs long and 1 furlong wide. It was worth £6. Now (it is worth) 100*s.*

(cxii) The wife of Hugh has 1 manor which is called Waia which 9 thegns held in parage on the day when King Edward was alive and dead and they could go with their lands to any lord and (the manor) paid geld T.R.E. for 4 hides and 1 virgate. Four ploughs can plough these. Thence the wife[41] of Hugh has 3 hides and 3 virgates and 2 ploughs in demesne and the bordars (have) ½ hide. There the wife of Hugh has 6 bordars and 3 serfs and 1 pack-horse and 2 cows and 9 pigs and 130 sheep and 1 mill which renders 10*s.* a year and 9 furlongs of meadow in length and 1 in width and 3 furlongs of pasture in length and 1 in width. To this manor belong 2 mills which render 25*s.* a year. This manor is worth 100*s.* a year and when Hugh received (it) it was worth £6.

(381) She herself holds WAIA [on the R. Wey, site unidentified]. Five thegns held (it) freely[42] T.R.E. and it paid geld for 6 hides. There is land for 5 ploughs. In demesne there are 2 ploughs with 1 serf and 1 villein and 10 bordars with 1 plough. There (are) 3 mills rendering 37*s.* 6*d.* and 25 acres of meadow. (There is) pasture 20 furlongs long and 3 furlongs wide. It was worth £7. Now (it is worth) £10.

(cxiii) The wife of Hugh has 1 manor which is called Waia which 5 thegns held on the day when King Edward was alive and dead, who could go to any lord with their lands, and (the manor) paid geld T.R.E. for 6 hides. Five ploughs can plough these. Thence the wife of Hugh has 4 hides and 1 virgate and 2 ploughs in demesne and the villeins have 2 hides[43] less 1 virgate and 1 plough. There the wife of Hugh has 1 villein and 10 bordars and 1 serf and 1 pack-horse and 330 sheep and 3 mills which render 37*s.* 6*d.* a year and 25 acres of meadow and 20 furlongs of pasture in length and 3 in width and it renders £10 a year and when Hugh received (it) it was worth £7.

(382) Azo holds WINTREBURNE [unidentified] of her. Almar held (it) T.R.E. and it paid geld for 1 hide. There is land for ½ plough. There are 2 bordars and 1 acre of meadow and 2 furlongs of pasture in length and 1 furlong in width. It is worth 10*s.*

(cxiv) The wife of Hugh has 1 hide of land in Wintreborna which Almar held on the day when King Edward was alive and dead and he could go to any lord with his land. Half a plough can plough this. Atso holds this (manor) of the wife of Hugh. There Atso has 2 bordars and 3 beasts and 100 sheep and 1 acre of meadow and 2 furlongs of pasture in length and 1 in width and it is worth 10*s.* a year.

(383) Hugh and William hold STAFORD [West Stafford] of her. Three thegns held (it) in parage[44] T.R.E. as 2 manors and it paid geld for 6 hides.

[36] 'iiii hidas' interlined.
[37] 'et iiii cotarios' interlined.
[38] 'filius Gripi' interlined.
[39] 'in paragio' interlined.
[40] 'in paragio' interlined.
[41] 'uxor' interlined.
[42] 'libere' interlined.
[43] 'hidas' interlined.
[44] 'in paragio' interlined.

There is land for 3 ploughs. In demesne there are 2 ploughs with 1 serf and 8 bordars. There (are) 24 acres of meadow and 16 furlongs of pasture and 8 acres.[45] It was worth £4. Now (it is worth) 70*s*.

(cxv) The wife of Hugh has 1 manor which is called Stafort which 2 thegns held in parage on the day when King Edward was alive and dead and they could go with their lands to any lord and (the manor) paid geld T.R.E. for 4 hides. Two ploughs can plough these. In the same manor the wife of Hugh has 2 hides of land which Leving held as 1 manor[46] on the day when King Edward was alive and dead, and he could go to any lord. One plough can plough these 2 hides. Hugh and William hold the aforesaid 2 manors of the wife of Hugh fitz Grip. Thence Hugh has 3 hides and 3 bordars and 1 cow and 300 sheep and 12 acres of meadow and 8 furlongs of pasture and 4 acres. In the aforesaid 3 hides which William holds of the wife of Hugh, he himself has 2 ploughs and 5 bordars and 1 serf and 3 pack-horses and 12 cows and 37 pigs and 400 sheep and 12 acres of meadow and 8 furlongs of pasture and 4 acres. Hugh's manor is worth 30*s*. a year and William's manor is worth 40*s*. a year and when Hugh fitz Grip received (them) these 2 manors were worth £4.

(384) The woman herself holds WINTREBURNE [unidentified]. Alric held (it) T.R.E. and it paid geld for 8 hides. There is land for 4 ploughs. In demesne there are 2 ploughs and 3 serfs and 3 villeins and 5 bordars with ½ plough. There (are) 9 acres of meadow and 200 acres of pasture. It was and is worth £6.

(cxvi) The wife of Hugh (has) 1 manor which is called Wintreborna which Alric held on the day when King Edward was alive and dead and it paid geld for 8 hides. Four ploughs can plough these. That Alric[47] could go with his land to any lord. Thence the wife of Hugh has 6 hides less 1 virgate and 2 ploughs in demesne and the villeins have 2 hides and 1 virgate and ½ plough. There the wife of Hugh has 3 villeins and 5 bordars and 3 serfs and 1 pack-horse and 6 cows and 10 pigs and 304 sheep and 9 acres of meadow and 200 acres of pasture and it is worth £6 a year and when Hugh received (it it was worth) as much.

(385) William holds MORDONE [Morden] of her. Alnod held (it) T.R.E. and it paid geld for 5 virgates of land. There is land for 1 plough—[*blank*].[48] It was worth 25*s*. Now (it is worth) 20*s*.

(cxvii) The wife of Hugh has 1 manor which is called Mordona which Alnod held on the day when King Edward was alive and dead and it paid geld for 5 virgates. One plough can plough these. William Chernet holds these of the wife of Hugh. Of these William has 3½ virgates in demesne and the villeins (have) 1½ virgate and when he received (it) it was worth 25*s*. a year and now it is worth 20*s*.

(386) She herself holds WINTREBURNE [unidentified]. Three thegns held (it) T.R.E. and it paid geld for 5 hides. There is land for 3 ploughs. In demesne there is 1 plough and 2 serfs and 5 villeins and 4 bordars. There (are) 4 acres of meadow and 5 furlongs of pasture in length and as much in width. It was worth 100*s*. Now (it is worth) 40*s*.

(cxviii) The wife of Hugh has 1 manor which is called Wintreborna which 3 thegns held on the day when King Edward was alive and dead and it paid geld for 5 hides. Three ploughs can plough these. These thegns could go to any lord with their lands. Thence the wife of Hugh has 3 hides and 1 plough in demesne and the villeins have 1½ hide. There the wife of Hugh has 5 villeins and 4 bordars and 2 serfs and 5 pigs and 100 sheep and 4 acres[49] of meadow and 5 furlongs of pasture in length and as much in width and it is worth 40*s*. and when the wife of Hugh received (it) it was worth 100*s*.

(387) Ralph holds 1½ virgate of land in WINTREBURNE [unidentified] of her. There is land for 3 oxen. Godwin held (it) T.R.E. and it was and is worth 3*s*.

(cxix) The wife of Hugh has 1½ virgate of land in Wintreborna which Godwin held on the day when King Edward was alive and dead. Three oxen can plough this. Ralph holds this of the wife of Hugh. This (manor) is worth 3*s*. a year and when Hugh received (it) it was worth as much.

(388) William holds WINBURNE [unidentified] of her. Aldwin held (it) T.R.E. and it paid geld for 1 hide. There is land for 1 plough. There are 2 bordars and ⅓ mill rendering 15*d*. There (is) pasture 4 furlongs in length and width. (There is) wood(land) 1 furlong in length and ½ furlong in width. It was worth 20*s*. Now (it is worth) 5*s*.

(cxx) The wife of Hugh has 1 manor which is called Winburna which Aldwin held on the day when King Edward was alive and dead and it paid geld for 1 hide. One plough can plough this. William de Creneto holds of her. There are 2 bordars and he has there ⅓ mill, that is, 15*d*. and 1 furlong of wood(land) in length and ½ (furlong) in width and 4 furlongs of pasture in length and width. This manor is worth 5*s*. a year and when he himself received (it) it was worth 20*s*.

(389) The same William holds HAME [Hampreston] of her. Agelward held (it) T.R.E. and it paid geld for 1 hide. There is land for 1 plough. There is 1 villein and 2 bordars and 2 acres of meadow and 1 furlong of wood(land) in length and another in width. It was and is worth 12*s*.

(cxxi) The wife of Hugh has 1 manor which is called Hame which Agelward held T.R.E. and it paid geld for 1 hide. William Chernet holds this and it can be ploughed by 1 plough and there is 1 villein and 1 bordar and 1 furlong of wood(land) in length and another in width and 2 acres of meadow. This manor is worth 12*s*. a year and when he received it it was worth as much.

(390) William holds BERE [Dodding's Farm in Bere Regis] of her. Leomer held (it) T.R.E. and it paid geld for ½ hide. There is land for ½ plough which is there and a mill rendering 20*s*. and 1 bordar and 6 acres of meadow and 6 acres of pasture. It is worth

[45] Supply 'silve'? For a comment on this passage and the corresponding entry in Exon. Domesday, see p. 4.

[46] 'pro i mansione' interlined.

[47] 'Alricus' interlined.

[48] Space in the text. For a comment, see p. 4.

[49] 'agros' interlined.

30*s*. William holds 1½ virgate[50] of land of her. It renders 20*s*.

(cxxii) The wife of Hugh has 1 manor which is called Bere which Leomar held T.R.E. and now William *de monasteriis* holds it and there neither is nor was more than ½ hide of land and it paid geld for so much T.R.E. and there William has ½ plough because it can be ploughed by so many. William has there 10 beasts and 45 sheep and 28 pigs and 1 pack-horse and 1 mill (rendering) 20*s*. and 1 bordar and 6 acres of meadow and 6 acres of pasture. This (manor) is worth 30*s*. a year.

(cxxiii) The wife of Hugh has 1½ virgate of land which William has of her and it renders 20*s*.[51] a year.

(391) Walter holds PIDELE [Turners Puddle] of her. Gerling held (it) T.R.E. and it paid geld for 6 hides. There is land for 3 ploughs. In demesne there are 2 ploughs and 4 serfs and 2 villeins and 4 bordars with ½ plough. There (are) 10 acres of meadow and 20 acres of wood(land). There (is) pasture 12 furlongs long and 6 wide. It was worth £3. Now (it is worth) £4.

(cxxiv) The wife of Hugh has 1 manor which is called Pidela which Jerling[52] held T.R.E. Hugh held this manor for 6 hides and there is ½ hide and 4 acres and 1 garden which never paid geld but it was concealed (*celatum est*). Three ploughs can plough these. There Walter Tonitruus, who holds this manor, has 2 ploughs and 4½ hides and his men (have) ½ hide and ½ plough and (he has) 20 animals and 12 mares with their foals (*aequas cum suis pullis*) and 2 pack-horses and 80 sheep and 20 pigs and 40 goats and 2 villeins and 4 bordars and 4 serfs and 20 acres of wood(land) and 10 acres of meadow and 12 furlongs of pasture in length and 6 in width and 1 mill (which renders) 10*s*. a year. This (manor) is worth £4 a year now and when Hugh received it (it was worth) £3.

(392) Hugh holds WINTREBURNE [Winterborne Houghton] of her. Ulgar held (it) T.R.E. and it paid geld for 2 hides and 1 virgate of land. There is land for 1½ plough. In demesne there is 1 plough with 1 serf and 2 villeins and 2 bordars with ½ plough. There (are) 14 acres of underwood and 6 furlongs of pasture in length and 6 in width. It was worth 20*s*. Now (it is worth) 30*s*. With this manor the same Hugh holds 1 virgate of land unlawfully which belongs to William of Moyon.

(cxxv) The wife of Hugh has 1 manor which is called Wintreborna which Wulgar held on the day when King Edward was alive and dead and it paid geld for 2 hides and 1 virgate. One plough and ½ (plough) can plough these. Thence the wife of Hugh has 2 hides less ½ virgate and 1 plough in demesne and the villeins (have) 1½ virgate and ½ plough. There the wife of Hugh has 2 villeins and 2 bordars and 1 serf and 300 sheep and 14 acres of underwood and 6 furlongs of pasture in length and as much in width. Hugh holds this of the wife of Hugh. This (manor) is worth 30*s*. a year and when Hugh fitz Grip received (it) it was worth 20*s*. With the aforesaid manor the same Hugh has a certain virgate of land unlawfully which belongs to the manor of William of Moyon.[53]

(393) Hugh holds 1 virgate of land at BRIGAM [Bridge in Weymouth, site lost] of the same woman. There is land for 2 oxen and there is 1 villein. It was and is worth 10*s*.

(cxxvi) The wife of Hugh has 1 virgate of land at Brigam which Almar held on the day when King Edward was alive and dead and it can be ploughed with 2 oxen. There the wife of Hugh has 1 villein. Hugh holds that (virgate) of the wife of Hugh. This (manor) is worth 10*s*. a year and when Hugh received (it) it was worth as much.

(394) William holds STERTE [Higher Sturthill in Shipton Gorge] of the same (woman). Alvric held (it) T.R.E. and it paid geld for 5 hides. There is land for 4 ploughs. In demesne there are 2 ploughs and 4 serfs and 2 villeins and 4 bordars with 1½ plough. There (is) a mill rendering 6*s*. 3*d*. and 27 acres of meadow. (There is) pasture 4 furlongs long and 1 furlong wide. It was worth £4. Now (it is worth) 100*s*.

(cxxvii) The wife of Hugh has 1 manor which is called Sterta which Alvric held on the day when King Edward was alive and dead and it paid geld for 5 hides. Four ploughs can plough these. William de Almereio holds it of the wife of Hugh. Of this William has 3 hides in demesne and 2 ploughs and the villeins (have) 2 hides and 1½ plough. There William has 2 villeins and 4 bordars and 4 serfs and 17 beasts and 7 pigs and 8 sheep and 1 mill which renders 6*s*. 3*d*. a year and 27 acres of meadow and 4 furlongs of pasture in length and 1 in width and it is worth 100*s*. a year and when Hugh received (it) it was worth £4.

(395) William holds GRAVSTAN [Graston in Burton Bradstock] of the same (woman). Alward held (it) T.R.E. and it paid geld for 2½ hides. There is land for 2 ploughs. In demesne there is 1 plough and 2 serfs and 1 villein and 8 bordars with ½ plough. There (is) a mill rendering 7*s*. 6*d*. and 16 acres of meadow. It was worth 40*s*. Now (it is worth) 60*s*.

(cxxviii) The wife of Hugh has 1 manor which is called Gravstan which Alward held on the day when King Edward was alive and dead and it paid geld for 2½ hides. Two ploughs can plough these. William holds this of the wife of Hugh. Thence William has 1½ hide in demesne and 1½ plough and the villeins (have) 1 hide and ½ plough. There William has 1 villein and 8 bordars and 2 serfs and 15 beasts and 7 pigs and 25 sheep and 1 mill which renders 7*s*. 6*d*. a year and 16 acres of meadow and it is worth £3 a year and when Hugh received (it) it was worth 40*s*.

(396) Ilbert holds ½ hide in FERNHAM [Farnham] of the same (woman). There is land for ½ plough but nevertheless there is 1 plough and 1½ furlong of pasture in length and 1 furlong in width. It is worth 10*s*. Alwin held this land of the church of Shaftesbury and he could not withdraw from it.

(cxxix) The wife of Hugh has ½ hide of land in Ferneham which Alwin held on the day when

[50] In the Exchequer text this 1½ virgate appears to be part of the entry relating to Dodding's Farm, but in Exon. Domesday it forms a separate entry.

[51] 'xx' interlined.

[52] So the MS.; the printed text has *Lerlincus*.

[53] See nos. 275 and lxxxv.

King Edward was alive and dead. Half a plough can plough this. Now Ilbert holds (it) of the wife of Hugh. There Ilbert has 1 plough and 1 cow and 6 pigs and 40 sheep and 20 goats and 1½ furlong of pasture in length and 1 in width and it is worth 10*s.* a year and when Hugh received (it it was worth) as much. This Alwin held this land of Shaftesbury Abbey on the day when King Edward was alive and dead and could not withdraw from the church.

(397) William holds POMACANOLE [Puncknowle] of the same (woman). Alward held (it) T.R.E. and it paid geld for 5 hides. There is land for 4 ploughs. In demesne there are 2 ploughs and 4 serfs and 4 villeins and 5 bordars with 2 ploughs. There (is) a mill rendering 12*s.* 6*d.* and 35 acres of meadow and 30 acres of wood(land) and 3 furlongs of pasture. It was worth 60*s.* Now (it is worth) 100*s.*

(cxxx) The wife of Hugh has 1 manor which is called Pomacanola which Alward held on the day when King Edward was alive and dead and it paid geld for 5 hides. Four ploughs can plough these. And now William *de monasterio* holds it of the wife of Hugh. Thence William has 3 hides and 2 ploughs in demesne and the villeins (have) 2 hides and 2 ploughs. There William has 4 villeins and 5 bordars and 4 serfs and 1 pack-horse and 12 beasts and 13 pigs and 153 sheep and 1 mill which renders 12*s.* 6*d.* and 30 acres of wood(land) and 35 acres of meadow and 3 furlongs of pasture. This (manor) is worth 100*s.* and when Hugh received (it) it was worth 60*s.*

(398) The woman herself holds 2 hides in TATENTONE [Tatton in Portesham] which were in the demesne of Cerne Abbey. T.R.E. 2 thegns held (them) for rent (*prestito*). Hugh took these against the abbot's will (*super abbatem*). It is worth 20*s.*

(cxxxi) The wife of Hugh has 2 hides in Tatentone[54] which on the day of King Edward's death belonged to Cerne Abbey and 2 thegns held them for rent on that day,[55] which Hugh took against the abbot's will and his wife still holds (them) and it is worth 20*s.* a year.

(399) Walter holds 1 hide at LODRAM [Matravers, formerly Loders Lutton, in Loders] of the same (woman). Two thegns held (it) T.R.E. There is land for 1 plough which is there in demesne with 1 serf and 1 villein and 4 bordars. There (are) 2 acres of meadow and 30 acres of pasture. It was worth 20*s.* Now (it is worth) 30*s.*

(cxxxii) The wife of Hugh has 1 hide at Lodram which 2 thegns held on the day when King Edward was alive and dead. Now Walter holds (it) of the wife of Hugh. This (hide) can be ploughed by 1 plough. Walter has this ½ hide in demesne and 1 plough and the villeins (have) ½ hide. There is 1 peasant (*rusticus*) and 4 bordars and 1 serf and 24 sheep and 2 acres of meadow and 30 acres of pasture. This (manor) is worth 30*s.* and when Hugh received (it) it was worth 20*s.*

(400) She herself holds ½ hide in TARENTE [unidentified]. There is land for 1 plough. There is 1 villein and 1 bordar and 2 acres of meadow and 3 furlongs of pasture in length and 1 furlong in width. It is worth 10*s.*

(cxxxiii) The wife of Hugh has ½ hide in Tarenta which Almar held on the day when King Edward was alive and dead, and he could go with his land to any lord. One plough can plough this. There the wife of Hugh has 1 virgate in demesne and 1 villein who dwells (*qui manet*) there has the other virgate and ½ plough and there the wife of Hugh has 1 villein and 1 bordar and 2 acres of meadow and 3 furlongs of pasture in length and 1 in width and it is worth 10*s.* a year and when Hugh received (it) it was worth the same amount.

(401) Robert holds DERVINESTONE [Durweston] of the same (woman). Alvric held (it) T.R.E. and it paid geld for 2 hides. There is land for 2 ploughs. In demesne there is 1 plough with 3 bordars. There (are) 8 acres of meadow and 4 furlongs of pasture in length and 2 furlongs in length (*sic*). It was and is worth 40*s.*

(cxxxiv) The wife of Hugh has 1 manor which is called Dervinestona which Alvric held on the day when King Edward was alive and dead. This (manor) paid geld for 2 hides. Two ploughs can plough these. And now Robert holds it of the wife of Hugh. Thence Robert has 1½ hide and 1 plough in demesne and the villeins (have) ½ hide and ½ plough. There Robert has 3 bordars and 14 pigs and 8 acres of meadow and 4 furlongs of pasture in length and 2 in width. This (manor) is worth 40*s.* and when Hugh received (it) it was worth as much.

(402) Robert holds WINTREBURNE [Winterborne Stickland] of the same (woman). Godwin held (it) T.R.E. and it paid geld for 1½ hide. There is land for 1½ plough. In demesne there is 1 plough with 1 serf and 4 bordars. There (is) a mill rendering 5*s.* (There are) 1½ furlong of wood(land) and 3 furlongs of pasture in length and 1 furlong in width. It is worth 30*s.*

(cxxxv) The wife of Hugh has 1 manor which is called Wintreborna which Godwin held on the day when King Edward was alive and dead. This (manor) paid geld for 1½ hide and can be ploughed with 1½ plough and now Robert holds it of the wife of Hugh. Thence Robert has 1 hide and 1 virgate and 1 plough in demesne and the villeins (have) 1 virgate. There Robert has 4 bordars and 1 serf and 1 cow and 172 sheep and 1 mill which renders 5*s.* and 1½ furlong of wood(land) and 3 furlongs of pasture in length and 1 in width. This (manor) is worth 30*s.* and when Hugh received (it) it was worth as much.

(403) In Wintreburne [Winterborne Stickland] Robert holds 1 hide and 1 virgate of land.[56] In demesne there is ½ plough with 1 bordar. It was worth 25*s.* Now (it is worth) 20*s.*

(cxxxvi) The wife of Hugh has 1 hide and 1 virgate of land in Wintreborna which Alvric held on the day when King Edward was alive and dead. And now Robert holds it of the wife of Hugh. There Robert has ½ plough and 1 bordar and 2 beasts and 88 sheep. This (manor) is worth 25*s.* a year and when Hugh received (it) it was

[54] 'Tatentone' interlined.

[55] 'et ii tani eas tenebant prestito ea die' interlined.

[56] The rest of this line in the text is left blank. For a comment, see p. 4.

worth 20*s*. And King William never had his geld from 1 virgate.

(404) Ralph holds TARENTE [Tarrant Rawston] of the same (woman). One thegn held (it) T.R.E. and it paid geld for 5 hides. There is land for 3 ploughs. In demesne there is 1 plough and 4 serfs and 2 villeins and 4 bordars with 1 plough. There (is) a mill rendering 30*d*. and 16 acres of meadow. (There is) pasture 3 furlongs long and 2 furlongs wide and in another place 8 furlongs of pasture. It was worth 100*s*. Now (it is worth) £4.

(cxxxvii) The wife of Hugh has 1 manor which is called Tarenta which 1 thegn held on the day when King Edward was alive and dead and it paid geld for 5 hides. Three ploughs can plough these and now Ralph holds (it) of the wife of Hugh. There Ralph has 4½ hides in demesne and 1 plough and the villeins (have) ½ hide and 1 plough. There Ralph has 2 villeins and 4 bordars and 4 serfs and 2 beasts and 20 pigs and 120 sheep and 1 mill which renders 30*d*. a year and 6 furlongs of wood(land) in length and 2 furlongs in width and 3 furlongs of pasture in length and 2 in width and 16 acres[57] of meadow and in another place 8 furlongs of pasture in length and width. This (manor) is worth £4 a year and when Ralph received it it was worth 100*s*.

(405) Berold holds TARENTE [unidentified] of the same (woman). One thegn held (it) T.R.E. and it paid geld for 1 hide and 3 virgates of land. There is land for 1½ plough. There are 3 bordars with 1 serf and 7 acres of meadow and 2 furlongs of pasture in length and 2 in width. It was worth 40*s*. Now (it is worth) 15*s*.

(cxxxviii) The wife of Hugh has 1 manor which is called Tarenta which 1 thegn held T.R.E. and he could go with his land to any lord and it paid geld for 1 hide and 3 virgates. One plough and ½ (plough) can plough these and now Berold holds it of the wife of Hugh. There Berold has 1½ hide in demesne and the villeins (have) 1 virgate. There are 3 bordars and 1 serf and 7 acres of meadow and 2 furlongs of pasture in length and 2 in width. This (manor) is worth 15*s*. a year and when Berold received (it) it was worth 40*s*.

(406) She herself holds LANGETONE [Langton Herring]. One thegn held (it) T.R.E. and it paid geld for 1½ hide. There is land for 3 ploughs. In demesne there are 2 ploughs with 1 serf and 1 villein and 7 bordars with 1 plough. There (are) 4 acres of meadow and 40 acres of pasture. It was worth 30*s*. Now (it is worth) 40*s*.

(cxxxix) The wife of Hugh has 1 manor which is called Langata which 1 thegn held on the day when King Edward was alive and dead and it paid geld for 1½ hide. Three ploughs can[58] plough this land. There the wife of Hugh has 3 virgates in demesne and 2 ploughs and the villeins (have) 3 virgates and 1 plough. There is 1 villein and 7 bordars and 1 serf and 6 pigs and 170 sheep and 1 pack-horse and 4 acres of meadow and 40 acres of pasture. This (manor) is worth 40*s*. a year and when Hugh received (it) it was worth 30*s*.

(407) Two knights hold ½ hide in RISTONE [Rushton in East Stoke] of the same (woman). Three thegns held (it) freely[59] T.R.E. and it paid geld for so much. There is land for ½ plough. There (are) 20 acres of meadow and 200 acres of pasture. It is worth 10*s*.

(cxl) The wife of Hugh has ½ hide of land in Ristona which 3 thegns held T.R.E. and they could go with this land to any lord and it paid geld for ½ hide. Half a plough can plough this. Two knights hold this of the wife of Hugh except for 16 acres of meadow which she herself holds in demesne. One of them, Turold, has there 10 beasts and 20 goats and 2 acres of meadow and 100 acres of pasture and the other knight (has) as many acres and pastures (*tantundem agrorum et pascuarum*) and no money (*nichil pecunie*) and this (manor) is worth 10*s*. a year.

(408) Hugh holds CELVEDUNE [Chaldon Herring or East Chaldon] of the same (woman). Nine thegns held (it) in parage[60] T.R.E. and it paid geld for 5 hides. There is land for 4 ploughs. In demesne there are 2 ploughs and 2 serfs and 5 villeins and 8 bordars with 2 ploughs. There (are) 3 acres of meadow and 7 furlongs of pasture in length and 5 furlongs in width. It was worth £10. Now (it is worth) £8.

(cxli) The wife of Hugh has 5 hides of land which are called Cealvaduna which 9 thegns held in parage[61] and this (manor) paid geld for 5 hides. Four ploughs can plough these. A certain knight of hers, Hugh,[62] holds these of her. Thence Hugh has 2½ hides and 2 ploughs in demesne and the villeins (have) 2½ hides and 2 ploughs. There Hugh has 5 villeins and 8 bordars and 2 serfs and 3 beasts and 302 sheep and 3 acres of meadow and 7 furlongs of pasture in length and 5 in width and it is worth £8 a year and when Hugh received it it was worth £10 and in Hugh's lifetime it rendered £11.

(409) Hugh holds RINGESTEDE [Ringstead in Osmington, site derelict] of the same (woman). Ulnod held (it) freely[63] T.R.E. and it paid geld for 1 hide. There is land for 1 plough. There are 2 villeins and 2 bordars and 8 acres of meadow and 2 furlongs of pasture in length and 1 furlong in width. It was worth 30*s*. Now (it is worth) 25*s*.

(cxlii) The wife of Hugh has 1 manor which is called Ringhesteta which 1 thegn, Ulnof, held on the day when King Edward was alive and dead, and he could go to any lord,[64] which paid geld for 1 hide. One plough can plough this. A certain knight of hers, Hugh,[65] holds this of the wife of Hugh. Of this Hugh has in demesne 3 virgates less 5 acres and the villeins (have) 1 virgate and 5 acres and ½ plough. There Hugh has 2 villeins and 2 bordars and 93 sheep and 8 acres of meadow and 2 furlongs of pasture in length and 1 in width and this (manor) is worth 25*s*. a year and when Hugh fitz Grip[66] received it it was worth 30*s*.

57 'agros' interlined.
58 'possunt' interlined.
59 'libere' interlined.
60 'in paragio' interlined.
61 'pariter' interlined.
62 'Hugo' interlined.
63 'libere' interlined.
64 'et hic poterat ad quemlibet dominum ire' interlined.
65 'Hugo' interlined.
66 'filius Gripi' interlined.

(410) Turold holds WARMEWELLE [Warmwell] of the same (woman). Almar held (it) T.R.E. and it paid geld for 1½ hide. There is land for 2 ploughs which are there in demesne and 5 bordars. There (is) a mill rendering 5*s*. (There is) pasture ½ league and 3 furlongs long and 3 furlongs wide. It was worth 30*s*. Now (it is worth) 40*s*.

(cxliii) The wife of Hugh has 1 manor which is called Warmewella which 1 thegn, Almar, held on the day when King Edward was alive and dead, and this (man) could go to any lord. This (manor) paid geld for 1½ hide and 1 virgate. Two ploughs can plough these. Turold, a certain knight of hers, holds this land of the wife of Hugh. Of these Turold has in demesne 1 hide and 1 virgate and 2 ploughs and the villeins (have) ½ hide. There Turold has 5 bordars and 10 pigs and 200 sheep and 1 mill which renders 5*s*. a year and ½ league and 3 furlongs[67] of pasture in length and 3[68] furlongs in width. This manor is worth 40*s*. a year and when Hugh received it it was worth 30*s*.

(411) Ralph holds RINGESTEDE [Ringstead in Osmington, site derelict] of the same (woman). Onowin held (it) T.R.E. and it paid geld for 1½ hide. There is land for 2 ploughs. In demesne there is 1 plough and 1 villein and 3 bordars with ½ plough and 4 furlongs of pasture. It is worth 40*s*.

(cxliv) The wife of Hugh has 1 manor which is called Ringhestede which Onowin, a thegn,[69] held on the day when King Edward was alive and dead, and he could go with his land to any lord. This (manor) paid geld for 1½ hide. Two ploughs can plough these. Ralph the steward (*dapifer*) holds this land of the wife of Hugh. Of these he himself has in demesne 1 hide and ½ virgate and 1 plough and the villeins (have) ½ virgate and ½ plough. There is 1 villein and 3 bordars and 1 pack-horse and 4 beasts and 10 pigs and 53 sheep and 4 furlongs of pasture in length and width. This manor is worth 40*s*. a year and when Hugh received it it was worth as much.

[f. 84]

(412) Robert holds CRIZ [East Creech in Church Knowle] of the same woman. Boln held (it) T.R.E. and it paid geld for ½ hide. There is land for ½ plough which is there with 4 bordars and 3 acres of meadow and 7 furlongs of pasture in length and 3 furlongs in width. It is worth 10*s*.

(cxlv) The wife of Hugh has 1 manor which is called Criz which Bolo held on the day when King Edward was alive and dead, and this (man) could go with his land to any lord. This (manor) paid geld for ½ hide. Half a plough can plough this. Robert the corn-dealer (*frumentinus*) holds this of the wife of Hugh. There Robert has ½ plough and 4 bordars and 1 pack-horse and 7 furlongs of pasture in length and 4 in width and 3 acres of meadow[70] and it is worth 10*s*. a year.

(413) Robert holds HERPERE [Hurpston in Steeple] of the same (woman). Alward held (it) T.R.E. and it paid geld for 3 hides. There is land for 3 ploughs. In demesne there are 1½ plough and 3 serfs and 2 coscets. There (is) a mill rendering 20*d*. and 9 acres of meadow and 4 furlongs of pasture and 1 furlong of wood(land) and 1 burgess rendering 8*d*. It was worth 100*s*. Now (it is worth) £4.

(cxlvi) The wife of Hugh has 1 manor which is called Harpera which Alward held on the day when King Edward was alive and dead which paid geld for 3 hides. Three ploughs can plough these. Robert the boy (*puer*) holds this of the wife of Hugh. Of this he himself has 3[71] hides and 1½ plough in demesne and 2 coscets and 3 serfs and 1 pack-horse and 6 beasts and 20 pigs and 103 sheep and 1 mill which renders 20*d*. a year and 1 furlong of wood(land) in length and as much in width and 9 acres of meadow and 4 furlongs of pasture and 1 burgess who renders 8*d*. a year. This manor is worth £4 and when Hugh received it it was worth 100*s*.

(414) In the same vill Robert holds ½ hide of the woman herself. Sawin held (it) as a manor T.R.E. There is land for ½ plough. It is worth 12*s*. 6*d*.

(cxlvii) In the same vill the wife of Hugh has 1 manor which Sawin held on the day when King Edward was alive and dead. This (manor) paid geld for ½ hide. Half a plough can plough this. This thegn could go with his land to any lord. Robert the boy holds this of the wife of Hugh. This land was entirely devastated (*omnino devastata est*) but nevertheless is worth 12*s*. 6*d*.

(415) She herself holds WILCESWDE [Wilkswood (Farm) in Langton Matravers]. Alward held (it) T.R.E. and it paid geld for 3½ hides and ⅔ virgate. There is land for 3½ ploughs. In demesne there is 1 plough and 2 serfs and 2 villeins and 4 bordars with 1 plough and 2 acres of meadow and 4 furlongs of wood(land). It was and is worth £4.

(cxlviii) The wife of Hugh has 1 manor which is called Wilceswda which 1 thegn, Alward, held on the day when King Edward was alive and dead and it paid geld for 3½ hides and ⅔ virgate. Three ploughs and ½ (plough) can plough these. Of these the wife of Hugh has in demesne 2½ hides and 1 plough and the villeins (have) 1 hide and 1 plough and 2 oxen. There are 2 villeins and 4 bordars and 2 serfs and 1 pack-horse and 16 sheep and 4 furlongs of wood(land) in length and width and 2 acres of meadow. This (manor) is worth £4 a year and when Hugh received it it was worth as much.

(416) She herself holds TACATONE [Acton in Langton Matravers]. Alward held (it) T.R.E. and it paid geld for 2½ hides. There is land for 2 ploughs. In demesne there is 1 plough and 3 serfs and 2 villeins and 1 bordar with 1 plough. There (is) a mill rendering 12*s*. 6*d*. (There is) wood(land) 2 furlongs long and 1½ furlong wide. It was worth 60*s*. Now (it is worth) 40*s*.

(cxlix) The wife of Hugh has 1 manor which is called Tacatona and it paid geld for 2½ hides. One thegn, Alward, held this T.R.E. Two ploughs can plough these. There the wife of Hugh has 2 hides in demesne and 1 plough and the villeins (have) ½ hide and 1 plough. There are 2 villeins and 1 bordar and 3 serfs and 4 beasts and 1 mill which

[67] 'et iii quadragenarias' interlined.
[68] 'i' interlined.
[69] 'tagnus' interlined.
[70] 'et vii quadragenarias pascue in longitudine et iiii in latitudine et iii agros prati' interlined.
[71] 'i' interlined.

renders 12*s*. 6*d*. a year and 2 furlongs of wood-(land) in length (and) 1½ furlong in width. This (manor) is worth 40*s*. a year and when Hugh received it it was worth 60*s*.

(417) Walter holds SWANWIC [Swanage] of the same (woman). Alward held (it) in parage[72] T.R.E. and it paid geld for 1½ hide. There is land for 1 plough which is there with 1 serf and 1 bordar. There (are) 7 acres of meadow. It was worth 20*s*. Now (it is worth) 25*s*.

(cl) The wife of Hugh has 1 manor which is called Swanwic which 1 thegn, Alward, held in parage[73] on the day when King Edward was alive and dead and it paid geld for 1½ hide. One plough can plough this. Walter Tonitruum holds this of the wife of Hugh. There Walter has 1 plough and 1 bordar and 1 serf and 20 sheep and 5 pigs and 7 acres of meadow. This (manor) is worth 25*s*. a year and when Hugh received it it was worth 20*s*.

(418) Ralph holds 3 virgates of land in WIRDE [Worth Matravers] of the same (woman). Two thegns held (it) in parage[74] T.R.E. and it paid geld for so much. There is land for ½ plough which is there with 2 bordars. It is worth 15*s*.

(cli) The wife of Hugh has 3 virgates of land in Wirda which 2 thegns held in parage on the day when King Edward was alive and dead and they paid geld for 3 virgates. Half a plough can plough these. A certain knight, Ralph,[75] holds these of her. There Ralph has ½ plough and 2 bordars and this (manor) is worth 15*s*. a year.

(419) Walter holds TORNE [unidentified] of the same (woman). Alvric held (it) in parage[76] T.R.E. and it paid geld for 1 hide. There is land for 1 plough—[*blank*].[77] It is worth 18*s*.

(clii) The wife of Hugh has 1 manor which is called Torna which 1 thegn, Alvric, held in parage on the day when King Edward was alive and dead and it paid geld for 1 hide. One plough can plough this (hide) which Walter Tonitruum holds of the wife of Hugh. Walter holds this entirely in demesne. This (manor) is worth 18*s*. a year.

(420) Robert holds TORNE [unidentified] of the same (woman). Sawin held (it) in parage[78] T.R.E. and it paid geld for 1 hide. There is land for 1 plough which is there in demesne. It was worth 10*s*. Now (it is worth) 20*s*.

(cliii) The wife of Hugh has 1 manor which is called Torna which 1 thegn, Saewin, held in parage on the day when King Edward was alive and dead and it paid geld for 1 hide. One plough can plough this. Robert, Hugh's nephew,[79] holds this of the wife of Hugh. There Robert has 1 plough and nothing more (*nichil amplius*). This (manor) is worth 20*s*. a year and when Hugh received it it was worth 10*s*.

(421) Hugh holds BRUNESCUME [Brenscombe (Farm) in Corfe Castle] of the same (woman). Algar held (it) in parage[80] T.R.E. and it paid geld for 1 virgate of land. There is land for 1 plough. There are 3 bordars and pasture ½ league long and 4 furlongs wide. (There is) wood(land) 4 furlongs long and 1 furlong wide. It is worth 10*s*.

(cliv) The wife of Hugh has 1 manor which is called Brunescume which 1 thegn, Algar, held in parage on the day when King Edward was alive and dead and it paid geld for 1 virgate. One plough can plough this. Hugh de Boscherbert holds this of the wife of Hugh. There Hugh has 3 bordars and 4 furlongs of wood(land) in length and 1 in width and ½ league of pasture in length and 4 furlongs in width. This (manor) is worth 10*s*.

(422) She herself holds HORCERD [Orchard in Church Knowle]. Four thegns held (it) T.R.E. and it paid geld for 1½ hide. There is land for 1½ plough. There are 2 bordars and an orchard (*virgultum*). Hugh gave this hide to the church of Cranborne for the sake of his soul and it is worth 20*s*. The wife of Hugh holds ½ hide. It is worth 20*s*.

(clv) The wife of Hugh has 1 manor which is called Horcerd which 4 thegns held in parage T.R.E. and it paid geld[81] for 1½ hide. One plough and ½ (plough) can plough these. Of these the wife of Hugh has ½ hide and 2 bordars and 1 orchard and this is worth 20*s*. a year. Hugh gave the aforesaid hide to the abbey of Cranborne for the sake of his soul and this is worth 20*s*. a year.

(423) Durand holds ½ hide in WILCHESODE [Wilkswood (Farm) in Langton Matravers] of the same (woman). There is land for ½ plough. It is worth 10*s*. Two thegns held (it) T.R.E. All the thegns who used to hold these lands T.R.E. could go to whichever lord they wished.

(clvi) The wife of Hugh has ½ hide in Wilchesoda which 2 thegns held T.R.E. and they could go to any lord. Half a plough can plough this. Durand the carpenter (*carpentarius*) holds this of the wife of Hugh and it is worth 10*s*. a year.

[THE LAND OF ISELDIS][82]

(424) Iseldis holds PITRICHESHAM [Petersham (Farm) in Holt] of the king. Wade held (it) T.R.E. and it paid geld for 1 hide. There is land for 1 plough. There are 11 bordars and a mill rendering 5*s*. 10*d*. and 7 acres of meadow. (There is) pasture 1 furlong long and ½ furlong wide. (There is) wood-(land) 1 furlong long and another in width. It is worth 15*s*.

LVI. THE LAND OF THE KING'S THEGNS

(425) Gudmund holds MIDELTONE [Milton on Stour in Gillingham]. The same (man) held (it) T.R.E. and it paid geld for 4½ hides. There is land for 3 ploughs. In demesne there is 1 plough and 2 serfs and 2 villeins and 8 bordars with 1 plough. There (is) a mill (rendering) 12*d*. and 10 acres of meadow. (There is) wood(land) 8 furlongs long and

[72] 'in paragio' interlined.
[73] 'pariter' interlined.
[74] 'in paragio' interlined.
[75] 'Radulfus' interlined.
[76] 'in paragio' interlined.
[77] Space in the text. For a comment, see p. 4.
[78] 'in paragio' interlined.
[79] 'nepos Hugonis' interlined.
[80] 'in paragio' interlined.
[81] 'gildum' interlined.
[82] The scribe omitted to give a name or a number to this fief. For this and similar omissions, see p. 6.

$\frac{1}{2}$ furlong wide. It was worth 60*s*. Now (it is worth) 30*s*.

(426) Chetel holds CHINTONE [Kington Magna]. Dodo held (it) T.R.E. and it paid geld for 3 hides and 3 virgates of land. There is land for 3 ploughs. In demesne there are 2 ploughs with 1 serf and 1 villein and 3 bordars. There (are) 15 acres of meadow and 5 acres of wood(land). It was and is worth 40*s*.

(427) Edwin holds 1 virgate of land in GELINGEHAM [Gillingham]. There is land for $\frac{1}{2}$ plough. It is worth 5*s*.

(428) Godric holds 1 virgate of land in GELINGEHAM [Gillingham]. There is land for $\frac{1}{2}$ plough. There are 4 bordars and 3 acres of meadow. It is worth 5*s*.

(429) Ulwin holds 1$\frac{1}{2}$ virgate of land in GELINGEHAM [Gillingham]. There is land for $\frac{1}{2}$ plough. It is worth 6*s*.

(430) Alvric holds 1 hide in WINTREBURNE [unidentified]. There is land for 1 plough. It is worth 10*s*.

(431) Bollo the priest[83] holds MAPLEDRE [Mappowder]. He himself held (it) with 7 other free[84] thegns T.R.E. and it paid geld for 5 hides and 3 virgates of land. There is land for 5 ploughs. In demesne there are 2 ploughs and 2 serfs and 8 villeins and 4 bordars with 3 ploughs. There (is) a certain amount (*aliquatenus*)[85] of meadow and wood(land) 4 furlongs long and 3 furlongs wide. It is worth £4.

(432) Bollo holds CICHERELLE [Chickerell]. Saulf held (it) T.R.E. and it paid geld for 3 hides and $\frac{1}{2}$ virgate of land. There is land for 3 ploughs which are there in demesne and 4 serfs and 1 villein and 6 bordars. There (are) 6 acres of meadow and 7 furlongs of pasture. It is worth 60*s*.

(433) Brictuin holds WAIA [unidentified]. He himself held (it) T.R.E. and it paid geld for 2 hides. There is land for 2 ploughs which are there in demesne and 3 serfs and 2 villeins and 4 bordars. There (is) a mill rendering 15*s*. and 3 acres of meadow and 2 acres of pasture. It is worth 40*s*.

(434) Brictuin holds 1$\frac{1}{2}$ hide in WINTREBURNE [unidentified]. He himself held (it) T.R.E. There is land for 1 plough which is there. It is worth 15*s*.

(435) Brictuin holds 1 virgate of land in LEWELLE [Lewell (Lodge) in West Knighton]. He himself held (it) T.R.E. It is worth 10*d*.

(436) Alvric holds CRAVEFORD [Tarrant Crawford] and Edward (holds it) of him. T.R.E. it paid geld for 2 hides. There is land for 1$\frac{1}{2}$ plough. However, there are 2 ploughs with 1 coscet and 3 serfs and $\frac{1}{4}$ mill rendering 30*d*. and 12 acres of meadow and 6 furlongs of wood(land) in length and 2 furlongs in width. It was worth 30*d*. Now (it is worth) 40*s*.

83 'presbyter' interlined.

84 'liberis' interlined.

(437) Ulvric holds MORDONE [Morden]. His father held (it) T.R.E. and it paid geld for 2$\frac{1}{2}$ hides. There is land for 2 ploughs which are there with 2 villeins and 6 bordars and 11*d*. from part of a mill and 5 acres of meadow and 1 league of pasture in length and width. It is worth 30*s*. The wife of Ulvric's brother has there 1 hide and $\frac{1}{2}$ virgate of land. There is land for 1 plough. It is worth 20*s*.

(438) Edwin holds BLENEFORDE [? Blandford St. Mary]. Alwin held (it) T.R.E. and it paid geld for 5 hides and 1$\frac{1}{2}$ virgate. There is land for 3 ploughs. In demesne there is 1 plough and 3 serfs and 2 villeins and 1 bordar and 3 cottars with 1 plough. There (are) 18 acres of meadow. (There is) pasture 8 furlongs long and 2 furlongs wide. It was worth £4. It is worth 40*s*.

(439) Alward holds TORNECOME [Thorncombe in Blandford St. Mary]. He himself held (it) T.R.E. and it paid geld for 2 hides. There is land for 1 plough which is there with 1 serf and 4 bordars. It is worth 20*s*.

(440) Ulviet holds WINBURNE [Wimborne St. Giles]. He himself held (it) T.R.E. and it paid geld for 1 hide. There is 1 plough with 1 serf. (There is) pasture 4 furlongs long and 1 wide. (There is) wood(land) 1 furlong long and $\frac{1}{2}$ furlong wide. It was worth 20*s*. Now (it is worth) 10*s*.

(441) Brictuin holds MELEBERIE [Melbury Sampford]. T.R.E. it paid geld for 5 hides. There is land for 4 ploughs. In demesne there are 2 ploughs and 5 serfs and 4 villeins and 9 bordars with 2 ploughs. There (are) 3 acres of meadow and 3 furlongs of wood(land) in length and 3 in width. It is worth 60*s*.

(442) Ulvric holds TORNEHELLE [Thorn Hill (Farm) in Wimborne Minster]. His father held (it) T.R.E. and it paid geld for $\frac{1}{2}$ hide. There is land for 1 plough which is there with 5 bordars and 5 cottars and 5 acres of meadow. It is worth 10*s*.

(443) Torchil holds HAME [Hampreston]. T.R.E. it paid geld for 3$\frac{1}{3}$ virgates of land. There is land for 1 plough. There is $\frac{1}{2}$ plough with 1 bordar and 6 acres of meadow and 2 furlongs of wood(land) and 2 furlongs of pasture in length and 1 furlong in width. It is worth 8*s*. The queen gave this land to Schelin.[86] Now the king has (it) in demesne.

(444) Dodo holds $\frac{1}{2}$ hide and it paid geld for so much T.R.E. There is land for $\frac{1}{2}$ plough. However, there is 1 plough and a mill rendering 10*s*. and 14 acres of meadow and $\frac{1}{2}$ acre of wood(land). (There is) pasture $\frac{1}{2}$ league long and 3 furlongs wide. It is worth 17*s*. 6*d*. The queen gave this land to Dodo in alms.

(445) The same (Dodo) holds 1 hide in WEDECHESWORDE [Wilksworth (Farm) in Colehill] and it paid geld for so much T.R.E. There is land for 1 plough which is there with 2 serfs and 2 villeins and 2 bordars having $\frac{1}{2}$ plough. There (are) 14 acres of meadow and 2 furlongs of wood(land) in length and 1 furlong in width. It is worth 10*s*.

85 'xvi' (? acres) interlined.

86 So the facsimile; the printed version has *Schelm*.

(446) Alward holds ⅓ virgate of land and it renders 30*d*.

(447) Ailrun holds WEDECHESWORDE [Wilksworth (Farm) in Colehill]. There is 1 hide. There is land for 1 plough which is there with 2 bordars and 2 serfs and pasture 4 furlongs long and 1 furlong wide and as much wood(land). It is worth 10*s*.

(448) Godwin the huntsman[87] holds WALTEFORD [Walford (Farm) in Colehill]. Almar held (it) T.R.E. and it paid geld for 1 hide. There is land for 1 plough which is there with 3 bordars and 7 acres of meadow and pasture 5 furlongs long and 2 furlongs wide and 1 furlong of wood(land). It is worth 15*s*.

(449) Ailward holds 1 virgate of land in RISTONE [Rushton in East Stoke]. There is land for 2 oxen. It is worth 30*d*.

(450) Godwin the reeve[88] holds 1 hide in WINTREBURNE [unidentified]. He himself held (it) T.R.E. There is land for 1 plough. There is 1 bordar. It is worth 12*s*. 6*d*.

(451) Godwin the huntsman[89] holds ½ virgate of land and 4 acres and there he has ½ plough with 5 bordars and 9 acres of meadow. It is worth 10*s*. Godric held (it) T.R.E.

(452) Swain holds WINTREBURNE [unidentified]. His father held (it) T.R.E. and it paid geld for 10 hides. There is land for 6 ploughs. In demesne there are 2 ploughs and 5 serfs and 7 villeins and 17 bordars with 3 ploughs. There (are) 10 acres of meadow. (There is) pasture 1½ league long and ½ (league) wide. (There is) wood(land) 1½ league long and 4 furlongs wide. It was worth 100*s*. Now (it is worth) £8. Robert holds (it) of Swain.

(453) The same Swain holds PLUMBERE [Plumber (Manor) in Lydlinch] and Ralph (holds it) of him. His father held (it) T.R.E. and it paid geld for 5 hides. There is land for 3 ploughs. In demesne there is 1 plough and 4 serfs and 3 villeins and 6 bordars with 1 plough. There (are) 15 acres of meadow. (There is) wood(land) 5 furlongs long and 3 furlongs wide. It was worth 30*s*. Now (it is worth) 60*s*.

(454) Ulvric the huntsman[90] holds 1 hide of the king. His father held (it) T.R.E. and it paid geld for so much. There is land for 1 plough. There are 3 bordars and 3 acres of meadow. It is worth 10*s*.

(455) Edwin holds BLENEFORD [? Langton Long Blandford]. Alwi held (it) T.R.E. and it paid geld for 5 hides. There is land for 4 ploughs. In demesne there is 1½ plough and 3 serfs and 3 villeins with a priest and 6 bordars and 3 cottars with 1 plough. There (is) a mill rendering 18*s*. 4*d*. and 18 acres of meadow. (There is) pasture 5 furlongs long and 2 furlongs wide. It is worth £4.

(456) Edwin holds WERNE [Lazerton Farm in Stourpaine]. Alward held (it) T.R.E. and it paid geld for 3 hides. There is land for 2 ploughs which are there with 1 villein and 3 coscets and 3 serfs. There (is) a mill rendering 2*s*. and 4½ furlongs of pasture in length and 2 furlongs in width. (There is) wood(land)
[f. 84b]
6 furlongs long and 2 furlongs wide. It was worth 60*s*. Now (it is worth) 30*s*.

(457) The same Edwin holds SILFEMETONE [Shilvinghampton in Portesham]. Alwi held (it) T.R.E. and it paid geld for 2½ hides. There is land for 2 ploughs. There is 1 villein and 5 serfs with ½ plough and 15 acres of meadow and 3 furlongs of pasture in length and width. It is worth 40*s*.

(458) Ulviet holds BLENEFORD [Langton Long Blandford]. He himself held (it) T.R.E. and it paid geld for 1 hide. There is land for 1 plough. There are 4 coscets and 3 acres of meadow and 5 acres of pasture. It was and is worth 10*s*.

(459) Brictuin holds CILTECOME [Chilcombe]. He himself held (it) T.R.E. and it paid geld for 3 hides. There is land for 3 ploughs. In demesne there are 2 ploughs and 5 serfs and 1 villein and 8 bordars with ½ plough. There (is) a mill rendering 5*s*. and 25 acres of meadow and 20 acres of pasture. It is worth 60*s*.

(460) The same (man) holds WADONE [Little Waddon in Portesham]. Alward held (it) T.R.E. and it paid geld for 2 hides. There is land for 2 ploughs which are there in demesne and 4 serfs and 1 villein and 3 bordars. There (are) 16 acres of meadow and 14 acres of pasture. It is worth 40*s*. Hugh fitz Grip[91] exchanged this land with Brictuin (for a manor) which the Count of Mortain now holds and the exchange itself is worth twice as much (*ipsum scambium valet duplum*).

(461) The same Brictuin holds 1 hide and 8 acres of land in MORTUNE [Moreton]. He himself held (it) T.R.E. There is land for 1 plough. Three villeins and 4 bordars have this there. There (are) 11 acres of meadow and 6 furlongs of pasture in length and 4 furlongs in width. It is worth 21*s*. 3*d*.

(462) The same Brictuin holds GAVELTONE [Galton in Owermoigne]. He himself held (it) T.R.E. and it paid geld for 2 hides and 1½ virgate of land. There is land for 2 ploughs. In demesne there is 1 plough and 3 serfs and 2 villeins and 6 cottars. There (is) a mill rendering 12*s*. 6*d*. and 2 acres of meadow and 8 furlongs of pasture in length and 3 furlongs in width. It is worth 40*s*.

(463) The same Brictuin holds 1 hide in RINGESTEDE [Ringstead in Osmington, site derelict]. He himself held (it) T.R.E. There is land for 1 plough. Six men hold it at farm. It is worth 25*s*.

(464) The same Brictuin holds 2½ virgates of land in STINCTEFORD [Stinsford] and Aiulf (holds) of him. There is land for ½ plough. There are 3 bordars. It is worth 7*s*.

(465) The same (man) holds 1 virgate of land in BRIGE [Bridge in Weymouth, site lost]. There is land

87 'venator' interlined.
88 'prepositus' interlined.
89 'venator' interlined.
90 'venator' interlined.
91 'filius Grip' interlined.

for 2 oxen. There are 2 fishermen. It is worth 5*s.* The same Brictuin used to hold these lands T.R.E.

(466) Edric holds 1 hide in RISTONE [Rushton in East Stoke] less ¼ virgate. Sawin held (it) T.R.E. There is land for 1 plough. There are 5½ acres of meadow. It is worth 9*s.* 2*d.*

(467) The same (man) holds 1 hide at HOLNE [East Holme]. There is land for 1 plough. It is worth 20*s.*

(468) The same (man) holds 1 hide at STOCHE [Stoke Wallis in Whitchurch Canonicorum, site lost]. There is land for 2 ploughs. In demesne there is 1 plough and 2 serfs and 1 villein and 8 bordars with ½ plough. There (is) a mill rendering 40*d.* and 14 acres of meadow and 16 acres of wood(land) and 12 acres of pasture. It is worth 30*s.*

(469) The same (man) holds 2 hides at SLITLEGE [Studley in Whitchurch Canonicorum, site lost].[92] There is land for 2 ploughs. In demesne there is 1 plough and 2 serfs and 2 villeins and 3 bordars with 1½ plough. There (are) 5 acres of meadow and 3 acres of wood(land) and 1 furlong of pasture in length and another in width. It is worth 25*s.*

(470) The same (man) holds PILESDONE [Pilsdon]. T.R.E. it paid geld for 3 hides. There is land for 4 ploughs. There are 7 villeins and 8 bordars with 3 ploughs and 12 acres of meadow and 100 acres of pasture. It was worth 20*s.* Now (it is worth) 40*s.*

(471) The same (man) holds 1 virgate of land at STODLEGE [Studley in Whitchurch Canonicorum, site lost]. There is land for ½ plough. It is worth 5*s.* Sawin held these lands of Edric T.R.E.

(472) Godric holds PIDELE [Briantspuddle in Affpuddle]. Azor held (it) T.R.E. and it paid geld for 5 hides. There is land for 3 ploughs. In demesne there is 1 plough and 7 serfs and 2 villeins and 4 bordars with 2 ploughs. There (is) a mill rendering 7*s.* 6*d.* and 38 acres of meadow and 12 acres of wood(land) and 11 furlongs of pasture in length and 4 in width. It is worth £4.

(473) Edric holds 1 virgate of land in TIGEHAM [Tyneham]. There is land for 2 oxen. It is worth 65*d.*

(474) Dodo holds 1 virgate of land in WELLACOME [Woolcombe (Farm) in Toller Porcorum]. There is land for 2 oxen. There are 2 acres of meadow and 3 furlongs of pasture in length and width. It was and is worth 20*d.*

(475) Alvric and Brictric hold ½ hide in LODRE [Uploders in Loders]. There is land for 1 plough. There (are) 5 acres of meadow and 20 acres of pasture. It was and is worth 10*s.*

(476) Alvric holds BLACHEMANESTONE [Blackmanston (Farm) in Steeple]. He himself held (it) T.R.E. and it paid geld for 1 hide. There is land for 1 plough.[93]

(477) Swain holds MELEBORNE [Milborne Stileham] and Osmund (holds it) of him. Swain's father held (it) T.R.E. There is land for 2 ploughs. There are 7 bordars with 1 serf and a mill rendering 25*d.* and 10 acres of meadow and 30 acres of pasture. It was and is worth 20*s.*

(478) Godric holds 1 hide in CANDELE [Stourton Caundle]. Leveron held (it) T.R.E. There is land for 1 plough. There are 2 serfs with 1 bordar and 6 acres of meadow and 10 acres of pasture and 2 furlongs of underwood. It is worth 10*s.*

(479) Saward holds 2½ virgates of land in CANDELE [Stourton Caundle]. He himself held (it) T.R.E. There is land for ½ plough. There is 1 acre of pasture. It is worth 5*s.*

(480) Two bordars hold ¼ virgate of land. It is worth 15*d.* They themselves held (it) freely T.R.E.

(481) Alvric holds COME [Coombe in Langton Matravers]. He himself held (it) T.R.E. and it paid geld for 5 hides and 1 virgate of land. There is land for 3 ploughs. In demesne there are 2 ploughs and 4 serfs and 1 villein and 4 bordars—[*blank*].[94] There (are) 6 acres of meadow and 4 furlongs of wood(land) in length and 2 furlongs in width. It is worth £6.

(482) Swain holds ALEOUDE [Ailwood in Corfe Castle]. Azor held (it) T.R.E. and it paid geld for 5 hides less 1 virgate. There is land for 6 ploughs. In demesne there are 3 ploughs with 1 serf and 1 villein and 1 coscet. There (are) 10 acres of meadow and 8 furlongs of pasture in length and 1 furlong in width. (There is) wood(land) 1 league long and as much in width. It was and is worth 40*s.* The wife of Hugh holds of Swain.

(483) Alvric holds BOVINTONE [Bovington (Farm) in Wool]. He himself held (it) T.R.E. and it paid geld for 4 hides. There is land for 3 ploughs. In demesne there is 1 plough with 1 serf and 3 villeins with 2 ploughs. There (are) 40 acres of meadow. (There is) pasture 1 league long and ½ league wide. It is worth 40*s.*

(484) Alvric holds WINTREBURNE [unidentified]. He himself held (it) T.R.E. and it paid geld for 1 hide. There is land for 1 plough. There are 5 bordars with 1 serf and 5 acres of meadow and 8 furlongs of pasture in length and 4 furlongs in width. It is worth 20*s.*

(485) Ten thegns hold CHIMEDECOME [Higher and Lower Kingcombe in Toller Porcorum]. They themselves held (it) T.R.E. as 1 manor and it paid geld for 1 hide and ¾ virgate. There is land for 1 plough which is there—[*blank*].[95]

(486) Alward holds WILLE [Wool]. He himself held (it) T.R.E. and it paid geld for 1½ hide. There is land

[92] See Fägersten, *Place-Names of Dorset*, 298, for this identification.

[93] This entry is repeated at no. 489. For a comment, see pp. 5, 8.

[94] Space in the text.

[95] The text breaks off at this point and a space has been left for the completion of the entry.

for 1 plough which is there in demesne with 1 villein and 2 bordars. There (are) 7½ acres of meadow and 2 acres of pasture. It is worth 15*s*.

(487) Almar holds WILLE [Wool]. Alward held (it) T.R.E. and it paid geld for 1 virgate of land. There is land for 2 oxen. It is worth 2*s*.

(488) Godwin holds CORISCUMBE [Corscombe]. Aldwin held (it) T.R.E. and it paid geld for 1 hide. There is land for 1½ plough. There is 1 villein with 1 plough and 4 bordars and 1 serf and ½ furlong of pasture and 2 furlongs of wood(land). It was worth 30*s*. Now (it is worth) 20*s*.

(489) Alvric holds 1 hide in BLACHEMANESTONE [Blackmanston (Farm) in Steeple]. He himself held (it) T.R.E. There is land for 1 plough. It is worth 20*s*.[96]

(490) Edward the huntsman[97] holds ½ virgate of land in GELINGEHAM [Gillingham]. Anschil held (it) T.R.E. There is land for 3 oxen. It is worth 30*d*.

All who held these lands T.R.E. could go to any lord they wished.

LVII. THE LAND OF THE KING'S SERJEANTS

(491) William Belet holds FROME [Frome Billet in West Stafford, now lost] of the king. Ulward and Bricsrid held (it) T.R.E. as 2 manors[98] and it paid geld for 3 hides. There is land for 2 ploughs. However, there are 3 ploughs and 6 serfs and 2 villeins with 1 bordar. There (is) a mill rendering 5*s*. and 23 acres of meadow. (There is) pasture 3 furlongs long and 2 furlongs wide. It is worth £6.

(492) Hugh holds 3 virgates of land in LIWELLE [Lewell (Lodge) in West Knighton]. Alward held (it) T.R.E. There is land for 2 oxen. There are 2 bordars rendering 20*d*.

(493) William holds WINTREBURNE [Winterborne Belet or Cripton, now lost]. Two thegns held (it) in parage[99] T.R.E. and it paid geld for 2½ hides. There is land for 1½ plough. However, there are 2 ploughs and 5 serfs and 18 acres of meadow. (There is) pasture 6 furlongs long and 3 furlongs wide. It was worth 40*s*. Now (it is worth) £4 15*s*.

(494) William de Dalmar holds the lands of 3 thegns [? part of Tarrant Crawford] which paid geld T.R.E. for 3 hides and 2½ virgates of land. There is land for 2 ploughs which are there and 5 serfs and 5 bordars. There (are) ¾ mill rendering 9*s*. and 4 acres of meadow. (There is) wood(land) 6 furlongs long and 3 furlongs wide. It is worth 60*s*.

(495) Hugh Gosbert[1] holds 1 virgate of land. Saulf held (it) T.R.E. It is worth 30*d*.

(496) The same Hugh holds WINTREBURNE [unidentified]. Two thegns held (it) T.R.E. and it paid geld for ½ hide. There is land for ½ plough. There are 2 villeins. It is worth 40*d*.

(497) The same Hugh holds 1 virgate of land in WIREGROTE [Worgret in Arne]. Almar held (it) T.R.E. There is land for 2 oxen. It was and is worth 12*d*.

(498) The same Hugh holds 3 virgates of land in WILECOME [Woolcombe (Farm) in Toller Porcorum]. Dode the monk held (it) T.R.E. and it paid geld for so much. There is land for 1 plough which is there with 2 bordars and 4 acres of meadow and 6 furlongs of pasture and 8 acres of underwood. It was worth 5*s*. Now (it is worth) 15*s*.

[f. 85]

(499) Hervey the chamberlain[2] holds WINBURNE [Wimborne St. Giles]. Brictric held (it) T.R.E. and it paid geld for 2½ hides. There is land for 3 ploughs. In demesne there is 1 plough and 5 villeins and 5 bordars with 2 ploughs. In the mill of the vill 22½ (*In molino ville xxii et dimidia*)—[*blank*].[3] There (are) 2 acres of meadow and pasture 1 league long and 3 furlongs wide. (There is) wood(land) 6 furlongs long and 2 furlongs wide. It was worth 30*s*. Now (it is worth) 50*s*.

(500) John holds WINTREBURNE [unidentified]. Alwold held (it) T.R.E. and it paid geld for 2 hides and 1½ virgate. There is land for 2 ploughs. In demesne there is 1½ plough and 3 serfs and 2 villeins and 3 bordars with ½ plough. There (is) pasture 5 furlongs long and as much in width. It was and is worth 40*s*.

(501) William de Dalmar holds WALDIC [Walditch in Bothenhampton]. Alwi held (it) T.R.E. and it paid geld for 2 hides. There is land for 1 plough which is there in demesne with 1 serf and 1 villein and 8 bordars with ½ plough. There (is) a mill rendering 45*d*. and 4 acres of meadow. (There is) wood(land) 4 furlongs long and 1 furlong wide. It was and is worth 40*s*.

(502) William Belet[4] holds NODFORD [France Farm, formerly Nutford Lockey, in Stourpaine]. Alnod held (it) T.R.E. and it paid geld for 1 hide and 2½ virgates of land. There is land for 1 plough. However, there are 2 ploughs and 3 serfs and 8 acres of meadow. (There is) pasture 3 furlongs long and 1 furlong wide. It was worth 15*s*. Now (it is worth) 30*s*.

(503) The same William holds WARDESFORD [Woodsford]. Levegar held (it) T.R.E. and it paid geld for 2½ hides. There is land for 2 ploughs which are there in demesne and 4 serfs and 2 villeins and 2 bordars. There (is) a mill rendering 6*s*. and 28 acres of meadow and 12 furlongs of pasture in length and width. It was worth 100*s*. Now (it is worth) 60*s*.

(504) The same William holds LIME [Lyme Regis]. Alveve held (it) T.R.E. and it paid geld for 1 hide.

96 This entry is repeated from no. 476. For a comment, see pp. 5, 8.

97 'venator' interlined.

98 'et Bricsrid pro ii maneriis' interlined.

99 'in paragio' interlined.

1 'Gosbert' interlined.

2 'cubicularius' interlined.

3 Space in the text. For a comment, see p. 22.

4 'Belet' interlined.

There is land for 1 plough. There is 1 villein with ½ plough and 14 salt-workers. There (is) a mill rendering 39*d.* and 3 acres of meadow. (There is) pasture 4 furlongs long and 1 furlong wide and 1 furlong of wood(land) in length and width. It is worth 60*s.*

(505) Hunger fitz Odin[5] holds WINDESORE [Broadwindsor]. Bondi held (it) T.R.E. and it paid geld for 20 hides. There is land for 20 ploughs. In demesne there are 2 ploughs and 7 serfs and 38 villeins and 12 bordars with 16 ploughs. There (are) 12 acres of meadow and 30 furlongs of wood(land) in length and 8 furlongs in width and 8 furlongs of pasture. It was and is worth £20.

(506) In the same vill Hunger has 1 hide of land which 1 free man held T.R.E.

(507) Osmund the baker[6] holds 1 hide and ½ virgate of land in GALTONE [Galton in Owermoigne]. Four free men held (it) T.R.E. There is land for 1 plough. There are 4 men rendering 12*s.* 4*d.* It was worth 15*s.*

(508) The same Osmund holds 3 virgates of land in WINDESTORTE [Woodstreet (Farm) in Wool]. Three free men held (it) T.R.E. There is land for 6 oxen. There are 2 bordars. It was and is worth 7*s.* 6*d.* (Those) who held these lands T.R.E. could go where they would.

(509) William Belet[7] holds 1 hide and 2½ virgates of land in STURE [Stourpaine] of the king. Alnod held (it) of Edward Lipe and he could not betake himself from his demesne.

(510)[8] Durand the carpenter[9] holds ALFRUNETONE [Afflington (Farm) in Corfe Castle]. Lewin held (it) T.R.E. and it paid geld for 1 virgate of land. There is land for ½ plough. It is worth 6*s.*

(511) The same (man) holds MOLEHAM [Moulham or Mowlem in Swanage, site lost].[10] Three thegns held (it) T.R.E. and it paid geld for 1 hide. There is land for 1 plough which is there with 1 cottar. There (is) a mill rendering 6*d.* and 1 acre of meadow. It was worth 5*s.* Now (it is worth) 30*s.*

(512) Godfrey the scullion (*scutularius*) holds 1 virgate of land in HERSTUNE [Herston in Swanage]. His father held (it) T.R.E. and it paid geld for 1 virgate of land and 4 acres. These (*Has*)—[*blank*].[11]

LVIII. THE LAND OF THE COUNTESS OF BOULOGNE

(513) The Countess of Boulogne holds BOCHEHANTONE [Bockhampton in Stinsford] of King William.[12] T.R.E. it paid geld for 4 hides. There is land for 3 ploughs. In demesne there is 1 plough with 1 serf and 4 villeins with 1 bordar have 2 ploughs. There (is) a mill rendering 5*s.* and 20 acres of meadow and 4 furlongs of wood(land) in length and 1 furlong in width. It is worth £3.

THE LAND OF THE COUNTESS OF BOULOGNE IN DORSET

(xxxvi) The wife of Count Eustace has 1 manor which is called Bochehamtona which Ulveiva held on the day when King Edward was alive and dead and it paid geld T.R.E. for 4 hides. Three ploughs can plough these. Thence the countess has 2 hides and 1 plough in demesne and the villeins (have) 2 hides and 2 ploughs. There the countess has 4 villeins and 1 bordar and 1 serf and 1 mill which is worth 5*s.* a year and 4 furlongs of wood(land) in length and 1 in width and 20 acres of meadow and it is worth £3 a year and when the countess received (it it was worth) as much.

(514) The same (countess) holds WINTREBURNE [Winterborne Monkton]. T.R.E. it paid geld for 6 hides. There is land for 5 ploughs. In demesne there are 2 ploughs and 4 serfs and 4 villeins and 2 bordars with 2 ploughs. There (are) 9 acres of meadow and 9 furlongs of pasture in length and 3 furlongs in width. It is worth £6.

(xxxvii) The Countess of Boulogne has 1 manor which is called Wintreborna which Ulvevia held on the day when King Edward was alive and dead and it paid geld for 6 hides. Five ploughs can plough these. Thence the countess has 4½ hides and 2 ploughs in demesne and the villeins (have) 1½ hide and 2 ploughs. There the countess has 4 villeins and 2 bordars and 4 serfs and 5 cows and 16 pigs and 105 sheep and 9 acres of meadow and 9 furlongs of pasture in length and 3 in width and it is worth £6 a year and when the countess received (it) it was worth as much.

(515) The same (countess) holds SONWIC [Swanage]. T.R.E. it paid geld for 1 hide and ⅓ virgate. There is land for 1 plough. One villein has this (plough) there and there (are) 4 acres of meadow. It is worth 15*s.* Ulveva held these 3 manors T.R.E. and she could go with the land where she would.

(xxxviii) The countess has 1 manor which is called Sonwich which Olveva held T.R.E. and she could go to any lord. This (manor) paid geld for 1 hide and for ⅓ virgate which 1 plough can plough, which 1 villein has in the same land and 4 acres of meadow, and it is worth 15*s.* a year. King William never had geld from this manor.

[5] 'filius Odini' interlined.
[6] 'pistor' interlined.
[7] 'Belet' interlined.
[8] Nos. 510–12 were added after the land of the Countess of Boulogne.
[9] 'carpentarius' interlined.
[10] According to Fägersten (op. cit. 127 and n. 2) 'De Moulham Road and Mowlem Institute in Swanage preserve the memory of the family which took their name from this place'.
[11] The entry, the last in the Dorset survey (see n. 8 above), breaks off at this point.
[12] 'de rege Willelmo' interlined.

DORSET GELD ROLLS

THE Geld Rolls preserved in Exon. Domesday relate to the five south-western counties originally covered by the volume. There are three differing versions of the Wiltshire roll, each the work of a separate scribe,[1] but the Geld Rolls for Dorset,[2] Devon, Cornwall, and Somerset[3] seem all to be written in one hand. At the foot of folio 82 in the Somerset roll a different hand appears and also writes folio 82b, but the detached portion of the Somerset roll[4] seems to be the work of the main scribe. Both hands can be recognized in Exon. Domesday itself. Three different hands at least can be identified in the Dorset section of Exon. Domesday, and two of these hands are identical with those of the Geld Rolls. The first scribe (A) who wrote the entry relating to Child Okeford on folio 25 can be identified as the main writer of the Geld Rolls. The second scribe (B) wrote the entry for Puddletown which follows that for Okeford on folio 25; he does not appear to have written any part of the Geld Rolls. The third scribe (C), who wrote the entries for Portland and Fleet on folio 26, seems to be the subsidiary scribe who wrote part of folio 82 and folio 82b in the Geld Rolls. In addition to these three hands a fourth scribe (D) seems to have written folio 47, covering the land of William of Moyon in Wiltshire and the beginning of his land in Dorset.

The Geld Rolls are arranged hundred by hundred. Under each hundred the number of hides in the hundred is entered first, followed by the total amount of exempt demesne held by the tenants-in-chief, which is then broken down into the demesne of each tenant-in-chief by name. The number of hides from which the king received or should have received geld follows and the amount of geld paid.[5] Lastly there are details of exemptions and defaults. In some hundreds the details of the account do not tally with the stated number of hides in the hundred. Usually the discrepancy is quite a minor one, a matter of one or two virgates, and in some cases fractions have been omitted from the total, but in two cases the difference is more serious. In *Langeberge* hundred, according to the Geld Roll, there should be 84 hides, but the details of the account add up to 88½ hides and 4 acres. In *Aileveswode* hundred there should be 73 hides, but the details add up to 78 hides, 1⅚ virgate. In the same way, but less frequently, the total amount of exempt demesne does not always tally with the sum of the individual demesnes. In *Canendone* hundred the king's barons are said to have 22 hides and ⅔ virgate in demesne, but in fact they held a total of 20 hides and 1⅔ virgate less 5 acres. In Puddletown hundred the king and his barons are said to have 47 hides less ½ virgate in demesne, but in fact they had 36 hides, 2½ virgates.[6] Occasionally the Geld Rolls include non-gelding carucates as part of the exempt demesne. In Yetminster hundred there were 47 hides. The Bishop of Salisbury had *tantum terre . . . quantum (possunt) arare vi carruce*. The barons had in demesne 6 hides, 1 virgate, and 6 carucates, and the bishop 6 carucates. These six carucates can easily be identified as the *terra vi*

[1] *Dom. Bk.* (Rec. Com.), iv. 1–6 (ff. 1–3b), 6–11 (ff. 7–9b), 12–18 (ff. 13–16). These 3 scribes did not write any other part of the Geld Rolls. For a further discussion of the palaeography of the Geld Rolls, see *V.C.H. Wilts.* ii. 169.

[2] *Dom. Bk.* (Rec. Com.), iv. 18–26 (ff. 17–24).

[3] Ibid. 56–74 (ff. 63–82).

[4] Ibid. 489–90 (ff. 526b, 527). An occasional word or two in the main section of the Geld Rolls (ff. 17–24 and 63–82) may be in another hand or hands.

[5] In a number of hundreds the amount of geld paid precedes the amount of exempt demesne.

[6] This error of a round 10 hides probably represents a slip on the part of the scribe. Another such slip can be observed in the account of *Haltone* hundred. There the king's barons have in demesne *xxxviii hidas et dimidiam et iii virgas*, that is 39 hides, 1 virgate. In fact they had 38 hides, 3 virgates. What the scribe meant to write was plainly *xxxviii hidas et dimidiam et i virgam.*

carucarum que nunquam geldavit T.R.E. which the Bishop of Salisbury had in demesne at Yetminster (no. 35). In Sherborne hundred there were *lxxv hide et dimidia* (*et xxv carucate*) . . . *Inde habent episcopus et sui monachi in dominio xxv carrucatas.* This land was at Sherborne itself (no. 37) where the bishop had 16 carucates in demesne and the monks had 9½ carucates. There is, however, no reference in Buckland hundred to the land for 8 ploughs *que nunquam geldavit* which the Abbot of Glastonbury had in demesne at Buckland Newton (no. 65), or in the hundred of Newton to the land for 14 ploughs *que nunquam gildavit* which the same abbot had in demesne at Sturminster Newton (no. 63). The Bishop of Salisbury had land for 2 ploughs which never paid geld at Charminster (no. 32) in Dorchester hundred, but it is not recorded in the Geld Roll for that hundred; he also had two such carucates at Stoke Abbott (no. 45), two at Beaminster (no. 46), and two at Netherbury (no. 47), all in Beaminster hundred, which are not recorded in the Geld Roll for Beaminster. There is only one, indirect, reference in the Dorset rolls to the manors of King Edward; in Whitchurch hundred, which must have included Burton Bradstock (nos. 2 and x), there were 84 hides and 3 virgates *preter firmam regis.* Otherwise the manors which rendered the night's farm are not mentioned at all.

It was only the tenants-in-chief whose demesnes were exempt from geld. Their mesne tenants were liable to the whole geld, on both demesne and the land of the *villani.*[7] The exemption of the baronial demesnes from geld seems to have been exceptional. It is obvious from the language of the Exchequer text and of Exon. Domesday that the usual practice had been for the whole manor to pay geld, and such seems to have been the custom in the 12th century also. On the occasion of this levy, however, the baronial demesnes were exempt, perhaps because the geld itself was levied at the unusually heavy rate of 6*s.* on the hide.[8] Other land was exempt in special instances, as appears from the Geld Rolls, although it is difficult at times to distinguish between exemptions and defaults. It is likely that when the text uses the phrase *nunquam habuit rex geldum* it is recording an exemption and that the phrase *non habet* (or *habuit*) *rex geldum* (*hoc anno*) indicated a default. This is not always true. In *Albretesberge* hundred the king did not have geld (*non habuit rex geldum*) from 1 hide which a widow had at farm of Humphrey the chamberlain, but the context shows that this was an exemption, not a default; the king had no geld because it had been remitted. Sometimes geld had been paid after the stated terms laid down for its collection. From Frampton hundred the king had £3 12*s.* 0*d.* from the land of Caen Abbey *post constitutos terminos.*[9] There are several references to these terms. The account of Badbury hundred makes it clear that there were two terms: *habuit rex lxiiii solidos* (*pro x hidis et dimidia et dimidia virga*) *intra ii terminos.* It is likely that the money was paid in two equal instalments, one at each term. Sometimes money which should have been paid at the first term was withheld until the second; sums of 12*s.* had been so withheld in Yetminster and Whitchurch hundreds.[10] One of the terms was Easter, as the Dorset rolls show. In *Canendone* hundred *de v hidis de terra Gode quam tenet Rotbertus de Oilleio ad firmam de rege habuit rex geldum post Pascha*; in Puddletown hundred *pro x hidis quas habet comes Alanus habuit rex lx et ii solidos et vi denarios post Pascha*; and in *Haltone* hundred *Rotbertus de Oilleio retinuit inde xv solidos usque post Pascha* (*quos nundum habet rex*).

[7] There is an exception to this in the case of Fifehead St. Quintin (no. 133) in Newton hundred. Chetel held this manor of the Abbess of Shaftesbury, but nevertheless was credited with 4½ hides and ⅜ virgate of exempt demesne in the account of Newton hundred. According to the Exchequer text he had 3½ hides in demesne.

[8] J. H. Round, 'Danegeld and the Finance of Domesday', *Domesday Studies*, ed. P. E. Dove, 97–98.

[9] Cf. Cadworth hundred (Wilts.) where *iiii denarios retinuerunt illi qui colligerunt geldum in constitutis terminis.*

[10] Cf. Thornhill hundred (Wilts.) where *de his denariis retinuerunt illi qui colligerunt geldum xv solidos et ii denarios usque ad istum terminum.* The phrases *istum ultimum terminum* in the Devon rolls and *in ultimo gildo* in Som. probably refer to these terms also.

From this last example it seems that Easter was the later of the two terms. Lady Day seems to have been an alternative date for this term; in Cogdean hundred *pro x et vii hidis et dimidia reddiderunt homines Rogerii de Bello Monte c et v solidos post festum sancte Marie.*

The collectors themselves were sometimes responsible for irregularities, either by collecting geld in one hundred which should have been paid in another, or, as in Gillingham hundred, failing to render money which they had received: *quia iiii congregatores huius pecunie non reddiderunt denarios quos receperunt dederunt vadimonium in misericordia ad reddendos denarios et ad emendandum forisfacturam.* In Uggescombe hundred the collectors had received 24*s.* *quos recipere non deberent,*[11] and moreover *iii solidi et vi denarii inventi sunt indicis eorum super numerum.* This same phrase occurs in the account of *Glochresdone* hundred, where the four collectors had received 12*s.* for land in another hundred, and in addition *indicis eorum inventi sunt vi solidi super numerum hidarum.* This may simply mean that the collectors had received money when they ought not to have done, for example from exempt land, but the references to the number of hides suggest that the body which checked the collectors' returns had a record of the geldable capacity of each hundred, perhaps derived from the accounts of an earlier levy of geld. Such a record might explain the not infrequent disparity between the number of hides said to be in a hundred and the details of the account. If the totals given in the geld rolls were derived from an earlier collection of geld they might have ceased to be accurate.

The accounts of both Gillingham and *Glochresdone* hundreds refer to four collectors, and four collectors are mentioned in the account of the Wiltshire hundred of Chippenham.[12] In Wiltshire they are sometimes called *congregatores*, as in Dorset, and sometimes *collectores.* In Somerset and Devon they are called *fegadri* and in Devon they seem to have been entitled to 1 geld-free hide, or to the geld from 1 hide. They seem also to have been called *hundremanni* in some Devon hundreds. In one of the hundreds of Cornwall there is a reference to 4 hides which never paid geld *secundum testimonium hundremannorum* and it is possible that these were the Cornish geld collectors. Individual collectors are mentioned twice, Celwi in Wiltshire and Ansger in Somerset.[13] The Somerset rolls mention a higher body to which the collectors were responsible, presumably the same body as that which checked the accounts of the hundreds of Uggescombe and *Glochresdone.* In Bedminster hundred (Som.) the *fegadri* had received the geld on ½ hide which they had not paid in and for this *vadiaverunt foris ante baronum regis.*[14] Both the Somerset and the Devon rolls mention the transportation of the geld to Winchester. In Somerset *illi qui portaverunt has* [*libras*] *Wintoniam* received 40*s.* These Somerset *portatores geldi* had received 1*s.* 3*d.* which the king did not have and *non potuerunt compotum reddere. Hos vadiaverunt sese reddituros legatis regis.*[15] In Devon William Hostius and Ralph de Pomario *debebant geldum portare ad thesaurum regis Wintonie.*[16] The Dorset rolls give the total amount of money collected but do not mention the transportation to Winchester. The three Wiltshire rolls show that two groups of persons, one headed by a certain Walter and one by Bishop William, supervised the collection of arrears, but some money was still outstanding.[17]

It is still a matter of controversy whether the Geld Rolls date from 1084 or 1086, but the view of most scholars is that they belong to 1084. In that year, according to the Anglo-Saxon Chronicle, a heavy geld of 6*s.* on the hide was levied and the Geld Rolls

[11] This seems to have been the geld on 4 hides belonging to Abbotsbury Abbey, which should have paid geld in Whitchurch and Redhone hundreds.

[12] *V.C.H. Wilts.* ii. 170.

[13] Ibid.

[14] *Dom. Bk.* (Rec. Com.), iv. 69 (f. 76b).

[15] Ibid. 489 (ff. 526b, 527).

[16] Ibid. 65 (f. 71).

[17] *V.C.H. Wilts.* ii. 171–2.

are the record of a tax assessed at that amount. It has been maintained, on the other hand, that the Geld Rolls are contemporary with Domesday and are based upon information collected by the Domesday commissioners,[18] but the arguments advanced in support of this conclusion do not seem strong enough to outweigh those for the traditional date.[19] Among the latter the silence of the Anglo-Saxon Chronicle, which makes no reference to the taking of a geld in 1086, is an important element.

One argument for 1086 as the date of the Geld Rolls is based on the supposition that three land-holders, Manasses the cook, Serle of Burcy, and Odin the chamberlain, died during the Domesday inquest and are referred to as already dead in parts of the Geld Rolls.[20] It is clear, however, that the compilers of the Geld Rolls and of Domesday were not consistent in their references to deceased tenants since Wulfweard White, for example, is mentioned in the Dorset Geld Rolls in terms which imply that he was dead while a passage in the Somerset Geld Rolls could be taken to mean that he was alive and was interpreted in that sense by Round.[21] As Ellis noted, the survey of Buckinghamshire treats Queen Maud as alive in 1086 while elsewhere in Domesday she is referred to as dead.[22] Similarly it might be inferred from Domesday that Earl Godwin, Earl Leofric, and Earl Aelfgar were all living in 1066.

The fact that the Dorset Geld Rolls indicate that Peter, Bishop of Chester, had died before the time of their compilation has also been cited as evidence that the Geld Rolls belong to 1086,[23] but the traditional date, 1085, for Peter's death, which is given by Stubbs, does not seem to be based on any contemporary source.[24] The compiler of the Burton annals gives the date of Peter's death as 1086, and he is followed by Thomas of Chesterfield (d. 1451).[25] This date conflicts with the accepted date for the election of Peter's successor, Robert de Limesey, who was chosen at the Christmas court in 1085[26] and consecrated a little later, probably early in 1086.[27] Wharton, Chesterfield's editor, accordingly corrected the date for Peter's death to 1085, which may be the source from which Stubbs derived his date. Chesterfield, however, again following the Burton annals, also dates the consecration of Robert de Limesey 1088 instead of 1086. He is thus two years out in his reckoning, and this mistake suggests that his date for Peter's death should also be corrected, to 1084, which is perfectly compatible with the traditional date for the Geld Rolls.

In Dorset, as in Wiltshire, the sizes of the baronial demesnes as given in the Geld Rolls and as given in Domesday sometimes coincide, but just as frequently differ. Out of 95 cases where direct comparison is possible, there are 51 instances where the demesnes do not agree. Sometimes the disparity is small, but sometimes serious. It has been argued that the differences between the demesnes of the Geld Rolls and those of Domesday are too great to be accounted for by a lapse of two years, but are 'precisely what we should expect to find when the records of a traditional tax, collected for twenty years, without the special procedure of inquisition, by local collectors, using rule-of-thumb methods, are set against the figures disclosed by the stringent and searching Domesday Survey'.[28] This is a matter of opinion, and neither view is capable of proof or disproof, but the fact that it is sometimes impossible to reconcile the information

[18] V. H. Galbraith, 'The Date of the Geld Rolls in Exon. Domesday', *E.H.R.* lxv; cf. Galbraith, *Making of Dom. Bk.* 87–101.

[19] *V.C.H. Wilts.* ii. 174.

[20] J. F. A. Mason, 'The Date of the Geld Rolls', *E.H.R.* lxix. 283–9.

[21] *V.C.H. Som.* i. 400.

[22] H. Ellis, *Domesday Tables*, i. 6; *Dom. Bk.* (Rec. Com.), i, f. 152b; cf. *V.C.H. Bucks.* i. 273.

[23] *E.H.R.* lxv. 7; cf. Galbraith, *Making of Dom. Bk.* 223.

[24] W. Stubbs, *Registrum Sacrum Anglicanum*, 38.

[25] *Ann. Mon.* (Rolls Ser.), i. 185; *Anglia Sacra*, ed. H. Wharton (1691), 433.

[26] Florence of Worcester, *Chron.* (Eng. Hist. Soc.), ii. 18.

[27] J. Earle and C. Plummer, *Two of the Saxon Chrons. Parallel*, i. 290; ii. 316.

[28] Galbraith, *Making of Dom. Bk.* 100–1.

given by the Geld Rolls with that given by Domesday makes it difficult to accept the contention that both are based on the same enquiry. The view has recently been advanced that the discrepancies between the demesnes of the Geld Rolls and those of Domesday arise because each document deals with a different kind of demesne, the latter with the manorial demesne or home farm (which could easily be changed from time to time by the addition or subtraction of land held by *villani* or by grants to tenants), and the former with fiscal demesne, the amount of the manor exempt for taxation purposes, which was 'fixed, traditional and very difficult to alter'.[29] This view also is hypothetical, having no evidence to support it, and does not explain why Domesday, which is careful to record all that pertains to geld, should count only the fluctuating manorial demesne and not the fixed fiscal demesne.

In some cases it is possible to put forward a reason for the difference in the size of the demesne. In *Canendone* hundred the abbey of Horton had 4 hides in demesne. Horton Abbey had only one manor in Dorset, Horton itself (no. 117), but according to Domesday there were only 2 hides in demesne. Domesday also records that the two best hides were held by the king in his forest of Wimborne. If this was also the case at the time of the Geld Rolls, there is no reason why they should not say so, since they record a similar afforestation in Wiltshire.[30] It seems at least possible that between 1084 and 1086 the king took 2 hides of the demesne at Horton into the forest of Wimborne. In Badbury hundred Schelin held 1 hide and 3 virgates in demesne and $\frac{2}{3}$ hide from which *nunquam habuit rex geldum*. The manor concerned must be Witchampton (nos. 20 and xxvi), which, according to Exon. Domesday, was held by Schelin of Queen Maud. There was $\frac{2}{3}$ hide which *nunquam reddebat gildum*, but both the Exchequer text and Exon. Domesday give the demesne as 2 hides and $1\frac{2}{3}$ virgate, not 1 hide and 3 virgates. In fact the $\frac{2}{3}$ hide which never paid geld had been added to the demesne. The case of Schelin has been used as evidence that the Geld Rolls and Exon. Domesday are based on the same materials but if this is so it is odd that they should give different amounts of demesne for the same manor. Further, there is no need to assume, as Eyton did, that Schelin's tenure of this manor and Edmondsham (nos. 18 and xxiv), which he also held of the queen, had ceased before the time of the Domesday survey, or that he necessarily held of her in fee. He may have held of her at farm, in which case the Exchequer text might omit his tenure just as it omitted other men who held land at farm. Schelin in the Geld Rolls accounted for the geld on these two manors just as Fulcred accounted for the geld of Fleet in Uggescombe hundred. In Badbury hundred also the king had $\frac{1}{2}$ hide in demesne. His manor must have been Wimborne Minster (nos. 21 and xxvii), assessed at $\frac{1}{2}$ hide, but the Exchequer text and Exon. Domesday give the demesne as 1 virgate, adding that, although the $\frac{1}{2}$ hide never belonged to the night's farm at Wimborne, it never paid geld. Here land regarded as demesne in the Geld Rolls is entered as an exemption in the Domesday records. In *Aileveswode* hundred Count Eustace is credited with 1 hide and $\frac{1}{3}$ virgate in demesne. This is the hidage of Swanage (nos. 515 and xxxviii), which was held by the Countess of Boulogne. According to Exon. Domesday she had no demesne in the manor and *rex Willelmus nunquam habuit geldum de hac mansione*. It seems as if in this instance the Geld Rolls recorded as exempt demesne land which should in fact have paid geld, and that the Domesday commissioners discovered and recorded the fact.

The Domesday survey appears to have uncovered certain other facts not known to the geld collectors. In Beaminster hundred William Malbank held of Earl Hugh a virgate from which *nunquam habuit rex geldum*. This land was at Catsley (no. 229)

[29] R. Welldon Finn, 'The Geld Abstracts in the Liber Exoniensis', *Bull. John Rylands Libr.* xlv. 370–89.

[30] *V.C.H. Wilts.* ii. 208 (Downton hundred).

where there was a virgate *de qua celatum est geldum T.R.W.* In Bere hundred Walter Tonitruus held ½ hide of the wife of Hugh fitz Grip from which *nunquam habuit rex geldum*. This was at Turners Puddle (nos. 391 and cxxiv) where, according to Exon. Domesday, there was *dimidia hida et quattuor agri et i ortus que nunquam gildavit sed celatum est*. It has been argued that these two instances show the dependence of the Geld Rolls on evidence uncovered by the Domesday inquest, since it would be illogical to describe as 'concealed' in 1086 land which had been known in 1084. But it seems more accurate to say that Domesday revealed here not the land but its liability to pay geld, of which the geld collectors were ignorant since they recorded it as exempt. There is also an exemption or default (the language is unclear) recorded in the Exchequer text but not in the Geld Rolls. At Warmwell (no. 226), which William held of Earl Hugh, there was a virgate *que nunquam gildavit*. Warmwell lay in *Celberge* hundred, but the virgate is not mentioned in the hundred account.

Some of the discrepancies between the Geld Rolls and the Domesday texts could be more easily explained if the Geld Rolls were assigned to 1084. In Knowlton hundred the mother of William of Eu is credited with 7½ hides in demesne, which was the demesne of Crichel (no. 266), held in 1086 by William himself. It would be natural to assume that in the interval between 1084 and 1086 William's mother had died and her land had passed to her son. In *Glochresdone* hundred Roger Arundel had 4 hides and a virgate in demesne. Two of his manors, Powerstock and Wraxall, can be assigned to this hundred, but in neither did he have any exempt demesne in 1086, since both were subinfeudated. William 'the Goat' (*capru*), who may have been one of the tenants, is mentioned in the geld account. It is possible that one or both of the manors was or were held by Roger in demesne in 1084 and subinfeudated between 1084 and 1086. In Badbury hundred Picot held of the Count of Mortain ⅓ hide which never paid geld. This can be identified as 1⅓ virgate at Witchampton (no. 188) on which geld had never been paid (*de qua nunquam dedit geldum*), but in 1086 Witchampton was held not by Picot but by Hubert. It seems possible that the land was taken from Picot and given to Hubert between 1084 and 1086. Several mesne tenants recorded as holding land in the Geld Rolls do not appear in the Domesday texts. In *Langeberge* hundred William Caisnell held 3½ hides of the wife of Hugh fitz Grip, but no man of that name is recorded among her tenants in 1086. Walchelin is twice recorded as a tenant of the Count of Mortain, but did not hold of him in 1086. In Winfrith hundred Robert had ½ hide of the count which never paid geld. Several manors were held of the count by persons named Robert in 1086, but none can be assigned to this hundred and none had such an exemption. In Whitchurch hundred Bollo the priest had ½ hide of Cerne Abbey, but he is not recorded as a tenant of that abbey in the Domesday texts.

Other contradictions between the Geld Rolls and the Domesday texts suggest that they drew upon different sources of information. According to the geld account of Buckland hundred Robert de Oilly did not pay geld on 2½ virgates which he took from a thegn *et posuit intra firmam regis in Melecoma*. The Exchequer text states that there were 3½ virgates in Buckland hundred attached to Bingham's Melcombe (no. 30) but according to this account they were held by three thegns T.R.E. and Countess Goda, who held the manor T.R.E., had been responsible for attaching them to Melcombe. In Badbury hundred the king had no geld from 8 hides and 3½ virgates *de terra geldanti* which had belonged to Aubrey. This land must be part of the manor of Gussage St. Michael in Dorset, which Aubrey de Couci once held and which was in the king's hand in 1086, but in Domesday it is entered not in Dorset but in Wiltshire. In Gillingham hundred there were 2½ virgates of exempt demesne belonging to Fulcred, which also appear in the Wiltshire section of Domesday. In Sherborne hundred the king had no geld from a hide and a virgate which Ansger the cook held *de dono regis*. No land answering this description is recorded in the Dorset Domesday in 1086, but Ansger the cook held 1 hide and 1 virgate in Somerset, attached to the royal manor of Martock. It is not uncommon to find persons mentioned in the Geld Rolls who do not appear in Domesday. In Hasilor hundred Robert fitz Ralph had 2 hides of exempt demesne. He is presumably to be identified with Robert fitz Ralph who held 1 hide, 2½ virgates, at Grafton (Wilts.) in 1086.[31] but he does not appear in the Dorset Domesday. In Whitchurch hundred Ulf held 1 hide and 1 virgate of William 'the Goat'. William does not appear as a tenant-in-chief in Dorset in 1086, although in *Glochresdone* hundred he is named as a tenant of Roger Arundel. He had extensive estates in Somerset, where Ulf was his Saxon predecessor on two small manors, but this holding of a hide and a virgate cannot be traced. In Cullifordtree hundred a priest held 1 hide of Bishop Peter's land, which cannot be traced in the Exchequer text, and there is ½ hide of thegnland in the king's farm in Bere hundred which cannot be identified in Domesday.

Like Exon. Domesday, the Geld Rolls supply a considerable amount of information not recorded in the Exchequer text. In Gillingham hundred the Abbess of Préaux had 3½ hides in demesne. She is not mentioned in the Domesday texts, but it seems that Roger de Beaumont gave his manor of Stour Provost (no. 231) to the abbey of St. Leger, Préaux.[32] In Puddletown hundred the abbey of Marmoutier had in demesne 5 hides and 3 virgates *de terra comitisse de Moritonio*. This land was at Piddlehinton (no. 168) which, according to the Exchequer text, the abbey held of the Count of Mortain. But the charter by which the count gave this land to the abbey shows that the land had belonged to the countess and was given to the abbey on her death.[33] In Pimperne hundred Humphrey the chamberlain had 5 hides in demesne, of which he had given ½ hide to the church. His manor must be Stourpaine (no. 356), but the Exchequer text does not record any gift to the church. In Pimperne hundred, also, the Abbess of Shaftesbury is said to have 1 hide and ½ virgate of land. The Exchequer text does not mention this land, but the 12th-century survey of the estates of Shaftesbury Abbey shows that 1 hide of the manor of Tarrant Hinton (no. 132) lay in Pimperne hundred.[34] In *Aileveswode* hundred the abbey of St. Stephen, Caen, had 1 hide which paid geld in another hundred. The Exchequer text does not record any land in Purbeck belonging to this abbey, but the confirmation charter of Henry I includes Purbeck as a member of the abbey's manors of Frampton and Bincombe.[35] Several persons holding land at farm are mentioned in the Geld Rolls but do not appear in the Domesday text. It is noticeable that Exon. Domesday on three occasions records people holding land at farm who are not mentioned in the Exchequer text and it seems almost as if the Exchequer scribe omitted such information as a matter of course, although he included the six men holding Ringstead (no. 463) at farm of Brictuin. All but one of the manors of Humphrey the chamberlain were at farm in the Geld Rolls. The widow holding 1 hide at farm of Humphrey in *Albretesberge* hundred is presumably Eddeva, who held Edmondsham (no. 354) of him in 1086, although the Exchequer text does not say she held at farm. In the same hundred an Englishman held 1 hide at farm of Humphrey, and in Badbury hundred another Englishman held 3 virgates at farm of him. The manors concerned must be Edmondsham (no. 353) and Hemsworth (no. 355) but no tenants are recorded in Domesday. In Combsditch hundred an Englishman held 1½ hide at farm of Aiulf the chamberlain. This was the hidage of his manor of Blandford

[31] *V.C.H. Wilts.* 166.

[32] See p. 141n.

[33] *Cal. Doc. France*, ed. Round, 435 (dated 1082–4); *Regesta Regum Anglo-Normannorum*, ed. C. Johnson and H. A. Cronne, i, no. 204.

[34] B.M. Harl. MS. 61, f. 58.

[35] Dugdale, *Mon.* vi (2), 1071.

St. Mary (no. 336), but no tenant is recorded in Domesday. In Uggescombe hundred a thegn held 2½ hides of Aiulf, probably at Tatton (no. 345). In Godderthorn hundred Berenger Giffard had 1½ hide and ⅓ virgate which his predecessor held of him at farm. Berenger's only Dorset manor was Bredy (Farm) (no. 317), held T.R.E. by Harding, but he is not recorded as a tenant in 1086. In Cullifordtree hundred William Belet had 1 hide in demesne and a thegn *cuius ipsa terra fuerat* held 5 virgates of him at farm. The manor in question must be Winterborne Belet (no. 493) which belonged to the hundred at a later date and which was held by two thegns T.R.E., but Domesday does not mention the tenure of this thegn in 1086. In *Canendone* hundred a thegn held 2 hides and 1 virgate at farm of the king. This is the hidage of Hampreston (nos. 19 and xxv) which William Belet held of the queen according to Exon. Domesday and which Saul held T.R.E. Neither Exon. Domesday nor the Exchequer text mentions the thegn. The Geld Rolls also reveal that Robert de Oilly held at farm the manors of Countess Goda which the king held in 1086.

The Geld Rolls also supply surnames for some of the persons mentioned only by their Christian names in the Exchequer text. In Whitchurch hundred William *de estra* is named as a tenant of the Count of Mortain, with 1 hide of land, half of which was in the king's farm. His manor can be identified as *Cerneli* (no. 212), where, according to the Exchequer text, ½ hide *fuit de dominica firma Cerne T.R.E.* In *Celeberge* hundred Robert fitz Ivo held 1 virgate which never paid geld, probably Morden (no. 172), and in Cullifordtree hundred the same Robert held ½ hide of the count, probably part of Stafford (no. 155). In Dorchester hundred Ralph the clerk held 2 hides, 1 virgate, which must be *Cerne* (no. 157), the only manor held of the count by a man called Ralph. In Beaminster hundred William Malbank had 1 virgate of Earl Hugh, which must be at Catsley (no. 229). In Dorchester hundred William Belet had 1 hide of William of Eu, probably part of Bradford Peverell (no. 257). In Combsditch hundred William *de monasterio* had 3 virgates of William de Aldrie which never paid geld. William de Aldrie does not appear as a tenant-in-chief in Dorset, but he was the steward of William of Eu and appears as his tenant in Wiltshire. In the Dorset Domesday William of Eu held Blandford St. Mary (no. 261), where there was ½ hide which never paid geld. Despite the difference in hidage this is likely to have been the piece of land mentioned in the Geld Rolls, since it was held of William of Eu by another William, probably either William de Aldrie or William *de monasterio*. In *Glochresdone* hundred William 'the Goat' had 3½ hides of Roger Arundel. The only land held of Roger by a man called William was three hides at Wraxall (nos. 328 and c) and this William can presumably be identified as William 'the Goat'. In *Hunesberge* hundred Alvred of Epaignes had 2½ hides of the abbey of Glastonbury, which must be the land held by Alvred at Okeford Fitzpaine (no. 64), although he is said in the Exchequer text to hold 2 not 2½ hides. This, however, is the only land of the abbey held by a man of this name. In Badbury hundred Hugh Maminot held 4 hides and 1 virgate of the Bishop of Lisieux (Gilbert Maminot). He is not recorded as the bishop's tenant in the Exchequer text, but it is not unlikely that he did hold of him since several of the bishop's manors went to endow Maminot's daughter.

The Geld Rolls are particularly helpful in the identification of the king's thegns since they supply distinguishing names such as 'the huntsman' or 'the reeve'. Edwin the huntsman (*venator*) had 2 hides and ½ virgate in demesne in Uggescombe hundred, 3 hides and ½ virgate in Combsditch hundred, 2 hides and 3 virgates in *Langeberge* hundred, and 2 hides and one virgate in Pimperne hundred. His manors in these hundreds can be identified as Shilvinghampton (no. 457), the two manors of *Bleneford*(*e*) (nos. 438 and 455), and Lazerton (no. 456) all held by Edwin according to Domesday. Ulviet the huntsman had 1 hide in demesne in *Albretesberge* hundred, which may be Wimborne St. Giles (no. 440), held by Ulviet in 1086. Ulvric the huntsman held 1 virgate in *Canendone* and 1½ hide in *Celeberge* hundred, where Ulveva had 3 virgates. His manor in *Canendone* is probably Thorn Hill (no. 442), and the one in *Celeberge* is probably Morden (no. 437), where his brother's wife, who may be the Ulveva (Wulfgifu) of the Geld Rolls, also held land. The Ulvric who held these two manors can therefore be identified with Ulvric the huntsman who held one hide of the king in an unspecified locality (no. 454). Alvric the huntsman held two hides in Bere hundred, 3 hides and 3 virgates in *Aileveswode* hundred, and 2 virgates in Hasilor hundred. His manors are probably *Wintreburne* (nos. 430 and 484), Coombe (no. 481), and Blackmanston (nos. 476 and 489). Godric the huntsman had 1 virgate in Gillingham hundred which must be the virgate in Gillingham (no. 428) held by Godric in 1086. Godric the priest held 4 hides less 10 acres in Bere hundred, probably the manor of Briantspuddle (no. 472). A man called Godric also held Stourton Caundle (no. 478), but it is not known whether he was Godric the priest or Godric the huntsman. Brictuin the reeve (*prepositus*) had 3 hides in Yetminster hundred, 1 hide, 3½ virgates, in Uggescombe hundred, 2½ hides in *Glochresdone* hundred, 3 hides, 1 virgate, in *Celberge* hundred, and 2 hides, 3½ virgates, in Cullifordtree hundred. These manors can be identified as Melbury Sampford (no. 441), Little Waddon (no. 460), Chilcombe (no. 459), Moreton (no. 461) and Galton (no. 462), and *Waia*, *Wintreburne*, and Lewell (nos. 433–5). If these identifications are correct, then the same Brictuin held all these manors, a fact which is not clear from the Exchequer text. Edric the reeve held 1 hide in demesne in Hasilor hundred, where both Holme (no. 467) and Tyneham (no. 473) seem to lie. Alward the reeve had 1 hide in demesne in Winfrith hundred where a beadle had 1 virgate. Alward's manor seems to be Wool (no. 486), one virgate of which (no. 487) was held by Almar, who may be the beadle of the Geld Rolls. Alward Colin(c) had 1 hide in Combsditch hundred, which was probably part of Thorncombe (no. 439); he had held the manor of Langton Herring (nos. 23 and xxix) T.R.E. In *Glochresdone* hundred two king's almsmen (*elemosinarii regis*) had ½ hide in demesne. It seems likely that the manor of Uploders (no. 475), assessed at ½ hide and held by Alvric and Brictric, may have lain in this hundred. They are classed as thegns in the Exchequer text, not as almsmen, but Dodo, who is also classed as a thegn, held ½ hide (no. 444) in alms of the queen. An unnamed thegn who held ½ virgate in *Glochresdone* hundred may be the same Dodo, who held 1 virgate at Woolcombe (no. 474) in *Glochresdone* hundred. In Combsditch hundred John the usher (*hostiarius*) had 1 hide and 1½ virgate in demesne, which must be at *Wintreburne* (no. 500), held by a man called John as a king's serjeant. Hervey *cubicularius*, who held Wimborne St. Giles (no. 499) in *Albretesberge* hundred, is called Hervey *camerarius* in the Geld Rolls. Similarly Anschitil fitz Ameline, a *francus* who held Tyneham (no. 369) in Hasilor hundred of the queen, is called Anschitil of Carisbrook (de Carisburgo) in the Geld Rolls.

ORDER OF DORSET HUNDREDS

I.	Yetminster	XX.	Handley
II.	Whitchurch	XXI.	Newton
III.	Uggescombe	XXII.	*Langeberge*
IV.	*Glochresdone*	XXIII.	Knowlton
V.	*Albretesberge*	XXIV.	Sixpenny
VI.	Badbury	XXV.	*Hunesberge*
VII.	*Canendone*	XXVI.	Pimperne
VIII.	Puddletown	XXVII.	Gillingham
IX.	*Stane*	XXVIII.	Brownshall
X.	Godderthorn	XXIX.	Hasilor
XI.	*Haltone*	XXX.	Winfrith
XII.	Beaminster	XXXI.	*Celberge*
XIII.	Redhone	XXXII.	Dorchester (St. George)
XIV.	Tollerford	XXXIII.	Modbury
XV.	Bere	XXXIV.	Sherborne
XVI.	Combsditch	XXXV.	*Ferendone*
XVII.	Cogdean	XXXVI.	Buckland
XVIII.	*Celeberge*	XXXVII.	Cullifordtree
XIX.	*Aileveswode*	XXXVIII.	Frampton

XXXIX. Loders

Glochresdone became Eggardon hundred; *Albretesberge*, with parts of *Canendone*, *Langeberge*, and *Hunesberge*, went to form the hundred of Cranborne; *Canendone* was amalgamated with Badbury hundred; *Stane* was amalgamated with Modbury to form Cerne, Totcombe, and Modbury hundred; *Haltone* was later called Whiteway hundred; *Celeberge* (Charborough) was later called Loosebarrow hundred; *Aileveswode* (Ailwood) was later called Rowbarrow hundred; Handley and Sixpenny were later amalgamated to form Sixpenny Handley hundred; *Hunesberge* and part of *Langeberge* were amalgamated with Pimperne hundred; *Celberge* was amalgamated with Winfrith hundred; *Ferendone*, with part of Gillingham, became the hundred of Redlane. The hundreds of Buckland and Newton were sometimes treated as one.[1]

I. YETMINSTER HUNDRED

[f. 17]

In hundreto Etheministre sunt xl et vii hide et tantum terre habet ibi Saresberiensis episcopus quantum (possunt)[2] arare vi carruce. Inde habent barones in dominio vi hidas et i virgam et vi carrucatas. Inde habet episcopus vi carrucatas et Rogerus Arondellus iii hidas et i virgatam et Bristuinus prepositus iii hidas et de xl hidis i virga minus habet rex xii libras decem et octo denarios et i obolum minus. Et de dimidia hida quam tenet Urso de Arnulfo de Hesdinc nunquam habuit rex Willelmus gildum et de dimidia hida quam tenet Dodemanus de comite de Moretonio non habuit rex gildum hoc anno. Sed xii solidi prescriptorum denariorum qui deberent esse redditi ad primum terminum non sunt redditi usque ad extremum.

In Yetminster hundred there are 47 hides and the Bishop of Salisbury has there as much land as 6 ploughs can plough. Of this the barons have in demesne 6 hides and 1 virgate and 6 carucates. Of this the bishop has 6 carucates, and Roger Arundel 3 hides and 1 virgate, and Brictuin the reeve 3 hides. And from 40 hides less 1 virgate the king has £11 18*s*. 5½*d*.[3] And from ½ hide which Urse holds of Ernulf of Hesdin King William never had geld and from ½ hide which Dodeman holds of the Count of Mortain the king did not have geld this year. But 12*s*. of the aforesaid pence which should have been rendered at the first term were not rendered until the last (term).

The Bishop of Salisbury's demesne in this hundred can be identified as the *terra vi carucarum que nunquam geldavit T.R.E.* at Yetminster (no. 35), which must have been the head of this hundred. It was assessed at 15 hides. Roger Arundel had 3 hides and 1 virgate in demesne at Melbury Bubb (nos. 323 and xcv), assessed at 6 hides. Brictuin had a manor called *Meleberie* (no. 441), assessed at 5 hides, but the extent of

[1] See O. S. Anderson (afterwards Arngart), *Eng. Hundred-Names: the South-Western Counties*, 104–41.

[2] In this section interlineations and marginal additions in the Latin text and interpolations in the English translation have been placed in round brackets.

[3] At 6*s*. on the hide, the geld on 39 hides and 3 virgates is £11 18*s*. 6*d*.

his demesne there is not known. Urse held 2 manors of Ernulf of Hesdin, 1 of which was called *Melesberie* (no. 246), and 1 of the manors held by Dodeman of the Count of Mortain was called *Melesberie* (no. 183). The manor of Urse was assessed at 4½ hides and the manor of Dodeman at 2½ hides. Eyton identified Brictuin's manor as Melbury Sampford and the manors of Dodeman and Urse as Melbury Osmond. In 1316 Woolcombe, held by John Mautravers, and Ryme, with Clifton and Trill, held by Humphrey de Bello Campo and Philip Maubank, lay in the hundred of Yetminster.[4] In 1086 Woolcombe (no. 262) was held by Hugh of William of Eu and Clifton Maybank, with 3 hides in Trill, was held by William (Malbank) of Hugh, Earl of Chester. Woolcombe was assessed at 5 hides, and Clifton Maybank (no. 225) at 6 hides. This gives a total of 47 hides, 6 carucates, the figure given in the Geld Roll.

II. WHITCHURCH HUNDRED

In hundreto Witchirce sunt lxxxiiii hide et dimidia (et i virgata) preter firmam regis. Inde habent barones regis in dominio xxi hidas et (dimidiam) virgam—[*blank*]. Abbas Cerneliensis habet inde v hidas. Hungerus filius Audoeni viii hidas et Edricius iii hidas et dimidiam et dimidiam virgam et Willelmus Belet iii virgas in dominio. (Abbas Abodesberiensis i hidam habet in dominio et Fulcredus vii virgas in dominio). Et de xl et viiii hidis (i virga et tercia parte alterius virge minus) habet rex xiiii libras et xvii solidos (et x denarios et i obolum) et de v hidis et dimidia quas habet Hungerus filius Audoeni de terra geldanti (has tenent villani) non habuit rex geldum et de iii hidis quas tenet abbas Cerneliensis (has tenent villani) non habuit rex geldum et de dimidia hida quam tenet Bollo presbiter de abbate Cerneliensi non habuit rex gildum. De i hida quam tenet Willelmus de Estra de comite de Moritonio (medietas huius hide est de firma regis) nunquam habuit rex geldum. De dimidia hida quam tenet Britellus de comite Moritonii

[f. 17b]

nunquam habuit rex geldum et de i hida et i virga quam tenet Ulfus de Willelmo Capru nunquam habuit rex gildum et de i hida et dimidia quam tenet Hugo de Aiulfo non habuit rex gildum hoc anno et abbas Abodesberie adquietavit in alio hundreto iii hidas terre et dimidiam quas ipse habet in hoc hundreto. Similiter fecit Turstinus filius Rolfi de vii virgis quas ipse habet in hoc hundreto. Et de denariis qui redditi sunt in hoc hundreto non sunt redditi xii solidi usque ad extremum terminum qui deberent esse redditi ad primum.

In Whitchurch hundred there are 84½ hides and 1 virgate besides the king's farm. Of this the king's barons have in demesne 21 hides and ½ virgate. The Abbot of Cerne has of this 5 hides, Hunger fitz Odin 8 hides, and Edric 3½ hides and ½ virgate, and William Belet 3 virgates in demesne. The Abbot of Abbotsbury has 1 hide in demesne, and Fulcred 7 virgates in demesne. And from 49 hides less 1⅓ virgate the king has £14 17*s.* 10½*d.*[5] And from 5½ hides of geldable land which Hunger fitz Odin has (the villeins hold these) the king did not have geld and from 3 hides which the Abbot of Cerne holds (the villeins hold these) the king did not have geld and from ½ hide which Bollo the priest holds of the Abbot of Cerne the king did not have geld. From 1 hide which William *de estra* holds of the Count of Mortain (half this hide belongs to the king's farm) the king never had geld. From ½ hide which Bretel holds of the Count of Mortain the king never had geld and from 1 hide and 1 virgate which Ulf holds of William 'the Goat' the king never had geld and from 1½ hide which Hugh holds of Aiulf the king did not have geld this year. And the Abbot of Abbotsbury was quit in another hundred for 3½ hides of land which he himself has in this hundred. Turstin fitz Rolf did likewise for 7 virgates which he himself has in this hundred. And of the pence which were rendered in this hundred 12*s.* were not rendered until the last term which should have been rendered at the first (term).

The Abbot of Cerne had 5 hides in demesne at Symondsbury (nos. 92 and lv), assessed at 19 hides. Hunger fitz Odin had only 1 manor, Broadwindsor (no. 505), assessed at 20 hides. Edric held several small manors as a *tainus*, and one of them, Pilsdon (no. 470), lay in Whitchurch hundred in 1303.[6] It was assessed at 3 hides, and even if he held it all in demesne it is not large enough to account for all his exempt demesne in this hundred. Another of his manors, *Stodlege* (no. 471), assessed at 1 virgate, was identified by Fägersten as Studley, in Whitchurch Canonicorum, the site of which is now lost. Fägersten also suggested that *Slitlege* (no. 469), assessed at 2 hides and also held by Edric, was a corrupt form referring to the same place.[7] The manor of William Belet is probably Lyme Regis (no. 504), which lay in Whitchurch hundred in 1212.[8] Lyme Regis was a divided vill, the other portions being held by Ulviet of Glastonbury Abbey (no. 68), and by the Bishop of Salisbury (no. 36). William Belet's portion was assessed at 1 hide, Ulviet's portion at 3 hides,[9] and the Bishop of Salisbury's portion was not assessed in hides and had never paid geld. The Abbot of Abbotsbury had 1 hide in demesne at Abbott's Wootton (nos. 114 and lxi). It was assessed at 2½ hides. His manor of Atrim (nos. 116 and lxiii), assessed at 2 hides, was held of the abbey by Bollo the priest and a widow, and it was probably this manor, with the geldable portion of Abbott's Wootton, which paid geld in another hundred. The account of Uggescombe hundred shows that it was there that these 3½ hides had paid geld. The land of Turstin fitz Rolf paid geld in Godderthorn hundred and consisted of his 2 manors of Stoke Wallis (no. 254) and Thurstanshay (no. 255), assessed at 1 hide and 3 virgates, the figure

[4] *Feud. Aids*, ii. 41.

[5] At 6*s.* on the hide, the geld from 47 hides and 2⅔ virgates is £14 6*s.*, not £14 17*s.* 10½*d.*

[6] *Feud. Aids*, ii. 38.

[7] A. Fägersten, *The Place-Names of Dorset*, 298.

[8] *Bk. of Fees*, 94.

[9] Later evidence shows Ulviet's manor to be Colway in Lyme Regis: see p. 56.

given in the Geld Roll. Fulcred held only 2 manors, *Waia* (no. 364), which probably belongs to Cullifordtree hundred, and Moorbath (no. 365), assessed at 2 hides, which is presumably in Whitchurch hundred. Bollo the priest is not recorded in the Domesday survey as a tenant of the Abbot of Cerne in Dorset. It is possible that he held part of Symondsbury. Hugh is not recorded as a tenant of Aiulf, but Aiulf's manor in this hundred is likely to have been Wootton Fitzpaine (no. 347),[10] assessed at 12 hides, with 4 carucates in demesne. Bretel held 2 manors in Wootton Fitzpaine of the Count of Mortain (nos. 211, 217), assessed at 2 hides and $\frac{1}{2}$ hide respectively. William, who is probably identical with William *de estra*, held *Cerneli* (no. 212), identified by Eyton as Catherston Leweston, where there was $\frac{1}{2}$ hide *que fuit de dominica firma CERNE T.R.E.* The king had no land at Cerne in 1086, but there seems to be no other manor of the Count of Mortain where there was $\frac{1}{2}$ hide *de firma regis*. The manor was assessed at $3\frac{1}{2}$ hides. William 'the Goat' is not recorded as a tenant-in-chief in Dorset in 1086, although he appears elsewhere in the Geld Rolls as a tenant of Roger Arundel. According to Exon. Domesday *Alseministre*, in Devon, was held of William 'the Goat' by Ulf; the Exchequer text gives the man's name as Eddulf, and the manor was assessed at 1 virgate.[11] This piece of land can scarcely be identical with the $1\frac{1}{4}$ hide mentioned in the Geld Roll for Whitchurch, and the matter must remain unsolved.

This hundred cannot be properly reconstructed. The manors enumerated above as likely to belong here amount to $74\frac{1}{2}$ hides. Later evidence suggests that some other manors lay in Whitchurch hundred at this date. In 1212 the hundred included Charmouth[12] which in 1086 was held by Robert of the Count of Mortain (no. 215) and was assessed at 3 hides. In 1316 Stockland, belonging to Milton Abbey, *Brigstoke*, and Stanton belonged to the hundred.[13] In 1086 Hervey fitz Ansger held Stockland (Devon) (nos. 106 and lxxx) of the abbey and it was assessed at 10 hides. *Brigstoke* is probably Burstock (no. 230) which William (Malbank) held of Earl Hugh in 1086, when it was assessed at 3 hides. *Stantone* (no. 210)[14] was held in 1086 by Alvred *pincerna* of the Count of Mortain. It was assessed at $\frac{1}{2}$ hide with land for 6 ploughs. This brings the hidage of the hundred up to 91 hides, instead of 84 hides, 3 virgates.

III. UGGESCOMBE HUNDRED

In Oglescumbe hundret sunt c hide et iiii. De his habent barones regis in dominio xl hidas et (ii partes i virge). De isto dominicatu habet abbas Abodesberie xiii hidas et abbas Cerneliensis iiii hidas et Hugo de Nemore Herberti v hidas et abbatissa de Monasterio Villari habet v hidas et dimidiam et Bristuinus prepositus i hidam et iii virgas et dimidiam et uxor Hugonis ii hidas et i virgam et ii partes unius virge et rex i hidam et dimidiam de terra regine Mathildis et Edwinus venator ii hidas et dimidiam virgam et comes de Moritonio v virgas et rex iii hidas—[*blank*] de terra Heroldi et Bollo presbiter dimidiam hidam de qua vadiavit regem adguarant. Et de lx et iiii hidis habet rex x et ix libras et vii solidos et vi denarios S (*sic*). Abbas Abodesberiensis adquietavit in hoc hundreto iiii hidas terre que sunt in alio hundreto. Et de ii hidis et dimidia quas habet i tagnus de Aiulfo non habet rex geldum et de hida et dimidia (de terra Heroldi) dedit Fulcredus geldum in alio hundreto et quia congregatores huius pecunie receperunt xxiiii solidos denariorum quos recipere non deberent et quia iii solidi et vi denarii inventi sunt indicis eorum super numerum dederunt vadimonium in misericordia regis.

In Uggescombe hundred there are 104 hides. Of these the king's barons have in demesne 40 hides and $\frac{2}{3}$ virgate. Of this demesne the Abbot of Abbotsbury has 13 hides, and the Abbot of Cerne 4 hides, and Hugh de Boscherbert 5 hides, and the Abbess of Montevilliers has $5\frac{1}{2}$ hides, and Brictuin the reeve 1 hide and $3\frac{1}{2}$ virgates, and the wife of Hugh 2 hides and $1\frac{2}{3}$ virgate, and the king $1\frac{1}{2}$ hide of Queen Maud's land, and Edwin the huntsman 2 hides and $\frac{1}{2}$ virgate, and the Count of Mortain 5 virgates, and the king 3 hides of Harold's land, and Bollo the priest $\frac{1}{2}$ hide on which he gave pledge to the king for warranty. And from 64 hides the king has £19 7*s*. 6*d*.[15] The Abbot of Abbotsbury was quit in this hundred for 4 hides of land which are in another hundred. And from $2\frac{1}{2}$ hides which 1 thegn has of Aiulf the king does not have geld and from $1\frac{1}{2}$ hide of Harold's land Fulcred paid geld in another hundred. And because the collectors of this money received 24*s*. of the pence which they ought not to have received, and because 3*s*. 6*d*. was found in their list above the number (of hides), they gave pledges, being in the king's mercy.

The Abbot of Abbotsbury's 13 hides in this hundred must be the combined demesnes of Abbotsbury (nos. 109 and lviii) and Portesham (nos. 112 and lix), assessed at 22 hides and 13 hides respectively. The manor of Cerne Abbey in this hundred is probably Littlebredy (nos. 85 and xlviii), which lay in this hundred in 1285,[16] although Exon. Domesday and the Exchequer text give the demesne as 5 hides, not 4 hides. It was assessed at 11 hides. Hugh de Boscherbert had only 2 manors, and since *Cernel* (no. 360) is too small to account for his exempt demesne the unnamed manor held by 2 brothers T.R.E. (no. 361) must belong here. It was assessed at 10 hides. The Abbess of Montevilliers had only 1 manor, Friar Waddon (no. 143), assessed at 6 hides, which was the gift of Hugh fitz Grip. Brictuin the reeve's manor is probably Little Waddon (no. 460), given him by Hugh fitz Grip in exchange for a manor worth twice as much. Langton Herring (nos. 23 and xxix), belonging to Queen Maud, was assessed at $1\frac{1}{2}$ hide, and probably

[10] R. W. Eyton (*Key to Domesday: Dorset*, 142) identifies this manor as Marshwood, but Fägersten (op. cit. 298) identifies it as Wootton Fitzpaine.

[11] *Dom. Bk.* (Rec. Com.), i, f. 111; iv. 378.

[12] *Bk. of Fees*, 94.

[13] *Feud. Aids*, ii. 45.

[14] The site is marked by St. Gabriel's House in Stanton St. Gabriel.

[15] The geld on 64 hides is £19 4*s*., with in addition the 3*s*. 6*d*. *super numerum*. The 24*s*. which the collectors should not have received represents the geld on the Abbot of Abbotsbury's 4 hides in another hundred.

[16] *Feud. Aids*, ii. 6.

represents her demesne here. Part of Langton Herring (nos. 406 and cxxxix) was held by the wife of Hugh fitz Grip. It was assessed at 1½ hide with 3 virgates in demesne. The rest of her demesne in this hundred probably lay at Tatton (nos. 398 and cxxxi), assessed at 2 hides. The other portion of Tatton was held by Aiulf the chamberlain (no. 345). It was assessed at 3 hides and was held by 1 thegn of Cerne Abbey T.R.E. This thegn may be the one who holds of Aiulf in the Geld Rolls. The manor of Edwin the huntsman is probably Shilvinghampton (no. 457), which lay in this hundred in 1285.[17] It was a divided vill in 1086, the other portions being held by the Count of Mortain (no. 216), which would account for his demesne in this hundred, and by the abbey of Abbotsbury (nos. 113 and lx). Edwin's manor was assessed at 2½ hides, the count's at 1 hide and 1 virgate (the amount of his exempt demesne), and Abbotsbury Abbey's manor, held of the abbey by Bollo the priest, at 1 hide and 1 virgate. Bollo's demesne in this manor is probably the land attached to the church of Fleet which he held (nos. 145b and xix). Fleet itself (nos. 11 and vii), which had belonged to Earl Harold, belonged to this hundred in 1212[18] and probably represents Earl Harold's land in this hundred, although Exon. Domesday and the Exchequer text give the demesne as 3½ not 3 hides. Exon. Domesday shows that Fulcred held the manor of Harold.

This brings the hidage to 82½ hides. In addition Elworth (no. 268) can be added to the hundred. In 1086 it was held by Ansfrid of William of Eu. In 1212 it lay in Uggescombe hundred, and belonged to the honor of Strigoil (later Chepstow).[19] In 1285 Puncknowle, Corton, and Bexington lay in this hundred.[20] In 1086 Puncknowle (nos. 397 and cxxx), assessed at 5 hides, was held by William *de monasterio* of the wife of Hugh fitz Grip. Corton (no. 238) was held by Vitalis of Roger de Courseulles, and Bexington (nos. 326 and xcviii) was held by Roger Arundel, although it is difficult to see why his demesne of 4 hides and ½ virgate was omitted from the Geld Roll. This brings the total hidage of the hundred to 104 hides, the Geld Roll total.

IV. EGGARDON HUNDRED

[f. 18]
In Glochresdone hundreto sunt lx et vi hide et dimidia. De his habent barones in dominio xx hidas et dimidiam et dimidiam virgam. De isto dominicatu habet abbas Cerneliensis xi hidas et Rogerus Arondellus iiii[21] hidas et i virgam (et) Brictuinus prepositus ii hidas et dimidiam et Hugo Gausbertus iii virgas. Comes de Moritonio hidam et dimidiam et ii elemosinarii regis dimidiam hidam et i tagnus dimidiam virgam. Et de iii hidis et dimidia non habuit rex geldum. Has tenet Willelmus Capru de Rogero Arondello. De reliqua terra habet rex totum geldum suum (scilicet xiii libras et x solidos et ix denarios) et quia iiii congregatores huius pecunie receperunt xii solidos pro terra alterius hundreti et quia indicis eorum inventi sunt vi solidi super numerum hidarum dederunt vadimonium in misericordia regis.

In Eggardon hundred there are 66½ hides. Of these the barons have in demesne 20½ hides and ½ virgate. Of this demesne the Abbot of Cerne has 11 hides, and Roger Arundel 4 hides and 1 virgate, and Brictuin the reeve 2½ hides, and Hugh Gosbert 3 virgates. The Count of Mortain 1½ hide, and 2 king's almsmen ½ hide, and 1 thegn ½ virgate. And from 3½ hides the king did not have geld. William 'the Goat' holds these of Roger Arundel. From the rest of the land the king has all his geld, that is £13 10*s*. 9*d*.[22] And because the 4 collectors of this money received 12*s*. for land in another hundred, and because in their list was found 6*s*. above the number of hides, they gave pledges, being in the king's mercy.

In 1285 the Abbot of Cerne had 4 manors in this hundred, Winterbourne Abbas, Long Bredy, Nettlecombe with Mappercombe, and Milton.[23] In 1086 Winterbourne Abbas (nos. 86 and xlix) was assessed at 10 hides, with 5 hides in demesne; Long Bredy (nos. 87 and l) was assessed at 9 hides, with 3 hides in demesne; Nettlecombe (nos. 88 and li) was assessed at 5 hides with 1½ hide and ½ virgate in demesne, and West Milton (nos. 89 and lii) was assessed at 4 hides with 2 hides in demesne. This brings the demesne of Cerne Abbey in this hundred to 11 hides, 2½ virgates. In 1285, also, Roger Arundel's heirs held some manors in this hundred, including Powerstock (nos. 327 and xcix) and Wraxall (nos. 328 and c).[24] Both manors were subinfeudated in 1086. Part of Wraxall was held of Roger by a man called William, who may be identical with William 'the Goat', although he held only 3 not 3½ hides. Powerstock was assessed at 6 hides and Wraxall at 10 hides. The manor of Chilcombe (no. 459), which lay in this hundred in 1285,[25] was held by Brictuin the reeve in 1086 and probably represents his exempt demesne here; it was assessed at 3 hides. Hugh Gosbert held the manor of Woolcombe (Farm) (no. 498), assessed at 3 virgates, the amount of his exempt demesne in the hundred. It was held T.R.E. by Dode the monk. In 1086 1 virgate in the same vill (no. 474) was held by Dodo, a king's thegn, who is probably the unnamed thegn with ½ virgate. The Count of Mortain held 2 manors assessed at 1½ hide, Brockhampton Green (no. 195) and Uploders (no. 206). Half a hide in Uploders (no. 475) was held in 1086 by Alvric and Brictric, 2 king's thegns. It is possible that they are the almsmen mentioned in the Geld Roll. Dodo held ½ hide in an unidentified locality of the king in 1086 (no. 444) and had held of the queen in alms. If Uploders is the almsmen's manor, then the count's manor is presumably Uploders also.[26]

[17] Ibid.
[18] *Bk. of Fees*, 93.
[19] Ibid.
[20] *Feud. Aids*, ii. 5–7.
[21] The MS. has 4 (*iiii*) hides, the printed version, 3 (*iii*) hides.
[22] This is the geld on 45 hides and ½ virgate. Since the collectors received 12*s*. (2 hides) for land in another hundred and 6*s*. (1 hide) *super numerum hidarum*, 42 hides and ½ virgate actually paid geld.
[23] *Feud. Aids*, ii. 3.
[24] Ibid. 1–3.
[25] Ibid. 3.
[26] See p. 131n.

This brings the hidage of the hundred to 50 hides. Later evidence suggests that Hooke (no. 207), Askerswell (nos. 119 and lxv), and Kingcombe (nos. 247, 485) lay in this hundred in 1086. They certainly lay here in 1285.[27] In 1086 Hooke, assessed at 2 hides, was held by William of the Count of Mortain; Askerswell, assessed at 3 hides, belonged to Tavistock Abbey, and Kingcombe was a divided vill, 3¼ virgates being held by Ernulf of Hesdin and 1 hide and ¾ virgate by 10 thegns. There remain 10½ hides to complete the hundred. Eyton supplied the deficiency in his table by postulating that the manor of Stapleford, which lay in the hundred in 1285,[28] when it was held by the heirs of Roger Arundel, was omitted from the Domesday survey and is to be identified as the manor held of Roger by William 'the Goat'.[29] He calculated its size as 6 hides, 1 virgate, and 3 acres, the amount necessary in his table to produce a total of 66½ hides. This is certainly a convenient way out of the difficulty.

V. *ALBRETESBERGE* HUNDRED

In Albretesberge hundret sunt xl(v)ii hide. De his habent barones in dominio xiii hidas et virgam unam. De isto dominicatu habet rex v hidas et dimidiam de terra regine Mathildis et abbas Creneburnensis ii hidas et iii virgas et Herveius camerarius hidam et dimidiam et comes de Moritonio hidam et dimidiam et Ulvietus venator i hidam et Eschelinus i hidam. Et pro reliqua terra habet rex vii libras et xiii solidos.[30] Et de i hida quam tenet i anglus ad firmam de Hunfrido camerario non habet rex geldum et de i hida quam tenet quidam vidua de Hunfrido camerario ad firmam non habuit rex geldum quia Aiulfus dicit reginam perdonasse pro anima Ricardi filii sui et de i hida et iii virgis quas tenuit[31] Ulwardus albus de ecclesia Glastiniensi non habuit rex geldum et pro iiii hidis et dimidia de terra regine Mathildis non habuit rex geldum.

In *Albretesberge* hundred there are 47 hides. Of these the barons have in demesne 13 hides and 1 virgate. Of this demesne the king has 5½ hides of Queen Maud's land, and the Abbot of Cranborne 2 hides and 3 virgates, and Hervey the chamberlain 1½ hide, and the Count of Mortain 1½ hide, and Ulviet the huntsman 1 hide, and Schelin 1 hide. And from the rest of the land the king has £7 13*s*. And from 1 hide which 1 Englishman holds at farm of Humphrey the chamberlain the king does not have geld and from 1 hide which a certain widow holds at farm of Humphrey the chamberlain the king did not have geld because Aiulf says that the queen remitted (it) for the soul of her son Richard, and from 1 hide and 3 virgates which Ulward White held of the church of Glastonbury the king did not have geld, and from 4½ hides of Queen Maud's land the king did not have geld.

The manor of Queen Maud in this hundred is probably Cranborne (nos. 16 and xxii), assessed at 10 hides, since *Albretesberge* was later absorbed into Cranborne hundred. Both Exon. Domesday and the Exchequer text give the demesne as 3½ hides, and state that 3 thegns held 3 hides. The Abbot of Cranborne had 2½ hides in demesne at Boveridge (no. 71), assessed at 5 hides. Hervey the chamberlain's only manor in Dorset was Wimborne St. Giles (no. 499), assessed at 2½ hides. The Count of Mortain had a manor, assessed at 1½ hide, called *Brochemtune* (no. 195), which Eyton identified with Brockhampton Green, now in Buckland Newton. Fägersten, however, identified it with Brockington Farm, in Knowlton hundred.[32] Ulviet the huntsman's manor is probably Wimborne St. Giles (no. 440), assessed at 1 hide, the amount of his exempt demesne. Schelin held Edmondsham (nos. 18 and xxiv) of the queen. There was 1 hide in demesne. Part of Edmondsham (no. 353) was held by Humphrey the chamberlain. Dodo held it T.R.E. and is presumably identical with the Dodo who held Schelin's manor also. He may be the thegn mentioned in the Geld Roll as holding of Humphrey at farm. The other portion of Edmondsham (no. 354) was held of Humphrey by Eddeva, who is probably to be identified as the widow holding of Humphrey in the Geld Rolls. Schelin's manor was assessed at 2 hides; Humphrey's manors were each assessed at 1½ hide. The manor which Wulfweard White held of Glastonbury Abbey was Pentridge (no. 67) which King William held in 1086. It was assessed at 6 hides. Woodyates (no. 66), another manor of the abbey, assessed at 4 hides, probably lay in this hundred in 1086. In the 13th century it was part of Upwimborne hundred, which was formed from part of *Albretesberge* hundred.[33] Eyton added to this hundred the manors of Leftisford and Langford (nos. 73, 74) belonging to Cranborne Abbey. Fägersten identified Leftisford as a place, now lost, in Cranborne, but Langford as Langford Farm in Stratton, in the hundred of St. George.[34] Of the many manors called *Winburne*, those belonging to Cranborne Abbey (no. 72) and held by William of the wife of Hugh (nos. 388 and cxx) were placed here by Eyton. Leftisford and Langford were assessed at ½ hide each, and the manors of *Winburne* were assessed at 5 hides (no. 72) and 1 hide (nos. 388 and cxx). Five hides remain. Eyton placed the land in 3 places held by Hugh de Lure (no. 362) in this hundred, but gave no authority for so doing.[35] It was assessed at 5 hides.

VI. BADBURY HUNDRED

In Bedeberie hundret sunt xxx et ii hide et i virga. Inde habent barones regis in dominio vi hidas et dimidiam (et i virgam). De his habet Aiulfus ii hidas

In Badbury hundred there are 32 hides and 1 virgate. Thence the king's barons have in demesne 6½ hides and 1 virgate. Of these Aiulf has 2 hides and 3

[27] *Feud. Aids*, ii. 2–3.
[28] Ibid. 2.
[29] Eyton, *Key to Domesday: Dorset*, 127–8.
[30] The geld on 25 hides and 2 virgates.
[31] The printed text has *tenent* (*sic*).
[32] Eyton, *Key to Domesday: Dorset*, 111–12; Fägersten, *Place-Names of Dorset*, 93.
[33] *Inq. Non.* (Rec. Com.), 55; Fägersten, op. cit. 99.
[34] Fägersten, op. cit. 101, 186.
[35] Eyton, op. cit. 111–12.

et iii virgas et Eschelinus i hidam et iii virgas et [f. 18b] Episcopus Londoniensis i hidam et dimidiam et rex dimidiam hidam et Godwinus venator i virgam. De viii hidis et iii virgis et dimidia de terra geldanti quas tenuit Albricus non habuit rex geldum et de iiii hidis et i virga quas tenet Hugo Maminot de episcopo Luxoviensi non habuit rex geldum et de tribus virgis quas i anglus tenet ad firmam de Hunfrido camerario non habuit rex geldum et de ii partibus unius hide quas tenet Eschelinus nunquam habuit rex geldum et de tercia parte unius hide quam tenet Piccotus de comite de Moritonio nunquam habuit rex geldum. De prescripto hundreto habuit rex lxiiii solidos (pro x hidis et dimidia et dimidia virga) intra ii terminos.

virgates, and Schelin 1 hide and 3 virgates, and the Bishop of London 1½ hide, and the king ½ hide, and Godwin the huntsman 1 virgate. From 8 hides and 3½ virgates of geldable land which Aubrey held the king did not have geld and from 4 hides and 1 virgate which Hugh Maminot holds of the Bishop of Lisieux the king did not have geld and from 3 virgates which 1 Englishman holds at farm of Humphrey the chamberlain the king did not have geld and from ⅔ hide which Schelin holds the king never had geld and from ⅓ hide which Picot holds of the Count of Mortain the king never had geld. From the aforesaid hundred the king had 64*s*. for 10½ hides and ½ virgate, at 2 terms.[36]

The manor of Aiulf in this hundred is probably *Selavestune* (no. 339), since it is the only manor large enough to cover his demesne which cannot be assigned to any other hundred. It was assessed at 4 hides and 1½ virgate. The manor of Schelin must be Witchampton (nos. 20 and xxvi), assessed at 4 hides, 2⅔ virgates, which he held of the queen. The demesne in the Exchequer text and Exon. Domesday is 2 hides, 1⅔ virgate, not 1 hide, 3 virgates, but Exon. Domesday states that Schelin *nunquam reddebat gildum de duabus partibus unius hide*, the 2⅔ virgates which never paid geld in the Geld Roll. Another part of Witchampton (no. 188) was held by Hubert of the Count of Mortain. It was assessed at 2 hides, 1⅔ virgate, and there was ⅓ hide (1⅓ virgate) *de qua nunquam dedit geldum*. This identifies Witchampton as the manor held of the Count of Mortain, though in the Geld Roll Picot, and not Hubert, was his tenant. The Bishop of London's only manor was *Odeham* (no. 62), assessed at ½ hide. This is not large enough to account for his exempt demesne in this hundred. The only other land which he held in Dorset in 1086 was 1 hide, 2½ virgates, at Hinton Martell (no. 31). Hinton lay in *Canendone* hundred, which was later amalgamated with Badbury, so it is possible that the bishop's land, which belonged to the church of Wimborne Minster, was in Badbury hundred. The king held ½ hide in Wimborne (nos. 21 and xxvii) which never paid geld, though it was not part of the farm of Wimborne. There was 1 virgate in demesne according to Exon. Domesday and the Exchequer text. Godwin the huntsman's demesne is probably the unnamed ½ virgate and 4 acres (no. 451). The land of Aubrey must be the manor of Gussage in Dorset, which had once belonged to Aubrey de Couci, sometime Earl of Northumbria. In 1086 it was held by the king, and was entered in the Wiltshire survey with Earl Aubrey's manors in that county. It was assessed at 10 hides. This is Gussage St. Michael, Gussage All Saints (no. 192) being held by the Count of Mortain. Hugh Maminot is not recorded in Domesday as a tenant of the Bishop of Lisieux in Dorset, but the bishop's manors of Tarrant Crawford and Preston (nos. 58, 59), assessed at 5 hides and 1 hide respectively, may belong to this hundred, since his 2 other manors of Tarrant Keyneston and Coombe Keynes (nos. 60, 61), which were the dowry of Hugh Maminot's daughter, lay in *Langeberge* and Winfrith hundreds respectively. No Englishman is recorded as the tenant of Humphrey the chamberlain either, but his manor of Hemsworth (no. 355) was held T.R.E. by 1 free thegn. This man may still have been holding of Humphrey at farm in 1084. Part of Hemsworth (no. 187) was held by Hubert of the Count of Mortain. It was assessed at 1 hide and Humphrey's manor at 1 hide also. This brings the total hidage to 32 hides and 1 virgate, the Geld Roll figure.

VII. *CANENDONE* HUNDRED

In Canendone hundret sunt xlviii hide et iii virge. Inde habent barones regis in dominio xxii hidas et ii partes (unius virge). De isto dominicatu habet abbas Hortonensis iiii hidas et abbatissa Wiltonensis ii hidas et iii virgas et rex vi hidas et i virgam de terra Gode. Issildis dimidiam hidam. Filius Eureboldi i virgam et Ulvritius venator i virgam et Dodo i hidam et dimidiam (virgam) et Goduinus venator ii partes unius hide iii agros minus et Aiulfus iii hidas dimidiam virgam minus et Radulfus de Creneborna iii virgas ii agros minus et comes de Moritonio i hidam et de ii hidis et i virga quas tenet i tagnus ad firmam de rege non habuit rex geldum et de v hidis de terra Gode quam tenet Rotbertus de Oilleio ad firmam de rege habuit rex geldum post Pascha. De prescripto hundreto habuit rex vi libras et x solidos et i denarium. Exceptis v hidis de quibus habuit xxx solidos post Pascha.

In *Canendone* hundred there are 48 hides and 3 virgates. Thence the king's barons have in demesne 22 hides and ⅔ virgate. Of this demesne the Abbot of Horton has 4 hides, and the Abbess of Wilton 2 hides and 3 virgates, and the king 6 hides and 1 virgate of Goda's land. Iseldis ½ hide. The son of Eurebold 1 virgate, and Ulvric the huntsman 1 virgate, and Dodo 1 hide and ½ virgate, and Godwin the huntsman ⅔ hide less 3 acres, and Aiulf 3 hides less ½ virgate, and Ralph of Cranborne 3 virgates less 2 acres, and the Count of Mortain 1 hide. And from 2 hides and 1 virgate which 1 thegn holds at farm of the king the king did not have geld and from 5 hides of Goda's land which Robert de Oilly holds at farm of the king the king had geld after Easter. From the aforesaid hundred the king had £6 10*s*. 1*d*. Excepting 5 hides from which he had 30*s*. after Easter.[37]

[36] The geld from 10½ hides and ½ virgate is 63*s*. 9*d*., not 64*s*.

[37] The total of exempt demesne in this hundred is given as 22 hides and ⅔ virgate; in fact it amounts to 20 hides, 1⅔ virgate (⅓ hide). The amount of geld received, £6 10*s*. 1*d*., is the geld on 21⅔ hides; if the hundred consisted of 48 hides and 3 virgates, there should be 21 hides and ⅓ virgate which paid geld.

The abbey of Horton had only 1 manor in Dorset, Horton itself (no. 117), assessed at 7 hides. According to the Exchequer Domesday there were 2 not 4 hides in demesne. The Abbess of Wilton had 2 hides and 3 virgates in demesne at Didlington (no. 139), assessed at 6 hides, and the king had 6 hides and 1 virgate in demesne at Countess Goda's manor of Hinton Martell (no. 31), assessed at 14 hides and 1 virgate. Iseldis held only 1 manor, Petersham (no. 424), assessed at 1 hide; another manor in the same vill (no. 375) was held by Odo fitz Eurebold. It was assessed at 3 virgates. Ulvric the huntsman's manor must be Thorn Hill (no. 442) which lay in this hundred in 1212.[38] It was assessed at ½ hide. Dodo held Wilksworth (no. 445), assessed at 1 hide, and ½ hide in an unspecified locality (no. 444), which he held in alms of the queen. It may have been part of Wilksworth. Another part of Wilksworth (no. 447) was held by Ailrun, and Alward held ⅓ virgate (no. 446) which may lie in the same vill since it is entered between Dodo's manor of Wilksworth and that of Ailrun. Ailrun's manor was assessed at 1 hide. Godwin held 3 manors, of which Walford (no. 448) seems most likely to belong here. Corscombe (no. 488) must have lain in Beaminster hundred, and the third manor (no. 451), which was unnamed, is too small to account for his exempt demesne. Aiulf's manor is probably Hampreston (no. 338), assessed at 6 hides. Part of this manor (nos. 19 and xxv) belonged to the king in succession to Queen Maud. It was assessed at 2 hides, 1 virgate, which is the amount of land held of the king at farm by a thegn, which had not paid geld. According to Exon. Domesday William Belet had held it of the queen. The queen gave 3⅓ virgates in the same vill (no. 443) to Schelin, but in 1086 Torchil held it of the king. One hide in the same vill (nos. 389 and cxxi) was held by William Chernet of the wife of Hugh fitz Grip. Ralph of Cranborne held the manor of West Parley (no. 371), assessed at 2 hides, and the Count of Mortain's manor seems to be Mannington, in Holt (no. 186), not far from Petersham. This brings the total hidage to 47 hides and ⅔ virgate. Eyton placed the manor of Dudsbury (no. 306) in West Parley in this hundred, which seems reasonable on geographical grounds, although, as usual, he gives no authority. It was assessed at 1 hide. In 1285 Leigh lay in the hundred of Badbury, which included *Canendone*.[39] It was held by Robert fitz Gerold in 1086 (no. 240) and was assessed at 1 hide.

VIII. PUDDLETOWN HUNDRED

[f. 19]
In Pideletone hundret sunt xc et i hide. Ex his habent rex et barones sui in dominio xlvii hidas dimidia virga minus. De isto dominicatu habet rex v hidas et dimidiam et i virgam (de terra Heroldi) et abbas de Maiore Monasterio v hidas et iii virgas de terra comitisse de Moritonio et Serlo de Burceio vi hidas et i virgam et abbas Mideltonensis ii hidas et abbas Abodesberiensis viii hidas et Matheus de Mauritania iiii hidas dimidiam virgam minus et comes Alanus v hidas. Et pro xl et iii hidis et dimidia et tercia parte unius virge habet rex xiii libras et x et viii denarios. Et pro x hidis quas habet comes Alanus habuit rex lx et ii solidos et vi denarios post Pascha. Et de i hida de terra Heroldi non habuit rex geldum.

In Puddletown hundred there are 91 hides. From these the king and his barons have in demesne 47 hides less ½ virgate.[40] Of this demesne the king has 5½ hides and 1 virgate of Harold's land, and the Abbot of Marmoutier 5 hides and 3 virgates of the Countess of Mortain's land, and Serle of Burcy 6 hides and 1 virgate, and the Abbot of Milton 2 hides, and the Abbot of Abbotsbury 8 hides, and Matthew de Moretania 4 hides less ½ virgate, and Count Alan 5 hides. And for 43½ hides and ⅓ virgate the king has £13 1*s.* 6*d.* And for 10 hides which Count Alan has the king had 62*s.* 6*d.* after Easter. And from 1 hide of Harold's land the king did not have geld.

Earl Harold's land in this hundred must include Puddletown itself (nos. 8 and ii), the head of the hundred, to which was attached the third penny of the whole shire. It was assessed at ½ hide with land for 15 ploughs. The manor of Little Puddle (nos. 14 and iii) was held by Earl Harold's mother T.R.E. It was assessed at 5 hides with 2½ hides in demesne. None of his other manors can be assigned to this hundred, but according to the geld account he held at least 6 hides and 1 virgate here. The Abbot of Marmoutier had only 1 manor, Piddlehinton (no. 168), assessed at 10 hides. He held it of the Count of Mortain in 1086, and the demesne consisted of 5 hides. A charter of King William granting Piddlehinton to the abbey gives the demesne as 6 hides and states that the manor had belonged to Maud, Countess of Mortain, and on her death was given to the abbey by her husband and brother-in-law for the sake of her soul.[41] Serle of Burcy had 6 hides and 1 virgate in demesne at Waterston (*Pidere* or *Pidra*) (nos. 334 and cvi), assessed at 10 hides. The Abbot of Milton had 2½ hides in demesne at Burleston (nos. 97 and lxx), assessed at 3 hides, and Little Puddle (nos. 107 and lxxxi), assessed at 2 hides. The abbey of Abbotsbury had 8 hides in demesne at Tolpuddle (nos. 110 and lvi). Matthew de Moretania's manor in this hundred must be Milborne St. Andrew (no. 320), assessed at 5 hides, since his other manor, Owermoigne (no. 321), was in *Celberge* hundred. Count Alan had only 1 manor, Dewlish (no. 148), assessed at 15 hides with 5 hides in demesne. Little Puddle (nos. 77 and xl), assessed at 3½ hides, must belong to this hundred. It was held of Cerne Abbey by William *de monasterio*. The 2 manors of *Pidele* (nos. 169, 170), held by Humphrey of the Count of Mortain and assessed at 1½ hide and 2½ hides respectively, must belong here. Athelhampton (no. 52), assessed at 4 hides, and Bardolfeston (no. 51), assessed at 4 hides, must also have lain in the hundred. They were held by Otbold and the wife of Hugh of the Bishop of Salisbury, and belonged to the hundred in 1285.[42] In 1285, also, Little Cheselbourne or Cheselbourne Ford lay in the hundred. In 1086 it was held by Roger Boissell of the wife of Hugh fitz Grip (nos. 378 and cx). In 1431 Tincleton lay in the hundred;[43] in 1086 it was assessed at 2 hides

[38] *Bk. of Fees*, 88.
[39] *Feud. Aids*, ii. 14.
[40] In fact there are 36 hides, 2½ virgates, in demesne.
[41] *Cal. Doc. France*, ed. Round, 435.
[42] *Feud. Aids*, ii. 16.
[43] Ibid. 16, 113.

(no. 222) and held by William of Earl Hugh. Eyton added Ilsington (no. 221), in Puddletown, to this hundred.[44] It was assessed at 2 hides and held by William of Earl Hugh. This would bring the total hidage to 90 hides, as opposed to 91 hides in the Geld Rolls, but the matter of Earl Harold's land remains unsolved.

IX. *STANE* HUNDRED

In Stane hundret sunt lx et iii hide et dimidia. Inde habent barones regis in dominio x et viii hidas (virgam et dimidiam minus). De isto dominicatu habet abbas Wintoniensis xvi hidas dimidiam virgam minus et abbas Cerneliensis ii hidas i virgam minus. Et pro xliii hidis et virga et dimidia habuit rex xiii libras et xx denarios. Et de ii hidis et dimidia quas tenet Bristuinus de abbate Cerneliensi non habuit rex geldum et de i virga quam tenent villani abbatis Wintoniensis non habuit rex geldum.

In *Stane* hundred there are 63½ hides. Thence the king's barons have in demesne 18 hides less 1½ virgate. Of this demesne the Abbot of Winchester has 16 hides less ½ virgate and the Abbot of Cerne 2 hides less 1 virgate. And from 43 hides and 1½ virgate the king had £13 1*s*. 8*d*. And from 2½ hides which Brictuin holds of the Abbot of Cerne the king did not have geld and from 1 virgate which the villeins of the Abbot of Winchester hold the king did not have geld.

The abbey of Winchester, that is, the New Minster (Hyde Abbey), held only 1 manor in Dorset, Piddletrenthide (no. 69), assessed at 30 hides with 15 hides, 2½ virgates, in demesne. Brictuin held 4 hides of thegnland of the abbey of Cerne at Cerne Abbas itself (nos. 76 and xxxix), assessed at 22 hides, but according to both Exon. Domesday and the Exchequer text the abbot's demesne was 3 hides, not 1 hide, 3 virgates. This hundred is very difficult to reconstruct. Eyton placed in it Alton Pancras (no. 33), assessed at 6 hides.[45] The manor lay in Sherborne hundred in 1285,[46] presumably because it belonged to the Bishop of Salisbury; it must have been an outlying portion of the hundred, and it was later a liberty.[47] Up Cerne (no. 34), held by Robert of the same bishop in 1086, also lay in Sherborne hundred in 1285. Eyton also identified *Cernel* (no. 147) as Godmanston, and placed it at this date in Modbury hundred,[48] with which *Stane* hundred was incorporated. Up Cerne was assessed at 2½ hides and *Cernel* at 3 hides. If both are included in *Stane* hundred they bring the total hidage to 63½ hides, the total given in the Geld Roll.

X. GODDERTHORN HUNDRED

In Goderonestona hundret sunt xx et viii hide et dimidia. Inde habent barones regis in dominio iii hidas et i virgam. De isto dominicatu habet Willelmus de Dalmereio i hidam et ii partes unius virge et Berengerius Giffardus i hidam et dimidiam et terciam partem unius virge (hanc tenet antecessor Berengerii de eo ad firmam) et comes de Moritonio dimidiam hidam. Et pro xxv hidis et i virga et pro vii virgis Turstini filii Rolfi que iacent in alio hundreto habet rex octo libras et x et viii denarios.

In Godderthorn hundred there are 28½ hides. Of this the king's barons have in demesne 3 hides and 1 virgate. Of this demesne William de Dalmar has 1 hide and ⅔ virgate, and Berenger Giffard 1½ hide and ⅓ virgate (Berenger's predecessor holds this of him at farm), and the Count of Mortain ½ hide. And for 25 hides and 1 virgate and for 7 virgates of Turstin fitz Rolf which lie in another hundred the king has £8 1*s*. 6*d*.[49]

William de Dalmar's manor in this hundred must be Walditch (no. 501) which lay in this hundred in 1212.[50] It was assessed at 2 hides. Berenger Giffard's only manor in Dorset was Bredy (Farm) (no. 317), assessed at 4 hides, where his predecessor was Harding. In 1285 Loders Lutton (later called Matravers, in Loders) *de feudo de Mortoyne* belonged to the hundred. The Count of Mortain's manor is therefore presumably *Lodre* (no. 190), assessed at 1 hide, of which the count held half and Alvred half. Another manor in *Lodre* (no. 189) was held of the count by Girard; it was assessed at 1 hide. *Lodram* (nos. 399 and cxxxii), assessed at 1 hide, which Walter Tonitruus held of the wife of Hugh fitz Grip, may belong here also, since in 1285 Giles Tonerre held part of Loders Lutton.[51] All these manors must be part of Matravers.[52] Sturthill (nos. 394 and cxxvii), which William de Dalmar held of the wife of Hugh fitz Grip, belonged to the hundred in 1212,[53] and Graston (nos. 395 and cxxviii), also held of the wife of Hugh by a man called William, lay in the hundred in 1285.[54] It was assessed at 2½ hides. The land of Turstin fitz Rolf in another hundred was his 2 manors of Stoke Wallis and Thurstanstay (nos. 254, 255) in Whitchurch hundred. Turstin's manor of Allington (no. 253), assessed at 3 hides, lay in Godderthorn hundred in 1285,[55] and the other manors probably paid geld here because of this. This brings the total hidage of the hundred to 19½ hides. Eyton added the manor of Swyre (no. 263), assessed at 9 hides. In 1275 it lay in Uggescombe hundred which was at one time amalgamated with Godderthorn.[56]

[44] Eyton, *Key to Domesday: Dorset*, 135–6.
[45] Ibid. 137–8.
[46] *Feud. Aids*, ii. 4.
[47] Fägersten, *Place-Names of Dorset*, 193.
[48] Eyton, *Key to Domesday: Dorset*, 133–4.
[49] The geld on 27 hides is £8 2*s*.
[50] *Bk. of Fees*, 93.
[51] *Feud. Aids*, ii. 10–11.
[52] See Fägersten, op. cit. 258. Eyton reversed the identifications, calling these 3 manors Uploders and the 2 lying in Eggardon hundred Loders Lutton i.e. Matravers.
[53] *Bk. of Fees*, 93.
[54] *Feud. Aids*, ii. 10–11.
[55] Ibid.
[56] *Rot. Hund.* (Rec. Com.), i. 102; *Inq. Non.* (Rec. Com.), 46.

XI. WHITEWAY HUNDRED

[f. 19b]
In Haltone hundret sunt lxxxvi hide et i virga. De his habent barones regis in dominio xxxviii hidas et dimidiam et iii virgas. De isto dominicatu habet rex x hidas et i virgam de terra Gode (et Heroldi) et abbatissa (Sancti Edwardi) v hidas et iii virgas. Abbas Abodesberiensis ix hidas et i virgam. Abbas Mideltonensis xiii hidas et dimidiam. Et pro xlv hidis habet rex xii libras et x(v) solidos sed Rotbertus de Oilleio retinuit inde xv solidos usque post Pascha (quos nundum habet rex). Exceptis supradictis denariis restant xv solidi de terra Heroldi que est terra villanorum.

In Whiteway hundred there are 86 hides and 1 virgate. Of these the king's barons have in demesne 38½ hides and 3 virgates.[57] Of this demesne the king has 10 hides and 1 virgate of Goda's and Harold's land and the Abbess of Shaftesbury 5 hides and 3 virgates. The Abbot of Abbotsbury 9 hides and 1 virgate. The Abbot of Milton 13½ hides. And for 45 hides the king has £12 15*s.* but Robert de Oilly retained 15*s.* of this until after Easter which the king does not yet have. Apart from the abovementioned pence, there remain 15*s.* of Harold's land, which is villein land.

The manor of Countess Goda must be Bingham's Melcombe (no. 30) since Hinton Martell is accounted for. It was assessed at 10 hides with 7 hides and 3 virgates in demesne. Ibberton (nos. 10 and v), which belonged to Earl Harold, had 2½ hides in demesne and 2½ hides held by the *villani*, which the Geld Roll says did not pay geld. The Abbot of Abbotsbury had 9 hides and 1 virgate in demesne at Hilton (nos. 111 and lvii), assessed at 18 hides. Two manors of the Abbess of Shaftesbury lay in the hundred in 1285, Cheselbourne and Stoke Wake.[58] In 1086 Cheselbourne (no. 138) was assessed at 16 hides with 2 hides and 3 virgates in demesne, and Stoke Wake (no. 136) was assessed at 5 hides with 3 hides and 1 virgate in demesne. Milton Abbas (nos. 94 and lxxiv) belonged to this hundred in 1212, and Woolland (nos. 102 and lxxvi) in 1285.[59] Milton Abbas was assessed at 24 hides with 9 hides and 3 virgates in demesne and Woolland at 5 hides with 2 hides in demesne. There remain 1 hide and 3 virgates of exempt demesne, possibly at Lyscombe (nos. 101 and lxxv), assessed at 3 hides with 2 hides in demesne. This brings the total hidage to 86 hides.

XII. BEAMINSTER HUNDRED

In Beieministre hundret sunt c hide et vi i virgata minus. De his habent barones regis in dominio viiii hidas i virgam (minus). De isto dominicatu habet episcopus Saresberiensis habet (*sic*) v hidas i virga minus que sunt de victu monacorum et Ricardus de Reveris iii hidas et dimidiam et Godwinus dimidiam hidam. Hungerus filius Audoeni adquietavit i hidam in alio hundreto quam habet in isto. De i hida et iii virgas quas tenet Aiulfus de Osmundo episcopo non habuit rex geldum et de hida et dimidia quam tenet Drogo de comite de Moritonio non habuit rex geldum et de i virga quam tenet Willelmus Malbeenc de comite Hugone nunquam habuit rex geldum. Et pro lxxxxii hidis et dimidia habet rex xxvii libras et xv solidos et ii denarios.

In Beaminster hundred there are 106 hides less 1 virgate. Of these the king's barons have in demesne 9 hides less 1 virgate. Of this demesne the Bishop of Salisbury has 5 hides less 1 virgate which are for the food of the monks, and Richard de Redvers 3½ hides, and Godwin ½ hide. Hunger fitz Odin was quit in another hundred for 1 hide which he has in this. From 1 hide and 3 virgates which Aiulf holds of Bishop Osmund the king did not have geld and from 1½ hide which Drew holds of the Count of Mortain the king did not have geld and from 1 virgate which William Malbank holds of Earl Hugh the king never had geld. And for 92½ hides the king had £27 15*s.* 2*d.*[60]

Beaminster (no. 46), belonging to the Bishop of Salisbury, must lie in this hundred. It was assessed at 16 hides, 1 virgate, with a demesne of 2 carucates. The 4 hides and 3 virgates of the bishop's exempt demesne are at Corscombe (no. 44), assessed at 9 hides, 3 virgates. Godwin also held part of Corscombe (no. 488), assessed at 1 hide, which must cover his exempt demesne in this hundred, and William held another manor called Corscombe (no. 213) of the Count of Mortain, assessed at 1 hide. The only manor of Richard de Rivers in Dorset was Mosterton (no. 366), assessed at 6 hides. Hunger fitz Odin's manor in this hundred must be his holding of 1 hide (no. 506), which presumably paid geld in Whitchurch hundred, along with Broadwindsor (no. 505) to which it was attached. William of Moyon held part of Little Windsor (nos. 282 and xcii), assessed at 4 hides. Aiulf is not recorded as a tenant of the Bishop of Salisbury in the Domesday survey. Drew held Toller Whelme (no. 214) of the Count of Mortain; it was assessed at 3 hides. Catsley (no. 229), assessed at 1 hide and 1 virgate, was held by William of Earl Hugh. There was 1 virgate *de qua celatum est geldum T.R.W.* In 1285 Chardstock, Netherbury, and Buckham, belonging to the Bishop of Salisbury, and Stoke Abbott, belonging to Sherborne Abbey, lay in this hundred.[61] In 1086 Chardstock (no. 49) was assessed at 12 hides and Netherbury (no. 47) at 20 hides with 2 carucates in demesne. Chardstock was subinfeudated, being held by Walter and William. Stoke Abbott (no. 45) was assessed at 6½ hides, with 2 carucates in demesne, and Buckham (no. 54) was assessed at 3 hides and was held by Walter of the bishop. In 1316 Bowood (no. 53), belonging to the Bishop of Salisbury, lay in this hundred,[62] which in 1086 was assessed at 6 hides and held by Godfrey, Osmar, and Elfric. In 1346 the hundred of Redhone, an

[57] In fact the demesnes add up to 38 hides and 3 virgates; for a comment on this discrepancy, see p. 115 n.
[58] *Feud. Aids*, ii. 13.
[59] *Bk. of Fees*, 90; *Feud. Aids*, ii. 13.
[60] The geld on 92½ hides is £27 15*s.*
[61] *Feud. Aids*, ii. 7.
[62] Ibid. 41.

offshoot of Beaminster, contained South Perrott, then held by Joan Maubank, and North and South Mapperton.[63] In 1086 William (Malbank) held South Perrott (no. 228) of Earl Hugh; it was assessed at 5 hides. Part of Mapperton (no. 248) was held by Ernulf of Hesdin and another part by William of Moyon (nos. 283 and xciii). William of Moyon had 3 hides in demesne, which the Geld Rolls do not mention. His portion of the vill was assessed at 5 hides and 1 virgate, and that of Ernulf at 3 hides and 3 virgates. This brings the total hidage of the hundred to 104 hides and 3 virgates. Eyton suggested that the hide in Wool attached to the manor of Buckham (no. 54) may have been counted as an outlying portion of Beaminster hundred,[64] which, if correct, would bring the total hidage to the Geld Roll figure of 105 hides and 3 virgates.

XIII. REDHONE HUNDRED

In Redehane hundret sunt vii hide. Pro iiii hidis et virga et dimidia habet rex xxvi solidos et vi denarios et de ii hidis et dimidia reddidit abbas de Tavestot geldum in alio hundreto. Similiter abbas Abodesberiensis de dimidia hida. Et pro dimidia virga quam tenet i anglus de Rogero Arundello non habuit rex geldum et pro dimidia virga quam tenet i anglus de Arnulfo de Hesdinc non habuit rex geldum.

In Redhone hundred there are 7 hides. For 4 hides and 1½ virgate the king has 26*s.* 6*d.*[65] And for 2½ hides the Abbot of Tavistock paid geld in another hundred. Likewise the Abbot of Abbotsbury for ½ hide. And for ½ virgate which 1 Englishman holds of Roger Arundel the king did not have geld and for ½ virgate which 1 Englishman holds of Ernulf of Hesdin the king did not have geld.

The abbey of Tavistock had 2 manors in Dorset in 1086, Askerswell (nos. 119 and lxv) and North Poorton (nos. 120 and lxvi). Askerswell was assessed at 3 hides, and North Poorton at 2 hides. In 1285 Askerswell lay in the hundred of Eggardon (formerly *Glochresdone*). In the Geld Roll for that hundred it is stated that the collectors received 12*s. pro terra alterius hundreti*, that is, the geld on 2 hides. This must be the land of the abbey of Tavistock which paid geld in another hundred, but, according to the account of Redhone, the amount of land in question was 2½ not 2 hides. North Poorton, assessed at 2 hides, must lie in Redhone, but is not large enough to account for all the abbot's land in this hundred, amounting to 2½ hides.

The Abbot of Abbotsbury's manor is probably *Bourtone* (nos. 115 and lxii), assessed at ½ hide and held by 2 *villani*. It paid geld in Uggescombe hundred, with Atrim, which the abbot had in Whitchurch hundred. Eyton identified *Bourtone* as Burcombe in North Poorton, but Fägersten regarded it as another form of Poorton.[66] Both Roger Arundel and Ernulf of Hesdin held manors in North Poorton in 1086. Roger's manor (nos. 329 and ci), assessed at 2 hides, was held of him by Wido, and Ernulf's manor (no. 249), assessed at ½ hide, was apparently held by Ernulf himself. Another part of North Poorton (no. 368), assessed at 1 hide and 2½ virgates, was held by Godeschal of David the interpreter. This hundred cannot be satisfactorily reconstructed.

XIV. TOLLERFORD HUNDRED

[f. 20]
In Tolreforde hundret sunt lix hide. De his habent barones regis in dominio xvii hidas et dimidiam et dimidiam virgam. De isto dominicatu habet Willelmus de Ou viii hidas (dimidiam virgam minus) et Hugo de Portu vi hidas et i virgam et Rogerus Arondellus iii hidas et dimidiam. Et pro xliii (hidis) et dimidia virga et iii hidis et iii virgis quas Hugo de Portu habet in alio hundreto sed adquietavit in isto habet rex xiiii libras et xvi denarios. Et pro iii hidis et dimidia quas tenet Waardus non habuit rex geldum et pro i hida quam tenet Rannulfus de Willelmo de Moione non habuit rex geldum.

In Tollerford hundred there are 59 hides. Of these the king's barons have in demesne 17½ hides and ½ virgate. Of this demesne William of Eu has 8 hides less ½ virgate, and Hugh de Port 6 hides and 1 virgate, and Roger Arundel 3½ hides. And for 43 hides and ½ virgate and 3 hides and 3 virgates which Hugh de Port has in another hundred but (which) were quit in this, the king has £14 1*s.* 4*d.*[67] And for 3½ hides which Wadard holds the king did not have geld and for 1 hide which Ranulf holds of William of Moyon the king did not have geld.

William of Eu's manor of Wynford Eagle (no. 264) lay in this hundred in 1303[68] and must therefore represent his demesne although, according to the Exchequer text, there were 6 hides in demesne, not 7 hides and 3½ virgates. It was assessed at 14 hides. Hugh de Port had only 1 manor in Dorset, Compton Valence (no. 357) in Frampton hundred. The exempt demesne credited to him in this hundred must be that of Compton Valence, and is the same as that credited to him in Frampton hundred. Ranulf held the manor of Chelborough (nos. 280 and xc) of William of Moyon. It was assessed at 3 hides, 1 of which *non dedit geldum*. Roger Arundel also held a manor called Chelborough (nos. 324 and xcvi), but Exon. Domesday gives the demesne as 3 not 3½ hides. Wadard held Rampisham (no. 55) of the Bishop of Bayeux. It was assessed at 6 hides. In 1303 the manors of Chilfrome and Cruxton lay in this hundred. They belonged to the fief of John de Mohun of Dunster. Maiden Newton, Toller Porcorum, and Frome Vauchurch also lay in the hundred at that date.[69] Chilfrome and Cruxton are identified by Eyton as *Frome* (nos. 278 and lxxxviii), assessed at 10

[63] Ibid. 60.
[64] Eyton, *Key to Domesday: Dorset*, 114 n.
[65] The geld on 4 hides, 1½ virgate, is £1 6*s.* 3*d.*
[66] Eyton, *Key to Domesdav: Dorset*, 137–8; Fägersten, *Place-Names of Dorset*, 281 n.
[67] The geld on 46 hides, 3½ virgates, is £14 1*s.* 3*d.*
[68] *Feud. Aids*, ii. 35.
[69] Ibid.

hides, and *Frome* (nos. 279 and lxxxix), both belonging to William of Moyon in 1086. Maiden Newton (no. 309) and Toller Porcorum (no. 310) belonged to Waleran in 1086 and were assessed at 6 hides and 5 hides respectively. Eyton identified Frome Vauchurch as *Frome* (no. 265) held by Ansfrid of William of Eu. It was assessed at 6 hides, which brings the total hidage of the hundred to 59 hides, the Geld Roll figure.

XV. BERE HUNDRED

In Bere hundret sunt xlix hide et i virga. Inde habet rex ix libras et viii solidos pro xxx et i hida et i virga et barones regis habent in dominio x et vii hidas i virgam minus. De isto dominicatu habet comes de Moritonio i hidam et Hugo Gausbertus i virgam et Aiulfus i hidam. Alvricius venator ii hidas. Abbas Mideltonensis i hidam. Godricus presbiterus iiii hidas x agros minus. Abbas Cerneliensis iiii hidas. Filius Eureboldi ii hidas. Et de i hida et dimidia quam tenet Osmundus de Sueno non habuit rex geldum et de dimidia hida quam tenet Walterus Tonitruus de uxore Hugonis nunquam habuit rex geldum et de dimidia hida terre que fuit tanglanda tempore regis Edwardi et est modo in firma regis nunquam habuit rex geldum et pro i virga et dimidia quam habet Edwinus venator in hoc hundreto reddidit geldum in alio.

In Bere hundred there are 49 hides and 1 virgate. Thence the king has £9 8*s*. for 31 hides and 1 virgate[70] and the king's barons have in demesne 17 hides less 1 virgate. Of this demesne the Count of Mortain has 1 hide and Hugh Gosbert 1 virgate and Aiulf 1 hide. Alvric the huntsman 2 hides. The Abbot of Milton 1 hide. Godric the priest 4 hides less 10 acres. The Abbot of Cerne 4 hides. The son of Eurebold 2 hides. And from 1½ hide which Osmund holds of Swain the king did not have geld and from ½ hide which Walter Tonitruus holds of the wife of Hugh the king never had geld and from ½ hide of land which was thegnland T.R.E. and is now in the king's farm the king never had geld. And from 1½ virgate which Edwin the huntsman has in this hundred he paid geld in another.

The Count of Mortain's manor is probably Bestwall (no. 197), assessed at 3 hides. In 1316 it lay in the hundred of *Hundredesberge*, an offshoot of Bere hundred.[71] Hugh Gosbert held 1 virgate in Worgret (no. 497). It was a divided vill, William of Briouze holding 1 hide and 3 virgates (no. 293), and Cerne Abbey 1 hide (nos. 84 and xlvii). Aiulf's manor must be Hethfelton (no. 349), since of his remaining manors *Brige* (no. 348) is too small and Chettle (no. 342) was subinfeudated. Hethfelton was assessed at 1½ hide. This is another divided vill, 2 hides being held by Robert of William of Briouze (no. 294) and 3 virgates by Cerne Abbey (nos. 83 and xlvi). Eyton identified the Abbot of Milton's manor as *Pidre* (nos. 107 and lxxxi), assessed at 2 hides, but if, as he says, this is part of Little Puddle, it must lie in Puddletown hundred. The abbey's manor of Clyffe (nos. 98 and lxxi), also assessed at 2 hides, may have lain in the hundred, but according to Exon. Domesday it was held by the *villani*. Alvric the huntsman held 2 manors called *Wintreburne* (nos. 430, 484), each assessed at 1 hide, which may represent his demesne in this hundred, since Winterborne Kingston lay here in 1285.[72] Godric the priest's manor must be Briantspuddle (no. 472), assessed at 5 hides, since his other manors are too small.[73] The Abbot of Cerne had 4 hides in demesne at Affpuddle (nos. 80 and xliii), assessed at 9 hides. Odo fitz Eurebold's manor of Milborne Stileham (no. 373), assessed at 2 hides, probably belongs here, since the manor which Osmund held of Swain was also Milborne Stileham (no. 477). Its hidage is omitted in the Domesday survey. Walter Tonitruus held Turners Puddle (nos. 391 and cxxiv) of the wife of Hugh. It was assessed at 6 hides and *ibi est dimidia hida et quattuor agri et i ortus que nunquam gildavit sed celatum est.* The ½ hide of thegnland in the king's farm is mysterious. At Hinton Martell (no. 31) there was 1 hide of thegnland which a priest had held T.R.E. but *modo est in dominio regis.* Edwin the huntsman's 1½ virgate is also difficult to identify. It has been suggested that it was the 1½ virgate attached to *Bleneforde* (no. 438),[74] assessed at 5 hides and 1½ virgate. *Bleneforde* is part of either Blandford St. Mary or Langton Long Blandford, and must lie either in Combsditch or *Langeberge* hundred, but neither account mentions 1½ virgate belonging to Edwin in another hundred. These manors amount to 32 hides, 2½ virgates. The manor of *Bere* (Dodding's Farm) (nos. 390 and cxxii) held by William *de monasteriis* of the wife of Hugh must belong here. It was assessed at ½ hide and 1½ virgate was attached to it. In 1316 Rushton lay in the hundred of *Hundredesberge*[75] already mentioned as an offshoot of Bere hundred. It was a divided vill in 1086. William of Briouze held 1½ hide (no. 292), Odo fitz Eurebold 3 virgates (no. 374), 2 knights held ½ hide of the wife of Hugh (nos. 407 and cxl), Alward held 1 virgate (no. 449), and Edward 3¾ virgates (no. 466). In 1431 Holton lay in the same hundred.[76] In 1086 it was assessed at ½ hide and held by William of Briouze (no. 286). Eyton placed Bovington (no. 483) here. It was assessed at 4 hides and held by Alvric. In modern times it lay in Winfrith hundred, but in 1086 the Frome seems to have been the boundary between Bere and Winfrith hundreds, and Bovington may have been in Bere. This brings the total hidage to 48 hides, 1¾ virgate.

XVI. COMBSDITCH HUNDRED

In (Con)cresdic hundret sunt lxx et vii hide et pro l et viii (hidis) habet rex x et vii libras et viii solidos et barones regis habent inde in dominio xiiii hidas et

In Combsditch hundred there are 77 hides and for 58 hides the king has £17 8*s*. and the king's barons have thence in demesne 14 hides and 1½ virgate. Of

[70] The geld on 31 hides and 1 virgate is £9 7*s*. 6*d*.

[71] *Feud. Aids*, ii. 42.

[72] Ibid. 12.

[73] An early variant of this manor's name was *Prestepidel(a)* ('priest's Puddle'), probably derived from its tenure by Godric the priest: Fägersten, op. cit. 167.

[74] R. Welldon Finn, 'The Making of the Dorset Domesday', *Proc. Dorset Nat. Hist. and Arch. Soc.* lxxxi. 155.

[75] *Feud. Aids*, ii. 42.

[76] Ibid. 113.

virgam et (dimidiam). De isto dominicatu habet comes de Moritonio v virgas et dimidiam et abbas Cerneliensis ii hidas. Mideltonensis abbas i hidam. Uxor Hugonis iii hidas et dimidiam. Johannes hostiarius i hidam et virgam et dimidiam. Godwinus prepositus i hidam.
[f. 20b]
Alwardus Colinc i hidam. Edwinus venator iii hidas et dimidiam virgam. Et pro dimidia hida quam tenet Britellus non habuit rex geldum et pro dimidia hida quam tenent villani Hugonis Gausberti non habuit rex geldum et pro iii virgis quas tenet Willelmus de monasterio de Willelmo de Aldreio nunquam habuit rex geldum et pro ii virgis et dimidia quas tenet Dodemanus de comite de Moritonio nunquam habuit rex geldum et pro i virga quam tenet Radulfus de uxore Hugonis non habuit rex geldum et pro hida et dimidia quam i anglus cuius illa terra fuerat prius tenet ad firmam de Aiulfo non habuit rex geldum.

this demesne the Count of Mortain has 5½ virgates and the Abbot of Cerne 2 hides. The Abbot of Milton 1 hide. The wife of Hugh 3½ hides. John the usher 1 hide and 1½ virgate. Godwin the reeve 1 hide. Alward Colinc 1 hide. Edwin the huntsman 3 hides and ½ virgate. And from ½ hide which Bretel holds the king did not have geld and from ½ hide which the villeins of Hugh Gosbert hold the king did not have geld and from 3 virgates which William *de monasterio* holds of William de Aldrie the king never had geld and from 2½ virgates which Dodeman holds of the Count of Mortain the king never had geld and from 1 virgate which Ralph holds of the wife of Hugh the king did not have geld and from 1½ hide which 1 Englishman, to whom this land previously belonged, holds at farm of Aiulf, the king did not have geld.

The Count of Mortain held 5½ virgates at *Wintreburne* (no. 184). Dodeman held 1½ hide of him in the same manor. The Abbot of Cerne had 2 hides in demesne at Bloxworth (nos. 79 and xlii), assessed at 5½ hides. The Abbot of Milton had 1 hide in demesne at *Wintreburne* (nos. 103 and lxxvii), assessed at 2 hides and 1 virgate. The wife of Hugh held *Wintreburne* (nos. 386 and cxviii), assessed at 5 hides, with 3 not 3½ hides in demesne, and Ralph held *Wintreburne* (nos. 387 and cxix), assessed at 1½ virgate, of her. John had only 1 manor, *Wintreburne* (no. 500), assessed at 2 hides, 1½ virgate. Godwin the reeve held 1 hide in *Wintreburne* (no. 450). Alward Colinc held Thorncombe (no. 439), assessed at 2 hides. Edwin the huntsman held 2 manors called *Bleneford(e)* (nos. 438, 455), 1 assessed at 5 hides, 1½ virgate, and 1 at 5 hides. It is not possible to decide which is Blandford St. Mary which lay in Combsditch[77] and which is Langton Long Blandford which lay in *Langeberge* hundred.[78] Aiulf held part of Blandford St. Mary (no. 336), assessed at 1½ hide, which Leveva (Leofgifu) held T.R.E. Bretel held the manor of Littleton (no. 176) of the Count of Mortain. It was assessed at 5 hides and belonged to the hundred in 1303.[79] Dodeman held part of *Wintreburne* (no. 184) of the Count of Mortain, as already stated, and also the manor of *Blaneford* (Blandford St. Mary) (no. 185), assessed at 1½ hide. Bretel also held a manor called *Bleneford* (no. 177), assessed at 1½ hide, of the Count of Mortain. William de Aldrie is not mentioned in the Dorset Domesday, either as a tenant-in-chief or as a mesne tenant. In the Wiltshire survey he appears as a tenant of William of Eu.[80] At *Bleneford* (part of Blandford St. Mary) (no. 261), which William (presumably William de Aldrie) held of William of Eu, there was ½ hide from which *non habuit rex geldum*. Possibly this is the manor referred to in the Geld Roll. Hugh Gosbert held a manor called *Wintreburne* (no. 496), assessed at ½ hide. Two thegns had held it T.R.E. and there were 2 *villani* in 1086. Of the many manors called *Wintreburne* it is impossible to decide which lay in Combsditch and which in Cullifordtree hundred. The manor of *Wintreburne* which Urse held of Waleran (no. 305) probably belongs to this hundred. In 1242–3 Winterborne Tomson and Winterborne Turbervileston (now Winterborne Muston in Winterborne Kingston)[81] were both *de feudo heredis Waleran*, and these same manors afterwards lay in the hundred of Combsditch.[82] Which of the 2 represents the manor held by Waleran in 1086 must remain doubtful. Since the other manors of *Wintreburne* cannot satisfactorily be identified, this hundred cannot be completed.

XVII. COGDEAN HUNDRED

In Cocdene hundret sunt lxxx et vi hide et pro xxxii hide habet rex ix libras et xii solidos (et iii denarios). Et pro x et vii hidis et dimidia reddiderunt homines Rogerii de Bello Monte c et v solidos post festum sancte Marie. Et barones regis habent inde in dominio xxxv hidas et virgam et dimidiam. De isto dominicatu habet Edwardus xvi hidas et dimidiam et Rogerus de Bello Monte xi hidas et dimidiam et Rotbertus filius Geraldi vii hidas et virgam et dimidiam et pro i virga quam Edwardus habet in hoc hundreto reddidit (geldum) in alio et pro dimidia virga villanorum (Rotberti) filii Geroldi (non habet rex) gildum.

In Cogdean hundred there are 86 hides and for 32 hides the king has £9 12*s*. 3*d*. and from 17½ hides the men of Roger de Beaumont rendered 105*s*. after Lady Day. And the king's barons have thence in demesne 35 hides and 1½ virgate. Of this demesne Edward has 16½ hides, and Roger de Beaumont 11½ hides, and Robert fitz Gerold 7 hides and 1½ virgate. And for 1 virgate which Edward has in this hundred he paid geld in another, and for ½ virgate belonging to the villeins of Robert fitz Gerold the king does not have geld.

Edward of Salisbury held 2 manors in Dorset, Canford Magna (no. 243), with 11½ hides in demesne, and Kinson (no. 244), now in Hampshire, with 5 hides and 1 virgate in demesne. Together they amount to 38 hides. Roger de Beaumont's manor must be Sturminster Marshall (no. 232), although the Domesday

77 *Inq. Non.* (Rec. Com.), 54.
78 See p. 138.
79 *Feud. Aids*, ii. 29.
80 *Dom. Bk.* (Rec. Com.), i, f. 71b.
81 Fägersten, op. cit. 71–72.
82 *Bk. of Fees*, 753; *Feud. Aids*, ii. 29, 43.

survey gives the demesne as 12½ not 11½ hides. It was assessed at 30 hides. Robert fitz Gerold had 7½ hides in demesne at Corfe Mullen (no. 239), assessed at 10 hides.[83] In 1303 Lytchett Matravers belonged to the hundred.[84] It was held by Hugh of William of Eu in 1086 (no. 260) and was assessed at 12 hides. This makes a total of 90 hides, as opposed to the 86 hides of the Geld Roll.

XVIII. LOOSEBARROW HUNDRED

In Celeberge hundret sunt xl et i hide et dimidia. Inde habet rex vi libras (et) vi denarios pro xx hidis iiii agris minus et barones regis habent in dominio —[*blank*]. Rex habet de isto dominicatu iii hidas et dimidiam de terra Heroldi. Hugo Gausbertus i virgam. Willelmus de Moione iii hidas et dimidiam iiii agros minus. Willelmus de Dalmereio iii hidas et virgam et dimidiam (et comes de Moritonio i virgam). Abbatissa Sancti Edwardi vi hidas et i virgam et ii agros et Ulvricius venator i hidam et dimidiam et Ulveva iii virgas. Walterus de Clavilla dimidiam hidam. Et pro i virga quam tenet Rotbertus filius Ivonis de
[f. 21]
comite nunquam habuit rex geldum. Pro hida et dimidia quam tenent villani de terra Heroldi non habuit rex geldum.

In Loosebarrow hundred[85] there are 41½ hides. Thence the king has £6 0*s*. 6*d*.[86] for 20 hides less 4 acres and the king's barons have in demesne—[*blank*]. Of this demesne the king has 3½ hides of Harold's land. Hugh Gosbert 1 virgate. William of Moyon 3½ hides less 4 acres. William de Dalmar 3 hides and 1½ virgate, and the Count of Mortain 1 virgate. The Abbess of Shaftesbury 6 hides and 1 virgate and 2 acres, and Ulvric the huntsman 1½ hide, and Ulveva 3 virgates. Walter de Claville ½ hide. And from 1 virgate which Robert fitz Ivo holds of the count the king never had geld. From 1½ hide which the villeins hold of Harold's land the king did not have geld.

The hundred takes its name from Charborough (nos. 9 and iv), a manor of 5 hides, previously held by Earl Harold but held by the king in 1086. It had 3½ hides in demesne. Hugh Gosbert's land must be his unnamed virgate (no. 495). William of Moyon's manor is probably Spetisbury (nos. 274 and lxxxiv). It was assessed at 7 hides, 1 virgate, and 6 acres, with 3 hides, 1 virgate, and 10 acres in demesne. The Count of Mortain also had a manor at Spetisbury (no. 173), of which he himself held 1 virgate and 3 acres and Robert held 3 virgates and 6 acres. It was assessed at 1½ hide. William de Dalmar held a manor in an unspecified locality (no. 494), assessed at 3 hides and 2½ virgates.[87] The Abbess of Shaftesbury had 7 hides and 1 virgate in demesne at Mapperton (in Almer) (no. 137), the nearest amount to that recorded in the Geld Roll. Mapperton was assessed at 11 hides. Ulvric the huntsman held Morden (no. 437), assessed at 2½ hides. In the same vill his brother's wife held 1 hide and ½ virgate. She is presumably identical with Ulveva. Walter de Claville held a manor called Morden (nos. 315 and clxi), but according to Exon. Domesday he had 1½ virgate in demesne, not 2 virgates. Aiulf held 3 virgates in Morden (no. 337) and William Chernet held 1 hide and 1 virgate in Morden of the wife of Hugh (nos. 385 and cxvii). Robert, perhaps Robert fitz Ivo, held 1 hide in Morden (no. 172) of the Count of Mortain. In 1303 Tarrant Crawford belonged to this hundred.[88] It was held in 1086 by Edward of Alvric (no. 436) and was assessed at 2 hides. This brings the hidage of the hundred to 40 hides, 3½ virgates, and 6 acres, just 2½ virgates short of the Geld Roll figure.

XIX. ROWBARROW HUNDRED

In Aileveswode hundret sunt lxx et iii hide. Inde habet rex xv libras et vii solidos et iii denarios pro l et i hidis et iii partibus unius virge et barones regis habent in dominio—[*blank*]. De isto dominicatu habet Rogerus (Arondellus) iii hidas et dimidiam et dimidiam virgam et abbatissa de Sancto Edwardo iii hidas quartam partem unius virge minus et Rogerus de Bello Monte ii hidas et dimidiam. Abbas Midiltonensis ii hidas dimidiam virgam minus. Serlo de Burceio ii hidas et dimidiam (i) agrum et dimidium minus et comes Eustachius i hidam et terciam partem i virge. Alvricitius venator iiii hidas i virgam minus. Uxor Hugonis v hidas. Durandus carpentarius (i) hidam. Et i hida que est sancti Stephani Cadomensis est adquietata in alio hundreto. Et pro i hida et dimidia villanorum de terra Heroldi non habuit rex geldum et pro dimidia hida quam tenet Durandus carpentarius de uxore Hugonis non habuit rex geldum.

In Rowbarrow hundred there are 73 hides. Thence the king has £15 7*s*. 3*d*.[89] for 51 hides and ¾ virgate, and the king's barons have in demesne—[*blank*]. Of this demesne Roger Arundel has 3½ hides and ½ virgate and the Abbess of Shaftesbury 3 hides less ¼ virgate and Roger de Beaumont 2½ hides. The Abbot of Milton 2 hides less ½ virgate. Serle of Burcy 2½ hides less 1½ acre, and Count Eustace 1 hide and ⅓ virgate. Alvric the huntsman 4 hides less 1 virgate. The wife of Hugh 5 hides. Durand the carpenter 1 hide. And 1 hide which belongs to St. Stephen, Caen, is quit in another hundred. And from 1½ hide belonging to the villeins of Harold's land the king did not have geld and from ½ hide which Durand the carpenter holds of the wife of Hugh the king did not have geld.

[83] Both Sturminster Marshall and Corfe Mullen, along with Canford Magna, lay in the hundred in 1212: *Bk. of Fees*, 90.

[84] *Feud. Aids*, ii. 28.

[85] The Domesday hundred took its name from the manor of Charborough, but was later called Loosebarrow.

[86] The geld on 20 hides is £6.

[87] This manor was probably part of Tarrant Crawford: see p. 22.

[88] *Feud. Aids*, ii. 28.

[89] The geld on 51 hides and ¾ virgate is £15 7*s*. 1½*d*.

Roger Arundel had 3½ hides and ½ virgate in demesne at Worth Matravers (nos. 330 and cii), assessed at 16 hides and 2½ virgates. He held another manor in the same vill (nos. 332 and civ), assessed at ½ hide. Ralph held 3 virgates in the same vill of the wife of Hugh (nos. 418 and cli). The Abbess of Shaftesbury held Kingston (no. 134), assessed at 16 hides, with 3 hides and 3 virgates in demesne. The king held 1 hide there, in which he had built Corfe Castle (*castellum Warham*), and William of Briouze held 1 virgate. It belonged to the hundred of Rowbarrow in the 14th century.[90] Roger de Beaumont held 2 manors at Afflington (nos. 236, 237), assessed at 2 hides and ½ hide respectively, the amount of his exempt demesne in this hundred. The manor of Milton Abbey is probably Ower (Farm) (nos. 105 and lxxix). Neither Exon. Domesday nor the Exchequer text gives the demesne of Ower, but it lay in the hundred in 1316.[91] It was assessed at 3 hides T.R.E. Serle of Burcy's manor must be Whitecliff (nos. 335 and cvii), assessed at 3 hides, with 2½ hides in demesne. Count Eustace (Count of Boulogne) does not appear in the Dorset survey, but his wife, the countess, held 3 manors, 1 of which, Swanage (nos. 515 and xxxviii), was assessed at 1 hide and ⅓ virgate. According to Exon. Domesday the countess had no demesne in this manor which was held by a *villanus*, but *rex Willelmus nunquam habuit geldum de hac mansione*. Walter Tonitruus held 1½ hide in Swanage (nos. 417 and cl) of the wife of Hugh. Alvric the huntsman held Coombe (no. 481), the only one of his manors, apart from Bovington in Bere hundred (no. 483), which is large enough to cover his exempt demesne. It was assessed at 5 hides and 1 virgate. Durand the carpenter held the manor of *Moleham* (no. 511), assessed at 1 hide, the amount of his exempt demesne in this hundred. The only manor which he held of the wife of Hugh was Wilkswood (nos. 423 and clvi), assessed at ½ hide. She herself held part of Wilkswood (nos. 415 and cxlviii), assessed at 3½ hides and ⅔ virgate, with 2½ hides in demesne. She also had 2 hides in demesne at Acton (nos. 416 and cxlix), assessed at 2½ hides. There was 1½ hide in Purbeck hundred attached to Earl Harold's manor of Puddletown (nos. 8 and ii), which is probably the 1½ hide held by the *villani* of Earl Harold. Six hides and 2½ virgates in Purbeck hundred (no. 296) were held of William of Briouze by Richard and the wife of Hugh. The hide held by St. Stephen, Caen, seems also to have laid in Purbeck, although the Domesday survey does not mention it. In Henry I's confirmation charter, however, *Pubich* is mentioned as a member of the abbey's manor of Bincombe in Cullifordtree hundred.[92] These manors add up to 66 hides and 1 virgate, with in addition 1 hide in Purbeck, belonging to St. Stephen, Caen. Studland and Rollington lay in this hundred at a later date. Studland (no. 209), assessed at 3½ hides, was held by Haimo of the Count of Mortain in 1086 and lay in the hundred of Rowbarrow in 1275,[93] and Rollington (nos. 331 and ciii), assessed at 2 hides and 1¾ virgate, was held by Robert of Roger Arundel in 1086 and lay in the hundred in 1303.[94] In 1431 Herston lay in Rowbarrow hundred.[95] In 1086 2 virgates in Herston (nos. 333 and cv) belonged to Roger Arundel, and 1 virgate in the same vill (no. 512) belonged to Godfrey the scullion. Fägersten linked the hundred name of *Aileveswode* with the manor of Ailwood (*Aleoude*) (no. 482), held of Swain by the wife of Hugh.[96] It must therefore lie in this hundred. It was assessed at 4 hides and 3 virgates. This brings the total hidage to 78½ hides and ¾ virgate. The Geld Roll gives the hidage as 73 hides, but in fact the details of the account add up to 78 hides and 1⅚ virgate.[97]

XX. HANDLEY HUNDRED

In Hanglege hundret sunt xx hide et pro xvi hidis et i virga quas homines abbatisse habent in hoc hundreto et pro vi hidis et dimidia quas ipsi habent in alio hundreto habet rex vi libras et xvi solidos et vi denarios et abbatissa habet inde in dominio iii hidas et iii virgas.

In Handley hundred there are 20 hides and for 16 hides and 1 virgate which the men of the abbess have in this hundred and for 6½ hides which they have in another hundred the king has £6 16*s*. 6*d*. and the abbess has thence in demesne 3 hides and 3 virgates.

This hundred consists only of the Abbess of Shaftesbury's manor of Sixpenny Handley (no. 125), assessed at 20 hides with 3 hides and 3 virgates in demesne.

XXI. NEWTON HUNDRED

In Newentone hundret sunt xl et vii hide. Inde habet rex x libras et vii solidos et vi denarios pro xxxiiii hidis et dimidia et tercia parte unius virge. Et pro vi hidis et dimidia quas tenent homines abbatisse habuit rex in alio hundreto xxx et ix solidos. Et abbatissa habet inde in dominio i hidam et dimidiam et Chetellus iiii hidas et dimidiam et ii partes unius virge.

In Newton hundred there are 47 hides. Thence the king has £10 7*s*. 6*d* for 34½ hides and ⅓ virgate. And for 6½ hides which the men of the abbess hold the king had 39*s*. in another hundred. And the abbess has thence in demesne 1½ hide, and Chetel 4½ hides and ⅔ virgate.

The hundred takes its name from the manor of Sturminster Newton (no. 63), held by the Abbot of Glastonbury. The abbot's demesne in this manor consisted of 14 carucates. It was assessed at 22 hides. The Abbess of Shaftesbury's manor must be Hinton St. Mary (no. 126) which lay in the hundred in 1212,[98]

90 *Feud. Aids*, ii. 44, 110.
91 Ibid. 44.
92 Dugdale, *Mon.* vi (2), 1071.
93 *Rot. Hund.* (Rec. Com.), i. 101.
94 *Feud. Aids*, ii. 37, 44.
95 Ibid. 109.
96 Fägersten, *Place-Names of Dorset*, 121.
97 Eyton added Brenscombe (nos. 421 and cliv), the 2 manors of *Torne* (nos. 419 and clii, 420 and cliii), and Woolgarston (no. 297) to this hundred.
98 *Bk. of Fees*, 87.

although the Domesday survey gives the demesne as 3 hides. Chetel's manor must be Lower Fifehead or Fifehead St. Quintin (no. 133) which he held of the abbey. It was assessed at 5 hides with $3\frac{1}{2}$ hides in demesne, and Hinton St. Mary was assessed at 8 hides. These manors amount to 35 hides only, but the rest of this hundred has not been reconstructed.

XXII. *LANGEBERGE* HUNDRED

In Langeberge hundret sunt lxxx et iiii hide. Inde habet rex xii libras et ii solidos et v denarios [f. 21b] pro xl hidis et i virga et viii agris et barones habent inde in dominio xxx et iiii hidas et i virgam. De isto dominicatu habet abbatissa Sancti Edwardi ii hidas et dimidiam et Aiulfus ii hidas et dimidiam et filius Eureboldi ii hidas iiii agros minus. Edwinus venator ii hidas et iii virgatas (et rex habet viii hidas et iii virgas de terra regine Mathildis). Radulfus de Creneborna i hidam et i virgam. Episcopus Luxoviensis v hidas et dimidiam et abbas Creneburnensis iiii hidas et dimidiam et Cadomensis abbatissa iiii hidas iiii agros minus et uxor Hugonis dimidiam hidam. Et pro iii hidis et dimidia quas tenet Willelmus Caisnellus de uxore Hugonis non habuit rex geldum et de vi hidis et iiii agris quas tenent villani abbatisse Cadomensis non habuit rex geldum et pro iiii hidis de terra regine non habuit rex geldum.

In *Langeberge* hundred there are 84 hides.[99] Thence the king has £12 2*s.* 5*d.*[1] for 40 hides and 1 virgate and 8 acres and the barons have thence in demesne 34 hides and 1 virgate. Of this demesne the Abbess of Shaftesbury has $2\frac{1}{2}$ hides, and Aiulf $2\frac{1}{2}$ hides, and the son of Eurebold 2 hides less 4 acres. Edwin the huntsman 2 hides and 3 virgates, and the king has 8 hides and 3 virgates of Queen Maud's land. Ralph of Cranborne 1 hide and 1 virgate. The Bishop of Lisieux $5\frac{1}{2}$ hides, and the Abbot of Cranborne $4\frac{1}{2}$ hides, and the Abbess of Caen 4 hides less 4 acres, and the wife of Hugh $\frac{1}{2}$ hide. And from $3\frac{1}{2}$ hides which William Caisnell holds of the wife of Hugh the king did not have geld and from 6 hides and 4 acres which the villeins of the Abbess of Caen hold the king did not have geld and from 4 hides of the queen's land the king did not have geld.

The Abbess of Shaftesbury had $2\frac{1}{2}$ hides in demesne at Tarrant Hinton (no. 132), assessed at 10 hides. Odo fitz Eurebold's manor must be Farnham (no. 372), assessed at 2 hides, his only remaining manor, and Aiulf's 2 manors of Farnham (nos. 343, 352), assessed at 2 hides and $\frac{1}{2}$ hide respectively, probably represent his exempt demesne in this hundred. The $\frac{1}{2}$-hide manor had belonged to Shaftesbury Abbey, as had the $\frac{1}{2}$ hide in Farnham held by the wife of Hugh (nos. 396 and cxxix). Edwin the huntsman held 2 manors called *Bleneford*(*e*), 1 of which must belong here, since Langton Long Blandford lay in this hundred in 1212.[2] The other lay in Combsditch hundred.[3] One (no. 438) was assessed at 5 hides, $1\frac{1}{2}$ virgate, and the other (no. 455) at 5 hides. The manors of Queen Maud in this hundred must be Ashmore (nos. 17 and xxiii), assessed at 8 hides with 4 hides in demesne, and the 3 manors of *Tarente*: (nos. 24 and xxx), assessed at $3\frac{1}{2}$ hides with 2 hides in demesne; (nos. 25 and xxxi), assessed at $\frac{1}{2}$ hide, held by the bordars; (nos. 26 and xxxv), assessed at 3 hides, 1 virgate, with 2 hides, 3 virgates, in demesne. This brings her exempt demesne to 8 hides, 3 virgates, as in the Geld Roll. Ralph, probably identical with Ralph of Cranborne, held the manor of *Tarente* (no. 370) as a *francus*. The Bishop of Lisieux had $5\frac{1}{2}$ hides in demesne at Tarrant Keyneston (no. 60), assessed at 10 hides and $\frac{2}{3}$ virgate, and the Abbot of Cranborne had $4\frac{1}{2}$ hides in demesne at Tarrant Monkton (no. 75), assessed at 10 hides. The Abbess of Holy Trinity, Caen, had only 1 manor in Dorset, Tarrant Launceston (no. 141), assessed at 10 hides with 4 hides less 4 acres in demesne. The wife of Hugh held $\frac{1}{2}$ hide at *Tarente* (nos. 400 and cxxxiii). Ralph held Tarrant Rawston (nos. 404 and cxxxvii), assessed at 5 hides, of the wife of Hugh, and Berold held 1 hide and 3 virgates in *Tarente* (nos. 405 and cxxxviii) of her. Aiulf held *Terente* (no. 340), assessed at 2 hides, and William held *Terente* (no. 267), assessed at $3\frac{1}{2}$ hides, of William of Eu. This brings the total hidage to 79 hides, $3\frac{2}{3}$ virgates. Eyton added Chettle (no. 342), assessed at 1 hide and held by Airard of Aiulf, Stubhampton (no. 341), assessed at 1 hide and held by Aiulf, and 2 manors in Langton Long Blandford, assessed at 1 hide and 5 hides respectively and held by Ulviet (no. 458) and by Robert Attlet of Roger Arundel (nos. 325 and xcvii), to bring the total hidage to 87 hides, $3\frac{2}{3}$ virgates.[4]

XXIII. KNOWLTON HUNDRED

In Chenoltune hundret sunt xxxvi hide et dimidia. Inde habet rex iiii libras et vii solidos pro xiiii hidis et dimidia et barones habent in dominio xx et i hidas et dimidiam. De isto dominicatu habet mater Willelmi de Ou vii hidas et dimidiam et comes[5] Moritonio xi hidas et dimidiam et de dimidia (hida) quam quidam mulier habet de comite de Moritonio nunquam habuit rex geldum et abbatissa Wiltonis habet ii hidas et dimidiam in dominio.

In Knowlton hundred there are $36\frac{1}{2}$ hides. Thence the king has £4 7*s.* for $14\frac{1}{2}$ hides and the barons have in demesne $21\frac{1}{2}$ hides. Of this demesne William of Eu's mother has $7\frac{1}{2}$ hides and the Count of Mortain $11\frac{1}{2}$ hides, and from $\frac{1}{2}$ hide which a certain woman has of the Count of Mortain the king never had geld and the Abbess of Wilton has $2\frac{1}{2}$ hides in demesne.

[99] In fact the details of the account amount to $88\frac{1}{2}$ hides and 4 acres.

[1] The geld on 40 hides and 1 virgate is £12 1*s.* 6*d.* The 8 acres therefore paid 11*d.*

[2] *Bk. of Fees*, 87.

[3] See p. 135.

[4] Eyton, *Key to Domesday: Dorset*, 131–2.

[5] Supply 'de' after *comes*.

The Abbess of Wilton held the manor of Philipston (*Winburne*) (no. 140), assessed at 3½ hides, the amount of her exempt demesne. William of Eu's mother does not appear in the Domesday survey, but William himself held 7½ hides in demesne at Long Crichel and Moor Crichel (no. 266), assessed at 12 hides. Aiulf held part of Crichel (*Chirce*) (no. 351), assessed at 4 hides. The Count of Mortain had only 1 manor large enough to have 11½ hides in demesne, Gussage All Saints (no. 192), which lay in this hundred in 1212.[6] His manor of Knowlton (no. 191), held of him by Ansger, must belong to this hundred also. It was assessed at 2 hides, which brings the total hidage to the Geld Roll figure of 36½ hides. A woman held *Cernel* (no. 153) of the count, assessed at 1½ hide, but it seems unlikely that this manor could belong to Knowlton hundred. It is more likely to have belonged to Dorchester hundred.

XXIV. SIXPENNY HUNDRED

In Sexpene hundret sunt l hide. Inde habet rex xi libras et xv solidos et vi denarios et abbatissa habet inde in dominio x hidas et iii virgas.

In Sixpenny hundred there are 50 hides. Thence the king has £11 15*s.* 6*d.*[7] and the abbess has thence in demesne 10 hides and 3 virgates.

This hundred was later amalgamated with Handley, also held entirely by the Abbess of Shaftesbury, to form Sixpenny Handley hundred. In the 13th century this combined hundred contained Iwerne Minster, Fontmell Magna, Melbury Abbas, and Compton Abbas as well as Handley. These 4 manors were held by the abbess in 1086 (nos. 128–31) and were assessed at 15 hides (Fontmell), 10 hides (Compton), 10 hides (Melbury), and 18 hides (Iwerne Minster), a total of 53 hides. The hidage of Iwerne Minster in the original bequest of King Alfred to the abbess was 15 hides,[8] which would make the total 50 hides. The total in demesne in the Domesday survey is 16 hides.

XXV. *HUNESBERGE* HUNDRED

In Hunesberge hundret sunt lxxix hide. Inde habet rex xvi libras et xviii solidos pro lvi hidis et i virga et tercia parte unius virge. Et barones regis habent inde in dominio xx hidas. De isto dominicatu comes de Moritonio habet viii hidas et i virgam et canonici Constantienses
[f. 22]
iii hidas et iii virgas. Willelmus de Moione iiii hidas et dimidiam iiii agros minus. Aiulfus iii hidas et dimidiam. Et pro ii hidis et dimidia quas Alvredus de Hispania tenet de Glastingeberiensi ecclesia non habuit rex geldum et de i virga quam tenet Rotbertus de uxore Hugonis nunquam habuit rex geldum.

In *Hunesberge* hundred there are 79 hides. Thence the king has £16 18*s.* for 56 hides and 1⅓ virgate. And the king's barons have thence in demesne 20 hides. Of this demesne the Count of Mortain has 8 hides and 1 virgate and the canons of Coutances 3 hides and 3 virgates. William of Moyon 4½ hides less 4 acres. Aiulf 3½ hides. And for 2½ hides which Alvred of Epaignes holds of the church of Glastonbury the king did not have geld and from 1 virgate which Robert holds of the wife of Hugh the king never had geld.

The only manor of the Count of Mortain, apart from Gussage All Saints, large enough to have 8 hides and 1 virgate in demesne is *Blaneford* (no. 194), which belonged to this hundred in 1212.[9] It was assessed at 10 hides. The canons of Coutances had only 1 manor in the whole of England, Winterborne Stickland (no. 142), assessed at 8 hides, with 3 hides, 3 virgates, in demesne. William of Moyon's manor is probably *Poleham* (nos. 276 and lxxxvi), assessed at 10 hides, with 4 hides, 1 virgate, and 6 acres in demesne, the nearest figure to the 4½ hides less 4 acres of the Geld Roll.[10] Alvred held 2 hides at Okeford Fitzpaine (no. 64) of Glastonbury Abbey, assessed at 8 hides. No other land was held of the abbey by a man of this name, so he must be Alvred of Epaignes, despite the discrepancy in hidage. Robert held the manor of *Wintreburne* (nos. 403 and cxxxvi) of the wife of Hugh. According to Exon. Domesday *de i virgata nunquam habuit Willelmus rex geldum suum*. It was assessed at 1 hide and 1 virgate. He also held the manor of *Wintreburne* entered immediately before this one (nos. 402 and cxxxv), assessed at 1½ hide. Probably both are part of Winterborne Stickland. Aiulf held part of Durweston (no. 346), assessed at 4½ hides. This manor lay in Pimperne hundred at a later date,[11] but since *Hunesberge* and Pimperne hundreds were amalgamated in the early 13th century Aiulf's manor could have lain in *Hunesberge* in the 11th century. This brings the hidage up to 43 hides, 1 virgate. Shillingstone (no. 367), held by Schelin and assessed at 16 hides, probably lay here also. It was originally called Shilling Okeford (*Alford*). Eyton added to this hundred Hammoon (nos. 277 and lxxxvii), held by Torstin of William of Moyon, Plumber (no. 453), held by Ralph of Swain, Fifehead Neville (no. 307), held by Ingelram of Waleran, and Turnworth (no. 319), held by Alvred of Epaignes. Each of these manors was assessed at 5 hides and they belonged to the hundred of Pimperne at a later date.[12] This brings the total hidage of *Hunesberge* hundred to 79 hides, 1 virgate, the Geld Roll total being 79 hides. The other 2 manors in Durweston, held by Robert of the wife of Hugh (nos. 401 and cxxxiv) and William of the Count of Mortain (no. 193), were assessed at 2 hides and 2½ hides respectively.

6 *Bk. of Fees*, 91.
7 This is the geld on 38 hides, 1 virgate.
8 See p. 42.
9 *Bk. of Fees*, 87.
10 Eyton (*Key to Domesday: Dorset*, 131–2) identified this manor as Hazelbury Bryan.
11 *Feud. Aids*, ii. 27.
12 Ibid. 27, 43.

XXVI. PIMPERNE HUNDRED

In Pinpre hundret sunt xxx et iiii hide et dimidia. Inde habet rex iii libras et x et viii solidos pro xiii hidis et barones regis habent in dominio xv hidas. De isto dominicatu habet rex vi hidas (et dimidiam et i virgam) de terra regine Matildis et abbatissa Sancti Edwardi i hidam et dimidiam virgam quam postea dedit cuidam suo servienti. Edwinus venator ii hidas et i virgam iiii agros minus et Hunfridus camerarius v hidas. De his v hidis dedit Hunfridus et (*sic*) ecclesie dimidiam hidam per assensum regis. Et de ii hidis et dimidia quas tenet David de Willelmo de Braiosa non habuit rex geldum et de iiii hidis quas tenent villani de terra regine Mathildis non habuit rex geldum.

In Pimperne hundred there are 34½ hides. Thence the king has £3 18*s*. for 13 hides and the king's barons have in demesne 15 hides. Of this demesne the king has 6½ hides and 1 virgate of Queen Maud's land and the Abbess of Shaftesbury 1 hide and ½ virgate which she afterwards gave to a certain serjeant of hers. Edwin the huntsman 2 hides and 1 virgate less 4 acres, and Humphrey the chamberlain 5 hides. Of these 5 hides Humphrey gave ½ hide to the church with the king's consent. And from 2½ hides which David holds of William of Briouze the king did not have geld and from 4 hides of Queen Maud's land which the villeins hold the king did not have geld.

The queen's manor of Nutford (Farm) belonged to the hundred in 1303[13] and can therefore be assumed to be part of her land in 1086. It was, however, assessed at only 2½ hides (nos. 28 and xxxiii), whereas the queen held 6 hides, 3 virgates, of exempt demesne and 4 hides of land held by *villani* in this hundred. The only other manor of the queen which cannot be assigned to another hundred[14] is Shitterton (nos. 27 and xxxii), assessed at 5 hides, with 3½ hides in demesne, which is still not large enough to cover her land. This problem seems to be insoluble. The demesne of the Abbess of Shaftesbury also does not tally with the Domesday account of the abbess's land. However, the later of the 2 surveys of the abbey's land, dating from the 12th century, says that the abbess had a hide in Pimperne attached to her manor of Tarrant Hinton (no. 132) in *Langeberge* hundred.[15] The Domesday survey mentions neither the land nor the fact that the abbess gave it to a serjeant. Steepleton Iwerne (nos. 281 and xci) lay in this hundred in 1303.[16] It was then held by William fitz Alexander of John de Mohun. In 1086 it was held by Geoffrey (Maloret) of William of Moyon and was assessed at 3 hides. The manor of *Iwerne* (no. 241) held by Robert of Robert fitz Gerold and also assessed at 3 hides seems to be Ranston.[17] It probably belonged to Pimperne as well at this date. Edwin the huntsman's manor is probably *Werne* (no. 456), identified as Lazerton (Farm) in Stourpaine.[18] Humphrey the chamberlain's manor must be Stourpaine (no. 356), since his other manors have been accounted for, and since it is the only one large enough to have 5 hides in demesne, being assessed at 6 hides, 1½ virgate. Part of Stourpaine was held by William Belet (no. 509); it was assessed at 1 hide and 2½ virgates. He also held *Nodford* (no. 502), formerly called Nutford Lockey but now France Farm in Stourpaine.[19] It was assessed at 1 hide and 2½ virgates. The Domesday account of Humphrey's manor of Stourpaine does not mention a gift to the church. The hundred cannot be completely reconstructed because of the confusion over the land of the queen and the difficulty of knowing which of the manors belonging to the later hundred of Pimperne lay in the Domesday hundred of Pimperne and which in the Domesday hundred of *Hunesberge*.[20]

XXVII. GILLINGHAM HUNDRED

In Gelingeham hundret sunt lxxix hide dimidia virga minus. Inde habet rex xi libras et x et viii solidos et ix denarios pro xl hidis ii partibus unius virge minus et barones regis habent inde in dominio xxvii hidas et dimidiam. De isto dominicatu habet Willelmus de Falesia vii hidas et dimidiam virgam et Godmundus iii hidas et dimidiam et Godricius venator i virgam et Fulcredus ii virgas et dimidiam et Chetellus iii hidas dimidiam virgam minus
[f. 22b]
et abbatissa Sancti Edwardi ix hidas et dimidiam et dimidiam virgam. Abbatissa Pratellensis iii hidas et dimidiam. Et de iii hidis et i virga quas tenet Urso de Arnulfo de Hesdinc non habuit rex geldum et de i hida quam tenet Drogo de comite de Moritonio non habuit rex geldum et de iii hidis et dimidia quas habet abbatissa Pratellensis non habuit [21] geldum et

In Gillingham hundred there are 79 hides less ½ virgate. Thence the king has £11 18*s*. 9*d*.[22] for 40 hides less ⅔ virgate and the king's barons have thence in demesne 27½ hides. Of this demesne William of Falaise has 7 hides and ½ virgate and Gudmund 3½ hides and Godric the huntsman 1 virgate and Fulcred 2½ virgates and Chetel 3 hides less ½ virgate and the Abbess of Shaftesbury 9½ hides and ½ virgate. The Abbess of Préaux 3½ hides. And from 3 hides and 1 virgate which Urse holds of Ernulf of Hesdin the king did not have geld and from 1 hide which Drew holds of the Count of Mortain the king did not have geld and from 3½ hides which the Abbess of Préaux has the king did not have geld and from 4 hides which the men of William of Falaise hold of him the king did not have geld. And because the 4 collectors of this money did

[13] *Feud. Aids.* ii, 28.
[14] Eyton placed Frome St. Quintin in this hundred, but it must lie in Modbury hundred: see p. 145.
[15] B.M. Harl. MS. 61, f. 58: *In Tarenta sunt x hidas* (sic) *quarum una est in Pimperne.* In 1212 the abbess held *i hyde terre in Pinpre*: *Bk. of Fees*, 87. Eyton (*Key to Domesday: Dorset*, 137–8) identified the land as Hyde.
[16] *Feud. Aids*, ii. 27.
[17] Fägersten, *Place-Names of Dorset*, 11–12.
[18] Eyton, op. cit. 137–8; Fägersten, op. cit. 59.
[19] Fägersten, op. cit. 58.
[20] *Hunesberge* contained 79 hides and Pimperne 34½ hides at the date at which the Geld Rolls were compiled, making a total of 113½ hides. This is the total hidage of the manors which can be assigned to the 2 hundreds.
[21] Supply 'rex' after *habuit.*
[22] The geld on 39 hides, 3⅓ virgates, is £11 19*s*.

de iiii hidis quas tenent homines Willelmi de Falesia de eo non habuit rex gildum. Et quia iiii congregatores huius pecunie non reddiderunt denarios quos receperunt dederunt vadimonium in misericordia ad reddendos denarios et ad emendandum forisfacturam.

not render the pence which they received they gave pledges (being) in (the king's) mercy for rendering the pence and for future good conduct.

William of Falaise held only 2 manors in Dorset, Silton (no. 271) and Milton on Stour in Gillingham (no. 272). Silton was assessed at 8 hides, and attached to it were a hide and $\frac{1}{2}$ virgate which Wulfweard White, William's predecessor, had in pledge and 1 hide which Wulfweard had bought from the Bishop of Exeter. Milton on Stour was assessed at 3 hides. Gudmund's only manor was Milton on Stour (no. 425), assessed at $4\frac{1}{2}$ hides. Godric the huntsman held 1 virgate in Gillingham (no. 428), and according to the Domesday survey of Wiltshire Fulcred held 3 virgates in Gillingham, which must be his manor in this hundred.[23] Bernard held part of Gillingham (no. 250), assessed at $3\frac{1}{2}$ hides, of Turstin fitz Rolf. Edwin held 1 virgate in Gillingham (no. 427), Ulwin $1\frac{1}{2}$ virgate (no. 429), and Edward the huntsman $\frac{1}{2}$ virgate (no. 490). Chetel held 3 hides and 3 virgates in Kington Magna (no. 426), his only manor in Dorset. Part of Kington Magna (no. 245), assessed at 6 hides and 1 virgate, was held by Urse of Ernulf of Hesdin, and Ranulf held Little Kington (Farm), in Kington Magna (no. 303), assessed at 3 hides, of Waleran. The Abbess of Shaftesbury had 9 hides, $2\frac{1}{2}$ virgates, in demesne at East and West Stour (no. 127), assessed at 17 hides. The Abbess of St. Leger, Préaux, is not recorded in the Domesday survey either as a tenant-in-chief or a mesne tenant. The abbey, with its companion house of St. Pierre, for monks, was founded by Humphrey de Vieilles, father of Roger de Beaumont, the Domesday tenant-in-chief.[24] Roger had the manor of Stour Provost (no. 231) in 1086, which in 1285 was held by the Abbess of Préaux of the Earl of Leicester.[25] It was assessed at 7 hides in 1086, and the Domesday survey gives the demesne as $4\frac{1}{2}$ not $3\frac{1}{2}$ hides, but this must have been the manor held by the Abbess of Préaux. It is possible that the abbess was Roger's daughter. It is known that Roger gave land to the abbey when his daughter became a nun there. Roger's son Robert, Count of Meulan, makes reference to his sister, Abbess Aubrey, in a charter to St. Mary de Pré, Leicester, and the name of the fourth abbess of Préaux is recorded as Alberée. She died in 1112.[26] Other manors which can be assigned to this hundred are Buckhorn Weston (no. 149), assessed at 7 hides and held by Haimo of the Count of Mortain, and Thorton (no. 256), assessed at 2 hides and held by William of William of Eu. Both manors lay in the hundred in 1212.[27] In 1285 Wyndlam, Fifehead Magdalen, and Todber lay in this hundred.[28] Wyndlam (nos. 322 and xciv), assessed at 2 hides, was held by Roger *de margella* of Roger Arundel; Fifehead Magdalen (no. 220), assessed at 5 hides, was held by Gilbert of Earl Hugh; and Todber (nos. 273 and lxxxiii), assessed at 2 hides, by Geoffrey Maloret of William of Moyon. In 1303 Nyland lay in the hundred.[29] It was a divided vill in 1086, 2 hides being held by Drew of the Count of Mortain (no. 150), 2 hides by Ranulf of Turstin fitz Rolf (no. 251), and 1 hide by Bernard of Turstin fitz Rolf (no. 252). This brings the total hidage to 82 hides, $3\frac{1}{2}$ virgates, 4 hides more than the Geld Roll figure.

XXVIII. BROWNSHALL HUNDRED

In Bruneselle hundret sunt lii hide et dimidia. Inde habet rex x libras et xiii solidos pro xxx(v hidis) et dimidia et barones habent in dominio x et vii hidas —[*blank*]. De isto dominicatu habent monachi Scireburnenses xi hidas et Godricius i hidam et Willelmus de Scoeia iii hidas et dimidiam dimidiam virgam minus et Hugo silvestris virgam et dimidiam et comes de Moritonio i hidam. Et de iii virgis quas tenet Manases quocus de terra Sireburnensium monachorum non habuit rex geldum.

In Brownshall hundred there are $52\frac{1}{2}$ hides. Thence the king has £10 13*s.* for $35\frac{1}{2}$ hides and the barons have in demesne 17 hides.[30] Of this demesne the monks of Sherborne have 11 hides and Godric 1 hide and William of Ecouis $3\frac{1}{2}$ hides less $\frac{1}{2}$ virgate and Hugh *silvestris* $1\frac{1}{2}$ virgate and the Count of Mortain 1 hide. And from 3 virgates which Manasses the cook holds of the land of the monks of Sherborne the king did not have geld.

Manasses held 3 virgates at Stalbridge (no. 42), belonging to the monks of Sherborne, *quas Willelmus filius regis tulit ab ecclesia sine consensu episcopi et monachorum*. The monks had 6 hides in demesne at Stalbridge, assessed at 20 hides, and 5 hides at Stalbridge Weston (no. 43), assessed at 8 hides. William of Ecouis had $3\frac{1}{2}$ hides in demesne at Stourton Caundle (no. 299), assessed at 5 hides. The only manor of Hugh *silvestris* was Stourton Caundle (no. 363), assessed at $\frac{1}{2}$ hide, which Leverone (Leofrun) held T.R.E. She had also held Stourton Caundle (no. 478), held in 1086 by Godric and assessed at 1 hide. The Count of Mortain held 1 hide in Stourton Caundle (no. 218), and Alwin held 3 hides there of him (no. 219). The count had given Purse Caundle (nos. 118 and lxiv) to Athelney Abbey, in exchange for Bishopston (Montacute) in Somerset. Purse Caundle was assessed at 4 hides, and Alvred *pincerna* held $1\frac{1}{2}$ virgate of the abbey. Hugh held Stourton Caundle (no. 270), assessed at $3\frac{1}{2}$ hides, of William of Eu and Wimer held Stourton Caundle (no. 301), assessed at 3 hides, of Walscin of Douai. In 1316 Stoke, in Caundle Haddon

[23] *Dom. Bk.* (Rec. Com.), i, f. 73b.

[24] See p. 49 n.

Earl of Leicester, Roger's grandson, Roger was the

[25] *Feud. Aids*, ii. 22. According to a charter of Robert, original grantor: *Neustria Pia*, 524.

[26] *Neustria Pia*, 552; Dugdale, *Mon.* vi (1), 467; Charpillon et Caresme, *Dictionnaire de l'Histoire de l'Eure*, ii. 686.

[27] *Bk. of Fees*, 91.

[28] *Feud. Aids*, ii. 22.

[29] Ibid. 33.

[30] There are in fact 16 hides and 3 virgates in demesne.

(another name for Stourton Caundle), lay in this hundred.[31] The Count of Mortain held *Stoches* (no. 200), assessed at 2 hides, and Hugh held 1 hide in *Stoches* (no. 269) of William of Eu, which Toli, William's predecessor, held in pledge *de terra Scireburne*. Both manors are probably represented by Stock Gaylard House. Stock Gaylard was formerly a separate parish in Brownshall hundred, but is now attached to Lydlinch.[32] This brings the total hidage to 53 hides and ½ virgate, as opposed to the 52½ hides of the Geld Roll. The details of the Geld Roll account, however, amount to 53 hides.

XXIX. HASILOR HUNDRED

In Haselore hundret sunt lxiiii (hide) et i virgata. Inde habet rex x libras et vi solidos et iii denarios pro xxxiiii hidis et virga et dimidia et barones habent inde in dominio xxx hidas. De isto dominicatu habet uxor Hugonis iii hidas et Walterus de Clavilla iii hidas et dimidiam et dimidiam virgam et Rogerus de (Be)llomonte vi hidas et dimidiam et dimidiam virgam et Durandus carpentarius i virgam et abbatissa Sancti Edwardi i hidam vi agros minus. Abbas Ceneliensis iii hidas et dimidiam virgam.
[f. 23]
Alvricius venator dimidiam hidam et Ascitillus de Carisburgo ii hidas et virgam et dimidiam. Rotbertus filius Radulfi ii hidas. Rotbertus filius Geroldi v hidas. Eddricius prepositus i hidam. Abbas Sancti Wandrigisili i hidam et comes de Moritonio dimidiam hidam.

In Hasilor hundred there are 64 hides and 1 virgate. Thence the king has £10 6*s.* 3*d.* for 34 hides and 1½ virgate and the barons have thence in demesne 30 hides. Of this demesne the wife of Hugh has 3 hides, and Walter de Claville 3½ hides and ½ virgate, and Roger de Beaumont 6½ hides and ½ virgate, and Durand the carpenter 1 virgate, and the Abbess of Shaftesbury 1 hide less 6 acres. The Abbot of Cerne 3 hides and ½ virgate. Alvric the huntsman ½ hide, and Anschitil de Carisburgo 2 hides and 1½ virgate. Robert fitz Ralph 2 hides. Robert fitz Gerold 5 hides. Edric the reeve 1 hide. The Abbot of St. Wandrille 1 hide and the Count of Mortain ½ hide.

The wife of Hugh held Orchard (nos. 422 and clv), assessed at 1½ hide. One hide belonged to Cranborne Abbey. The manor lay in the hundred in 1431.[33] The other 2½ hides of exempt demesne held by the wife of Hugh in this hundred cannot be identified, since her remaining manors were all subinfeudated in 1086. Eyton placed Hurpston in Steeple (nos. 413 and cxlvi) in this hundred. It was held by Robert the boy (*puer*) of the wife of Hugh, and assessed at 3 hides.[34] Walter de Claville had 1 hide and 1 virgate in demesne at Church Knowle (nos. 312 and clviii), assessed at 2 hides, and his manor of Afflington (nos. 311 and clvii), which he held in demesne, was assessed at 2 hides, 1½ virgate. Church Knowle lay in this hundred in 1212, along with Steeple and East Creech.[35] Roger de Beaumont held land in all 3 vills in 1086, 2½ hides in Steeple (no. 234), 2 hides in East Creech (no. 233), and 3½ hides in Church Knowle (no. 235). Beulf held 1 hide in Church Knowle (no. 308) of Waleran, and Walter held 1 hide in the same vill (no. 291) of William of Briouze. Bretel held 2 hides in East Creech (no. 202) of the Count of Mortain, Walter held ½ hide there (no. 289) of William of Briouze and Robert *frumentinus* another ½ hide (nos. 412 and cxlv) of the wife of Hugh. Durand the carpenter's virgate must be his manor of Afflington (no. 510), assessed at that amount. Three and a half virgates in Afflington were held by Walter of William of Briouze (no. 290). The Abbess of Shaftesbury's land in this hundred is difficult to identify. In 1285 she held the manors of Arne, Blashenwell (Farm), and Encombe (the 2 latter in Corfe Castle parish). In the second survey of the abbey's lands, dating from the latter part of the 12th century, Blashenwell and Encombe were appendages of her manor of Kingston, and Arne in Purbeck consisted of a hide of land occupied by salt-pans. Encombe consisted of ½ virgate and Blashenwell of 1½ hide.[36] Both the Domesday survey and the 12th-century survey give the hidage of Kingston (no. 134) as 16 hides. It lay in Rowbarrow hundred at this date. The Abbot of Cerne held Kimmeridge (nos. 90 and liii), which lay in the hundred in 1285, and Renscombe (nos. 91 and liv), which lay there in 1316.[37] Kimmeridge was assessed at 5 hides with 2 hides, 2½ virgates, in demesne and Renscombe at 5 hides, 1 virgate, with 2 hides, 3 virgates, in demesne. Part of Kimmeridge was held by Richard of William of Briouze (no. 288). It was assessed at 1½ hide. Alvric the huntsman held Blackmanston (nos. 476, 489), assessed at 1 hide. Anschitil de Carisburgo must be the man called Anschitil fitz Ameline in the Exchequer text. He held only 1 manor, Tyneham (no. 369), assessed at 3 hides. It was a divided vill, 3½ hides being held by Bretel of the Count of Mortain (no. 203), 1 hide and 1 virgate by William of Earl Hugh (no. 227), and 1 virgate by Edric (no. 473). The last-named is presumably Edric the reeve, but Tyneham is too small to cover his exempt demesne in this hundred. He also held East Holme (no. 467), assessed at 1 hide, which lay in the hundred in 1285.[38] Walter de Claville also held 2 hides and 1 virgate in East Holme (nos. 313 and clix), with ½ virgate in demesne. Robert fitz Gerold's manor in the hundred must be Povington (no. 242), assessed at 8½ hides, which lay there in 1212.[39] Robert fitz Ralph does not appear in the Dorset survey, either as a tenant-in-chief or as a mesne tenant. A Robert fitz Rolf or Ralf held 3 manors in Wiltshire,[40] but none of them could have been included in Hasilor hundred. The land of the abbey of St. Wandrille must be the hide attached to the church of Wareham (nos. 124 and xx). The Count of Mortain had ½ hide attached to a mill at Stoborough (no. 201). The manor of Bradle (no. 344), assessed at 4 hides and

31 *Feud. Aids*, ii. 40.

32 Fägersten, *Place-Names of Dorset*, 219 n.

33 *Feud. Aids*, ii. 110.

34 Eyton, *Key to Domesday: Dorset*, 129–30. For the identification of *Herpere* or *Harpera* as Hurpston in Steeple, see Fägersten, op. cit. 136.

35 *Bk. of Fees*, 89.

36 *Feud. Aids*, ii. 23; B.M. Harl. MS. 61, f. 61v.

37 *Feud. Aids*, ii. 23–24, 44.

38 Ibid. 23–24.

39 *Bk. of Fees*, 89.

40 *V.C.H. Wilts.* ii. 154.

belonging to Aiulf the chamberlain, lay in the hundred in 1285,[41] and Eyton also placed in it Smedmore (House) (no. 295), assessed at ½ hide and held by Richard of William of Briouze.[42] It lay in Kimmeridge. This brings the hidage to 62 hides, but the hundred cannot be properly reconstructed because of the difficulties over the land of the Abbess of Shaftesbury and Robert fitz Ralph.

XXX. WINFRITH HUNDRED

In Winfrode hundret sunt xlix hide et i virga. Inde habet rex c et vii solidos et iii denarios pro x et viii hidis dimidia virga minus et rex et sui barones habent inde in dominio xxvi hidas. De isto dominicatu habet rex viii hidas et dimidiam (de terra Heroldi). Episcopus Luxoviensis vi hidas et i virgam et Aiulfus vii hidas (et) i virgam et comes de Moritonio ii hidas dimidiam virgam minus. Walterus de Clavilla dimidiam hidam. Osmundus pistor iii virgas. Alwardus prepositus i hidam et i bedellus i virgam. Et de dimidia hida quam tenet Rotbertus de comite de Moritonio nunquam habuit rex geldum. De iiii hidis et dimidia de terra Heroldi non habuit rex geldum.

In Winfrith hundred there are 49 hides and 1 virgate. Thence the king has 107*s.* 3*d.* for 18 hides less ½ virgate, and the king and his barons have thence in demesne 26 hides. Of this demesne the king has 8½ hides of Harold's land. The Bishop of Lisieux 6 hides and 1 virgate, and Aiulf 7 hides and 1 virgate, and the Count of Mortain 2 hides less ½ virgate. Walter de Claville ½ hide. Osmund the baker 3 virgates. Alward the reeve 1 hide, and a beadle 1 virgate. And from ½ hide which Robert holds of the Count of Mortain the king never had geld. From 4½ hides of Harold's land the king did not have geld.

Harold's manor in this hundred must be Chaldon Herring or East Chaldon (nos. 12 and viii), assessed at 13 hides, which lay in this hundred in 1275,[43] but both Exon. Domesday and the Exchequer text give the hidage in demesne as 6 hides. The Bishop of Lisieux had 6 hides and 1 virgate in demesne at Coombe Keynes (no. 61), assessed at 10 hides. Walter de Claville held part of Coombe Keynes (nos. 314 and clx), assessed at 3 hides, but Exon. Domesday gives his demesne as 2 hides. The Count of Mortain held 2 manors in Lulworth (nos. 198, 199), assessed at 3½ hides and 2 hides, respectively, which probably represent his demesne in this hundred, since Lulworth lay in Winfrith hundred in 1212.[44] Aiulf the chamberlain held a manor in Lulworth (no. 350), assessed at 8 hides and 3 virgates. Wool lay in the hundred at the same date. Alward held 1½ hide in Wool (no. 486) in 1086, and had held a virgate in the same vill T.R.E. which in 1086 was held by Almar (no. 487) who may be the beadle mentioned in the Geld Roll. One hide and 3 virgates in Wool (no. 208) were held of the Count of Mortain by Bretel and Malger in 1086. This may be the land held of the count by Robert in the Geld Roll, but no part of the land seems to have been exempt from geld. Osmund the baker held 3 virgates at Woodstreet (no. 508) in Wool. Hugh held 5 hides at Chaldon Herring (nos. 408 and cxli) of the wife of Hugh. This brings the total hidage to 49½ hides, 1 virgate more than the Geld Roll total.

XXXI. *CELBERGE* HUNDRED

In Celberge hundret sunt l et i hide et dimidia. Inde habet rex x libras et xii denarios pro xxx et iii hidis et dimidia. Inde habent rex et sui barones in dominio x et viii hidas et dimidiam. De isto dominicatu habet rex i hidam de terra regine Mathildis et abbas Cerneliensis i hidam et Hugo de Sancto Quintino hidam et dimidiam et dimidiam virgam et Willelmus Belet i hidam et dimidiam. Matheus de Mauritania vi hidas et dimidiam virgam. Bristuinus prepositus iii hidas (et i virgam) et Osmundus pistor i hidam et dimidiam virgam et abbas Mideltonensis iii hidas dimidiam virgam minus.

In *Celberge* hundred there are 51½ hides. Thence the king has £10 0*s.* 12*d.* for 33½ hides. Thence the king and his barons have in demesne 18½ hides. Of this demesne the king has 1 hide of Queen Maud's land, and the Abbot of Cerne 1 hide, and Hugh de St. Quintin 1½ hide and ½ virgate, and William Belet 1½ hide. Matthew de Moretania 6 hides and ½ virgate. Brictuin the reeve 3 hides and 1 virgate, and Osmund the baker 1 hide and ½ virgate, and the Abbot of Milton 3 hides less ½ virgate.

Queen Maud's manor of Watercombe (nos. 29 and xxxiv) was assessed at 1 hide. The Abbot of Cerne's manor is probably Poxwell (nos. 81 and xliv) assessed at 6 hides, although both Exon. Domesday and the Exchequer text give the demesne as 1½ hide. It lay in the hundred of Winfrith in 1285.[45] *Celberge* had been amalgamated with Winfrith hundred by that date, and since the Abbot of Cerne had no exempt demesne in Winfrith hundred in 1084 Poxwell was presumably then part of *Celberge*. Holworth, Ringstead (now deserted), Woodsford, Warmwell, and Morton also lay in Winfrith hundred in 1285. Ringstead in 1086 was a divided vill. Hugh de St. Quintin had 2 hides there (no. 359) and Brictuin the reeve 1 hide (no. 463). This cannot be part of the latter's demesne in this hundred, since 6 men held it of him at farm. Hugh held 1 hide in Ringstead (nos. 409 and cxlii) of the wife of Hugh and Ralph the steward 1½ hide there of the same woman (nos. 411 and cxliv). William Belet held 2½ hides at Woodsford (no. 503) and Bristuin held 2½ hides in the same vill (nos. 82 and xlv) at farm of Cerne Abbey. Matthew de Moretania's manor in this hundred must be Owermoigne (no. 321), assessed at 9 hides and 3 virgates. Brictuin the reeve held 1 hide at

[41] *Feud. Aids*, ii. 23–24.

[42] Eyton, op. cit. 129–30; Fägersten, op. cit. 135.

[43] *Rot. Hund.* (Rec. Com.), i. 103.

[44] *Bk. of Fees*, 89.

[45] *Feud. Aids*, ii. 9.

Moreton (no. 461) and Robert 3 hides in the same vill (no. 204) of the Count of Mortain. The rest of Brictuin's demesne in this hundred must be at Galton (no. 462), assessed at 2 hides, 1½ virgate, since Osmund the baker's manor in this hundred must be Galton (no. 507), assessed at 1 hide and ½ virgate, the amount of his exempt demesne. The Abbot of Milton held Holworth (nos. 104 and lxxviii), assessed at 5 hides, but both Exon. Domesday and the Exchequer text give the demesne as 3 hides. Warmwell was a divided vill in 1086, 1 hide being held by Robert of the Count of Mortain (no. 205), 1½ hide by Turold of the wife of Hugh (nos. 410 and cxliii), and 2½ hides by William (Malbank) of Earl Hugh (no. 226). William (Malbank) held 1 virgate at Warmwell which never paid geld, but the Geld Roll does not mention it. In 1275 Mayne, belonging to the Knights Hospitallers, lay in the hundred of Winfrith.[46] In 1285 Mayne *Ospitalis* (Fryer Mayne) and Mayne Syrard (Little Mayne (Farm)) lay in Cullifordtree hundred and Mayne Martel (Broadmayne) in the hundred of St. George.[47] It is possible, however, that the 2 manors of Broadmayne and Little Mayne lay in *Celberge* hundred in 1084. Both were held by William (Malbank) of Earl Hugh in 1086 (nos. 223, 224) and were assessed at 3 hides and 2 hides respectively. This gives a total hidage of 49 hides and 3 virgates, 1 hide and 3 virgates short of the Geld Roll figure.

XXXII. DORCHESTER HUNDRED (ST. GEORGE)

In Dorecestre hundret sunt lxxiii hide et i virga. Inde habet rex xvi libras et ix solidos et ii denarios pro lv hidis dimidia virga minus. Inde habent barones in dominio xiiii hidas. De isto dominicatu habet uxor Hugonis iii hidas et i virgam et comes de Moritonio v virgas et Hugo de Nemore Herberti i hidam et dimidiam virgam.
[f. 23b]
Hugo de Sancto Quintino ii hidas. Comitissa Boloniensis iiii hidas. Willelmus Belet ii hidas et virgam et dimidiam. Et de i hida quam tenet Walchelinus de comite de Moritonio non habuit rex geldum et de ii hidis et i virga quas tenet Radulfus clericus de comite de Moritonio non habuit rex geldum et de dimidia virga quam tenet Ansgerus de comite de Moretonio non habuit rex geldum et de i hida quam tenet Willelmus Belet de Willelmo de Ou non habet rex geldum.

In Dorchester (St. George) hundred there are 73 hides and 1 virgate. Thence the king has £16 9*s.* 2*d.*[48] for 55 hides less ½ virgate. Thence the barons have in demesne 14 hides. Of this demesne the wife of Hugh has 3 hides and 1 virgate, and the Count of Mortain 5 virgates, and Hugh de Boscherbert 1 hide and ½ virgate. Hugh de St. Quintin 2 hides. The Countess of Boulogne 4 hides. William Belet 2 hides and 1½ virgate. And from 1 hide which Walchelin holds of the Count of Mortain the king did not have geld and from 2 hides and 1 virgate which Ralph the clerk holds of the Count of Mortain the king did not have geld and from ½ virgate which Ansger holds of the Count of Mortain the king did not have geld and from 1 hide which William Belet holds of William of Eu the king did not have geld.

The wife of Hugh had 3 hides in demesne at *Wintreburne* (nos. 376 and cviii), the nearest figure to the Geld Rolls. This manor must be Martinstown in Winterborne St. Martin which lay in the hundred in 1285.[49] It was assessed at 6 hides. The numerous manors called *Cerne* may be presumed to lie in this hundred. The Count of Mortain held 2½ hides in *Cerne* (no. 158) which probably represents his exempt demesne; Ralph held *Cerne* (no. 157) of him, and since this is the only manor in Dorset held of the count by a man called Ralph he must be identical with Ralph the clerk. Ansger held 2 manors called *Cerne* (nos. 156, 159) of the count. Ralph's manor was assessed at 3 hides, and the manors of Ansger at 3 hides and 2 hides respectively. Walchelin is not recorded as a tenant of the count in the Domesday survey. Hugh de Boscherbert's manor in this hundred must be *Cernel* (no. 360), assessed at 1½ hide, since his only other manor must lie in Uggescombe hundred. Hugh de St. Quintin's manor in this hundred must be Stinsford (no. 358), assessed at 2 hides, 2½ virgates. It lay in the hundred of St. George in 1285, when it belonged to the heirs of John Quintin.[50] Part of Stinsford was held by Aiulf of Brictuin (no. 464). It was assessed at 2½ virgates. The Countess of Boulogne held the manor of Bockhampton (nos. 513 and xxxvi), assessed at 4 hides. According to Exon. Domesday there were 2 hides in demesne. William Belet held Frome Billet (no. 491), assessed at 3 hides. In 1285 Frome Billet, Frome Whitfield, Bradford Peverell, and Charminster lay in the hundred.[51] Bradford (no. 257), assessed at 17 hides, was held by William of William of Eu. This is probably the manor held of William of Eu by William Belet. Frome Whitfield was *de baronia Winterborne St. Martin.* Immediately following Martinstown in the Domesday survey is a manor called *Frome* (nos. 377 and cix) held by William of the wife of Hugh. This may be Frome Whitfield. It was assessed at 4 hides. The Bishop of Salisbury held Charminster (no. 32), assessed at 10 hides, with 2 carucates in demesne. This brings the hidage of the hundred to 59 hides and 1 virgate. Bretel held *Frome* (no. 160), assessed at 1 hide, of the Count of Mortain and William held *Frome* (no. 154), assessed at 4 hides, of the same. Eyton identified these 2 manors as Frome Bonvile or Bomston, now represented by Bhompston Farm in Stinsford.[52] A woman held 1½ hide in *Cernel* of the count (no. 153), and another woman held 1½ hide in *Cernel* of the Bishop of Salisbury (no. 50). Aiulf held 1½ hide in *Cerne* of Milton Abbey (nos. 108 and lxxxii). This brings the total to 68 hides, 3 virgates, 4½ hides below the Geld Roll total.

[46] *Rot. Hund.* (Rec. Com.), i. 103.
[47] *Feud. Aids*, ii. 18–19, 31.
[48] The geld on 55 hides less ½ virgate is £16 9*s.* 3*d.*
[49] *Feud. Aids*, ii. 17.
[50] Ibid. 18.
[51] Ibid. 17.
[52] Eyton, *Key to Domesday: Dorset*, 123–4; cf. Fägersten, *Place-Names of Dorset*, 184.

XXXIII. MODBURY HUNDRED

In Morberge hundret sunt lxiii hide. Inde habet rex xii libras et ix solidos et ix denarios pro xl et i hidis et dimidia et dimidia virga. Inde habent rex et sui barones in dominio xx et i hidas et virgam et dimidiam. De isto dominicatu habet rex xi hidas de terra regine Mathildis et abbas Mideltonensis x hidas et i virgam et dimidiam.

In Modbury hundred there are 63 hides. Thence the king has £12 9*s*. 9*d*. for 41½ hides and ½ virgate. Thence the king and his barons have in demesne 21 hides and 1½ virgate. Of this demesne the king has 11 hides of Queen Maud's land and the Abbot of Milton 10 hides and 1½ virgate.

The queen had 10½ hides in demesne at Frome St. Quintin (nos. 15 and xxi), assessed at 13 hides. It later lay in the hundred of Tollerford,[53] but since the hundreds adjoin and the queen had no demesne in Tollerford at this date the manor may then have lain in Modbury. Cattistock and Compton Abbas (West) lay in the hundred of Modbury in the 13th century.[54] Both manors belonged to Milton Abbey in 1086. Cattistock (nos. 96 and lxix) was assessed at 10 hides with 3 hides in demesne and Compton Abbas (West) (nos. 95 and lxviii) at 5 hides with 3 hides in demesne. In 1303 the hundred of Cerne, Totcombe, and Modbury, which consisted of the Domesday hundreds of *Stane* and Modbury, included Sydling St. Nicholas.[55] In 1086 this manor also was held by Milton Abbey (nos. 93 and lxvii), and was assessed at 29 hides with 6 hides in demesne. This gives the abbey a total demesne of 12 hides, not 10 hides, 1½ virgate. Ansger held 5 hides in Sydling of the Count of Mortain (no. 174) and Amund held 1 hide in the same place of the count (no. 175). This brings the total hidage of the hundred to 63 hides, the Geld Roll figure.

XXXIV. SHERBORNE HUNDRED

In Sireburne hundret sunt lxxv hide et dimidia (et xxv carucate). Inde habet rex x et viii libras et xii solidos et iiii denarios pro lxii hidis. Inde habent episcopus et sui monachi in dominio xxv carrucatas que nunquam reddiderunt gildum et monachi habent in dominio ix hidas et i virgam et de i hida et i virga quas tenet Ansgerus quocus de dono regis non habuit rex geldum et de ii hidis et virga et dimidia quas tenent villani Osmundi episcopi non habuit rex geldum et de dimidia hida et dimidia virga quas tenet Sawarus de rege et habet eas in dominio non habuit rex gildum.

In Sherborne hundred there are 75½ hides and 25 carucates. Thence the king has £18 12*s*. 4*d*.[56] for 62 hides. Thence the bishop and his monks have in demesne 25 carucates which never paid geld and the monks have in demesne 9 hides and 1 virgate. And from 1 hide and 1 virgate which Ansger the cook holds of the king's gift the king did not have geld and from 2 hides and 1½ virgate which the villeins of Bishop Osmund hold the king did not have geld and from ½ hide and ½ virgate which Saward holds of the king, and he has them in demesne, the king did not have geld.

The demesne of the bishop and his monks was at the manor of Sherborne (no. 37), the head of the hundred, assessed at 43 hides, where the bishop held 16 and the monks 9½ carucates, making a total of 25½ carucates. The rest of the monks' demesne lay at their 4 manors of Oborne, Thornford, Bradford Abbas, and Over Compton (nos. 38–41), all of which lay in this hundred in 1285.[57] At Oborne, assessed at 5 hides, there were 2 hides in demesne, at Thornford, assessed at 7 hides, 3 hides in demesne, at Bradford Abbas, assessed at 10 hides, 1½ hide in demesne, and at Over Compton, assessed at 6 hides, 3 virgates, 1 hide and 3 virgates in demesne, a total of 8 hides and 3 virgates, not 9 hides and 1 virgate as in the Geld Roll. Saward's only manor was *Candele*, possibly Stourton Caundle (no. 479), assessed at 2½ virgates. In 1212 Hervey de Candel had ½ hide in Sherborne hundred from which he paid 1*d*. a year *aput Gellingeham*, by the gift of King William.[58] The land of Ansger the cook presents difficulties. He does not appear in the Dorset survey, but according to the Somerset survey he held 1 hide and 1 virgate in Compton, attached to the king's manor of Martock.[59] Round identified this manor as Compton Durville and Eyton as Stapleton.[60] Two vills called Compton lay in Sherborne hundred, Over Compton and Nether Compton. It is possible that Ansger's manor of Compton did in fact lie in Sherborne hundred, and was attached to the manor of Martock in Somerset, just as 1½ hide in Purbeck was attached to the manor of Puddletown (nos. 8 and ii). Sinod held 1 hide at Sherborne (no. 37) which Alward had held of King Edward T.R.E. but which had previously belonged to the bishopric. This brings the total hidage of the hundred to 74 hides, 2½ virgates, 3½ virgates less than the total given in the Geld Roll.

XXXV. *FERENDONE* HUNDRED

In Ferendone hundret sunt xxx et vii hide. Inde habet rex iiii libras et xi solidos pro xv hidis et duabus partibus unius virge et rex et sui barones habent inde in dominio xx hidas (et) dimidiam (et

In *Ferendone* hundred there are 37 hides. Thence the king has £4 11*s*. for 15 hides and ⅔ virgate and the king and his barons have thence in demesne 20½ hides and ½ virgate. Of this demesne the king has

[53] *Inq. Non.* (Rec. Com.), 45.
[54] Ibid. 48.
[55] *Feud. Aids*, ii. 39.
[56] The geld on 62 hides is £18 12*s*.
[57] *Feud. Aids*, ii. 5.
[58] *Bk. of Fees*, 90.
[59] *Dom. Bk.* (Rec. Com.), i, f. 87: *De hoc manerio* [Martock] *est ablata i hida et una virgata terre in CONTONE. Ansgerus (cocus) tenet.*
[60] *V.C.H. Som.* il 440; Eyton, *Domesday Studies: Som.* i. 213.

dimidiam) virgam. De isto dominicatu habet rex iii hidas et iii virgas de terra Heroldi et comes de Moritonio vi hidas (et) i virgam et Balduinus vicecomes iiii hidas et dimidiam et dimidiam virgam et Walerannus venator iiii hidas et Osbertus Gifardus ii hidas. Et de v virgis de terra Heroldi non habuit rex geldum.

3 hides and 3 virgates of Harold's land, and the Count of Mortain 6 hides and 1 virgate, and Baldwin the sheriff 4½ hides and ½ virgate, and Waleran the huntsman 4 hides, and Osbern Giffard 2 hides. And from 5 virgates of Harold's land the king did not have geld.

Harold's manor in this hundred must be Child Okeford (nos. 7 and i), assessed at 5 hides, with 3 hides in demesne. It lay in the hundred in 1212.[61] The Count of Mortain held 5 hides in Child Okeford (no. 152) and the manor of Hanford (no. 151), assessed at 4 hides, which also lay in the hundred in 1212. Baldwin, Sheriff of Devon, held only 1 manor in Dorset, Iwerne Courtney or Shroton (no. 316), assessed at 8 hides. It lay in Gillingham hundred at a later date, but was in *Ferendone* hundred in 1212.[62] Sutton Waldron (no. 304), which was held by Waleran in 1086, also lay in *Ferendone* hundred in 1212. It was assessed at 8 hides in 1086. Osbern Giffard's only manor in Dorset was Hill (Farm) (no. 318), assessed at 2 hides. Manston (no. 302), which Warenger held of Waleran, belonged to Gillingham hundred in 1285.[63] *Ferendone* became part of Gillingham hundred, and it is quite likely that Manston lay in *Ferendone* at this date. If so, this brings the total hidage to the Geld Roll figure of 37 hides.

XXXVI. BUCKLAND HUNDRED

In Bochene hundret sunt xxx et viiii (hide) una virga minus. Inde habet rex ix libras xii denarios et i obolum minus pro xxx hidis i virga minus.
[f. 24]
Inde habent barones regis in dominio vii hidas et dimidiam dimidiam virgam minus. De isto dominicatu habet Rainboldus (presbiter) ii hidas et Willelmus de Braiosa ii hidas et Bolo presbiter iii hidas dimidiam virgam minus et rex dimidiam hidam de terra Heroldi. Et de dimidia hida et dimidia virga quas Rotbertus de Oilleio abstulit i tagno et posuit intra firmam regis in Melecoma non habuit rex geldum et de i hida quam tenet Walchelinus de comite de Moritonio non habuit rex geldum.

In Buckland hundred there are 39 hides less 1 virgate. Thence the king has £8 18*s*. 11½*d*.[64] for 30 hides less 1 virgate. Thence the king's barons have in demesne 7½ hides less ½ virgate. Of this demesne Rainbald the priest has 2 hides, and William of Briouze 2 hides, and Bollo the priest 3 hides less ½ virgate, and the king ½ hide of Harold's land. And from ½ hide and ½ virgate which Robert de Oilly took from a thegn and placed in the king's farm of Melcombe the king did not have geld and from 1 hide which Walchelin holds of the Count of Mortain the king did not have geld.

Rainbald the priest had only 1 manor in Dorset, Poleham (no. 146), assessed at 10 hides, with 4 not 2 hides in demesne. In 1303 Henry de Glaunvyle held Glanvilles Wootton in this hundred of William de Brewes.[65] William of Briouze held 2 manors in Glanvilles Wootton in 1086 (nos. 284, 285), assessed at 3 hides and 2 hides respectively. Both were held of him by Ralph. Bollo the priest's manor in this hundred must be Mappowder (no. 431), assessed at 5 hides and 3 virgates, since Chickerell (no. 432) belonged to Cullifordtree hundred. The Count of Mortain held 3½ virgates and 7 acres of Mappowder (no. 171). Perhaps this is the manor said to be held by Walchelin in the Geld Roll, though he does not appear as the count's tenant in the Domesday survey. Hugh held 3 virgates in Mappowder (no. 259) of William of Eu. The land which Robert de Oilly added to the king's manor of Bingham's Melcombe (no. 30) must be the 3½ virgates in Buckland hundred attached to it. Domesday, however, states that Countess Goda, who held the manor T.R.E., was responsible for the addition and that previously the land was held by 3 free thegns. Robert held Bingham's Melcombe and Hinton Martell (no. 31) at farm of the king.[66] Earl Harold's land must be the ½ hide in Mapperton attached to Puddletown (nos. 8 and ii), although Mapperton lay in Loosebarrow hundred. Fifteen hides remain to be found. This is the hidage of Buckland Newton (no. 65), the head of the hundred, belonging to Glastonbury Abbey. The abbot's demesne consisted of 8 ploughlands which never paid geld.

XXXVII. CULLIFORDTREE HUNDRED

In Cuferdestroue hundret sunt c et viiii hide. Inde habet (rex) xiiii libras et x et vii solidos pro xlix hidis et dimidia et rex et sui barones habent inde in dominio liiii hidas dimidia virga minus. De isto dominicatu habet rex in dominio i hidam et dimidiam et uxor Hugonis xvi hidas et Fulcredus ii hidas et Bristuinus prepositus iii hidas dimidiam virgam minus et abbas Cerneliensis i hidam et dimidiam et Bolo presbiter ii hidas et dimidiam et dimidiam virgam et abbas Cadomensis vii hidas et i virgatam

In Cullifordtree hundred there are 109 hides. Thence the king has £14 17*s*. for 49½ hides and the king and his barons have thence in demesne 54 hides less ½ virgate. Of this demesne the king has in demesne 1½ hide, and the wife of Hugh 16 hides, and Fulcred 2 hides, and Brictuin the reeve 3 hides less ½ virgate, and the Abbot of Cerne 1½ hide, and Bollo the priest 2½ hides and ½ virgate, and the Abbot of Caen 7 hides and 1 virgate, and the Countess of Boulogne 6 hides, and William Belet

[61] *Bk. of Fees*, 91.
[62] Ibid.
[63] *Feud. Aids*, ii. 22.
[64] The correct geld would be £8 18*s*. 6*d*.
[65] *Feud. Aids*, ii. 30.
[66] See pp. 129, 132.

et comitissa Bolonie vi hidas et Willelmus Belet i hidam et abbas Mideltonensis vii hidas et dimidiam virgam et Hugo Gausbertus iii virgas. Willelmus de Scoeia iiii hidas et i virgam et quidam presbiter i hidam quam tenuit Petrus episcopus. Et de v virgis quas tenet i tagnus cuius ipsa terra fuerat de Willelmo Belet ad firmam non habuit rex geldum et de dimidia hida quam tenet Rotbertus filius Ivonis de comite de Moritonio non habuit rex geldum et de iii hidis et i virga quas tenent villani de abbate Cadomensi non habuit rex geldum.

1 hide, and the Abbot of Milton 7 hides and ½ virgate, and Hugh Gosbert 3 virgates. William of Ecouis 4 hides and 1 virgate, and a certain priest 1 hide, which Bishop Peter held. And from 5 virgates which 1 thegn, to whom the land belonged, holds at farm of William Belet the king did not have geld and from ½ hide which Robert fitz Ivo holds of the Count of Mortain the king did not have geld and from 3 hides and 1 virgate which the villeins of the Abbot of Caen hold the king did not have geld.

The manor of the king in this hundred is probably *Waia* (nos. 22 and xxviii), which Hugh fitz Grip had held of the queen. It was assessed at 1½ hide, the amount of his exempt demesne. The wife of Hugh held 2 manors called *Waia* (nos. 380 and cxii, 381 and cxiii),[67] assessed respectively at 4 hides and 1 virgate, with 3 hides and 3 virgates in demesne, and 6 hides, with 4 hides and 1 virgate in demesne. These 2 manors account for 8 hides of her exempt demesne. She held 5 hides and 3 virgates in demesne at *Wintreburne* (nos. 384 and cxvi), assessed at 8 hides, and 3 hides and 1 virgate in demesne at Buckland Ripers (nos. 379 and cxi), assessed at 4 hides. Buckland Ripers lay in this hundred in 1285.[68] This gives her a total demesne of 17 not 16 hides. Fulcred held *Waia* (no. 364), assessed at 2½ hides. Brictuin held 3 small manors which probably lay in this hundred, *Waia* (no. 433), assessed at 2 hides, *Wintreburne* (no. 434), assessed at 1½ hide, and 1 virgate at Lewell (no. 435). The Abbot of Cerne had 1½ hide in demesne at Radipole (nos. 78 and xli), assessed at 3 hides, and Bollo the priest's manor must be Chickerell (no. 432), assessed at 3 hides and ½ virgate, which lay in the hundred in 1285. The Abbot of St. Stephen, Caen, held the manor of Bincombe (no. 122), assessed at 8 hides with 5 hides in demesne. This must be the abbot's manor in this hundred, since the abbey's only other Dorset manor was Frampton, in Frampton hundred. The Geld Roll for Cullifordtree, however, credits the abbot with 7 hides and 1 virgate in demesne and 3 hides and 1 virgate held by his *villani*, a total of 10½ hides, which is 2½ hides more than the total hidage of Bincombe. There were 2 hides attached to Frampton (no. 121), given by Queen Maud, which do not seem to have lain in Frampton hundred; they may have lain in Cullifordtree. The Countess of Boulogne held the manor of Winterborne Monkton (nos. 514 and xxxvii), assessed at 6 hides, although Exon. Domesday gives the hidage in demesne as 4½ hides. William Belet's manor in this hundred must be Winterborne Belet (no. 493), assessed at 2½ hides, which lay in the hundred in 1285.[69] It was held T.R.E. by 2 thegns, 1 of whom is presumably the man holding of William at farm in the Geld Roll. The Abbot of Milton held Osmington (nos. 99 and lxxii), assessed at 10 hides with 4 hides in demesne, and Whitcombe (nos. 100 and lxxiii), assessed at 6 hides with 4 hides in demesne. Both belonged to the hundred in 1285.[70] This gives him a total demesne of 8 hides, not 7 hides and ½ virgate. Hugh Gosbert's manor must be his 3 virgates in Lewell (no. 492). William of Ecouis's manor must be West Knighton (no. 298), assessed at 6 hides, since Stourton Caundle (no. 299), his only other manor, belongs to Brownshall hundred. Peter, Bishop of Chester, died before the Domesday survey, and is not mentioned in the Dorset section of Domesday.[71] The hide of land which he held cannot be identified. The manor which Robert fitz Ivo held of the Count of Mortain is probably Stafford (no. 155), assessed at 3 hides, or *Wai* (no. 164), assessed at 3 hides, 3 virgates. Stafford lay in the hundred in 1285. Part of it was held in 1086 by Hugh and William of the wife of Hugh fitz Grip (nos. 383 and cxv). It was assessed at 6 hides. Dodeman held 2 hides at *Wai* (no. 162) of the Count of Mortain and Amun held 4 hides at *Wai* (no. 163) of the same. Holwell (no. 165) lay in the hundred in 1275.[72] In 1086 it was assessed at 2 hides, and held by Bretel of the Count of Mortain. The 3 small manors in *Brigam* or *Brige*, identified by Fägersten as the lost village of Bridge[73] near Weymouth, must have lain in this hundred. One virgate was held by Aiulf (no. 348), 1 virgate by Hugh of the wife of Hugh fitz Grip (nos. 393 and cxxvi), and 1 virgate by Brictuin (no. 465). This brings the total hidage to 96 hides and 3½ virgates. The remaining manors in the hundred must be sought for among the Winterbornes, but it is not possible to tell which manors of that name should lie in Cullifordtree and which in Combsditch.

XXXVIII. FRAMPTON HUNDRED

In Frontone hundret sunt xxxv hide. Inde habuit rex post constitutos terminos iii libras et xii solidos de terra Cadomensis abbatis et Hugo de Portu adquietavit in alio hundreto iii hidas et iii virgas geldantis terre quas habet in hoc hundreto. Abbas Cadomensis habet xiii hidas in dominio et Hugo de Portu vi hidas et i virgam in dominio.

In Frampton hundred there are 35 hides. Thence the king had, after the constituted terms, £3 12*s.* from the land of the Abbot of Caen and Hugh de Port was quit in another hundred for 3 hides and 3 virgates of geldable land which he has in this hundred. The Abbot of Caen has 13 hides in demesne, and Hugh de Port 6 hides and 1 virgate in demesne.

[67] It has not been possible to identify all the manors of *Wai(a)* and *Wintreburne*. Eyton supplies identifications for all of them, but gives no authority for his decisions, and in the cases where his identification cannot be substantiated the names have not been used; see Eyton, *Key to Domesday: Dorset*, 121–2.

[68] *Feud. Aids*, ii. 19.

[69] Eyton (op. cit. 121–2) states that the manor was later called Cripton. Fägersten does not mention this manor, but a Cripton Barn, in Winterborne Came, is marked on O.S. Map 1/25,000 SY 78 (1958).

[70] *Feud. Aids*, ii. 19.

[71] He is mentioned in the Somerset Domesday: see p. 40 n.

[72] *Rot. Hund.* (Rec. Com.), i. 101.

[73] Fägersten, *Place-Names of Dorset*, 161; see also p. 23 n.

The manor of the Abbey of St. Stephen, Caen, is Frampton itself (no. 121), assessed at 25½ hides. The Domesday survey gives the demesne as 9½ not 13 hides. There were 2 hides attached to the manor which do not seem to have lain in this hundred. They were probably in Cullifordtree hundred with the abbey's manor of Bincombe (no. 122). Hugh de Port had only 1 manor in Dorset, Compton Valence (no. 357), assessed at 10 hides. It paid geld in Tollerford hundred. This gives a total of 35½ not 35 hides. The abbey was said to hold 10½ hides of land in Cullifordtree hundred. Bincombe was assessed at 8 hides; with the 2 hides of land attached to Frampton there is still ½ hide remaining. It is odd that the abbey should have ½ hide too little in one hundred and ½ hide too much in another.

XXXIX. LODERS HUNDRED

In Lodre hundret sunt xx hide. De his habet rex viii hidas in dominio de terra Heroldi et villani tenent inde x hidas de quibus rex non habuit geldum et ii hide quas tenuerunt tagni tempore regis Edwardi sunt addite huic mansioni de quibus rex non habuit geldum.

In Loders hundred there are 20 hides. Of these the king has 8 hides in demesne of Harold's land and the villeins hold thence 10 hides from which the king did not have geld, and 2 hides which thegns held T.R.E. were added to this manor from which the king did not have geld.

This hundred consists of the manor of Loders (nos. 13 and ix), held by Earl Harold T.R.E. There were 8 hides in demesne, 10 hides held by the *villani*, and 2 hides of thegnland *que non ibi pertinent* which 2 thegns held T.R.E.

In Dorseta habuit rex de geldo suo cccc et xv libras et viii solidos et viiii denarios et i obolum. Adhuc debentur regi xl—[*blank*].

In Dorset the king had from his geld £415 8*s*. 9½*d*. There is still owing to the king 40—[*blank*].

The money recorded in the actual geld accounts amounts to £422 6*s*. 5½*d*., the geld on 1,407 hides, as opposed to 1,394 hides.

SUMMARIES OF FIEFS IN EXON. DOMESDAY

These summaries, relating to the manors of certain tenants-in-chief in the five south-western counties, are entered at the end of Exon. Domesday. The entries include the Dorset manors of Glastonbury Abbey and Robert fitz Gerold, translated below.[74]

[f. 527b]
Ecclesia Glastiniensis habet ii mansiones dominicas in Dorseta de xxii hidis et iii virgis et dimidia. Ibi sunt xxii carrucate terre non gheldantis. Ibi sunt ix carruce in dominio et xliii villani et lxxii bordarii et x (et) ix servi et xiii coliberti habentes xx carrucas. Hec terra appreciata est xlv libras. Milites abbatis habent in Dorseta v mansiones de xxxi hidis et virga et dimidia. In his sunt xiiii carruce in dominio et xxxvii villani et xlvi bordarii et xix servi habentes xxi carrucas. Hec terra appreciata est xxix libras. Duo tagni tenent de predicta terra i manerium v hidarum. In his sunt ii carruce in dominio et xii villani et xxvi bordarii et iiii servi habentes iii carrucas. Hec terra appreciata est iiii libras et x solidos. Hec terra sufficit c et v carrucis et est peiorata de xl solidos.

The church of Glastonbury has 2 demesne manors in Dorset of 22 hides and 3½ virgates. There are 22 carucates of land (which is) not liable to geld. There are 9 ploughs in demesne and 43 villeins and 72 bordars and 19 serfs and 13 coliberts having 20 ploughs. This land is valued at £45. The knights of the abbot have in Dorset 5 manors of 31 hides and 1½ virgate. In these there are 14 ploughs in demesne and 37 villeins and 46 bordars and 19 serfs having 21 ploughs. This land is valued at £29. Two thegns hold of the aforesaid land 1 manor of 5 hides. In these there are 2 ploughs in demesne and 12 villeins and 26 bordars and 4 serfs having 3 ploughs. This land is valued at £4 10*s*. This land is enough for 105 ploughs, and it has deteriorated by 40*s*.

Notes

(1) The abbey of Glastonbury had 6 manors in Dorset in 1086, 1 of which was held by the king. In demesne the abbot had 10 hides at Sturminster Newton (no. 63) and 5 hides, 2½ virgates, at Buckland Newton (no. 65). In addition he had in demesne land for 14 ploughs *que nunquam geldavit* at Sturminster Newton, and land for 8 ploughs *que nunquam geldavit* at Buckland Newton. These non-gelding teamlands are presumably the 22 carucates of the summary. The abbot had 43 *villani*, 40 bordars, and 32 cottars (the 72 bordars), 13 coliberts, and 19 *servi*. As the account of Sturminster Newton does not give the number of ploughs in demesne and among the men these totals cannot be checked. The value of the land in demesne amounted to £45.

(2) Two manors, Okeford Fitzpaine (no. 64) and Woodyates (no. 66), were held in entirety by Norman tenants. Okeford was divided between the wife of Hugh, Alvred of Epaignes,[75] and Chetel; Woodyates was

[74] See also *V.C.H. Wilts*. ii. 218, 220, 221.

[75] The Domesday survey calls him simply Alvred, but the Geld Roll for *Hunesberge* hundred shows that he was Alvred of Epaignes.

held by the wife of Hugh. Their joint hidage amounted to 12 hides. The abbot's knights held 8 hides at Sturminster Newton, divided between Waleran, Roger, and Chetel. Goscelm the king's cook also held 4 hides at Sturminster Newton and the wife of Hugh 7 hides and 1½ virgate at Buckland Newton. These manors and parts of manors amount to 31 hides, 1½ virgate, as stated in the summary. Since the account of the knights' 8 hides at Sturminster Newton does not mention either peasantry or ploughs, the figures cannot be checked. Neither can the joint value be checked, since the land of Hugh's wife at Buckland Newton was valued jointly with that of Warmund, who must be 1 of the 2 thegns mentioned. Warmund held 2 hides at Buckland and Ulviet held Colway (no. 68), assessed at 3 hides, and held it T.R.E. also. Five hides is the amount mentioned in the summary as being held by the 2 thegns. The joint value for the land of the thegns and knights in the summary is £33 10*s*. The total value of all the subinfeudated land in Domesday is £34 10*s*.

(3) As stated in the summary, there is land for 105 ploughs on the 5 manors of Sturminster Newton, Okeford Fitzpaine, Buckland Newton, Woodyates, and Colway.

[f. 530b]
Rotbertus filius Giroldi habet in Wiltesira et in Dorseta x et viii mansiones. In his habentur lxx et vii hide. Hec terra sufficit l et iiii carrucis et dimidie et est appreciata lxxx et iiii libras et x solidos. De his habet R. xx et viii hidas et iii virgas in dominio et valet sibi xx et vii libras et x solidos. Cetera habent homines sui. Idem Rotbertus habet ii mansiones in Sumerseta in quibus habentur xv hidas quas possunt arare xx et ii carruce et valet R. xx et iii libras. Cetera habent homines sui. Robertus filius Giroldi habet in Wiltesira et in Dorseta et in Sumesiseta (*sic*) xx mansiones. In his habentur nonaginta et ii hidas. Hec terra sufficit lxx et vi carrucis et dimidie et est appreciata c et xiii libras et x solidos. De his habet R. filius Giroldi xxx et viii hidas et iii virgas in dominio et valet sibi l libras et x solidos. Cetera habent homines sui.

Robert fitz Gerold has 18 manors in Wiltshire and Dorset. In these he has 77 hides. This land is sufficient for 54½ ploughs and is valued at £84 10*s*. Of these Robert has 28 hides and 3 virgates in demesne and it is worth £27 10*s*. to him. His men have the rest. The same Robert has 2 manors in Somerset in which he has 15 hides which 22 ploughs can plough and it is worth £23 to Robert. His men have the rest. Robert fitz Gerold has in Wiltshire and Dorset and Somerset 20 manors. In these he has 92 hides. This land is sufficient for 76½ ploughs and is valued at £113 10*s*. Of these Robert fitz Gerold has 38 hides and 3 virgates in demesne and it is worth £50 10*s*. to him. His men have the rest.

Notes

(1) Robert fitz Gerold had 4 manors in Dorset (nos. 239–42) and 10 manors in Wiltshire. One of his Wiltshire manors had been held *pro ii maneriis* T.R.E., and of his manors in Dorset, Corfe Mullen was held by Wada and Egelric T.R.E., Leigh was held by 2 thegns T.R.E., and Ranston by 2 brothers in parage T.R.E. If each of these 3 manors was counted as 2 then the figure of 18 manors given in the summary would be correct.

(2) The total hidage of Robert's Dorset and Wiltshire manors was 77 hides and 2½ virgates, approximating to the 77 hides of the summary, and there was land for 59½ not 54½ ploughs. Robert had 7½ hides in demesne at Corfe Mullen and a total of 28 hides and 1 virgate in demesne in Wiltshire, considerably more than the 28 hides and 3 virgates given in the summary. The total value of these manors is £84 10*s*., as in the summary.

(3) The 2 manors of Robert fitz Gerold in Somerset were assessed at 15 hides, with land for 22 ploughs, 6 hides being in demesne. The total value T.R.E. was £28. In 1086 Charlton Musgrove rendered £6, and the other manor 100 cheeses and 10 bacons.

(4) The combined assessment of Robert's manors in the 3 counties is 92 hides, 2½ virgates, which 81½ ploughs could plough. The total value of the manors in 1086 was £90 10*s*., 1 of the Somerset manors not being valued in money. The total demesne in the Exchequer text was 41 hides, 3 virgates, not 38 hides, 3 virgates.

INDEX OF PERSONS AND PLACES IN THE DOMESDAY SURVEY AND THE GELD ROLLS

'No[s].' followed by arabic numerals indicates entries in the translation of the Exchequer text of the Dorset Domesday. 'No[s].' followed by small roman numerals indicates entries in the translation of Exon. Domesday. Large roman numerals standing alone refer to the hundreds as numbered in the text and translation of the Geld Rolls. *Elemosinarius*, *francus*, *serviens*, and *tainus* indicate that persons so described are listed in those categories in Domesday. 'T.R.E.' after a personal name indicates a person entered as holding land in 1066. '1084' or '1086' after a personal name indicates a person entered as holding land at the date when the Geld Rolls were compiled or at the time of the Domesday survey. The forms of place-names in the original texts are printed in italic type and cross-referenced to their modern forms except where the places themselves have not been identified. If a place recorded in Domesday is not a parish at the present time (see p. 61), the name of the modern parish in which it lies has been added to the index entry.

INDEX

TO VOLUMES II AND III

NOTE. The index presupposes that the corrections printed on p. 189 have already been made. The following abbreviations have been used: adv., advowson; abp., archbishop; agric., agriculture; Alex., Alexander; And., Andrew; Ant., Anthony; archd., archdeacon; Bart., Bartholomew; Ben., Benjamin; bp., bishop; br., brother; cast., castle; Cath., Catherine, Catholicism; cath., cathedral; chant., chantry; chap., chapel; Chas., Charles; Chris., Christopher; ch., church; coll., college; ctss., countess; Dan., Daniel; D. & C., Dean and Chapter; d., died; dioc., diocese; div., division; dchss., duchess; Edm., Edmund; Edw., Edward; Eliz., Elizabeth; fam., family; fl., flourished; Fred., Frederick; Geo., George; Geof., Geoffrey; Gilb., Gilbert; Hen., Henry; hosp., hospital; ho., house; Humph., Humphrey; hund., hundred; inc., inclosure; ind., industry; Jas., James; Jos., Joseph; Kath., Katherine; Lawr., Lawrence; ld., lord; man., manor; Marg., Margaret; m., married; Mat., Matthew; Nic., Nicholas; nonconf., nonconformity; *n*, note; par., parish; pk., park; Pet., Peter; Phil., Philip; pop., population; Prot., Protestant; Ric., Richard; riv., river; Rob., Robert; Rog., Roger; Rom., Roman; Sam., Samuel; sch., school; Sim., Simon; s., son; Steph., Stephen; Thos., Thomas; vct., viscount; Wal., Walter; w., wife; Wm., William. A dagger (†) preceding a page number indicates a plate facing that page.

CORRIGENDA TO VOLUME II

page 5, lines 13–14, *for* Sherborne and Ramsbury . . . became again united *read* Sherborne and Ramsbury were united

,, 6, line 4, *for* 904 *read* 964

,, 7, note 70, *for* the manors of Sherborne, Oborne *read* $9\frac{1}{2}$ carucates in Sherborne and the manors of Oborne

,, 39, line 11 from end, *for* James *read* Joseph

,, 49*a*, line 18 from end, *for* had taken six *read* retained it by force

,, 49*b*, lines 14–15, *for* Granston *read* Graston

,, 49*b*, line 15, *for* Poeyeto *read* Poryete

,, 49*b*, line 20, *for* Hornington *read* Horsington

,, 52*a*, line 21, *for* Chandler *read* Nevill

,, 52, note 58, *for* Chandler, fol. 67 *d read* Nevill, ii, fol. 67 *d*

,, 54, line 3 from end, *for* 'Vergroth' *read* 'Vergroh'

,, 55*a*, lines 9 and 5 from end and last line, *for* Wootton *read* Watton

,, 55, note 24, *delete* pt. 1, m. 6;

,, 56*a*, line 9, *for* 1337 *read* 1537

,, 60*a*, line 32, *for* Hunsworth *read* Hemsworth

,, 63*a*, lines 19–20, *for* about the year 903 *read* between 946 and 951

,, 63*b*, line 3, *for* two *read* three

,, 64*a*, lines 5–6, *for* Sherborne with $9\frac{1}{2}$ carucates of land *read* $9\frac{1}{2}$ carucates of land in Sherborne

,, 64*b*, last 2 lines, *for* Lyme and Fleet (Dorset), Littleham and Carswell (Devon) *read* Lyme (Dorset), 'Fleote' (in Seaton), Littleham, and Carswell (Devon)

,, 66, note 46, *for* Edw[ard] I *read* Edw[ard] II

,, 69*a*, line 10, *for* 1261 *read* 1260

,, 69*a*, line 18, *for* 1348 *read* 1349

,, 69*b*, line 3, *for* north *read* south

,, 69*b*, line 13 from end, *for* Flixton *read* Henton

,, 69, note 97, *for* Edw[ard] I *read* Edw[ard] II

,, 74*a*, line 19, *for* Downton *read* Dinton

,, 78*a*, line 10, *for* Donington *read* Dinton (Wilts.)

,, 82*b*, line 2, *for* Hada *read* Adam

,, 87*b*, line 4, *after* All Saints, *insert note* [6]

,, 87*b*, lines 13–14, *for* at Fordham Serlon[6] *read apud fordam Serlonis*

,, 102*b*, line 5 from end, *for* Robert *read* Richard

,, 102, note 64, *for* Hutchins, *Hist. of Dorset*, ii, 416 *read Cal. Pat.* 1350–4, 69

,, 105*b*, line 24, *for* John *read* Roger

,, 106, note 142, *for* Leicester *read* Lancaster

,, 110, line 11 from end, *for* Chalbury *read* Chilbridge

,, 110, note 38, *delete* Pat. 28 Edw. III, pt. 2, m. 10 *and for* Close, 14 Hen. IV, m. 28 *read Cal. Pat.* 1354–8, 279; *Cal. Close*, 1409–13, 394, 396–7

,, 114*a*, line 8 from end, *for* Sefton *read* 'Sefton'

,, 122*a*, last line, *for* Sussex *read* Surrey

,, 130, line 9 from end, *for* Affrington *read* Afflington

,, 145, line 10, *for* Wolly *read* Wolley

,, 145, note 2, *for* p. 223, *read* p. 594

,, 166, line 6, *for* 1677 *read* 1665

,, 240, lines 5 and 26, *for* Waterson *read* Waterston

,, 292, line 9, *for* Dulham *read* Pulham

,, 296, line 13 from end, *for* Moram *read* Morden

,, 308, note 4, *for* from 1883 to 1886 *read* from 1883 to 1885

,, 320*a*, line 6, *for* larmers *read* lanners

,, 334*b*, lines 13–17, *delete sentence* Occasionally . . . craft.

,, 334, note 32, *delete note*

,, 344*b*, line 6, *for* Blackenwell *read* Blashenwell

PRINTED IN GREAT BRITAIN
BY ROBERT MACLEHOSE AND CO. LTD
THE UNIVERSITY PRESS, GLASGOW